Palgrave Studies in Economic History

Series editor
Kent Deng
London School of Economics
London, UK

Palgrave Studies in Economic History is designed to illuminate and enrich our understanding of economies and economic phenomena of the past. The series covers a vast range of topics including financial history, labour history, development economics, commercialisation, urbanisation, industrialisation, modernisation, globalisation, and changes in world economic orders.

More information about this series at
http://www.palgrave.com/series/14632

Jianyong Yue

China's Rise in the Age of Globalization

Myth or Reality?

palgrave
macmillan

Jianyong Yue
London School of Economics and Political Science
London, UK

Palgrave Studies in Economic History
ISBN 978-3-319-63996-3 ISBN 978-3-319-63997-0 (eBook)
https://doi.org/10.1007/978-3-319-63997-0

Library of Congress Control Number: 2017964225

Printed on acid-free paper

This Palgrave Macmillan imprint is published by Springer Nature
The registered company is Springer International Publishing AG
The registered company address is: Gewerbestrasse 11, 6330 Cham, Switzerland

Acknowledgments

This book is developed on the basis of a Ph.D. thesis completed during my studies at the London School of Economics and Political Science (LSE). It is the result of a decade-long observation and intellectual thinking about the interactive relationship between China's domestic politics and international politics. My own experience as a manager in Chinese and Western firms and as a journalist and political economy analyst in domestic media provided me with a unique "insider advantage" in assessing the gains and losses of China's "reform and opening" from a scholar's as well as a practitioner's perspective. Relevant research had been done concerning globalization and China's economic development and foreign policy in the past two decades.

I am deeply grateful to my two supervisors, Dr. Chun Lin and Professor Odd Arne Westad. Both scholars taught me how to make the thesis a seminal work by broadening the theoretical perspective not limited to political science but involving the paradigms of international relations and development studies, and by having greater historical depth.

I am also very thankful to Professor Guoguang Wu (University of Victoria), LSE Professors Kent Deng, Robert Wade, Michael Cox, MacGregor Knox, David Held, Chris Alden, and Peter Wilson, and Professor Peter Nolan (University of Cambridge). Discussions with them, their advice on my work, and their outstanding academic contributions in their respective fields are valuable sources of inspiration for my book writing from a multidisciplinary perspective.

During the doctoral research and the book writing, in particular, I interviewed a lot of old friends, who introduced me to new friends in academia and government institutions. For understandable reasons, I cannot divulge their names; however, I very much appreciate their enthusiastic assistance to my research. Also, I am very grateful to our department's Research Student Award and the Dorothy Hodgkin Award that funded my research at LSE. Lastly, I am heavily indebted to my dear wife Diana, who gave me love, confidence, and the most unselfish and warm-hearted support. Without her, this book would never have been completed.

About the Book

China's reform and opening from the late 1970s is considered an irreversible process of the country's integration into the capitalist world system. After nearly 40 years of sustained rapid growth, China arguably has risen by riding the waves of globalization and is poised to overtake the USA as the new global hegemon in the not-too-distant future. Skeptical of this "rise of China" thesis, this book will shed new light on the mystified reform and opening process. The author argues that the particular way the Chinese Communist regime quested for legitimacy after the Tiananmen Incident in 1989 dramatically radicalized its previous experiment of market socialism in the 1980s into an unbridled capitalism. By politicizing growth performance as its top priority, the Chinese regime implemented a de facto shock therapy reform from the mid-1990s onward at the expense of social justice. Deng Xiaoping played a crucial role in this transformative process. The demise of socialism and the softening of the strong Leninist party state as a result of *state capture* by the nomenclatura elite fatally eroded the social and institutional foundations for internal integration, making it extremely difficult for China to achieve a self-sustaining growth on a self-reliant basis. Deeper integration into the world economy, therefore, became the logical solution to achieving an export-led growth. This was made possible by the regime's renouncement of economic nationalism that underpinned China's national development strategy throughout the 1990s in terms of ceasing import substitution and liberalizing trade and investment on a massive scale in exchange for wider access to developed countries' markets. China's radical embrace of neoliberalism was well in line with the US grand strategy of fully integrating China into the international system precisely through globalizing the Chinese economy. The unholy alliance formed between Chinese market Leninism and global capitalism led to crony comprador capitalism flourishing at the turn of the century. Set on a dependent path of development, China, despite having achieved an amazing Ricardian growth miracle since the WTO accession in 2001, has failed thus far to escape dependency in any meaningful way. Far from being an economic success story, the incomplete economic transformation of China has engendered increasing social and political instability, which as a consequence prompted the Chinese regime's intuitive "totalitarian turn." This, along with an illusory global power shift toward China, casts a shadow on the country's democratic transition and a lasting world peace. Nevertheless, stuck in a quagmire of dependent development, what circumstances would incentivize China to overturn the existing liberal order that has enabled its "success"—and with which the market Leninist regime has been deeply contented—remains an open question.

Important Moments from Mao Zedong to Xi Jinping

1949	The founding of the People's Republic of China (PRC)
1950	Sino-Soviet alliance
1950–1953	China joined the Korean War
1953–1956	The socialist transformation
1953–1957	The first "Five-Year Plan"
1958–1961	The Great Leap Forward
1966–1976	The Cultural Revolution
1969	Climax of Sino-Soviet split
1971	The PRC's lawful seat in the United Nations restored
1972	Nixon visited China
1976	Death of Mao; the arrest of the Gang of Four; Hua Guofeng as party chairman
1978	The Third Session of the 11th CCP Central Committee, reform begins
1979	Sino-US diplomatic relations established; Deng Xiaoping visited the USA; Sino-Vietnamese border war
1980	Chen Yun and "feeling the stone to cross the river"
1982	China's "one-child policy"; Chen Yun's "birdcage" theory
1984	Sino-UK agreement on handover of Hong Kong in 1997
1987	The 13th National Party's Congress; Zhao Ziyang's "preliminary stage of socialism"
1989	Tiananmen crackdown; Zhao Ziyang was removed from the General Secretary post; Jiang Zemin became the new General Secretary
1992	Deng Xiaoping's journeys to southern provinces; the 14th National Party's Congress: legalizing "market economy"
1993	Zhu Rongji's market Leninist reform begins
1997	End of Deng Xiaoping era; the 15th National Party's Congress; UK handover of Hong Kong to China
1998	Zhu Rongji became Premier
1999	US bombing of Chinese embassy in Belgrade; Sino-US deal on WTO
2000	Jiang Zemin's "Three Represents" theory
2001	Sino-US relations improved after 9/11; China joined the WTO
2002	The 16th National Party's Congress; Jiang Zemin stepped down; Hu Jintao became the new General Secretary
2003	Zhu Rongji stepped down; Wen Jiabao became the new Premier; Hu Jintao's "scientific development outlook" and "peaceful rise" of China
2004	Hu Jintao's "harmonious society"
2005	First Sino-US Strategic and Economic Dialogue (S&ED) held in Beijing

2006	China's "Indigenous Innovation" Program
2007	The 17th National Party's Congress; Hu Jintao began his second term in office
2008	Olympic Games in Beijing
2009	The four-trillion stimulus package
2010	China overtook Japan to become the second largest economy
2012	The fall of Bo Xilai; Chongqing Model (2007–2012)
2012	The 18th National Party's Congress; Xi Jinping became the new General Secretary; Xi Jinping and "China Dream"
2013	Xi Jinping's "One-Belt, One Road" Program
2013	The Third Session of the 18th CCP Central Committee: deepen the reform: Let markets determine
2017	The 19th National Party's Congress, Xi Jinping began his second term in office

China's Per Capita GDP (1952–2016)

Year	Nominal GDP (RMB Yuan)	Equiv. (USD)	Real GDP 1952 = 100	GDP growth (%)
1952	119	54	100	–
1953	142	54	113.13	15.6
1954	144	55	115.14	4.3
1955	150	58	120.33	6.9
1956	166	64	135.56	15.0
1957	168	65	138.85	5.1
1958	201	77	164.29	21.3
1959	217	83	175.35	9.0
1960	220	90	174.51	0.0
1961	187	76	128.12	–27.3
1962	175	71	119.94	–5.6
1963	183	74	128.98	10.3
1964	210	85	149.03	18.2
1965	242	98	170.31	17.0
1966	257	104	183.40	10.7
1967	238	97	168.56	–5.7
1968	225	91	157.50	–4.1
1969	246	100	179.13	16.9
1970	279	113	208.05	19.3
1971	292	119	216.68	7.1
1972	296	132	219.39	3.8
1973	313	157	231.28	7.8
1974	314	160	231.78	2.3
1975	332	178	247.52	8.7

Year	Nominal GDP (RMB Yuan)	Equiv. (USD)	Real GDP 1952 = 100	GDP growth (%)
1976	321	165	239.77	−1.6
1977	344	185	254.54	7.6
1978	385	229	280.47	11.7
1979	423	272	297.78	7.6
1980	468	312	317.03	7.8
1981	497	291	329.18	5.1
1982	533	282	353.63	9.0
1983	588	298	386.02	10.8
1984	702	302	438.92	15.2
1985	866	295	491.68	13.4
1986	973	282	527.65	8.9
1987	1123	302	580.11	11.7
1988	1378	370	635.36	11.2
1989	1536	408	652.06	4.2
1990	1663	348	667.65	3.9
1991	1912	359	719.85	9.3
1992	2334	423	812.60	14.2
1993	3027	525	915.27	13.9
1994	4081	473	1023.34	13.0
1995	5091	610	1123.57	11.0
1996	5898	709	1222.20	9.9
1997	6480	782	1321.38	9.2
1998	6860	829	1411.55	7.8
1999	7229	873	1505.98	7.7
2000	7942	959	1620.11	8.5
2001	8717	1053	1741.86	8.3
2002	9506	1149	1887.52	9.1
2003	10,666	1289	2063.75	10.0
2004	12,487	1509	2258.24	10.1
2005	14,368	1754	2499.86	11.4
2006	16,738	2100	2801.36	12.7
2007	20,505	2697	3182.34	14.2
2008	24,121	3473	3470.76	9.7
2009	26,222	3839	3772.43	9.4
2010	30,876	4561	4153.39	10.6
2011	36,403	5636	4523.46	9.5
2012	40,007	6338	4852.63	7.9
2013	43,852	7081	5199.82	7.8
2014	47,203	7684	5551.17	7.3
2015	50,251	8068	5904.12	6.9
2016	53,974	8126	–	6.7

Contents

List of Abbreviations

AIP	Automotive Industrial Policy
AMC	Asset Management Company
AMF	Asian Monetary Fund
AML	Anti-monopoly Law
APEC	Asia-Pacific Economic Cooperation
ASEAN	Association of Southeast Asian Nations
ASEM	Asia–Europe Meeting
BOD	Board of Directors
BWS	Bretton Woods System
CAE	Chinese Academy of Engineering
CAS	Chinese Academy of Sciences
CASS	Chinese Academy of Social Sciences
CBRC	China Banking Regulations Commission
CCP	Chinese Communist Party
CCTV	China Central Television
CDIC	Central Disciplinary and Inspection Committee
CDS	Coastal Development Strategy
CFALG	Central Foreign Affairs Leading Group
CFELG	Central Finance and Economy Leading Group
CFO	Chief Financial Officer
CMC	Central Military Commission
CoCom	Coordinating Committee for Export to Communist Countries
COD	Central Organization Department

COMECON	Council for Mutual Economic Assistance
Comintern	Communist International
CPPCC	Chinese People's Political Consultative Committee
CPSU	Communist Party of the Soviet Union
CRS	Contract Responsibility System
CWG	China Work Group
DRC	Development and Research Centre under the State Council
EEC	European Economic Community
EOI	Export-Oriented Industrialization
ESM	European Single Market
ETMA	Exchange for Technology with Market Access
EU	European Union
FDI	Foreign Direct Investment
FIEs	Foreign-Invested Enterprises
FIFs	Foreign-Invested Firms
GATS	General Agreement on Trade in Services
GATT	General Agreement on Tariffs and Trade
GDP	Gross Domestic Product
GEACS	Greater East Asian Co-prosperity Sphere
GLF	Great Leap Forward
GNP	Gross National Product
Gosplan	State Planning Commission of the Soviet Union
GPA	Agreement on Government Procurement
GPL	Government Procurement Law
GSP	Generalized System of Preferences
HKMT	Hong Kong, Macau, and Taiwan
IIP	Infant Industry Protection
IMF	International Monetary Fund
IPE	International Political Economy
IPR	Intellectual Property Rights
IR	International Relations
ISI	Import-Substituting Industrialization
IT	Information Technology
ITO	International Trade Organization
JCCT	Joint Commission on Commerce and Trade
JVs	Joint Ventures
KMT	Kuomintang
LDCs	Less-/Least-Developed Countries

LDP	Liberal Democratic Party
LMEs	Large- and Medium-Sized Enterprises
M&A	Mergers and Acquisitions
MBO	Management Buy-Out
MDG	Millennium Development Goal
MFA	Ministry of Foreign Affairs
MFA	Multi-fiber Agreement
MFN	Most Favored Nation
MFT	Ministry of Foreign Trade
MITI	Ministry of International Trade and Industry
MLP	Medium- and Long-Term Plan
MNCs	Multinational Corporations
MOA	Ministry of Agriculture
MOFCOM	Ministry of Commerce
MOFTEC	Ministry of Foreign Trade and Economic Cooperation
MOR	Ministry of Railway
MOST	Ministry of Science and Technology
MRC	Modernization Research Centre
NAFTA	North American Free Trade Agreement
NATO	North Atlantic Treaty Organization
NCCPC	National Chinese Communist Party's Congress
NDCs	Now-Developed Countries
NDPC	National Development and Planning Commission
NDRC	National Development and Reform Commission
NEP	New Economic Policy
NIEO	New International Economic Order
NIEs	Newly Industrialized Economies
NIPEO	New International Political and Economic Order
NOEs	Nationally Owned Enterprises
NPC	National People's Congress
NPLs	Non-performing Loans
NSI	National System of Innovation
NTBs	Non-tariff Barriers
OECD	Organization for Economic Cooperation and Development
OEM	Original Equipment Manufacturing
PBOC	People's Bank of China
PLA	People's Liberation Army
PNTR	Permanent Normal Trade Relations

POEs	Privately Owned Enterprises
PPP	Purchasing Power Parity
PRC	The People's Republic of China
PSC	Politburo Standing Committee
PSS	Preliminary Stage of Socialism
QFII	Qualified Foreign Institutional Investors
R&D	Research and Development
RMA	Revolution in Military Affairs
RMB	Renminbi
ROC	Republic of China
S&ED	Strategic and Economic Dialogue
SAAB	State Asset Administration Bureau
SAIC	State Administration of Industry and Commerce
SASAC	State-Owned Assets Supervision and Administration Commission
SCMP	South China Morning Post
SDT	Special and Differential Treatment
SEC	State Economic Commission
SERC	State Economic Restructuring Commission
SETC	State Economic and Trade Commission
SEZ	Special Economic Zone
SMEs	Small and Medium-Sized Enterprises
SOEs	State-Owned Enterprises
SPC	State Planning Commission
SSRI	State System Reform Institute
TFP	Total Factor Productivity
TRIMs	Trade-Related Investment Measures
TRIPs	Trade-Related Aspects of Intellectual Property Rights
UIBE	University of Business and Economics
UN	United Nations
UNCTAD	United Nations Conference on Trade and Development
USSR	Union of the Soviet Socialist Republics
USTR	United States Trade Representative
WOS	Wholly Owned Subsidiaries
WTO	World Trade Organization

List of Tables

1
Introduction

China Says No to Fukuyama

Precisely before the end of the Cold War, the American political scientist Francis Fukuyama propounded his most famous thesis of so-called end of history in the summer issue of *The National Interest* in 1989. He announced with full confidence the eventual triumph of liberal democracy and predicted with extraordinary courage the inevitable "universalization of Western liberal democracy as the final form of human government."[1] His arguments resonated in the post-Cold War years when more and more countries joined the ranks of democracies furthering the flow of the third-wave democracy that had begun in 1974. But history did not end. It has since moved in many directions with competing ideologies—bar Communism—remaining tenacious in many parts of the world, be it Islamic fundamentalism, re-animated totalitarian tendencies in countries such as Russia[2] and China, or the non-ideological "Clash of Civilizations." History has also returned in the traditional form of revived geopolitical competition between the great powers.[3] Among these divergences, the rise of China and its implications on both the country's

J. Yue, *China's Rise in the Age of Globalization*, Palgrave Studies in Economic History, https://doi.org/10.1007/978-3-319-63997-0_1

domestic politics and international politics have posed the greatest challenge to Fukuyama's historical determinism.

Like Marxists, Fukuyama views material force such as the markets as the driver for a "Darwinian evolution" of the political infrastructure, although in an entirely different direction.[4] He has noted uneasily the hardening of Chinese authoritarianism that sufficed to render his theory invalid. Yet he tends to believe that events that had incurred *temporary setbacks* (return of history) will not alter the predestined historical process in the long term. Sensing the growing bottom-up pressures for political liberalization within Chinese society, Fukuyama traveled to Beijing on April 23, 2015, to interview Wang Qishan—one of the most powerful figures in charge of China's anti-graft campaign and member of the new Standing Committee of the Chinese Communist Party's (CCP) Politburo formed in late 2012 after the closing of the 18th National Party's Congress—in the hope of getting the right kind of answer he needed. Wang was an outstanding technocrat with rich administrative experience, skilled at handling thorny issues. He was fond of history books and did read extensively. His most recent reading was *The Old Regime and the Revolution* written by Alexis de Tocqueville in 1856. These credentials had won him a lot of applause among Chinese intellectuals, many of whom viewed him as the hope of pushing China in the right direction of liberal democracy. His forthcoming dialogue with Fukuyama became the weather vane of Chinese politics—and he did give Fukuyama and the Chinese intellectuals the most straightforward answer. Wang began by acknowledging the "excellent DNAs" of "the nation, the rule of law, and accountability" rooted in the Chinese civilization, which "should play a role in China's modernization." He frankly admitted that uprooting corruption by the party itself was extremely difficult. Yet in response to Fukuyama's suggestion that the rule of law and an independent judiciary be established so as to eradicate corruption institutionally, Wang replied in an unquestionable tone that the one-party leadership will never be abandoned and the judicial system must be run under the leadership of the Communist Party.[5] What would have further frustrated Fukuyama, as revealed later, was the internal remarks made by Wang ten days earlier at the CCP's Central Disciplinary and Inspection Committee (CDIC). These remarks ranked this allegedly most enlightened Communist politician among the most conservative ultra-leftists in the defense of the totalitarian party-state regime and the Marxist capitalism it created in the reform era, a "socialism of (rather than with) Chinese characteristics," as he repeatedly reiterated.[6]

The CCP's blatant rejection of democracy and the strong measures of Xi Jinping, the all-powerful paramount leader, like Putin's Re-Stalinization in Russia, to reestablish totalitarian rule in China, provided a potent counterargument to Fukuyama's "end of history" thesis. The post-Mao China had instead presented to the outside world an alternative model of "Marxist capitalism"—a distinctive Chinese way of creating "wealth without freedom."[7] This sort of market Leninism has to date created a stunning economic miracle, which as a consequence enormously bolstered the authoritarian regime. Unlike in other authoritarian states in which civil society had kept growing up hand in hand with the economy, the Chinese party state had all the while kept a tight grip over the society and exhibited persistent totalitarian tendencies throughout the reform years. As Wu Guoguang noted, the perplexing paradox was that the Chinese Communist regime intuitively resisted any political change for fear of losing power during an economic crisis, and it felt no need to launch any political reform with a view to increasing its legitimacy during an economic boom.[8] Anyway, as historians often argue, nothing is impossible. In the future, Fukuyama might still have the chance to witness sudden dramatic change in China, like the one that took place in Communist Romania in 1989. That sort of abrupt change might occur not necessarily because of the power of his liberal-materialistic deterministic logic, but because of accidents, such as a major economic crisis, which is a high probability event as a result of the country's deep integration into the global economy. But China might also change in other directions. With democracy having being strenuously demonized by China's Marxist regime, Maoism, in one form or another, might be brought back as a solution to the alienation into New Class of the ruling Marxist capitalists or "capitalist roaders." History is not linear; it can be reversed, and "repeats itself," as Marx claimed.

Furthermore, with relevance to China, Fukuyama's broadly termed "temporary setbacks" might not be "temporary" in global historical terms. It is worth remembering that even the triumph of liberal democracy as proclaimed by Fukuyama in the late 1980s is not preordained. Ideology often makes people blind to historical truths. The moral high ground that liberal democracy holds today has never guaranteed its triumph over other "evil" forms of government as a historical inevitability. It is inconceivable that a liberal democratic order would have been put in place after World War II without the USA. Had the USA not existed, the industrial democracies in Western Europe would have had little chance to vanquish the German Reich in the two world wars. Without a USA committing itself to the European security and recovery after World War II, the capitalist Western Europe would probably have been engulfed in a pro-Communist revolution. In the absence of a powerful industrial democracy of the USA, other forms of government might have prevailed, thereby legitimating multiple pathways of development other than the currently dominant free-market capitalism based on liberal democracy. Take World War I as an example: should the democracies have failed, a most likely outcome without the US intervention, the German Reich would have been better able to project its economic and ideological powers beyond the *Mitteleuropa*, the German-centered Central-European Customs Union. The "New Capitalism" of Germany, an organized authoritarian capitalism characterized by state-led industrialization and welfare-state building, would unequivocally have become the most attractive model of development to late-developing countries in the decades or even centuries that ensued.[9]

Imperial Germany had in actuality offered an alternative form of government and a unique model of development that were deemed not inferior to competing regime types and economic models at the time.[10] The particular way imperial Germany rapidly industrialized in the late nineteenth century had appeared "universalistic" to many late-developing countries that were institutionally weak and thus had to rely on a strong authoritarian state to foster a Gerschenkronian growth to overcome economic backwardness. The German "Asiatic model" of authoritarian capitalism had since been successfully emulated, though to varying degrees, by late-industrializers in East Asia, namely, Japan, South Korea and Taiwan before and after the two world wars. The discrediting of this model, as Liven argued, was not because of its "being less modern and efficient" but because of its being "overthrown by military defeat" in the

World War I.[11] Seen from a broader historical perspective, industrialization without liberal democracy had been the norm. The USA was the only exception among the now-developed countries (NDCs) to have managed to "simultaneously meet the demanding prerequisites of both economic development and a democratic process."[12] For most NDCs, industrialization, which stands for "a brutal and exploitative process" in the takeoff phase, was meant to suppress "redistributive claims on wealth" so as to enable the requisite capital formation and investment by "less democratic or authoritarian regimes" to foster economic and social transformations.[13] This is precisely why Park Chung-hee's hard authoritarian approach to harnessing rapid industrialization in the 1970s was hailed by Samuel Huntington, who, in delving into the turbulent modernization process of "changing societies," underscored the necessity of maintaining order at the critical moment of profound economic change.[14] But even so, both the East Asian regimes (South Korea and Taiwan)' eventual transition to democracy from the late 1980s onward was driven not so much by the "Darwinian evolution process" as by political pressures from the USA, which both the regimes found hard to resist given the acute vulnerabilities of their respective smaller-sized export-dependent economies.[15] The overwhelming primacy of liberal democracy was established only after the sudden collapse of the Soviet Union in 1991. It is worth noting nonetheless that it was Gorbachev's reform blunders and grave miscalculation that caused the collapse of the Soviet system and empire, a momentous event that was in no sense unavoidable.[16]

There is little doubt, therefore, that it is those accidental "events"—military victories of American-led liberal democracies in the two world wars and the largely accidental demise of Soviet Communism in the Cold War—that had made the precarious historical process seem inevitable. If the global Cold War had politicized the discourse of development, making it part of the international relations, the triumph of liberal democracy in the late 1980s, coupled with the failure of the "Southern Challenge," an effort of the less-developed countries (LDCs) to establish a new international economic order (NIEO) in attempt to reform the dominant Western liberal economic order from the 1970s till the mid-1980s, naturally legitimized the neoliberal paradigm as the dominant and only "correct" model of development. Neoliberalism initially arose as the antithesis of Keynesianism. It was a kind of "market fundamentalism," as Stiglitz termed it,[17] that strongly disparaged the role of the state in regulating the market and, in particular, in enforcing industrial policies to foster catch-up. This new paradigm created a superstitious belief that went against the historical truths about how modernization had been achieved by Western powers from the late eighteenth century onward. As Ha-Joon Chang pointed out, "virtually all NDCs" had carried out "interventionist industrial, trade, and technology (ITT) policies" to encourage industrialization at the critical stage of takeoff.[18] Robert Wade noted that even Britain, the first industrial country, had intervened by erecting trade barriers against textile imports from the Dutch. Successful late-industrializers, either the democratic USA or the despotic Germany, had used tariff protection to prop up domestic producers in the late nineteenth century.[19] Even today, the US administration still plays a crucial role in sponsoring innovation of home-grown high-tech firms.[20] Even more often overlooked is the fact that few NDCs nowadays take free trade seriously.[21] Yet the political "triumph of liberal democracy" had effectively discredited all other alternatives to modernity in ideological and practical terms, rating them as economically inefficient and politically retrogressive. This "neoliberal turn" tremendously fostered the global expansion of the liberal order and, as a consequence, confined the developmental options of *late* late-industrializers such as China within a narrow range, subjecting them to increasing systemic pressures for economic liberalization. These late-developing countries were now told that for their economies to succeed, they must orient their economies externally! The rise of China, as depicted by this narrative, is such a good template.

External Orientation: Bound for Economic Success?

China's spectacular economic growth, averaging at 10% from 1978 to 2008, was recognized by the World Bank as being "unprecedented" in economic history.[22] This is not without controversy given the authenticity of the dubious Chinese statistics.[23] Economic historian Harry Wu contended that the newly industrialized economies (NIEs) in East Asia had achieved no less high growth rate in the long 1960s and 1970s.[24] Whatever the truth is, according to most estimates, the Chinese economy had grown faster than most of the OECD (Organization for Economic Cooperation and Development) countries in the Golden Age of economic growth (1950–1973), averaging 4.6% per annum after the end of the Second World War.[25] China's growth miracle was impressive as it was achieved under the same Leninist party-state institutions that have been consistently inimical to enforcement of intellectual property rights (IPR) and protection of private property, the very institutional infrastructures that had led to the rise of the West. The famous "Qian Xuesen question"—China's most distinguished missile scientist, trained in the USA in the 1940s and returned to the People's Republic of China (PRC) in the late 1950s, raised the question with the then Premier Wen Jiabao in 2005 why Chinese universities had been unable to cultivate world-class talents[26]—hinted at China's innovation-hampering institutions that could only engender, as a logical consequence, a pattern of extensive growth, which is part and parcel of China's economic miracle. Extensive growth is by definition "input-driven" as Krugman generalized it.[27] "Input-driven" signifies a nation's dependence on heavy inputs of manpower and raw materials rather than on the increases in total factor productivity (TFP) to generate growth. Extensive growth is difficult to sustain in the long term for being subject to the law of diminishing return. The long-lasting pattern of extensive growth distinguishes China from the Bismarckian Germany in the late nineteenth century where economic growth was driven by rapid industrialization, which was in turn fostered by the country's strength of its preeminence in science and technology. This kind of innovation-driven growth made Germany "the largest and most dynamic economy in Europe" prior to the outbreak of the World War I.[28]

Nevertheless, high growth was possible in the initial stage of socialist industrialization, first and foremost because the brutal revolutionary leader was capable of forcing growth at whatever cost that other types of regime could hardly afford. In addition, forced growth, according to Kornai, is what characterized the socialist system that had to substantiate its superiority over capitalism to legitimize the regime's monopoly of power.[29] Yet forced growth was bound to lose its potency in the long term when the old way of capital formation through harshly curtailing ordinary people's consumption became more and more unlikely in the post-totalitarian era. Except for the hereditary Communist regimes like North Korea, virtually all the second-generation Communist leadership introduced certain sort of "social contract" in a bid to relegitimize the regime through exchanging material benefits for people's political obedience. This entailed some sort of welfare-state building ironically on the back of the high accumulation accomplished in the totalitarian era. In the absence of TFP increases, however, the depletion of accumulation began to retard the economic growth. Without overhauling the entire system of the command economy, some limited market-driven reforms were far from sufficient to stem the general trend of economic decline or even stagnation, as had been evidenced by the failures of market socialist experiments in Poland and Hungary, and in a way the Soviet Union from the 1960s until the 1980s.

China by contrast had waged the most far-reaching economic reform since the late 1970s. The reform did have weakened central planning by unleashing substantial market forces beyond state control throughout the 1990s. However, forced growth as the most crucial institutional vestige of the Chinese socialist system remains. The administrative decentralization from the 1980s onward and the central state's inability to integrate the national market in a constitutional way gave rise to economic balkanization. It is the provinces rather than the central state that had since become the key agents of industrialization and the dominant resource allocators. They, assisted by another institutional legacy—regional autarky inherited from Mao's era—have every incentive to meet and even exceed the regime's preset growth target by mobilizing all available resources, domestic (sponsoring big state-owned enterprises; SOEs) or foreign (encouraging foreign direct investment [FDI]) at all costs, within their spheres of influence. This was particularly the case after 1992 when the economic growth was decidedly linked to political legitimacy. This sort of de-centered "whole-nation" system was distinctly the institutional feature of the Chinese "socialist market economy." Anyhow, with the unfolding of marketization reform throughout the 1990s, especially the fiscal and banking reforms since the mid-1990s, which were in part designed to contain the so-called soft budget constraint, the ending of the shortage economy from 1996 onward called forced growth into serious question.

Conventional wisdom more often than not accredited Chinese long-lasting "most rapid" growth to the country's gradualist approach to enforcing the market-oriented reform, arguing that China had managed to keep the economy growing rapidly while keeping the market forces at bay and maintaining social order forcefully—and, by so doing, China successfully prevented the precarious reform process from going out of control. This line of argument was partly true. Economic liberalization was indeed piecemeal in the 1980s but became radicalized throughout the 1990s in the key areas of either the price reform (1993–1994) or the privatization of the SOEs from the mid-1990s onward. On the surface, China's supply-side reforms did not result in the magnitude of transitional decline that had engulfed many of the former socialist economies in the Soviet Bloc. But the brutal fact is that Chinese public sector industries did decline precipitously in the most turbulent reform years of the 1990s.[30] The domestic industrial decline had led to massive layoffs of SOEs' workers, leading to substantial shortfall in consumption, which in turn caused the economy to shrink. Economic hardships resulting from the painstaking restructuring of SOEs could be felt everywhere across the country. Paradoxically, the deflationary Chinese economy at the macro-level continued to grow robustly. What had made up for the domestic demand shortfall was the country's dramatic turning to external orientation from the early 1990s onward. This decisive shift, though in a way inheriting the coastal development strategy of the late 1980s, formed the basis of China's new national development strategy within which an export-led growth had become its central preoccupation.

China's external-oriented development strategy has been widely considered an imitation of the newly industrialized economies (NIEs) in East Asia that used export trade as the engine of growth from the early 1960s until the 1980s.[31] The so-called East Asian model is a problematic term since it covers four economies of South Korea, Taiwan, Hong Kong and Singapore that differed significantly in regard to the role of the state in economic development. Bar the laissez-faire Hong Kong, the other three states were all interventionist, though to varying degrees. Unlike the city-state of Singapore that heavily relied on FDI to spur industrial development, South Korea and Taiwan promoted exports while closing the door to market-seeking foreign investors. The rise of the East Asian NIEs occurred in the early 1980s when many Latin American countries were being plunged into a severe debt crisis. Against the backdrop of global neoliberal turn, the striking developmental divergences between East Asia and Latin America had to a great extent discredited the structuralist dependency theory many Latin American countries had subscribed to with a view to escaping from the entrenched world-system structure of global capitalism. The World Bank cited the East Asian NIEs as the template of liberal developmentalism, accrediting their success to "free markets, free trade and an export-oriented development."[32] As leading proponents of neoliberalism, the World Bank and the International Monetary Fund (IMF) extolled the East Asian NIEs' export-oriented industrialization (EOI) approach as being superior to that of the inward-looking, market-distorting, and catch-up oriented import-substituting industrialization (ISI) that the economically nationalist Latin American countries had carried out from the late nineteenth century onward. The logic behind this neoliberal assertion was unequivocally what Stiglitz called "market fundamentalism."[33] Within the new paradigm, GDP growth became the central criterion in the 1980s to measure performance[34]; technology was regarded as being costless and thus given no place; catch-up was disavowed intellectually; and export-led growth was dictated as the only correct way to economic success.[35]

However prevalent those liberal interpretations of the East Asian model were at the "neoliberal turn" in the 1980s and 1990s, they came to be confronted by a new generation of Western-based development economists who theorized the pathway of East Asian development of South Korea and Taiwan (excluding the two city-states, Hong Kong and Singapore) as having adopted an illiberal state-centered approach of economic development called the "developmental state," the forerunner of which was Japan.[36] This was a unique planning-rational approach, through which the strong state utilized both the institutional advantages of capitalism and socialism to direct the country's industrialization based on private property and a regulated market. Except Hong Kong, markets were not entirely free in the tiger economies, and nor was trade. State intervention was pervasive and powerful in coercing a state corporatist public–private partnership to serve the purpose of attaining national technological independence by nurturing the productive capabilities of the local firms. Behind these market-distorting measures lay the staunchest belief in economic nationalism, particularly the notion of infant industry protection (IIP), no less resonant than that in Latin America in the 1950s. Ironically, these left-wing intellectual critiques had been seldom heard or even deliberately ignored in the Communist-led China throughout the whole reform era. By contrast, where Friedrich List was everywhere in South Korea in the 1960s and 1970s,[37] Adam Smith and David Ricardo were omnipresent on Chinese university campuses and had captured the hearts and minds of the decision-makers from the 1990s until today.[38] China's sheer misperception of the vaguely termed East Asian model was rooted in its own preference for external orientation on political grounds when Deng Xiaoping made his "opening-up" irreversible in 1992.[39] What China had overlooked is the fact that all the East Asian NIEs were resource-poor economies whose internal markets were much smaller, making it an economic imperative for external orientation so as to achieve the required economies of scale. The three economic superpowers—the USA, Germany and Japan—resource-rich or poor, had industrialized through import substitution based on their relatively large domestic markets.[40] Ignoring its inborn advantage as a (potential) large economy backed up by a huge domestic market, China carried out an outward-oriented development strategy that is naturally suited for small economies.

Like the NDCs in their capitalist development, the East Asian regimes are strong states. For late-comer industrializers, a strong state is essential for modernization.[41] The developmental states of South Korea and Taiwan had industrialized first and foremost because they had a strong state apparatus staffed by competent bureaucrats exercising selective interventions. Both had used export promotion to dynamize their economies to foster the industrial transformation, the importance of which was far greater than mere economic growth. In contrast, the strong party state of China and its external orientation have, to date, failed to create an advanced industrial economy as sophisticated as the East Asian developmental states, not to mention the three economic superpowers. Institutional differences between China and the East Asian developmental states were self-evident and do matter significantly given the former's entrenched legacy of anti-intellectualism in the PRC's history. What deserves to be particularly highlighted is the ad hoc international context that accommodated their respective external orientations. For the East Asian NIEs, however efficient and effective their strong state institutions turned out to be, they might not be able to make their external orientation work unless under favorable international conditions. As a *late* late-industrializer, in contrast, the outward-oriented China was facing a considerably harsher external developmental environment than the tigers economies did at similar stage of economic development.

It is argued that both China and the East Asian Tigers had benefited enormously from the liberal order that the USA established after World War II. This line of argument is plausible in narrow economic growth terms. Yet development is not merely about growth; it is more importantly about "catching up and getting even."[42] This inevitably entails industrial policies characteristic of economic nationalism with a view to nurturing domestic players or even national champions as the agents of industrialization. At the core of the postwar liberal order lay the Bretton Woods System (BWS) jointly created by the USA and Britain in 1944. This was a multilateral institutional arrangement based on the principle of so-called embedded liberalism. This was a kind of enlightened liberalism that stands for the grand compromise between the Smithian free trade doctrine and the Keynesian interventionism. By detaching international trade from domestic policies, known as "shallow integration," countries were expected to interact with the global economy most actively while preserving sufficient policy autonomy at home for the sake of full employment. This kind of so-called Keynesian enlightened liberalism[43] that combined shallow integration with welfare state ushered in a golden age of two-decade-long economic prosperity in the capitalist First World after World War II.

From the late 1950s and early 1960s, South Korean and Taiwanese economies began to take off. Both countries shifted to export orientation after the first stage of ISI was completed. They exported huge amounts of low value-added manufactured products to developed countries in exchange for capital goods to be used for their second stage of ISI to further their industrial deepening and economic diversification. They were fortunate enough to see their export boom assimilated by the global trade expansion as a result of the unprecedented prosperity within the capitalist

First World. Taiwan, in the name of the Republic of China (ROC), was the founding member of the General Agreement on Tariffs and Trade (GATT), one of the three Bretton Woods institutions overseeing international trade. It withdrew membership from GATT only until 1972, when the ROC was replaced by the PRC in the United Nations (UN). South Korea joined GATT in 1967 with the help of the USA. As the few developing countries that joined the Rich Countries' Club, Taiwan and South Korea took a free ride on the multilateral tariff cuts of industrial goods negotiated by the developed countries. In addition, as the strategic allies of the USA, both tigers were accorded unilateral preferences in terms of exporting to US market without being asked for reciprocity. This was accompanied by the US tolerance of their restrictions on FDI with an aim to protect domestic infant industries, which was another significant unilateral preference the US reserved specifically for the tigers. Furthermore, the USA provided huge amount of economic and military aids and transferred technologies to the two East Asian allies. The total amount of aid provided for the tigers was even greater than what had been provided for the African nations as a whole.[44]

Given the extent of economic backwardness of the two East Asian tigers prior to their takeoff, even though they had inherited considerable Japanese developmental state institutional legacies, it is not beyond doubt that they could have succeeded without the massive sponsorship of the USA. Although their developmental outcomes had rendered the dependency theory, which viewed the dynamic international relations as ahistorical and static, practically obsolete, their success was largely accidental since this was the result of "development by invitation"—a deliberate US Cold War policy that made their external orientation work.[45] In other words, external orientation per se does not guarantee economic success. Their economic success only demonstrates that even within the entrenched world-system structure of global capitalism, escaping dependency is still possible so long as later-comer industrializers were the lucky "chosen few" of the USA.[46] This in no sense implies that countries not being the chosen few of the USA would never have the chance to modernize, but evidently a much less favorable international context would no doubt make an outward-oriented development much more difficult.

As a Communist great power, China was extremely backward economically in the early 1970s. It had never been among the "chosen few" even when it allied with the USA to oppose the Soviet Union in the later years of the Cold War. From the Sino-US rapprochement until the 1980s when the two powers were in strategic honeymoon, the post-Bretton Woods world economy had been gloomy, international trade grew slowly, and protectionism was on the rise within the entire First World. From the early 1980s onward, even the tigers were forcibly "graduated" from US unilateral preferences. When Western Europe and Japan, along with a couple of Second World Communist countries, extended to China the treatment of generalized system of preferences (GSP) normally accorded to the least-developed countries (LDCs) in Africa, the Caribbean, and the Pacific, the USA did not follow suit. Instead, it granted China a conditional most-favored-nation (MFN) trading status subject to annual review by the Congress as per the 1974 Jackson-Vanik Amendment that linked MFN with free emigration. The end of the global Cold War in 1989 terminated the Sino-US strategic partnership. The falling apart of the Soviet Union in 1991 ushered in the unipolar moment whereby the USA became the sole superpower. The central focus of the American foreign policy after the Cold War has been to prevent the emergence of peer rivals from challenging its hegemonic leadership.[47] Parallel to this realist instinct stood the liberal belief in inducing desired change inside China through strategic engagement. The hybrid of containment and engagement, or "congagement," became part and parcel of US grand strategy under Bill Clinton (1993–2001) with a view to fully integrating China into the international system of global capitalism. Central to this objective was integrating China into the global economy. As a matter of fact, committing China to deep integration by fusing its trade and domestic policies reflects the joint effort of both the USA and the Bretton Woods institutions to finalize the neoliberal turn in economic and strategic terms. Ignoring its own history of industrialization through tariff protection, the USA, by taking advantage of China's desperate need for membership with the World Trade Organization (WTO), exerted heavy pressures on China in the late 1990s, committing it to liberalizing trade and investment in an extremely radical way.[48] Compared with GATT, the WTO had legally removed substantial policy space left for less-developed countries. According to Ha-Joon Chang, the new development regime, epitomized by the WTO's neoliberal rules, was anti-developmental in terms of virtually outlawing industrial policies to facilitate catch-up.[49] Against such a backdrop, in what way could China make globalization work to its own benefit?

Two Dominant Interpretations

Michael Pillsbury, the former "panda hugger"—a bantering appellation for pro-Beijing China expert—who also has close ties with Washington's national security apparatus, all of a sudden changed his attitude toward China in 2015 by publishing a new book titled *The Hundred-Year Marathon: China's Secret Strategy to Replace America as the Global Superpower*. In this shocking book, Pillsbury, based on interviews with Chinese defectors and declassified US national security documents, described how an aspiring China has been following a grand strategy since 1949 of rising to a global superpower within 100 years at the expense of the USA. According to him, "For more than forty years, the United States has played an indispensable role helping the Chinese government build a booming economy, develop its scientific and military capabilities, and take its place on the world stage, in the belief that China's rise will bring us cooperation, diplomacy, and free trade."[50] Deeply grudgingly, Pillsbury contended that China, on the one hand, had used strategic deception to "manipulate perceptions of dominant world power" and, on the other hand, had promoted mercantilism by erecting high tariff barriers to build up its industrial strength.

Pillsbury's assertion about China's "secret strategy" is dubious as this may have confused the verbally aggressive nationalist rhetoric of the Chinese Communist Party (CCP), overt or covet, with China's actual economic and foreign policies. As a matter of fact, seldom has there been a country like China in which the leadership after Deng Xiaoping has been so obsessed with free trade economically and imbued with idealistic pacifism politically.[51] The class-struggle-minded Mao Zedong might once have had a fanciful plan of global domination primarily through projecting ideological power and sponsoring Third World revolutions beyond

Chinese borders.[52] Post-Mao leaders, including Deng, were short-sighted pragmatists who had neither the vision nor the statecraft to construct a new world order superior to the liberal order crafted by the USA after World War II. Their intellectual background had given them neither proper knowledge of, nor real insights into, what the current liberal order meant, how it came about, and in what way could it be overturned.[53] Pillsbury emphasized the indispensable "helping" role of the USA in China's economic and military modernization. But he avoided mentioning the fact that forcing China to relinquish economic nationalism had been crucial to the US grand strategy of fully integrating China into the international system; and globalizing the Chinese economy along neoliberal line was exactly grounded in the belief that the rule-based multilateral order was "easy to join but hard to overturn."[54]

It is fairly doubtful that the USA really believed that economic liberalism would lead to modernity since there is no such precedent in economic history, itself being the best example of development through mercantilism—tariff protection, to be more specific. Not being among the chosen few, had China been "helped" by the USA to escape dependency through the neoliberal rules of the WTO that were "deeply anti-developmental" in nature?[55] That sounds incredibly bizarre. Was the US administration, determined to prevent peer rivals from emerging after the Cold War, so easily cheated as to have utterly ignored China's repeated attempts to modernize along mercantilist lines over such a long period of time? In fact, although misjudging China's evolutionary trajectory, the USA was by no means altruistic in integrating China into the global economy from the very outset. The US producers, by focusing on high value-added activities in the global supply chain, had "done equally well or even better" than their Chinese counterparts that had little choice but to engage in low-tech assembly with razor-thin profit margins.[56] Chinese firms, despite great strides in many respects, still lag far behind the US global firms in innovation terms.[57] The weird dichotomy that "China gains trade surplus; the US gains trade profits" highlights a seriously asymmetrical economic interdependence as a result of a hugely uneven distribution of relative gains. This sort of bilateral trade relationship has rendered the Chinese economy more vulnerable to the precarious Sino-US relations.

Nevertheless, like Pillsbury's, the prevailing views, either for or against free market and unfettered globalization, held that "China was globalization's greatest success story during the last quarter century."[58] This contrasts China with a good many developing and transition economies that had been devastated by globalization in its finest hours (1986–2005). Joseph Stiglitz reprehended hyperglobalization for those misfortunes. He contended that globalization was a neutral force that was neither good nor bad.[59] As such, Pillsbury's highly politicized "Hundred-Year Marathon" discourse can be reduced to a relatively neutral question: China and globalization: who has taken advantage of whom? This has already invoked entirely divergent interpretations on what actually led to China's economic miracle in the post-Cold War era of liberal globalization.

To the market liberals, there is nothing peculiar with the Chinese model of development. China succeeded because "globalization works."[60] China's and India's "successful move to the market" in terms of "economic liberalization" and "international integration" was the necessary if not the sufficient condition for their economic success.[61] The widely cited "historically unprecedented poverty reduction"[62] of China in the past three decades was the most compelling evidence of the efficacy of liberal globalization.[63] The market skeptics interpreted the Chinese miracle in a more nuanced way from a statist perspective. They were inspired by the extraordinarily strong state capacity of China that had intervened to stem the economy from falling further amidst the most devastating global financial crisis after World War II in the years of 2008 and 2009. Thanks to the intervention, the Chinese economy not only resumed momentum but grew faster. Its GDP overtook that of Germany in 2009 and Japan in 2010 to become the second largest economy. In March 2011, China outpaced the USA to be the "world's top manufacturing country by output."[64] It had been widely expected ever since to become the largest economy by 2020 or even as early as 2016.[65]

The market skeptics, predominantly left-wing development economists, were generally not opposed to globalization per se. They were for "mild globalization" and against so-called hyperglobalization, a variant of what Stiglitz called "market fundamentalism."[66] Mild globalization was the product of the Bretton Woods System that had existed mainly in the capitalist First World until the mid-1970s. National governments were allowed to play a proactive role in regulating the markets and cross-border capital flows. This sort of "embedded liberalism" that characterized the Bretton Woods System had made globalization manageable and less harmful. Having witnessed the wide-ranging failures of the neoliberal Washington Consensus[67] in Africa, Latin America and the transition economies, the market skeptics accredited the success of the East Asian countries, including China, to "their ability to take advantage of globalization, without being taken advantage of by globalization."[68] As they understood it, China was truly exceptional in terms of dancing with the new wave of liberal globalization. Rodrik argued that by gradually opening its markets for imports and foreign investors, China "shielded itself from the global economy," thereby averting the negative impact of the volatile world economy. Meanwhile, China made efforts to "build a modern industrial base" through "fostering domestic capabilities." For this sake, China "welcomed foreign companies" but "used a number of policies to ensure that technology transfer would take place and strong domestic players would emerge."[69] Rodrik asserted that "China played the globalization game by Bretton Woods rules rather than the post-1990 rules of deep integration."[70] Stiglitz and Lall held similar views. Both agreed that China was cautious enough not to "remove tariff barriers" too quickly and refused to fully liberalize the capital account.[71] Golub maintained that China had adopted an EOI strategy that was "modeled on the neo-mercantilist strategies of earlier East Asian developmental states." This, along with its "gradual integration into the world capitalist economy," had generated strong and sustained growth "over long periods." He argued that China's successful pathway was somewhat similar to "US economic expansion in the nineteenth century."[72] In short, the market skeptics considered China's success to be rooted in its incompliance with the neoliberal Washington Consensus.

The above two prevailing views converged on the positive effect of globalization on the Chinese economy, but diverged on the role of the Chinese state in managing globalization. Both arguments are flawed in logical and/or empirical terms. The market liberals overlooked the fact that major reduction of poverty was achieved in the 1980s when China's integration in the world economy was "shallow" and the market forces were considerably weaker as compared with the 1990s and beyond. And deep integration that began from the early 1990 until beyond China's accession to the WTO did not expedite the reduction of poverty but rather increased "the number of people living in extreme poverty.[73] In addition, despite the fact that China had attained most of the United Nations Millennium Development Goals (MDGs) in early 2015,[74] the absolute number of people living in extreme poverty remains huge as per the World Bank criterion of living on and less than US $1.25 per day rather than China's own.[75] In response to the critics from the market skeptics regarding the failures of the Washington Consensus, in particular the increased number of people living in extreme poverty (excluding China) during the heyday of globalization,[76] the market liberals resorted to so-called post-Washington Consensus, arguing that institutions matter in the first place. In other words, late-developers should "get the institutions rights" before "getting the prices right." While blaming the institutional failures in many parts of the world for the dysfunction of globalization, they turned a blind eye to the conspicuously "bad" institutions of the Chinese state. Had globalization worked to China's economic growth through the country's "bad" institutions, why had it not worked to China's innovation and catch-up, the two key indicators of development?

The market skeptics rightly took note of the critical role of the state in economic development. Their deep distrust of market fundamentalism made them inclined to believe that China must have vigorously resisted the dogma of the Washington Consensus in terms of regulating the market, sponsoring the SOEs and reining in imports and FDI to spur domestic industrial development in a proactive way. They got major facts seriously wrong. Statism is not the emblem of China's wholesale rejection of the Washington Consensus,[77] nor is it the synonym for the country's commitment to economic nationalism. As mentioned earlier, the Chinese authoritarian regime has promoted privatization and trade and investment liberalization in a strongly statist way. There is no doubt that the Chinese regime has been intervening extensively in the economy, which naturally gives the semblance of a strong state. But the purpose of the intervention is the key to understanding the nature of the Chinese state. It is arguable that the state per se is predatory in nature.[78] A strong state is particularly prone to be predatory in light of its powerful extractive capacity. A developmental state is first and foremost a strong state that aims to achieve the overwhelming national objective of modernization. For this purpose, authoritarian regimes in Taiwan and South Korea, the two typical developmental states, were not hesitant in controlling corruption heavy-handedly. By contrast, a strong state is not necessarily a developmental state. It could denigrate into a "soft state," as Myrdal called it,[79] whose overriding task is to enrich itself.[80]

For more than a decade, the Chinese government has been repeatedly ranked among the most corrupt regimes in the world.[81] Compared with the developmental states in East Asia, the Chinese bureaucracy, which is much bigger in size in both absolute and relative terms, is far more corrupt and less competent.[82] One crucial aspect of the Chinese state's self-enrichment was precisely large-scale privatization of the SOEs from the mid-1990s onward in the name of "corporate restructuring" and building "modern enterprise system (corporate governance)," which was well in line with the Washington Consensus prescription. This type of state-led nomenclatura privatization had led to rampant "asset stripping" rather than "wealth creation."[83] The regime's conversion to the Washington Consensus was further manifested in its radical liberalization of trade and investment before and after the country's entry into the WTO. The Chinese state was strong enough to overcome fierce oppositions at home by accepting harsh conditions for WTO membership. China's deep integration in terms of forgoing economic nationalism, embodied by its drastic tariff cuts, removal of non-tariff barriers (NTBs) and liberalization of inbound FDI, was hard to reverse as it had been highly institutionalized not only by its extensive market access commitments but also by the mechanisms specifically created inside the USA and the WTO to monitor China's compliance on a routine basis. These institutional constraints suffice to make any attempt of the member state to evade its obligations beyond the WTO's legal limits extremely difficult if not completely impossible. Blind to these crude facts, the market skeptics put China in the wrong time and space, imaging that it could still play by the "Bretton Woods rules." They seriously overstated the policy space left for China's development within the WTO's legal framework, or what Rodrik called the "post-1990s rules of deep integration." Comparing China to the nineteenth-century USA that industrialized through tariff protection entirely missed the point. The USA was genuinely mercantilist; China was not! It was far more economically internationalist (liberal) than nationalist.

Are There Alternative Pathways of Development in the Age of Liberal Globalization?

"External orientation" of a national economy does not guarantee economic success on both theoretical and empirical grounds. Therefore, before delving into alternative solutions, the neo-Marxist dependency and world-system theories deserve to be revisited: Are they still valid, or to what extent are they relevant under current circumstances?

Drawing inspirations from the dependency theory that emerged and came into fruition in the 1950s and 1960s, Emmanuel Wallerstein developed the world-system theory in the 1970s. Wallerstein sees capitalism as a world system from the time of its inception in the sixteenth century. Both the dependency and world-system theorists agree that the capitalist world system has structured a rigid international division of labor between the developed nations (core) and the developing nations (periphery). The core exports high value-added industrial goods while importing primary goods from the periphery, thereby generating vastly disproportionate wealth to the core. Such an exploitative relationship based on unequal exchange makes the rich nations richer and the poor nations poorer, hence the "development of underdevelopment."[84]

Nevertheless, from the 1960s onward, both schools acknowledged that the capitalist system allowed some room for development, and that the international division of labor did not always take place between the secondary-producing core and primary-producing periphery, but "between countries with different degrees of industrialization."[85] Wallerstein, who views the capitalist world economy as a dynamic system that changes over time, adds a new level in the world-system hierarchy: semi-periphery or semi-industrialized countries that serve as a buffer between the core and the periphery. Created by the world system, they are "both the exploiter and the exploited" that exist to "make a capitalist world-economy run smoothly."[86] This evokes the notion of "dependent development," as propounded by Peter Evans,[87] to characterize those previously underdeveloped countries that had managed to find a "pathway from the periphery" but were finding it still difficult to become the core.

Different from the neoclassical economists in the 1940s who eschewed "confronting enormously complex questions about the causes of poverty or the persistence of inequality" and focused instead on economic growth alone as the "benchmark of progress,"[88] dependency theorists made an important distinction between economic growth and economic development. For them, economic activity that takes place within a dependent state may not benefit the nation as a whole. "Social indicators" such as "life expectancy, literacy, infant mortality, education, and the like" are far more important.[89] Underlining national economic and political independence, they saw the need to sever ties, at least partially, with the capitalist system. But delinking was extremely difficult because of the existence of a "comprador class" that allied themselves with global capitalists in the metropolitan core. Many of the elites were trained in the West. They "voluntarily" maintained the dependency relationship not necessarily because they "consciously" betrayed national interests or interest of the poor, but because they sincerely believed that "the key to economic development lies in following the prescriptions of liberal economic doctrine."[90]

Among a plethora of critiques of the dependency theory, the most cogent was about its grave oversight of "internal factors." As Wilson and Economides convincingly argued, "Corruption, government mismanagement, nepotism and the systemic denial of civil liberties have been common ills in the body politic of many Third World states since they achieved their independence in the 1960s and 1970s. … It is these ills, rather than 'structural imperialism', or the inherently exploitative nature of the world capitalist system that account for their continued impoverishment."[91] With or without these "internal factors," nonetheless, the theory's central contention about the structural rigidity of the capitalist world system remains vibrant. This can be seen clearly from the strong presence of the powerful "comprador class" in many developing and transition economies. They were the building blocks to the global neoliberal turn since the turn of the 1980s. Collaborating with elites in the core, they have to varying degrees captured the state to adopt policies to the detriment of national economic interests. But far more importantly, nonetheless, it is the core states, led by the USA, that engineered an unprecedented institutional entrenchment of global capitalism in the aftermath of the Cold War by setting in motion the deeply anti-statist, anti-developmental "post-1990s rules of deep integration." Given the size of the externally integrated Chinese economy, its actual developmental outcome has become the best testing stone of the dependency theory in the present day. Is China's amazing Ricardian growth miracle the hard evidence of irresistible rise or dependent development after all?

The prevailing preconception that China has risen was to a huge extent misguided by the country's high growth rate achieved thus far that had made China exceptional in terms of outperforming many other developing and transition economies in the "golden age" of hyperglobalization. Yet unlike the East Asian developmental states that had industrialized in one generation, China has to date not escaped dependency. It remains a semi-peripheral country whose various attempts to upgrade into more sophisticated high value-added knowledge-intensive industrial activities have been largely unsuccessful.[92] This sort of "growth without development" (hereby narrowly defined as catch-up),[93] which is typical of a dependent development,[94] underlined the fact that China is far from being fully industrialized into an advanced high-income economy. Rather, it is being faced with an increasing peril of falling into the so-called middle-income trap.[95] This is a brutal reality even the authoritarian Communist leaders and bureaucrats, whose basic instinct was to overstate the positives and understate or cover up the negatives, were reluctant to deny.[96] China's current status as an incomplete economic powerhouse as evidenced by the still large population living in extreme poverty,[97] ever-enlarging wealth gap between the rich and poor,[98] low per capita GDP in both exchange rate and purchasing power parity (PPP) terms,[99] and most importantly, the enduring technological dependency of its domestic industries, did not make the country unique among the developing nations in their unsuccessful quest for modernization through deep external integration. This has once again called the prevailing paradigm of liberal globalization, an outward-oriented pathway of liberal developmentalism, into question.

Are there alternative pathways of development in the post-Bretton Woods age of liberal globalization at all? Or to be more specific, were there feasible alternatives available to China in the reform era that began from the late 1970s? Let us begin with the non-integration approach. It has been widely accepted that "economic autarky is not the road to prosperity."[100] This is plausible from a long-term perspective because first and foremost no country could attain complete self-sufficiency in everything. The Soviet model of rapid industrialization from the 1920s through the 1930s was a rare example of an early phase near-autarkic industrial development propped up by the country's comprehensive resource endowments and relatively strong science and technology capacity. However, the long process of modernization, embodied in the form of constant industrial upgrading and economic diversification, will sooner or later generate greater demand for raw materials not necessarily available at home, and larger markets a trade-exclusive autarkic development would be hard to satisfy. Even Nazi Germany, highly advanced in synthesizing chemical compounds to substitute imports, was ultimately incapable of achieving an empire-wide strategic autarky.[101] That the resource-abundant USA embraced liberal internationalism after World War II was in large part driven by the need to ensure its economic security through free access to strategically important raw materials and larger markets beyond national borders.[102] For late-comer industrializers, albeit many of them were richly endowed with natural resources, development, normally defined as catch-up through industrial upgrading, requires a lengthy and complicated learning process to be completed through the importation of capital goods and new technologies, and, perhaps more importantly, of institutions from the advanced economies. The importation of capital goods requires hard currencies that must be earned through exports. In addition, as the late-developers' "restricted national markets" are not large enough for new industries that "heavily relied on" "the scale of a global market," "global integration" becomes an economic imperative.[103] Hence, economic autarky is neither possible nor desirable nor viable for development. The dirigist inward-looking ISI strategy many Latin American nations had carried out from the 1930s until the late 1980s was not autarkic all the way through. Their second-stage import substitution of capital goods had involved substantial participation of FDI. As most liberal reformist strand dependency theorists had recognized, delinking from the capitalist world system is by no means the solution to underdevelopment.[104] This is particularly true when globalization, as far as its positive aspect is concerned, has drastically facilitated the diffusion of knowledge through cross-border movement of goods, capital and information, making it possible for developing nations to skip certain stages of development to expedite catch-up.[105]

Anyhow, import substitution is what national industrialization, autarkic or not, is predicated upon. The strategy of ISI is by definition to sponsor the growth of "nationally owned enterprises" (NOEs),[106] or "local industrial sector"—to put it another way—as the "the source of innovation" and for creating the "spillover effect on the rest of the economy."[107] According to Stiglitz, those "short-term inefficiencies" arising from the market-distorting infant industry protection "are more than offset by long-term dynamic gains."[108] And one such gain is unequivocally the establishment of an independent technological-industrial base which lays the very foundation of national economic modernization. It has been argued that the lateness of switching to export orientation is what had caused the failure of ISI in Latin America. Raul Prebisch had presciently advocated such a policy turn as early as the late 1950s at the rightful moment when the East Asian tigers' export drive was just to begin. Unlike the resource-poor East Asian NIEs whose domestic markets were relatively small that they had to orient their economies externally, many Latin American NIEs were rich in natural resources whose domestic markets were much larger, making it still possible to carry on ISI further. As a matter of fact, far from being a failed strategy that is doomed from the very start, ISI had achieved enormous success in quite a number of Latin American countries, especially the large ones, in terms of effecting rapid economic and social transformations. As Rodrik argued,

> ISI countries experienced rapid productivity growth as their economies diversified away from traditional agriculture into manufacturing activities. … Our best studies indicate that during the sixties and seventies economy-

> wide productivity grew more rapidly in import-substituting Latin America than it did in export-oriented East Asia. Latin America's economies expanded at a slower clip than East Asia's not because they experienced slower technological progress but because they invested a lower share of their national income.[109]

Contrary to the cliché of the neoliberal paradigm that contraposed EOI with ISI, the export-oriented "East Asian Miracle" was rooted in successful import substitution of, first, labor-intensive non-durable consumer goods, then skill-intensive capital and durable consumer goods, each being followed by substantial export promotion drive of the authoritarian state that carried out a strategic rather than a deep integration approach to protecting their domestic industries and to liberalizing trade and investment in an incremental way. As Sanchez argued, "Economic development is the result of a much more complex matrix of factors,"[110] or the combination of export promotion and import substitution,[111] to say the least. Neither EOI nor ISI alone can guarantee economic success. The USA and Germany achieved unprecedented prosperity in the late nineteenth century as a result of the most successful ISI, which was sustained by a massive export boom thanks to the first wave of globalization in human history.[112] Henceforth, which of the two approaches, EOI or ISI, is to emerge as the dominant strategy is contingent upon the market size of the late-developer concerned and the international context at that very moment to accommodate its development strategy. For the Latin American NIEs during the Cold War, even if they had turned to export orientation in a timely fashion, to what extent would they have been able to gain from the global trade boom in the 1960s—a prerequisite for achieving the needed global economies of scale for their new industries so as to make the EOI strategy work—remains an outstanding issue. For one thing, not being among the "chosen few" would make privileged access to the huge US domestic market entirely unwarranted. The same can be said for the East Asian developmental states. Given their much smaller home markets, had they not been among the "chosen few," they would have had a much smaller chance to succeed in industrial development without being accorded special treatment of the USA, be it access to the US market on unilateral basis, the US sponsorship in terms of helping both countries to normalize diplomatic relations with Japan, or the American strategic tolerance to their import substitution at home.

Achieving EOI is conceivably difficult for China given its "empire's" size and huge population. First and foremost, the liberal order created by the USA after World War II could only accommodate "one or two Japans" given the global stock of raw materials, and the USA is neither willing nor likely to "guarantee China's access to sufficient primary products."[113] This is reinforced by the fact that although the liberal order did offer the chance of "upward mobility" for late-comer industrializers, development is by no means non-ideological. Either the reemergence of Japan or the rise of the East Asian NIEs was the result of "development by invitation," which was part of the US Cold War grand strategy to roll back global Communism. For China, even if it allied with the USA during the Cold War or even evolved itself into a capitalist state after the Cold War, the country's population size per se suffices to make the liberal order ill afford its EOI approach as far as the availability of and/or accessibility to raw materials and the potentiality of global export markets were concerned. Such conspicuous strategic vulnerability as entailed by external orientation, coupled with the "deeply anti-developmental" constraints of the global institutions, such as the WTO, informs that so long as the PRC aims to achieve an autonomous modernization, it would have little alternative but to reflect again on its old approach of national self-reliance and proceed with a market-based, resource-efficient ISI through deepening *internal* integration and engaging with the global economy via shallow (strategic) *external* integration.[114]

Upon delving into conditions for development based on the East Asian model, Robert Wade made an important distinction between two forms of integration: internal integration and external integration. He argued that "the development of a national economy is more about internal integration than about external integration."[115] The economy with a high internal integration requires "a dense set of links between sectors." Meanwhile, robust political coalitions between the capitalists and workers become likely in that wages are not just the cost of production but also the source of consumption. As a result, "export demand is not the main source of economic growth."[116] In contrast, for an economy with a low internal integration, domestic sectors are loosely connected. As wages are "seen simply as a cost, not also source of demand," economic growth relies on export such that sectors producing for foreign market are further detached from the domestic market. Such a low internal integration economy, Wade argued, "has no basis for class alliances and democratic regimes."[117] Thus, by defining development as a normative process of autonomous modernization based on domestic sectoral integration through backward-forward linkages and social cohesion under the auspices of progressive (though not necessarily democratic) regimes, Wade established a link between development and social democracy. To put it another way, a statist-oriented internal integration not only lays the foundation for autonomous national development but also enhances the possibility for peaceful democratic transformation afterward.

In defiance to the prevailing neoliberal paradigm that tends to view deep (external) integration as panacea to development, Wade dismissed the possibility that external integration will bolster internal integration, which is the most essential prerequisite for development. Quite the contrary, Wade argued, "more external integration can erode more internal integration."[118] Nevertheless, he did not regard the two forms of integration as mutually exclusive. He favored instead a national development strategy that would "operate in the zone where the two forms of integration reinforce rather than undermine each other." As he saw it, the best strategy for developing nations was to "combine the principle of comparative advantage and the principle of import replacement."[119] Such an approach, well-grounded both theoretically and empirically, stands for a consensus reached by a handful of world's most famous development economists, including Wade himself, Amsden, Sanchez, and some others. It appears a particularly appealing option for large developing nations like China to prioritize ISI over EOI through deepening internal integration. Such an option signifies that by boosting backward and forward linkages to nurture densely linking local sectors within the protected home markets and by fostering class alliance between capitalists and workers, the national state will be in a very strong position to achieve a demand-driven autonomous development. Extrapolating from this vantage point, it can be clearly seen that China is naturally suited for ISI. The country's huge market potential, the remaining socialist legacies in terms of both job security and a highly egalitarian income distribution inherited from Mao's era, a still rich endowment in raw materials in the early years of reform and opening, a "large scientific community,"[120] and, perhaps most crucially, a well-established and integrated national industrial system founded in the pre-reform era, which was rare among the developing nations at comparable stage of economic development, all constitute favorable conditions for national development on a *refreshingly* self-reliant basis.

"Refreshingly" refers to the reality that in the era of reform and opening, an ISI based on internal integration is by no means autarkic. Although less dependence on foreign markets incurred by ISI at the take-off stage may mitigate temptation for radical deep integration into the world economy, a shallow integration is indispensable in expediting China's catch-up. Yet as a late late-industrializer that remained located at the lower stage of economic development throughout the 1980s and 1990s, China would see its vital national economic interests better served by eschewing pressure over *reciprocal* market access, one of the neoliberal justifications for a premature deep integration under the pretext of establishing the "global level playing field." The complication was that in the new age of liberal globalization that accompanied the ending of the Cold War, non-democratic developing nations, no matter how deeply their national economies had been internally integrated, would have to face a dual challenge of deep integration (befalling all developing nations except the least-developed countries notwithstanding), on the one hand, and political liberalization, on the other. Both were set to undermine the state in its quest for autonomous national development at the moment when the new paradigm, dubbed "market fundamentalism" began to prevail. As mentioned earlier, virtually all the NDCs were interventionist at their take-off stage. Except that of the USA, all the NDCs' industrialization drive had been associated with less democratic regimes. In other words, a democratic transition, under most circumstances, follows rather than precedes the modernity-oriented economic transformation. This was particularly true for "changing societies," in which, as Huntington argued, a premature democratic transition could be socially and economically destabilizing, thereby retarding rather than facilitating the country's modernization drive.[121] Despite these facts, the impact of the "Global 1989"[122] that witnessed the collapse of Communism in the Soviet Bloc accorded global capitalism moral commanding heights in an unprecedented way, rendering in both ideological and practical terms the blending of either democratic or authoritarian strong states with economic nationalism anachronistic.

Against such a backdrop, how to cope with the global diffusion of democracy had become an unavoidable political economy issue facing the Chinese authoritarian regime in the post-Cold War era. Among all possibilities, no matter whether the "Communist" system is essentially reformable or not, a managed political transformation in the sense of creating a "law-based state" under an enlightened authoritarianism is not only possible[123] but also essential to keeping the Chinese strong state intact for the purpose of autonomous development. Such progressive transformation would also pay off diplomatically, enhancing China's international respectability. This would translate into more room for China to maneuver on the world stage, thereby improving her bargaining position vis-à-vis the industrial democracies in low politics. This is entirely conceivable in practical terms because first and foremost China is a great power in political terms. It is the largest developing economy with immense growth potential as well. The country's huge geographic extent and population suffice to enable the Chinese state to leverage technology transfer at relatively low costs from the advanced economies by playing one off against the other.[124] In addition, with China's increasing interaction with the outside world, insightful leaders might come to the realization that in the post-Cold War era, a more democratic China would be better accommodated by the two civilian great powers: the European Union (EU) and Japan. Both were peer rivals of the USA in economic and technological terms possessing enormous hard and soft powers and global clout. Unlike the realist hegemonic American power bent on preserving its leadership at all costs, both the EU and Japan were largely regional powers overwhelmingly obsessed with domestic affairs and much less ambitious geopolitically. As such, for China, being more democratic would increase the likelihood of collaborating with both powers strategically to jointly shape a more stable world. The EU's dire quest for a multipolar world in the wake of the Cold War,[125] along with Japan's unyielding perseverance against the USA on both bilateral and global occasions in defending its distinct state-centered development paradigm, which had become one of the key sources of Japan's soft power ever since the 1980s,[126] was precisely what China could take advantage of diplomatically to serve the purpose of curbing American hegemony through soft balancing, on the one hand, and changing back the former's greater receptiveness to its shallow integration approach, on the other.[127] By so doing, China would be in a better position to not only retain large "development (policy) space"[128] in a legitimate way through diplomacy, making it still possible to play by the Bretton Woods rules to a considerable extent, but also present herself as a peaceful and responsible great power.

In a nutshell, despite the immense institutional as well as intellectual constraints preventing China from seeking alternatives in the age of liberal globalization, China, in comparison with many developing nations, has a lot more choices to circumvent them given its great power status and as the largest developing economy. Assisted by its intrinsic advantage in geographic extent and size of population, China will see an active embrace of democracy, though in a manageable way, rather than a stubborn aversion to it—the least costly and viable solution to cope with the challenge of modernity in the post-Cold War era. This implies that an alternative pathway of autonomous national development is not only existent in theory but also available to China in practical terms so long as the leadership never runs short of the requisite statecraft in engaging the increasingly globalized world.

Overview of the Book

This book aims to shed new light on the mystified reform and opening process that *allegedly* had led to the "rise" of China in the past four decades. By delving into how the current pathway of development took shape, which is hardly an economic success story in the strict sense, and why alternative approaches were precluded all the way throughout the reform period, the author will examine the political dynamism behind China's deep integration into the international system of global capitalism. The author argues that the particular way the CCP quested for political legitimacy after the Tiananmen crackdown in 1989 radicalized the regime's previous experiment of market socialism in the 1980s into an unbridled capitalism. By making high GDP growth the top priority, the Chinese regime that embraced market Leninism in lieu of market socialism implemented a de facto Washington Consensus-type marketization reform from the mid-1990s onward at the expense of social justice. Deng Xiaoping played a crucial role in this transformative process. The demise of socialism and the softening of the strong state as a result of "state capture" by nomenclatura elite fatally eroded the social and institutional foundations for internal integration, making it extremely difficult to achieve and sustain rapid economic growth on a self-reliant basis. Deep integration into the world economy, therefore, became the logical solution to achieving a Ricardian export-led growth. This was enabled by China's abandonment of economic nationalism at home by means of not only ceasing import substitution but also liberalizing trade and investment on a massive scale in exchange for wider access to developed countries' markets. China's radical embrace of neoliberalism was well in line with the US grand strategy of fully integrating China into the international system precisely through inducing and coercing the latter's deep integration into the global economy. The complicated interaction of Chinese domestic politics and the international politics eventually resulted in an unholy alliance between Chinese market Leninism, or "Communist capitalism," a new type of state capitalism rejecting both Marxism and liberal democracy,[129] and global capitalism, leading to the flourishing of a crony comprador capitalism at the turn of the century. Set on a dependent path of development from the late 1990s onward, China, although having achieved a striking *wirtschaftswunder* (economic miracle) after the WTO accession in 2001, has failed to escape dependency in any meaningful way. Such a process of reform and opening is by no means preordained. It had been made irreversible in large part due to the changing character of the Communist state and the technocratic leadership's acute myopia in making the fateful choice concerning Chinese modernity in the age of liberal globalization.

Following the Introduction, Chap. 2 starts with China's deeply questionable accession to the WTO at the turn of the century. The WTO accession was the "apex" of China's reform and opening and has been widely regarded as being responsible, in large part, for the rise of China through globalization (external integration). This chapter will first provide a detailed account of China's economic diplomacy during the accession talks in the late 1990s, then specify a series of abnormal state behavior before and after the country's WTO entry. Devoid of a convincing economic rationale, the WTO deal China accepted on extremely harsh terms was essentially the product of the political decision made by the top leadership. This was a momentous decision that would irreversibly integrate China into the international system in both low politics and high politics terms. Such a dubious accession raises a set of important questions: Why did the politically threat-sensitive, risk-averse authoritarian regime make such a big gamble when the whole set of rules made by the Bretton Woods institution had become much less favorable to global development after the Cold War? Why did Chinese intellectuals differ so much from their counterparts around the world in the sense that they gave the autocratic regime virtually unreserved support for the accession, and for that matter, turned a blind eye on the ostensibly undemocratic manner in which the regime stroke the deal irrespective of all opposition from within and forced upon the nation an "unequal treaty"? What has been the underlying logic behind the reform and opening that had prompted the Communist regime's "intimate embrace" with neoliberalism?[130] These questions can be reduced to one key question: was the radical deep integration inevitable?

Chapter 3 traces the origin of China's deep integration to the 1980s when the reform and opening just began. How to deal with the legacies of Mao's revolutionary state was then a crucial issue facing the post-totalitarian regime. The devastation of the Cultural Revolution and the extreme poverty of the nation made economic reform not only necessary but also much easier relative to its Communist counterparts in the Soviet Bloc. But the high consensus on the necessity of reform, which was based on a vague vision of the self-perfection of the Chinese socialism toward a "developed socialism" with a human face, did not eclipse the intensifying power struggle between the planning faction led by Chen Yun and the market faction led by Deng Xiaoping on how to modernize the economy through what kind of reform. The balance of power between Deng and Chen, the two political heavyweights within the CCP, set limits on how far the market reform could go. Moreover, the intra-party ban on open factionalism against the backdrop of Deng–Chen condominium made it highly unlikely that a *strategic compromise* would be reached between the major factions in terms of pursuing a market-based development through some sort of state reinvention to deepen national economic reintegration, first and foremost removing provincial autarky, with a view to creating a socialist developmental state. Deng's close aide, Premier Zhao Ziyang, was the de facto chief architect of the market-driven reform in the 1980s. Thwarted by the old regime, he came to be obsessed with neoliberal notions in outmaneuvering the planners. He did two things that had deep implications for China's reform and development well into the 1990s and beyond: devolving central government power to the provinces and deepening external integration in coastal areas, both contributing to instant economic dynamism and the dissolution of the planning system afterward. However, the potential damage his approach incurred to internal integration—the very foundation of China's autonomous development—was deliberately ignored and dismissed then and has been so even until the present day. In addition, the deadlocked market reform by the late 1980s alienated the liberal intellectuals, who, inspired by Mikhail Gorbachev's glasnost and perestroika, became radicalized and called for greater political openness. The failing price reform in the fall of 1988 and the sudden death of the deposed liberal-minded General Secretary Hu Yaobang six months later triggered off a nationwide pro-democracy movement which nearly brought down the regime in the summer of 1989.

Chapter 4 discusses the Tiananmen Incident in 1989 and its implications on China's reform and development in the 1990s. Had it not been for Deng Xiaoping and the personal loyalty of the armed forces to him, the regime might have crumbled anyway in the very summer of 1989. The collapse of Communism in Eastern Europe and the breaking apart of the Soviet Union in particular had an enormous impact on the Chinese Communist rulers, who were now faced with the most onerous task of regime re-legitimation. Despite backlashes from the planners and the ideologues, either diehard Stalinists or Maoists, against his reform in the wake of the crackdown, Deng's grip on power remained firm. He chose to retreat for the sake of political stability, but never gave up. Failure of the central planners to reignite prosperity through recentralizing the economy during the three-year stabilization (1989–1992) enabled Deng to strike back in early 1992. Eagerness to leave his imprint on history as a great reformer and the immense impact of the Global 1989, however, prompted Deng to impose his reform agenda on the party with the backing of the People's Liberation Army (PLA). Seeing that Communism had lost its appeal both as a belief system and an alternative to modernity, Deng came to the conclusion that the most reliable way to keep the Communist regime in power permanently was sustaining rapid economic growth at all costs. This, as he understood it, could only be achieved through embracing (global) capitalism in an unprecedented way by going much beyond the sort of Lenin's New Economic Policy (NEP) in the 1920s' Soviet Russia—a rather limited experiment with state capitalism under acute international isolation—to forcibly carry out an efficiency-biased marketization reform alongside a radicalized nationwide outward-oriented development strategy. The three big lessons that Deng had drawn from the Tiananmen crackdown, namely, no democracy, no appeasing the people, and appeasing the West, provided the requisite justification for the changing track of Chinese reform and development along neoliberal lines throughout the 1990s. Still a socialist, albeit in an abstract sense, Deng placed hope on the guardianship of the state machine to defend socialism as the last resort. What he failed to envision was that he had let the genie out of the bottle: an unbridled crony, comprador capitalism that the "socialist" state machine was not only unable to rein in, but even became part of it.

Chapter 5 looks into the truth behind China's reform and development in the 1990s. "Development is the hard truth," an imposed consensus in the aftermath of Deng's southern tour in 1992, addressed the overriding concern of the third-generation leadership led by Jiang Zemin about regime legitimacy. Educated before the Cultural Revolution and traumatized by it, most members of the new leadership were technocrats with an engineering background, having neither insightful vision for the future of China nor true belief in Communism. More opportunistic than Deng, who cleared the way to the capitalist convergence, they turned out to be far more resolute and ruthless in discarding socialism in practical terms. As a result, the Brezhnev-type "social contract" in the 1980s gradually gave way to an elite coalition between the nomenclatura, business people, and the intellectuals by the late 1990s, with egalitarianism, the basic principle of socialism, being removed from the reform agenda. The hardening of authoritarianism enabled a de facto shock therapy neoliberal reform, either the radical price reform in 1993–1994 or the nomenclatura privatization of the SOEs from the mid-1990s onward, to proceed without meeting significant resistance from the urban working class. This sort of Washington Consensus-type marketization reform was driven by the self-serving bureaucracy that first and foremost benefited themselves via institutionalized rent-seeking. The resultant rampant corruption and rapidly expanding income disparity led to severe and persistent underconsumption, reinforcing the country's external orientation for sustaining an export-led rapid growth. The erosion of internal integration resulting from the changing socialist industrial relations was further aggravated by the intensification of economic balkanization (federalism) that Zhao's fiscal decentralization reinforced in the 1980s. Zhu Rongji as first Deputy Premier was the key figure presiding over China's economic reform and industrial development in the 1990s. Despite remarkable success in regaining fiscal power to the central state, he had made little effort to foster internal integration through eliminating provincial autarky institutionally. Rather, his previous experience as the mayor and party boss of Shanghai inclined him to base China's national development strategy on deep external integration characterized by the blending of export promotion with import and investment liberalization, a strange EOI strategy that put the local firms at stake. By the late 1990s, the dramatic decline of the SOEs reinforced China's dependence on FDI. Lacking the will to develop on an autonomous basis, however, the Chinese regime, faced with the quagmire of underconsumption and stagnant industrialization, was forced to seek a "globalization plus" approach to institutionalizing deep integration through joining the WTO in the hope of increasing exports and FDI to reverse the declining economic momentum.

Chapter 6 examines the significant role the USA had played in inducing China's deep integration into the global economy. It has been a consistent US–China policy, since President Nixon, of not isolating China but of bringing it back to the "community of nations" since the early 1970s. By drawing China out rather than fencing it in economically and diplomatically, this grand strategy was designed to transform Communist China from a challenger of the international system of global capitalism into a stakeholder, and if possible, to make China more democratic. Throughout the 1980s, the USA was hugely successful in influencing the mindsets of the Chinese ruling and intellectual elites who were led to believe that deep integration in the form of reciprocal market opening rather than self-reliance was the road to prosperity. After Tiananmen, President Bush shortly lifted economic sanctions, lest that would force China to seek alternative path to modernity. Deng's southern tour remarks in the spring of 1992 sent strong signals to the USA that the regime had no other alternatives but to deepen market reforms and to orient the economy entirely externally. This fit squarely into the US grand strategy of liberal integration. But the USA had never had the intention of helping to build an empire-sized non-Western China into another Germany or Japan, no matter whether it had allied with China or not before and after the Cold War. Bent on preserving its hegemonic primacy, the USA allowed China to bandwagon with the liberal order to achieve an export-led growth precisely on the condition that it renounce economic nationalism in an institutionally irreversible way. This realist element of US liberal engagement policy under President Clinton was complemented by a series of hard balancing arrangements against China. Although such a posture of preemptive deterrence had triggered defensive realist reactions on the part of China and further fed into the latter's resurgent anti-American nationalism, the substantial success the USA ultimately achieved in fully integrating China into the global economy, epitomized by the country's dire quest for WTO membership at the turn of the century, rendered Chinese nationalism hollow and meaningless in practical terms.

Chapter 7 follows up China's political and economic development after the WTO accession, on the basis of which it deconstructs the "rise of China" myth. From 2005 onward, the "rise of China" has become a global consensus. Thawing of relations with the USA after 9/11 and the export boom led Chinese decision-makers, especially the fourth-generation leadership led by Hu Jintao (2003–2013), to firmly believe that their predecessors' liberal globalization approach had worked. They envisioned that by staking in global capitalists at home and bandwagoning with the liberal order abroad China would be able to achieve a peaceful rise. As a matter of fact, it will be argued that globalization, although having stimulated a Ricardian growth miracle in the 2000s by exploiting China's comparative advantage in cheap labor, has hindered Chinese firms' industrial upgrading and catch-up by locking them in at the low end of the global value chain. This sort of dependent development was also contributed to, if not more importantly, by the party state that became much more repressive and exploitative after the WTO entry. With Chinese crony capitalism and its unholy alliance with global capitalism becoming well entrenched, the soft party state was not only powerless to stem household consumption in proportion to GDP declining further but also incapable of enforcing strong intellectual property protection to stimulate indigenous innovation, the two pillars of internal integration on the basis of which a profound economic transition from an extensive investment-and-export-driven growth to that of an intensive consumption-and-innovation-driven growth was to be accomplished.

The year 2008 was the critical one when the sudden drop in growth rate in the last quarter effectively brought the widely acclaimed Chinese model of market Leninism to an end. Yet similar to what had motivated the Communist regime to desperately join the WTO a decade earlier, the country's developmental quandary further radicalized the Chinese leadership's embrace of globalization. Such a "globalization paradox"[131] had significantly constrained the Chinese leadership's vision and statecraft in seeking an alternative intellectually and institutionally. Despite the resumed yet short-lived prosperity propped up by heavy state investments in infrastructure in the wake of the global financial crisis, the intensifying power struggle over leadership succession prior to the 18th National Party's Congress in late 2012 highlighted the comprehensive sociopolitical crisis China's crony capitalist development had inflicted upon the Chinese society and the party itself. The looming large of a major economic crisis, characterized by a prospective bubble-bursting in virtual economy, along with an ongoing deindustrialization in the real economy, got on the nerves of the market Leninist regime that has been intransigent in rejecting democratic power-sharing and preserving the party's monopoly on power at all costs. The rulers' growing sense of insecurity about rising social disturbances and color revolution added fuel to resurgence of political conservatism and even a totalitarian turn. Meanwhile,

China's external orientation to such an astonishing extent also backfired in the form of unprecedented global imbalance, which had to be addressed forcefully by the international society, and the country's strategic vulnerability of increasing resource shortage at home, a difficult endgame that made the liberal order less able to accommodate its peaceful "rise"—or continued dependent development, to put it another way. More importantly, far from being another Germany or Japan in terms of its actual industrial strength, China possesses neither sufficient hard power nor sufficient soft power to overturn the existing "fundamental order of the international system." In the face of US' overwhelming preponderance of military power and toughening-up of foreign policy, is there still room for China to rise peacefully within the capitalist world system? Or will China evolve into an inward-looking "restless empire" in pursuit of domination strictly within its own national boundary?

Notes

1. Francis Fukuyama (1989), "The End of History?" *The National Interest*, Summer.
2. Re-Stalinization, special issue of *Communist and Post-Communist Studies*, March 2016, 49:1, pp. 1–112.
3. Robert Kagan (2008), *The Return of History and the End of Dreams*, London: Atlantic Books.
4. Eliane Glaser (2014), "Bring Back Ideology: Fukuyama's 'End of History' 25 Years On," *The Guardian*, 21/03/2014. http://www.theguardian.com/books/2014/mar/21/bring-back-ideology-fukuyama-end-history-25-years-on
5. "Wang Qishan Sent out Blurred Signal," *Radio France Internationale (RFI)*, 12/05/2015. http://cn.rfi.fr/%E4%B8%AD%E5%9B%BD/20150512-%E4%B8%AD%E7%BA%AA%E5%A7%94%E4%B9%A6%E8%AE%B0%E7%8E%8B%E5%B2%90%E5%B1%B1%E4%BC%9A%E8%A7%81%E6%97%A5%E8%A3%94%E5%AD%A6%E8%80%85%E9%87%8A%E6%94%BE%E6%A8%A1%E7%B3%8A%E2%80%9C%E4%BF%A1%E5%8F%B7%E2%80%9D
6. https://www.youtube.com/watch?v=yWJWCoVYF_Q, posted on 24/02/2016.

7. Timothy Stanley and Alexander Lee (2014), "It's Still Not the End of History," *The Atlantic Monthly*, September 1. http://www.theatlantic.com/politics/archive/2014/09/its-still-not-the-end-of-history-francis-fukuyama/379394/
8. Wu Guoguang interviewed by NTDTV, 2/05/2011. http://www.ntdtv.com/xtr/gb/2011/05/30/a65981.html.-%E3%80%90%E9%80%8F%E8%A7%86%E4%B8%AD%E5%9B%BD%E3%80%91%E5%90%B4%E5%9B%BD%E5%85%89%3A-%E6%97%A0%E6%B3%95%E9%80%9A%E8%BF%87%E7%9A%84%E3%80%9D%E7%AA%84%E9%97%A8%E3%80%9E.html
9. Lieven (2003), Empire, p. 45. An example of this was the exportation of German welfare state spreading "across Atlantic to America" from the late nineteenth century onward. See Richard M. Ebeling, "Marching to Bismarck's Drummer: The Origins of the Modern Welfare State," FEE (Foundation for Economic Education), 1/12/2007. https://fee.org/articles/marching-to-bismarcks-drummer-the-origins-of-the-modern-welfare-state/
10. Ibid. with Lieven, p. 45.
11. Lieven (2003), Empire, pp. 44–45.
12. Richard Franklin Bensel (2008), *The Political Economy of Industrialization, 1877–1900*, NY: Cambridge University Press, Preface: xvii.
13. Ibid., pp. 1–2.
14. Bruce Cumings (1984), "The Origins and Development of the Northeast Asian Political Economy," *International Organization*, 38:1, pp. 1–40.
15. Ibid.
16. Dylan Finlay (2012), "Gorbachev's Miscalculation and the Collapse of the Soviet Union," *Foreign Policy*, November 22. https://thestateofthecentury.wordpress.com/2012/11/22/gorbachevs-miscalculation-and-the-collapse-of-the-soviet-union/
17. Joseph Stiglitz (2002), *Globalization and Its Discontents*, London: Penguin Books, p. 14.
18. Ha-Joon Chang (2003), *Kicking away the Ladder—Development Strategy in Historical Perspective*, London: Anthem Press, pp. 17–18.
19. Robert Wade (2003), *Governing the Market—Economic Theory and the Role of Government in East Asian Industrialization* (2nd ed.), NJ: Princeton University Press, introduction, p. xv.
20. Joseph Stiglitz (2007), *Making Globalization Work: The Next Steps to Global Justice*, London: Penguin Books, p. 19.

21. Ha-Joon Chang (2009), "Hamlet without the Prince of Denmark: How Development Has Disappeared from the 'Development' Discourse?" 15/02/2009. http://hajoonchang.net/wp-content/uploads/2012/01/HamletwithoutthePrinceofDenmark-revised.pdf
22. "Building Engines for Growth and Competitiveness in China: Experience with Special Economic Zones and Industrial Clusters," https://openknowledge.worldbank.org/handle/10986/2501
23. Thomas G. Rawski, "What's Happening to China's GDP Statistics?" 12/09/2001. http://www.pitt.edu/~tgrawski/papers2001/gdp912f.pdf (hyperlink no longer available); Lester Thurow, "A Chinese Century? Maybe It's the Next One," *New York Times*, 19/08/2007. http://www.nytimes.com/2007/08/19/business/yourmoney/19view.html
24. *The Wall Street Journal*, 18/06/2014.
25. Nick Crafts (1994), "The Golden Age of Economic Growth in Western Europe, 1950–1973," Warwick Economic Research Paper, No. 427. https://www2.warwick.ac.uk/fac/soc/economics/research/workingpapers/1989-1994/twerp_427.pdf
26. http://news.ifeng.com/history/phtv/tfzg/detail_2010_03/24/403443_0.shtml
27. Paul Krugman (1994), "The Myth of Asia's Miracle," *Foreign Affairs*, 73:6, November/December, pp. 62–78.
28. Lieven (2003), Empire, p. 44.
29. Janos Kornai (1992), *The Socialist System: The Political Economy of Communism*, Oxford: Clarendon Press, pp. 197–198.
30. The bulk of private enterprises were technologically backward, managerially inadequate, thus were of limited significance in national economy, according to Cheng Xiaonong (2003) in "Reinterpreting China's Economy," Modern China Studies, No. 1.
31. Shaun Breslin (2005), "Power and Production: Rethinking China's Global Economic Role," *Review of International Studies*, 31:4, pp. 735–753.
32. Cristóbal Kay (2002), "Why East Asia Overtook Latin America," *Third World Quarterly*, 23:6, pp. 1073–1102.
33. Stiglitz, J (2002), *Globalization and Its Discontent*, p. 14.
34. Charles Gore (2000), "The Rise and Fall of the Washington Consensus as a Paradigm for Developing Countries," *World Development*, 28:5, pp. 789–804.
35. Kay (2002), pp. 1073–1102; Henry J. Bruton (1998), "A Reconsideration of Import Substitution," *Journal of Economic Literature*, 36:2, June, pp. 903–936.

36. Charmers Johnson (1982), *MITI and the Japanese Miracle: The Growth of Industrial Policy, 1925–1975*, Redwood: Stanford University Press.
37. Robert Wade, professor of development studies, recalled his past personal experience in his lectures at the London School of Economics (LSE) in the 2008–2009 session.
38. Interviews and discussions with Chinese counterparts from 2005 until recently.
39. Jianyong Yue (2016), "China, Global Capitalism, and the Quest for Political Legitimacy," *International Politics*, 53:6, November, pp. 752–774.
40. Michael Lind (2016), "Taking Modernization Seriously—How to Think About Global Industrialization," *Breakthrough Journal*, Issue 6, Summer. https://thebreakthrough.org/index.php/journal/issue-6/taking-modernization-seriously
41. Mancur Olson (1982), *The Rise and Decline of Nations: Economic Growth, Stagflation, and Social Rigidities*, New Haven: Yale University Press; Wade (2003), introduction: xlviii.
42. Meredith Woo-Cuming (1999), "Introduction: Charmers Johnson and the Politics of Nationalism and Development," in *The Developmental State*, ed. Woo-Cumings, Ithaca and London: Cornell University Press, p. 10.
43. Peter Preston (2011), *Theories of Development*, London: Routledge, p. 41.
44. UNCTAD (2013), "The Asian Developmental State and the Flying Geese Paradigm," November, p. 13. http://unctad.org/en/PublicationsLibrary/osgdp20133_en.pdf
45. Bruce Cumings (1984), "The Origins and Development of the Northeast Asian Political Economy," *International Organization*, 38:1, pp. 1–40.
46. Ibid.
47. Michael Mastanduno (1997), "Preserving the Unipolar Moment: Realist Theories and US Grand Strategy after the Cold War," *International Security*, 21:4, pp. 49–88.
48. Yue Jianyong (2011), "The Myth of the Chinese Model," *Leaders* (Hong Kong), 40, June, pp. 11–27.
49. Ha-Joon Chang (2009), "Hamlet without the Prince of Denmark: How Development Has Disappeared from the 'Development' Discourse?" 15/02/2009. http://hajoonchang.net/wp-content/uploads/2012/01/HamletwithoutthePrinceofDenmark-revised.pdf
50. Michael Pillsbury (2014), *The Hundred-Year Marathon: China's Secret Strategy to Replace America as the Global Superpower*, New York: Henry Holt and Co.

51. Interview with an informed source 20/06/2004.
52. Jung Chang and Jon Haliday (2006), *Mao, The Unknown Story*, Hong Kong: Open Press, p. 373.
53. Interviews and discussions with insiders from 2005 until 2015.
54. John Ikenberry (2011), *Liberal Levithan: The Origins, Crisis, and Transformation of the American World Order*, NJ: Princeton University Press, p. 9.
55. Ha-Joon Chang (2009), "Hamlet without the Prince of Denmark," http://hajoonchang.net/wp-content/uploads/2012/01/HamletwithoutthePrinceofDenmark-revised.pdf
56. Edward Steinfeld (2010), *Playing Our Game—Why China's Rise Doesn't Threaten the West*, NY: Oxford University Press, p. 18.
57. Thomson Reuters: Top 100 Global Innovators 2015. http://www.reuters.com/article/tr-pr-innovations-idUSKCN0T72RA20151119
58. Dani Rodrik (2011), *The Globalization Paradox*, Oxford: Oxford University Press, p. 273.
59. Joseph Stiglitz (2002), *Globalization and Its Discontent*, p. 20.
60. Martin Wolf (2004), *Why Globalization Works—The Case for the Global Market Economy*, New Haven and London: Yale University Press, pp. 144–146.
61. "China had Lifted 680 Million People out of Poverty between 1981 and 2010," *The Economist*, 1/06/2013. http://www.economist.com/news/briefing/21578643-world-has-astonishing-chance-take-billion-people-out-extreme-poverty-2030-not
62. World Bank Policy Research Working Paper 4253, June 2007. http://core.ac.uk/download/pdf/6615660.pdf
63. Danny Quah (2011), "The Global Economy's Shifting Centre of Gravity," *Global Policy*, 2:1, pp. 3–9.
64. "China Noses ahead as Top Goods Producer," *The Financial Times*, 13/03/2011.
65. Various predictions in recent years made by *The Economist*, Standard Chartered Bank, Deutsche Bank, PricewaterhouseCoopers, and so on claimed that China will overtake the USA by 2020. The international Monetary Fund (IMF) predicted most recently that China will become the largest economy in 2016. See report "The Age of America Ends in 2016: IMF Predicts the Year China will Surpass U.S.," *Daily Mail*, 26/04/2011. http://www.dailymail.co.uk/news/article-1380486/The-Age-America-ends-2016-IMF-predicts-year-Chinas-economy-surpass-US.html. "The Dating Game," *The Economist*, 27/12/2011 (2018). http://www.economist.com/blogs/dailychart/2010/12/save_date

66. Joseph Stiglitz (2002), *Globalization and Its Discontents*, p. 221.
67. The term "Washington Consensus" is often used interchangeably with "neoliberalism" and "globalization". http://www.cid.harvard.edu/cidtrade/issues/washington.html
68. Joseph Stiglitz (2007), *Making Globalization Work: The Next Steps to Global Justice*, London: Penguin Books, p. 31.
69. Dani Rodrik (2011), *The Globalization Paradox*, pp. 149–153.
70. Ibid., pp. 155–156.
71. Joseph Stiglitz (2007), *Making Globalization Work*, p. 10; Sanjaya Lall (2004), "Reinventing Industrial Strategy: The Role of Government Policy in Building Industrial Competitiveness," UNCTAD G-24 Discussion Paper Series No. 28, April, pp. 1–46.
72. Philip Golub (2013), "From the New International Economic Order to the G20," *Third World Quarterly*, 34:6, pp. 1000–1015.
73. Helen Clark addressed the LSE audience in the capacity of the United Nations Development Programme (UNDP) on March 12, 2010, "if we took China's figures out of the equation, the number of people living in extreme poverty is actually estimated to have increased between 1990 and 2005 by about 36 million." Helen Clark: Meeting Development Challenges in the 21st Century," http://www.undp.org/content/undp/en/home/presscenter/speeches/2010/03/12/helen-clark-meeting-development-challenges-in-the-21stcentury.html
74. "China's Success on Millennium Development Goals Provides an Example for Others to Follow for the Post-2015 Development Agenda, Says New UNDP Report," http://www.undp.org/content/undp/en/home/presscenter/articles/2015/02/17/china-s-success-on-millennium-development-goals-provides-an-example-for-others-to-follow-for-the-post-2015-development-agenda-says-new-undp-report0.html; The Millennium Development Goals Report 2015. http://www.un.org/millenniumgoals/2015_MDG_Report/pdf/MDG%202015%20rev%20(July%201).pdf
75. China's latest poverty line was raised upward from 1196 yuan set in 2008 to 2300 yuan in 2011, equivalent to US 1$ per day, which was lower than the World Bank criterion. The number of people living in extreme poverty would increase from 26.88 million in 2010 to 128 million by the end of 2011. (http://news.ifeng.com/mainland/detail_2011_11/30/10997300_0.shtml); In November 2015, the Chinese government vowed to eradicate poverty by 2020 which implies that still 74 million

people would have to be lifted out of poverty within five years' time. http://opinion.huanqiu.com/opinion_china/2015-12/8082333.html. Premier Li Keqiang admitted on 15/03/2015 during the annual National People's Congress that China still had 200 million people living in poverty as per relevant World Bank criterion (*People's Daily* online, 15/03/2015). http://lianghui.people.com.cn/2015npc/n/2015/0315/c394537-26695251.html

76. UN (2009), *Rethinking Poverty—Report on the World Social Situation 2010*, Chap. 2: Poverty: The Official Figures, p. 15: "Without the rapidly growing developing economies of Brazil, the Russian Federation, India and China, the absolute number of people living in extreme poverty actually went up, from 619 million in 1981 to about 699 million in 2005." http://www.un.org/esa/socdev/rwss/docs/2010/chapter2.pdf; http://www.un.org/esa/socdev/rwss/docs/2010/fullreport.pdf (full report)
77. The ten policy prescriptions of the Washington Consensus were normally simplified as "deregulation, privatization, and liberalization."
78. Alice Amsden (2007), *Escape from Empire—The Developing World's Journey through Heaven and Hell*, Cambridge: MIT Press, p. 131.
79. Gunnar Myrdal (1968), *Asian Drama: An Inquiry into the Poverty of Nations*. London: Allen Lane The Penguin Press, p. 208.
80. Chalmers Johnson (1999), "The Developmental State: Odyssey of a Concept," in *The Developmental State*, ed. Meredith Woo-Cumings, Ithaca and London: Cornell University Press, p. 48.
81. Transparency International Annual Report. https://www.transparency.org/whatwedo/publications/doc/ar/
82. Peter Nolan (2001), "China, the US and the WTO: Battle of the Giants or Defeat of the Pygmies?" (manuscript).
83. Stiglitz contended most convincingly that "privatization without the necessary institutional infrastructure in the transition countries led to asset stripping rather than wealth creation … By contrast, privatization accompanied by regulation, corporate restructuring, and strong corporate governance has led to higher growth." Stiglitz (2002), p. 220; Also see Yusuf (2007), Under New Ownership: Privatizing China's State-Owned Enterprises; He Qinglian (2003), *The Pitfall of Modernization* (new edition), Sunnydale: Broad Press, pp. 53–89.
84. Andre Gunder Frank (1966), *The Development of Underdevelopment*, Boston: New England Free Press.
85. *The Princeton Encyclopedia of the World Economy* (Two volume set) (2009), NJ: Princeton University Press, p. 271.

86. Immanuel Wallerstein (1979), *The Capitalist World-Economy*, Cambridge University Press, p. 21.
87. Peter Evans (1979), *Dependent Development: The Alliance of Multinational, State, and Local Capital in Brazil*, NJ: Princeton University Press.
88. Michael Latham (2011), *The Right Kind of Revolution: Modernization, Development, and US Foreign Policy from the Cold War to the Present*, Ithaca: Cornell University Press, p. 50.
89. Vincent Ferraro (2008), "Dependency Theory: An Introduction," in *The Development Economics Reader*, ed. Giorgio Secondi, London: Routledge, pp. 58–64.
90. Ibid.
91. Economides, S and Wilson, P (2003), *The Economic Factor in International Relations: A Brief Introduction*, London: I.B. Tauris, p. 60.
92. CASS Blue Paper 2014, *Xinhuawang*, Beijing, 10/12/2013. http://news.xinhuanet.com/world/2013-12/11/c_125838153.htm; Wang Bao'an (Deputy Minister of Finance): "How to Forge an Upgrading of the Chinese Economy?" Qiushi (*Seeking Truth*, one of the most authoritative mouthpieces of the CCP), 1/01/2014. http://www.qstheory.cn/zxdk/2014/201401/201312/t20131230_307459.htm; Yao Jingyuan: Chinese Manufacturing "Big but not Strong," See report "'Made in China' in Unprecedented Crisis," 9/02/2015. http://finance.qq.com/a/20150209/057597.htm; Yao Jingyuan argued that China's extensive mode of growth in the past decades driven by three "massive inputs," namely, capital, resource, and labor force, has become unsustainable. Although it can outproduce the rest of the world combined in more than half of the 440 kinds of UN-identified major industrial products, China is still running short of "Core Technologies," *Jiemian*, 20/08/2016. http:www.jiemian.com/article/809384.html; "Miao Wei (Minister of Industry and Information Technology): 'Chinese Manufacturing still in the Third-tier in the World'," *China News Agency*, 18/11/2015. http://www.chinanews.com/cj/2015/11-18/7630207.shtml; Chen Ming, "Chinese Manufacturing "Big but not Strong" not Changed," 11/01/2017. http://www.jfdaily.com/news/detail?id=41829
93. Yue, J (2016), "China, Global Capitalism, and the Quest for Political Legitimacy," *International Politics*, pp. 752–774.
94. Peter Evans (1979), *Dependent Development*, Princeton University Press.
95. (Finance Minister) Lou Jiwei's speech at the School of Economics and Management, Tsinghua University, 24/04/2015. http://www.sem.tsinghua.edu.cn/portalweb/sem?__c=fa1&u=xyywcn/69292.htm

96. Chinese media reports.
97. The newly upward adjusted poverty line set by the World Bank would increase China's poverty-stricken population from 70.71 million (China's own criterion of measuring extreme poverty was set at just 2300 yuan, even lower than the US 1.25$ standard) to 200 million. "Ending Poverty—An Empty Victory?" *China Economic Review* (online), 16/10/2015. http://www.chinaeconomicreview.com/spicy-hotpot/ending-poverty%E2%80%94-empty-victoryhttp://www.chinaeconomicreview.com/spicy-hotpot/ending-poverty%E2%80%94-empty-victory
98. *The Chinese Livelihood Development Report 2015*, issued by the Peking University, was released on January 13, 2016. The report shows that China's income gap has been expanding rapidly in the past three decades which rose from 0.3 in the early 1980s to over 0.45 in recent years. In 2012, China's income Gini coefficient reached 0.49, far above the widely recognized alert level of 0.4. China's family wealth inequality was even more acute. The top 1% families possessed one third of the country's total wealth, while the bottom 25% families owned just 1%. China's family wealth Gini coefficient had risen from 0.45 in 1995 to 0.73 in 2012. *Yicaiwang* (yicai.com), 13/01/2016. http://www.yicai.com/news/2016/01/4738424.html
99. http://www.cia.gov/library/publications/the-world-factbook/geos/ch.html
100. Omar Sanchez (2003), "The Rise and Fall of the Dependency Movement: Does it inform Underdevelopment Today?" *EIAL (Estudios Interdisciplinarios de América Latina y el Caribe)*, 14:2, July to December.
101. Richard Evans, "Autarky: Fantasy or Reality?" http://www.richardjevans.com/lectures/autarky-fantasy-reality/; Hitler's Confidential Memo on Autarky (August 1936), German History in Documents and Images, vol. 7. Nazi Germany, 1933–1945. http://germanhistorydocs.ghi-dc.org/pdf/eng/English61.pdf
102. John Ikenberry (2011), *Liberal Levithan: The Origins, Crisis, and Transformation of the American World Order*, NJ: Princeton University Press, pp. 169–174.
103. Jeffrey A. Frieden (2006), *Global Capitalism—Its Rise and Fall in the Twentieth Century*, NY: Norton, p. 63.
104. Ronaldo Munck (2012), *Contemporary Latin America* (3rd ed.), NY: Palgrave Macmillan, p. 77.
105. Joseph Stiglitz (2003), *Globalization and Its Discontents*, pp. 4, 20–21, 214.

106. Alice Amsden (2001), *The Rise of "The Rest": Challenges to the West from Late-Industrializing Economies*, NY: Oxford University Press, p. 16.
107. Joseph Stiglitz (2007), *Making Globalization Work*, p. 72.
108. Ibid.
109. Dani Rodrik (2011), *The Globalization Paradox*, pp. 169–170.
110. Sanchez (2003), "The Rise and Fall of the Dependency Movement: Does It Inform Underdevelopment Today?" *EIAL*, 14:2. http://eial.tau.ac.il/index.php/eial/article/view/893/946
111. Robert Wade (2003), "Introduction to the 2003 Paperback Edition," in *Governing the Market*, p. i.
112. "Industrialization of the 19th century latecomers was in fact frequently accompanied by both tariff protection and a vigorous export drive which threatened the previous dominant position of the old established industrial countries in a number of important markets." (p. 25) See Albert O. Hirschman (1968), "The Political Economy of Import-Substituting Industrialization in Latin America," *The Quarterly Journal of Economics*, 82:1, pp. 1–22; Tony Pierenkemper and Richard Tilly (2004), *The German Economy during the Nineteenth Century*, Chap. 10: The International Economy, London: Berghahn Books, pp. 145–156.
113. Kenneth Pomeranz (2001), "Is there an East Asian Development Path?" *Journal of the Economic and Social History of the Orient*, 44:3, pp. 322–362.
114. Unless otherwise specified, "shallow integration" and "external integration" only refer to external integration.
115. Wade (2003), introduction: p. xlviii.
116. Ibid.
117. Ibid.
118. Ibid.
119. Wade (2003), intro, p. 1.
120. Harry Oshima (1986), "The Transition from an Agricultural to an Industrial Economy in East Asia," *Economic Development and Cultural Change*, 34:4, pp. 783–809.
121. Samuel Huntington (1965), "Political Development and Political Decay," *World Politics*, 17:2, pp. 386–430.
122. George Lawson, Chris Armbruster, and Michael Cox (eds.) (2010), *The Global 1989—Continuity and Change in World Politics*, Cambridge: Cambridge University Press.
123. As to whether a "law-based state" is congruent with "a socialist state," please refer to Sergio De Sanctis (1993), "*Legal and Criminal Law Reform: Another Failure of Perestroika?*" (p. 152) in Stephen White, Rita

Di Le, and Ottorino Cappelli (co-ed.), *The Soviet Transition: From Gorbachev to Yeltsin* (Special Issue of the "Journal of Communist Studies," 9:1), London: Routledge.

124. From a hindsight perspective, it is the EU rather than the USA that has long been China's largest destination for exports and the top source of high technology, thus being more crucial to China's modernization drive. See also Wen Jiabao speech in 2012 in which he claimed that EU was China's largest export market and the biggest source of technologies. "Keynote address by Wen Jiabao, Premier of the State Council of the People's Republic of China, at the 8th EU-China Business Summit, on 20 September 2012, in Brussels," https://tvnewsroom.consilium.europa.eu/event/eu-china-summit-september-2012/8th-eu-china-business-summit-wen-jiabao-part-1
125. Ivan Krastev, "The Crisis of the Post-Cold War European Order," 10/09/2008. http://www.eurozine.com/the-crisis-of-the-post-cold-war-european-order/. Charles Grant with Tomas Valasek (2011), "Preparing for the Multipolar World—European Foreign and Security Policy in 2020," Centre for European Reform. http://www.cer.eu/sites/default/files/publications/attachments/pdf/2011/e783_18dec07-1376.pdf
126. Robert Wade (1996), "Japan, the World Bank, and the Art of Paradigm Maintenance: The East Asian Miracle in Political Perspective," *New Left Review*, 1:217, May–June, pp. 3–36.
127. Yue, J (2014), "EU: China's Lost 'Ally'?" *Phoenix Weekly*, No. 18, 25/06/2014.
128. Wade (2003) used "development space," which can be used interchangeably with "policy space."
129. Cheng Xiaonong (2015), "Capitalism Making and its Political Consequences: A Comparative Political Economy of China's Communist Capitalism," in *China's Transition from Communism—New Perspectives*, ed. Guoguang Wu and Helen Lansdowne, Oxon: Routledge.
130. Leong Liew (2005), "China's Engagement with Neo-liberalism: Path Dependency, Geography and Party Self-Reinvention," *The Journal of Development Studies*, 41:2, pp. 331–352.
131. This was the term used by Dani Rodrik in his book that interpreted the divergent development outcomes in the age of globalization in a different way.

2

Process of China's WTO Accession: A Questionable Integration

China's accession to the World Trade Organization (WTO) in 2001 was acclaimed by the communist regime as the third and highest stage of the country's "reform and opening," a fateful choice of political correctness that allegedly was bound to lead China to "the wealth of the nation." It had been contended by liberal economists in the Soviet Bloc in the 1980s that the market reform in socialist states was essentially a process of transition "from capitalism to capitalism."[1] This was nonetheless neither a simple restoration of prewar unregulated capitalism nor a creation of "national capitalism," as both Lenin and Gilpin called it,[2] similar to Lenin's New Economic Policy (NEP), which developed in isolation. It was rather a process that would integrate the socialist economies into the capitalist global economy rebuilt by the USA after World War II. Much less constrained ideologically in the aftermath of the Cultural Revolution and the Sino-Soviet split from the late 1960s, China, unlike the *late* communism in the Second World, had greater incentive to embrace global capitalism to dynamize the economy. What merits attention is not why China joined the WTO but why it sought WTO membership in an increasingly radical way at a time in the late 1990s when the country was still situated in a low stage of economic development, despite rapid

J. Yue, *China's Rise in the Age of Globalization*, Palgrave Studies in Economic History, https://doi.org/10.1007/978-3-319-63997-0_2

growth in the past two decades, and, of particular importance, when the whole economic rules of the game made by the Bretton Woods institutions were turning against development as a result of the Uruguay Round negotiations of the General Agreement on Tariffs and Trade (GATT) (1986–1994).

In 1986, China applied to rejoin the GATT, the precursor of the WTO; it was also the same year in which the last and lengthiest round of GATT negotiations began. It took China 15 years to join the WTO. During this process, China suffered a series of setbacks and humiliations. Rapid economic growth in the past two decades did not seem to have increased China's bargaining position vis-à-vis its main adversaries, the USA and the European Union (EU). Despite active collaboration on renminbi (RMB) policy in 1998 and Premier Zhu's contentious trip to Washington at the climax of NATO's intervention in Kosovo in 1999, China failed to secure the USA's return favor on generous terms of WTO accession. Rather, the USA, even after the subsequent bombing of the Chinese embassy in Belgrade in May 1999, insisted that deals be struck "strictly on commercial terms." China's grave miscalculation in dealing with great power relations led the EU to cooperate closely with the USA. Desperate for the membership, the Chinese regime kept domestic firms in the dark; nor did it make sophisticated gain-and-loss calculations regarding impacts on the domestic economy prior to and amid negotiations. And the final approval by the National People's Congress (NPC) was procedurally unconstitutional. Lacking sufficient economic rationale, China's accession looks like a big gamble.

Lost Opportunities in the 1970s?

China is the founding member of the GATT more than half a century ago. In 1947, the nationalist government of the Republic of China (ROC) under the Kuomintang (KMT) sent a delegation to attend the preparatory meetings for the United Nations Conference on Trade and Employment held in Geneva. China participated in the drafting of the charter for the International Trade Organization (ITO) and held tariff reduction talks with 18 founding members. China reduced tariffs on 188 of all its 627 categories of products, 80 of which were reduced according to US demands. Boycotted by the US Senate, the ITO eventually aborted. As a temporary agreement concluded by 23 nations that aimed at removing trade barriers, the GATT remained intact and came into being on January 1, 1948. China joined the second round of tariff reduction talks in Annecy, France, and cut down tariffs on 66 categories of products.

With the crumbling of the KMT regime in the Chinese civil war (1946–1949) and the ensuing founding of the People's Republic of China (PRC) led by the Communist Party of China (CCP) in October 1949, the government of the ROC retreated to Taiwan, despite continually enjoying broad diplomatic recognition abroad, and lost legitimacy as a sovereign state representing all constituent parts of China in practical terms. Losing all the trade interests in the mainland and fearing that the PRC would benefit from the GATT, Taiwan withdrew its membership in the name of China on March 6, 1950.[3] Accordingly, a dozen of the GATT signatories that had cut deals with the ROC withdrew their tariff reduction commitments to the ROC in Taiwan. GATT requested the PRC to take over the seat vacated by Taiwan. The PRC government made no reaction due to its deep ideological enmity to this "rich people's club."[4]

In 1964, the GATT launched the Kennedy Round multilateral trade talks, a time when Taiwan was in a golden age of economic takeoff. Taiwan declared rejoining the GATT in 1965. But this attempt was boycotted by the GATT, which only accorded Taiwan an observer status to enable it to present at GATT conferences. Sino-US rapprochement in the early 1970s led to successive resumption of China's membership in the United Nations and a set of international organizations. With the eviction of Taiwan from the UN in 1971, the GATT terminated Taiwan's observer status accordingly. This brought China a rare opportunity of overtaking Taiwan as a full member of the GATT. Premier Zhou Enlai gave instructions to the Ministry of Foreign Trade (MFT) and the Ministry of Foreign Affairs (MFA) to research on how to view the GATT and what position China should take. Both Ministries argued in their respective report that joining the GATT was economically and politically favorable to China in the long term. But the GATT's most-favored-nation (MFN) principle would disrupt China's country-specific policy; and GATT's requirement on market access was disadvantageous to China too. Thus, the best option for China was to defer the accession.[5] The genuine reason for China's "not to join" decision was understandably ideological. On the one hand, China perceived the GATT as a "rich-nation club" overwhelmingly composed of the First World capitalist industrial nations with which China was not at all affiliated politically. On the other hand, the GATT espoused free trade and market economy, which in the eyes of the Chinese were dirty words synonymous with exploitative capitalism.[6] These were insurmountable ideological barriers during the Cultural Revolution, on which China was unable to compromise in the early 1970s.

The thawing of relations with the USA in the wake of Nixon's visit in 1972 ended China's largely self-imposed isolation ever since the outbreak of the Korean War (1950–1953). But it was not until the end of the Cultural Revolution in 1976 that a far-reaching market-oriented economic reform became likely. Ahead of the market reform in the urban areas, China's foreign trade regime experienced significant transformation in the early 1980s. Its trade policy guideline was no longer "to trade haves with have-nots" as a supplement to the socialist economy but "to join the international division of labor" in order to serve wider economic and political purposes. Institutionally, the national monopoly of foreign trade was decentralized to the provincial administrations. In 1982, China acquired the observer status from the GATT. Given the fact that the trade volume between China and GATT members had reached some 80% of its total trade thanks to the end of international isolation, its interest in securitizing its trade links through full GATT membership grew exponentially. But to avert a marathon bargaining with regard to the GATT reentry, China, after intensive internal discussions, thought it more favorable to restore its contracting party status with the GATT than to rejoin it. To this end, China spelled out three principles for reentry: (1) China requested to resume its contracting party status rather than to rejoin GATT; (2) China was willing to conduct substantive negotiations regarding the terms of the resumption; and (3) China was a socialist developing country—henceforth, China should enjoy equal rights with other developing nations.[7]

Marathon Talks with GATT and WTO—"Black Hair Becomes White"

China submitted application for the resumption of its contracting party status with the GATT in 1986, two years after it launched the economic reform in the urban sector. For those technocrats of MFT, the initial aim for securing GATT membership was to obtain permanently for China a universal MFN trading status, thereby steering clear of the US annual review mechanism targeting China and other communist states. Negotiations between China and GATT went on swiftly at the outset, but were suspended due to the Tiananmen Incident in the summer of 1989, the year that witnessed the end of the Cold War and the onset of successive regime changes in the Soviet Bloc. When the negotiations on China's reentry were back on track in April 1991, the demand terms from GATT became tougher. Concomitant to the GATT negotiations, bilateral talks between China and the USA on market access were launched. Nine rounds of tough negotiations had since been conducted. Vexed by the growing trade deficits with China, the USA pressed China hard to open the domestic market and threatened to wage a trade war in early 1992. After hard bargaining, both countries signed a memorandum of understanding on October 10, 1992. China promised to increase transparency in making available all the policy documents and regulations regarding foreign trade in a frequent and timely manner. China committed to drastically cutting down on the tariffs that had been raised since 1988 and to phasing out most of the import licenses and quota, known as the non-tariff barriers (NTBs), within the next two to three years. Moreover, China agreed to "cease implementing import substitution on all products permanently." As a quid pro quo, the USA committed to loosen high-tech export control in computers and telecommunication equipment and to stop the 301 investigation against Chinese products. The MFN trading status of China was renewed as a result of this agreement.[8]

To China's great ebullience, the USA committed to "staunchly" supporting China to join the GATT. The US gesture in this regard was to compensate for the sales of F-17 fighters to Taiwan, a provocative act in clear violation of the 8.17 communiqué signed in 1982 by China and the USA that set limits on US sales of weaponry to Taiwan. President George Bush promised to the Chinese in private that the fighters sold to Taiwan were not advanced enough to shift the cross-strait military balance in China's disadvantage. The arms sale was not to offend China but for election purposes only, to woo the military-industrial complex in Texas, the hometown and power base of the president.[9] The signal was clear: a trade war with China was not what he actually wanted in an election year. For China, a trade war with the USA was even less desirable as it would unequivocally hit China harder. Compared with just 2% of US total exports to China, the ratio was 25% for Chinese exports to the USA. Moreover, if the "old friend" Bush lost the election to Bill Clinton, a left-wing politician whom the Chinese communists disliked intuitively, relations with the USA might severely deteriorate. Hence, both sides wanted to compromise. In general, the agreement was an explicit American diplomatic victory in terms of its long-term implications on China's economic development. China's external orientation was locked in by its commitment on import liberalization. Its commitment to renouncing import substitution induced further liberalization of investment.

Targeting China's market access, both negotiations held in parallel were complementary and mutually reinforced one another? in pressing for China's commitments on trade liberalization. Where the Sino-US talks focused on trade issues, the GATT talks placed greater emphasis on China's trading system, in particular its transition to the market economy. When informed by the Chinese delegates immediately after the closing of the 14th National Party's Congress in October 1992 that the CCP had just proclaimed to build a "socialist market economy," reviewers of the GATT's China Work Group (CWG) were excited and gave a warm and lengthy applause. But the elation disappeared shortly. They began putting forth harsher questions breathlessly with the Chinese delegates regarding China's "market economy" rhetoric: what is a "socialist" market economy? What is the difference between a *socialist* market economy and a *capitalist* market economy? When Long Yongtu, the vice chief negotiator, replied that China had established various functional markets such as the steel market, cereal market, and so on, he was impatiently interrupted and told that those sorts of "markets" had nothing to do with a market economy.[10]

Nevertheless, China's ideological break-off with planning no longer beset the Chinese negotiators who had long been at pains to defend the so-called planned commodity economy, a puzzling expression referring to a de facto market economy which was nonetheless overruled by state planning. The changing face in economic ideology, however, only made China's reentry slightly better in that major powers and the GATT were too demanding—their terms on China's membership varied unpredictably and kept increasing endlessly. The GATT and some of its member states were deeply concerned about the Sino-US talks, fearing that a bilateral arrangement could eclipse China's negotiations with the GATT. Hence, the outcome of Sino-US talks on market access was prone to being mutilateralized into China's negotiations with the GATT. Meanwhile, China's attempt to take advantage of the GATT's unconditional MFN treatment and the dispute settlement mechanism to steer clear of US arbitrary protectionism was discerned by the USA, which ironically was the dominant rule-setter of GATT from the very outset. As such, China's bid for GATT membership was susceptible to the escalating demand terms of the USA, thereby placing China in an increasingly difficult position.

Given the USA's written promise of "staunchly" supporting China's reentry into GATT, the whole country of China was immersed in an extremely optimistic atmosphere in late 1992 that a reentry was imminent. As the GATT was to be replaced by the WTO on January 1, 1995, China made strenuous efforts in removing the trade barriers and restructuring its trading system in a bid to enter the GATT before it was overtaken by the WTO. On January 1, 1993, the Commission on Tariff Regulation under the State Council decided to reduce tariff rates for 3371 kinds of commodities. On January 1, 1994, China unified the renminbi exchange rate, a key step to facilitating its reentry. But the USA raised further demands by insisting that China's poor market access and a murky trade regime disqualify it for the membership, and that China ought to join the GATT as a developed rather than a developing country subject to the terms of a wider market access. China was hugely disappointed, claiming, "China will seek a principle of balancing rights with obligations and will not trade off our fundamental interests for the sake of reentry into the GATT."[11] China was ultimately denied the membership by the GATT for not meeting the criteria before the WTO was put in place.

The WTO was established on January 1, 1995, on the basis of the 18 agreements concluded at the Uruguay Round. At the urging of the Global North countries, the WTO curtailed the Special and Differential Treatment (SDT) reserved for the developing countries under the GATT and left it only to the least-developed countries. More than that, this reinvented Bretton Woods institution incorporated wide-ranging issues such as trade-related investment and intellectual property, financial services, distribution, and government procurement into its regulatory framework. China's attempt to resume its membership with GATT did not come to fruition with the creation of the WTO, which subjected prospective members to the "Single Undertaking," or acceptance of the whole package of the GATT agreements concluded at the Uruguay Round. Compared with the pro-development agenda of GATT, the neoliberal agenda of the WTO, particularly the "three capstone agreements," as Wade coined it, namely, Trade-Related Investment Measures (TRIMs), Trade-Related Aspects of Intellectual Property Rights (TRIPS), and the General Agreement on Trade in Services (GATS), as well as the much-strengthened dispute settlement mechanism, rendered the kind of industrial policies that had been successfully implemented by the late industrializers in East Asia like Taiwan and South Korea illegitimate. New members like China were requested not only to radically liberalize trade and investment but also to massively restructure their domestic legal systems and regulatory regimes to ensure full compliance with their market access commitments, thereby making their deep integration irreversible institutionally. This "globalization plus" feature of the WTO—legal compliance at home—suggests that China would have to encounter much tougher terms of accession than ever before.

Deeply frustrated by the denial of entry in 1994 and facing much tougher terms of accession thereafter, China seemed to become much less enthusiastic to join the WTO and the accession talks proceeded very slowly. Yet, starting from late 1995, China made new initiatives. President Jiang Zemin announced at the APEC (Asia-Pacific Economic

Cooperation) meeting in Osaka, Japan, that China would cut tariffs for 4000 products by 30% by the end of 1997 and would abolish quotas for 170 categories of products, about one-third of all commodities. In September 1997, China and Japan struck a deal on trade in goods as part of the bilateral agreement on market access yet to be finalized during Japan's Prime Minister Ryutaro Hashimoto's visit to China. By the end of the year 1997, China reached agreements with six countries, including South Korea, Japan, and four developing countries. At the Asia–Europe Meeting (ASEM) in 1998, China announced further tariff cuts to an average of 10% by 2005.

The outbreak of financial crisis in Thailand in July 1997 quickly spread over the entire East Asian region and devastated the export-oriented Tiger economies. Thanks to tight control on capital account, China remained virtually intact except for a couple of the local government-affiliated non-bank financial institutions that suddenly became insolvent for overborrowing short-term capital to finance long-term projects. But the Chinese economy was facing distinct hardship and was on the verge of a recession due to the sluggish demand at home, declining FDI and flood in the summer of 1998. With the successive currency devaluation in the neighboring countries, the Chinese renminbi (RMB) was under intense pressure of depreciation. The depreciation of the Japanese yen at this critical moment added to China's economic plight. Japan's economy was six times larger than that of China and had long been the locomotive of the economic growth of East Asian region. The bubble bursting in the early 1990s plunged the Japanese economy into a long recession. By Japan's calculation, an export boom would contribute to its economic recovery, which would in turn be capable of sucking in more imports from the devastated East Asian economies. The Clinton administration condemned Japan's self-interested act, dismissing it as being "irresponsible." Japan had its own agenda and moved on its way. It tacitly furnished massive financial assistance to Association of Southeast Asian Nations (ASEAN) countries—its traditional economic partners that had been hardest hit in this financial crisis.[12] The USA turned to China and flattered the latter for its critical role to be played in helping alleviate the East Asian financial crisis. The USA claimed that an RMB devaluation could trigger a competitive devaluation of the currencies in the region, thus making matters worse.

China took the USA's flattery seriously and was deeply intoxicated by a perceived bigger role and a greater international respectability in the region and in the world. Despite widespread speculation at home and abroad about an imminent RMB devaluation for the sake of Chinese exporters' interests, China committed to keeping the RMB stable at all costs. China not only echoed the US censure on Japan for "irresponsibly" depreciating the yen regardless of "international appeals," which were mainly from the USA, but joined hands with the USA in crippling the efforts of Japan to establish the Asian Monetary Fund (AMF), which was initiated not by Japan but by Malaysia.[13] Chinese Premier Zhu Rongji even openly asked the USA to put pressure on Japan.[14] As a matter of fact, China's decision not to devalue the RMB at the expense of its export interests was not driven by an outright altruistic internationalism. An enhanced political clout in the region as a result of being a "responsible great power" was China's primary objective. In addition to the need to bail out the newly returned Hong Kong, also severely devastated by the crisis, China was also in the hope of making its accession to the WTO easier as a reward for its active collaboration. Unfortunately, this once again turned out to be the wishful thinking of the Chinese leaders. In June 1998, US Trade Representative (USTR) Charlene Barshefsky stated in Shanghai, "The WTO is not a political but a commercial institution. Accession should be on a commercially meaningful basis. There will be no favors. … No Sweetheart Deal!"[15] Hence, little progress was made in China's bilateral talks with the USA. China was rather dispirited, and for not a short while, it displayed a "no rush" attitude.

Toward the closing of the year, Chinese officials switched their attitudes all of a sudden. They emphasized the need for an earlier WTO membership. Chief negotiator Long Yongtu told the *People's Daily*, "Some people have misunderstood that the Chinese government no longer treats the accession to the WTO as a priority. I think the earlier China joins the WTO, the better."[16] Entering 1999, China became so impatient that it did not attempt to cover up its deep anxiety for the accession. The Chinese government declared early in the year that Premier Zhu Rongji would visit the USA in April. Speculations were circulating in the diplomatic communities in both capitals that a deal could be struck shortly during Zhu's visit. Barshefsky briefed the press, "Upcoming visit of Premier Zhu Rongji to U.S. in April will be the last chance for China to accede, otherwise it will be left behind for years as a second class economy!"[17] It is hard to gauge to what extent this statement had affected China's calculation and tactics for the accession talks. But the USTR's words did generate psychological impact on Chinese leaders. At the press conference following the closing of the annual session of the National People's Congress (NPC) on March 15, 1999, Premier Zhu Rongji started with a humorous metaphor: "China's negotiations for entry into the GATT and WTO has lasted over a decade. Black hair has gotten white. Isn't it the time to finish this negotiation?"[18] To the surprise of all attending the press conference, Zhu declared in a blunt outspoken tone, "in order to push the WTO accession talks forward, China is ready to make maximum concessions." He said that the division between China and the USA and EU, though still large, had been reduced, and "hope is high of reaching an agreement so long as both sides make certain concessions by taking into account the vital importance of bilateral relations and of jointly maintaining the prosperity and stability of the world market."[19]

Zhu's eagerness to strike the deal was no more pronounced by the above statement. To downplay China's entreaties to the USA in the accession talks, Zhu began to play the Russian card, emphasizing China's good relations with Russia. He said, China and Russia "are warm and sincere friends. This time when I go to America, I think I will receive the same warm welcome rather than walking through the minefield. Maybe, I will not be hugged by President Clinton; but if we shake hands tightly, it must have the same meaning."[20] Zhu's words sounded like a warning to the USA not to press China too hard. Yet his caveat went little noticed by the USA, with the exception of one senior diplomat at the US embassy in Beijing who responded that such a way of expression would cause displeasure by many people in Washington if Zhu spoke like that in the USA.[21] Nevertheless, the Premier's statecraft in handling great power relation would soon be tested by a major global crisis concomitant to his journey to the USA.

Zhu's trip to the USA began at the very moment when NATO's military intervention in Kosovo reached a climax. China and Russia condemned NATO's intervention as violating the UN principles and international law, and thus endangered world peace. Both countries concluded a "coordinated strategic partnership" in 1997 to counterbalance the reinforced US–Japan alliance. Ironically, China concluded a "constructive strategic partnership" with the USA during President Jiang

Zemin's state visit to Washington the same year. Jiang was appointed General Secretary in June 1989 in the aftermath of the Tiananmen Incident. One year later, he took over the presidency and chairmanship of the Central Military Commission (CMC). Even so, he was fairly weak politically and lived cautiously under the shadow of Deng Xiaoping. In 1997, Deng passed away and Jiang as the core of the third-generation leadership was able to make decisions. Jiang's ambition to make China a respectable great power was reflected in his new thinking of so-called great power diplomacy (*daguo waijiao*). To this end, China concluded *strategic* partnerships with all major powers. This new thinking was ostensibly pointless in that an indiscriminate global partnership was by no means strategic. It further raised the key question of whom China was to strategically ally with to oppose whom.

The triangle relationship between China, Russia, and the USA in the late 1990s was no longer the one in the 1980s from which China reaped maximal strategic gains through maintaining roughly equal distance with the two superpowers. With the end of the Cold War, China's strategic value to the USA vanished. Thanks to increasing economic links, however, China viewed maintaining good and stable relations with the USA the top priority of its foreign policy. The Russians thought likewise. Both China and Russia regarded access to the market and technology of the West as being crucial to their respective modernization drive. The economic links between China and Russia were fairly weak, with trading volume negligible compared with that between China and the USA. Thus, despite NATO's eastward expansion and the USA's increasing assertiveness in the West Pacific that engaged Russia and China geopolitically, their *strategic partnership* was more apparent than substantive. As a matter of fact, both powers had made it clear from the outset of negotiating the partnership that a political-military alliance was unlikely and the strategic partnership was not targeted against any third party. More than that, mutual suspicion and distrust between the two powers were deeply rooted in the long past, exacerbated by a never-ending overt and covert geopolitical rivalry in the Far East. With the USA's and EU's arms embargo hanging on, China had no other sources but Russia from which to acquire advanced weaponry. Although China's security concern was partly addressed by Russia's delivery of advanced weaponry, the Russians delivered more sophisticated weaponry to its traditional ally, India—China's historic foe—which geopolitically outflanks China from the south. The Kosovo crisis became the testing stone of the reliability of the strategic partnership in the post-Cold War era.

At the news of NATO's bombing of Yugoslavia, Russia's Prime Minister Yevgeny Primakov was en route to Washington on a planned visit. On the order of President Boris Yeltsin, he canceled his visit to the USA and flew back in protest. Meanwhile, several Chinese scholars and students living in the USA wrote an open letter to Premier Zhu Rongji, asking him to defer or cancel his visit to Washington to echo Russia's response. The letter stated that if the Premier insisted on visiting Washington, he should not bow to the US accusation on China's human rights abuse and he should draw attention to the USA's hypocrisy for illegally using the UN-banned uranium-depleted bombs against Yugoslavia.[22] At this juncture, President Jiang Zemin was on a state visit in Europe. He did not suspend his visit and return home as anticipated in protest of NATO's bombing. The Chinese Foreign Ministry only issued oral protest. After coming back to Beijing, Jiang chaired the Politburo meeting and decided that Zhu visit the USA as scheduled. This highlighted the frailty of Sino-Russian relations, which were eclipsed by the far greater importance China attached to its relations with the USA. China had kept a low profile since 1989 according to Deng Xiaoping's dictate to "abide the time to build our strength." By distancing itself from Russia in the Kosovo crisis and making friendly overtures toward the USA, China bowed its head even lower. Moreover, given the China-bashing atmosphere in the USA, China saw logical links between greater concessions on the WTO accession and improvement of Sino-US relations. Zhu stated in the press conference on March 15, "since they [Americans] had anger on China, let them vent anger (*xiaoxiaoqi*) on me when I visit the U.S."[23]

Zhu's "Walk to Canossa"—Journey to the USA

On the eve of his departure, China announced that it would accord license to two of the USA's largest insurance companies, John Hancock and Chubb, very soon. Meanwhile, China decided to import US $150 million worth of equipment and technology products as a major step toward reducing the US-concerned trade deficits. These were explicit attempts to create a friendly atmosphere for Zhu's visit.[24] In such settings, Zhu boarded the plane heading to the USA with the mission of finalizing negotiations on China's WTO entry. To the astonishment of foreign observers in China, Zhu did not bring with him ministers from the line departments. He included in his delegation only subordinates that shared his liberal views on WTO accession, such as Wu Yi, State Councilor and former head of the Ministry of Foreign Trade and Economic Cooperation (MOFTEC); Wang Zhongyu, Director General of the State Council and head of the State Economic and Trade Commission (SETC); Zeng Peiyan, Director General of the National Development and Planning Commission (NDPC); and Shi Guangsheng, Minister of MOFTEC. Such composition of delegation was rumored to be Zhu's personal decision,[25] with the discernible intent to make quick decisions by issuing orders directly to his closest aides without being hampered by the suspicious line department heads.

Upon arrival in the USA, the Chinese delegation declared its intention to lift the import ban on citrus, meat, and wheat of seven states at the US Pacific Northwest. This was to please the US agribusiness, prompting them to lobby for China's WTO entry. Zhu further extended extremely generous offers by promising to (1) lower agricultural tariffs to 17% by 2004; (2) reduce tariffs on chemicals, wood and paper to the level of other WTO members; (3) equally open markets for semiconductors, computers and computer equipment, telecom and other high-tech products; (4) reduce tariffs on cars from 80–100% to 25% by 2005, cut tariffs on car parts to an average of 10%, as well as phase out quotas on car imports by 2005; (5) extend distribution rights of films to 40 a year and allow full foreign ownership; (6) phase out all geographic restrictions on foreign banks in 5 years; (7) lift restrictions on foreign insurance companies upon the accession; (8) double airline landing rights to foreign firms.[26]

Nevertheless, to avoid creating a disgraceful image of pleading for a WTO deal with an increasingly bellicose USA, Zhu downplayed his personal role in recklessly coming to the USA to negotiate the deal at an improper moment of NATO's escalating bombing and Russian defiance. Clearly aware of opposition at home and abroad, Zhu told the press,

"Actually I didn't want to come at all. But President Jiang (Zemin) is China's Number One. He ordered me to come, so I dared not disobey." Zhu's words reminded shrewd China observers of similar remarks made by Zhao Ziyang, then CCP's General Secretary, to the visiting Soviet leader Mikhail Gorbachev in May 1989 that Deng Xiaoping was the de facto paramount leader who pulled the string from behind the curtain. Zhao's words and his ambiguous attitudes toward the demonstrators irritated Deng and led to his downfall. Although President Jiang lacked Deng's authority and was unable to sack the disobedient Premier at will, the tricks the Premier played by diverting all possible blame to the president put himself on a political tightrope; in alienating Jiang, who gave him full backing in negotiating the WTO deal with the USA, Zhu made the contentious negotiation his one-man show rather than the gamble of the Chinese leadership as a whole. Zhu's adventurism was also derived from his misconception of a US–EU rift in the Kosovo crisis. He was misguided by official think-tank "strategists" who made the Premier believe that the US military intervention in Kosovo was a currency war against the EU.[27] Caught in a bitter strife with its European ally, Zhu calculated that the USA, eager to preserve its dollar supremacy, needed China at this very juncture. Therefore, making overtures toward the USA could exchange a return favor from the latter—that is, China's WTO accession.

For domestic political reasons—in particular, pressures from protectionist interest groups and charges against China for spying on US military technology—President Bill Clinton, who was undermined by the impeachment proceedings in 1998, rejected Zhu's generous offer and instead raised further demands. This went far beyond the Premier's expectation and bottom line. The USA demanded further concessions on anti-dumping, banking and textiles. It insisted that China remain a non-market economy for ten years instead of the five years that had been accepted by China in previous negotiations. To make matters worse, an alleged draft agreement was uploaded to the Internet by somebody inside the US administration, indicating that China had accepted all the points listed in this agreement. This immediately sparked an uproar in the Chinese-language media in North America and put Premier Zhu Rongji and the Chinese delegation in an extremely awkward position. Zhu's aide and

MOFTEC Minister Shi Guangsheng denied the existence of such an agreement, claiming that the Chinese side had not agreed to all the points on the list unilaterally released by the US side, despite the fact that much progress had been made. The USA's back-stabbing of Zhu gave no better excuse for those overseas Chinese Maoists who lashed out at Zhu's "anger-venting diplomacy" (*xiaoqi waijiao*) and his traitorous WTO deal that was poised to sell too many Chinese national interests to US imperialism. A pen-named leftist writer summarized the online "agreement" into 21 points to refer to the notorious "Twenty-one Demands" that imperial Japan intended to impose on the Yuan Shi-kai regime in 1915.[28] These harsh attacks did not instantly reach the Premier and the Chinese delegation. But they could sense the hostility from their political intuition. Sandwiched by the leftist censure at home and abroad, and the US ingratitude for China's offer, Premier Zhu and the Chinese delegation had no other choice but to suspend the talks and leave the USA empty-handed for Canada.

Both Shi Guangsheng and Long Yongtu later recalled that Clinton's decision to decline Zhu's offer frustrated many of the US negotiators, some of whom even wept for having missed such a good deal.[29] Shi and Long spared no efforts to describe how Clinton quickly regretted the decision after the Chinese delegation had left. His phone call chased Zhu to Canada, pleading him to reopen talks in Washington. They flattered the Premier by claiming that he displayed exquisite statecraft, who told Clinton that negotiation could be reopened but only in Beijing. It is more likely that Zhu's decline to the American president's extension of an olive branch is that the Premier had been disempowered to conduct any negotiations with the USA on China's WTO accession.[30] However it is viewed, Zhu's failed trip to the USA dealt a heavy blow to his prestige and cast a long shadow on his career. However, face-saving is an imperative politically since the visit was collectively decided anyway. In response to mounting suspicions of Zhu's journey of self-humiliation and criticisms within and without the party that would also implicate President Jiang himself, propaganda was waged to obviate the negative image of selling China to the USA. The *Outlook Weekly* (*liaowang*), one of the CCP's major mouthpieces, printed a flattering cover story article titled "Premier Zhu Visit the U.S. to Declare Righteousness" (*Zhu zongli fangmei shenming dayi*), asserting that the visit "achieved [the] expected result" in the sense that relations improved and the WTO negotiations made substantial progress. The article cited Foreign Minister Tang Jiaxuan's words as saying that the Premier's visit had "achieved consummate success."[31]

To make this sort of propaganda more persuasive, the *Outlook Weekly* that carried this article decorated the cover sheet with a big photo of the confident Premier Zhu who spread out his hands and wore a big smile. Underneath the photo was a splash subtitle in big Chinese characters—"The Successful Visit of Premier Zhu to the USA (*zhu zongli chenggong fangmei*)." A scholar of international relations (IR) at the Chinese Academy of Social Sciences (CASS), the biggest official think tank, echoed the official position by detailing why it was necessary that Premier Zhu should go to America in spite of mounting hostilities in Washington. He made no reference to China' overzealous anticipation to strike the WTO deal with the USA at an improper moment. Instead, he argued that "despite the hostilities, Premier Zhu should go to America to clarify our position on the Kosovo question and the truth of Sino-US trade relations and other issues with our patience and sincerity to reduce their misunderstanding."[32] Sarcastically, the CASS author was not at all convinced by his own reasoning. He complained in private that he did not actually believe this but was compelled to write such a thing by order of the "above."[33]

The propaganda collapsed only one week later on May 8, 1999, when the Chinese embassy in Belgrade was hit by five laser-guided missiles launched from three US strategic bombers. The whole nation was infuriated. Only the leadership kept silent. None of the senior leaders turned out for several days to pacify public sentiments until Vice-President Hu Jintao, the heir apparent of Jiang, read soberly a brief and carefully worded government statement on the state television (CCTV) to denounce the "purposeful bombing" by the USA. Hu warned the demonstrators that they must not go to the extreme, especially not be "used" by "hostile foreign forces." He cautioned that the Chinese people should cherish the nation's "current good political climate" of "stability and unity" (*anding tuanjie*). Hu's speech suggested that what really worried the leadership was not so much the diplomatic crisis as the resurgence of an unbridled nationalism to backfire at the regime. The leadership did have good reason to worry since wrath and cynicism were on the rise in the past years among the underclass and young college students who increasingly resented the regime's overt pro-Western stance and low-profile foreign policy. Many Chinese, especially young adults, did not refrain from displaying their anger at and contempt for the leaders, in particular President Jiang Zemin and Premier Zhu Rongji. Zhu's humiliating trip to Washington and the embassy bombing added fuel to the nationalist backlashes against not only the West but also the Chinese regime that to legitimate itself had ironically spared no effort in instigating anti-Western nationalism in ideological terms in the aftermath of the Tiananmen Incident in 1989.

Thanks to the bombing, the scheduled talks in Beijing were suspended. However, the suspension did not lead to either China's revocation of its previous commitments or the US retreat from the terms it had demanded from China. Zhu's position within the party state was severely undermined by the bombing. His draconian reforms to re-streamline the central state apparatus were largely derailed; the "strike-hard" campaign waged against massive smuggling in coastal areas offended vested interests of local administrations and even the military. His pro-Western stance and a less-bellicose gesture toward the breakaway province of Taiwan also made him the target of the nationalists. Therefore, during the Beidaihe Conference in June 1999, Zhu was harshly attacked by many attendants for his economic and reform policies. In addition, his improper remarks in the USA concerning the SOE's restructuring were the focus of criticism by his Politburo colleagues such as Li Peng and Hu Jintao.[34] Shortly after, news leaked from the summer resort that Zhu had submitted his resignation at the conference. The stock market plummeted accordingly. However, Jiang declined his resignation owing to the fact that Zhu's courage and capability were after all indispensable to forging ahead with a profound economic change in the nation at the turn of the century. For the Premier, those fatal setbacks at home and abroad frustrated and subdued him permanently.

Triad Feud and China's Miscalculation

With domestic discontent over the embassy bombing abating, China resumed the WTO talks with the USA, less than one week before President Jiang Zemin met with President Bill Clinton at the APEC summit in New Zealand on September 11, 1999. China's eagerness to strike the

WTO deal with the USA in the first place was no more evident. In theory, China needed to hold bilateral talks with all the 100-strong WTO members. In reality, however, only 37 members were ready to hold bilateral negotiations with a view to addressing their particular concerns on trading with China. According to WTO's universal principle of MFN, all the commitments China made in the bilateral talks would be automatically applicable to all members. The most important adversaries in the negotiations were the three largest trading powers, the USA, the EU and Japan, known as the Triad. The Triad "had traditionally controlled the agenda of the global trading regime until the Doha Round (in 2005)."[35] They shared the strategic vision of integrating China into the rule-based international system. However, they diverged regarding respective priority concerns on trade. Their strategic focus and attitudes toward China's transition differed as well. Thus, they did not develop a coordinated approach in negotiating with China when China started to engage in intensive economic diplomacy, with regard to China's WTO entry, until the middle of 1999.

China's calculation was twofold: First and foremost, it viewed relations with the USA as being the most crucial amid its great power relations. Secondly, it viewed the USA as the most formidable adversary in the bilateral talks on its WTO entry. Chinese decision-makers judged that striking a deal with the USA in the first instance would make subsequent talks much easier. They made a big mistake. The USA, the EU and Japan had competing economic and trade interests on the emerging market of China. The USA was the late-comer market intruder in East Asia that had competed fiercely with Japan since the late 1970s. Japan maintained a large trade surplus with China; therefore, it did not have the same concerns as the USA with regard to addressing rapidly expanding trade deficit through China's wider market access. Japan struck the second WTO deal on trade in services with China in September 1999. Japan was clearly aware that its moderation was to the displeasure of the USA, which insisted on harsh terms regarding China's accession. The USA was unhappy with Japan's free riding on its efforts to integrate China into the global trading regime. But Japan had its own calculation: as a civilian power and a most reliable ally of the USA, Japan had to address its security concerns through realignment with the USA. Since a great part of its security concern was associated with China,[36] Japan wished to use its moderation on the terms of China's WTO entry in exchange for the latter's acquiescence in its new defense guideline with the USA. Japan also expected to play a constructive role in facilitating the thawing of Sino-US relations after the embassy bombing through the completion of her WTO agreement with China.[37]

The EU endorsed Japan's view that "the US was too harsh on a transitional country like China." Although it also endorsed the US position that standards should be set for China's WTO accession, the EU disagreed to identify China as a developed nation and to exert too much pressure on China, which was in a difficult process of reform.[38] The EU's leniency was not out of altruism. Its general trade performance was rather good, which more than compensated its sizable trade deficit with China. This contrasted with the USA, which recorded enlarging trade deficit as a whole, a large part of which was accrued to its trade with China. In addition, the EU had less incentive to force open China's market since its industrial products were less competitive than those of the USA and Japan.[39] Thus, it did not want the USA to gain the upper hand on China's market.

For the part of China, acquiring technologies from either of the Triad powers made little difference. These First World trading powers were the most advanced industrial economies, each of which was the source of technology and the export destination of the developing nations. Relative to the USA and Japan, the EU was the most generous high-tech provider to China. A lesser demanding Japan and EU on either political or economic grounds offered a rare opportunity for China to play one trading power off against the other. The multifaceted Triad feud was what China could take advantage of in order to facilitate its national development. China could have chosen to reach the WTO deal with either one or two of the Triad powers—namely, Japan and the EU—on favorable terms to enforce ISI on the basis of internal integration in conjunction with the legitimate retention of sufficient policy space for autonomous national development. This implies that given the country's great power status, its empire's size and market potential, continuing to play by the Bretton Woods rules even without the WTO membership was still possible for China in the age of liberal globalization. Reaching the deals with Japan and the EU would translate into a stronger bargaining position for China to pursue less harsher terms of accession with remaining countries, particularly the USA, by locking in those favorable terms to seek the compliance of the USA. Should the USA insist on its demand terms and refuse to compromise, it could risk losing China's potential market to other two trading powers and America's political clout in China in the long term. For China at that juncture, even if it failed to secure US compromise in this regard, its access to advanced technology and overseas markets would not be adversely affected, considering that an alternative pathway of development had been set in motion blending ISI with shallow integration. Resisting the tide of hyperglobalization through diplomacy would also pay off politically in terms of creating a favorable image of China as a pacifist responsible great power.

From the above inference, China, after concluding the WTO deal with Japan on generous terms, could immediately enter into negotiations with the EU to cut the deal before resuming talks with the USA. This was by no means an unrealistic dream given the "good cop" role played by the EU.[40] It is highly likely that, misguided by its foreign policy, which took the maintaining of good relations with the USA as the top priority, China ignored the EU's kind gestures from time to time and, as always, devoted all its attention to negotiating with the USA, the toughest adversary in the first place. China's aloofness infuriated and alienated the EU. That "there was no close cooperation between the United States and Europe on China"[41] gave way to the two largest trading powers cooperating closely in coercing China to much harsher terms of the accession.

In such a setting, the USA called for much harsher terms after the negotiations were restarted in September 1999, despite the embassy bombing. Premier Zhu Rongji commented on USTR Barshefsky's negotiating style during his visit in April: "When we give away a point, she wants another," or *decun jinchi* in Chinese phraseology.[42] In the last round of negotiations held in Beijing in November 1999, Chinese and US negotiators engaged in tough bargaining for six nights and days centering on eight big issues concerning agriculture, the opening of capital market, telecommunications, financial services, insurance, auto industry, anti-dumping, safeguards, and the rights of foreign trade. Several times, the US delegation, wary of Chinese negotiators' insistence, threatened to wind up the negotiations and had their luggage transported to the Beijing Capital Airport for departure. At this critical moment, the "master strategist"—Premier Zhu—appeared according to the "special decision" made by President Jiang Zemin, who urged the Premier twice to "rush to the negotiation."[43] He intervened to talk directly with Barshefsky. And the talks continued! In the first instance, Zhu dissuaded the Americans by deferring some outstanding issues such as agricultural subsidies to the future; then he made even larger concessions in some critical areas concerning US particular interests on which MOFTEC negotiators could not decide to exchange for the latter's acceptance of China's priority concerns on some fragile sectors, like the auto industry.[44] After hard bargaining until the last minute, China made substantial concessions on market access and concluded the bilateral agreement with the USA on November 15, 1999. China backed away further from the terms the USA had demanded in April.[45]

The Sino-US agreement was extolled with fanfare on the state-controlled media as the country's latest "achievements in reform and opening."[46] Jiang Zemin called the deal a win–win for both sides which was "good, historic and realistic" when he turned out to meet with US chief negotiator Ms. Barshefsky immediately after the signing ceremony.[47] The *People's Daily* hailed the deal as "a great event in the Chinese history" and the leader's great achievement.[48] The full text was not made public to Chinese citizens, but the main points of China's commitments were immediately released on the Western media and transmitted back through emails to those Chinese researchers and scholars having foreign connections. To China's great astonishment, the EU sharply changed its attitude and became a much more formidable adversary than the USA in the ensuing bilateral talks. The EU's trade commissioner Pascal Lamy declared that the EU "was 80 percent satisfied with the US–China deal."[49] There is reason to believe that before starting bilateral talks with China in Brussels in January 2000, the EU had obtained the full text of the Sino-US agreement from the USA. As a matter of fact, the full text was uploaded online by the USA on March 13, 2000. The EU raised a number of fresh demands beyond the Sino-US agreement. But for the Sino-US agreement to take effect, the US must grant China Permanent Normal Trade Relations (PNTR) trading status, which was, nonetheless, conditioned on the conclusion of bilateral agreement between China and the EU in the first place. Thus, the US administration urged the EU to strike an early deal with China during May 2000 so that it would be able to present its own package to the House of Representatives to replace the old conditional MFN legislation. However, the EU refused to rush into an agreement with China, in that it had resolved to extract further concessions on the basis of what China and the USA had agreed.[50] Under these circumstances, China completely lost the bargaining power vis-à-vis the EU and had no other choice but to make further concessions to satisfy EU's special concerns with regard to China's market access. The European Commission claimed that China's change of mind was the result of close cooperation between Brussels and Washington.[51] On May 18, 2000, China and the EU reached an agreement based on the tougher terms of the EU.[52] Five days later, US House voted and approved China's PNTR status.

The EU achieved three extra gains in the agreement beyond the American deal: more than 150 industrial and agricultural products of European concern, wider market access to insurance industry and telecommunication industry, which was EU's major concern.[53] Amid the euphoria in China's state-controlled media, positive aspects from the WTO accession were stressed while forthcoming challenges ahead were little mentioned.[54] Nonetheless, given growing suspicions and criticisms from the domestic industries and the leftist intellectuals, and to avoid the image of being extorted by Western powers, the state propaganda on China's agreement with the EU was much more restrained than six months earlier when the Sino-US agreement was concluded.

To cover up the decision-makers' substantial miscalculation in alienating the previously moderate EU into a tough opponent, one of China's chief negotiators later tried to disassociate the US–EU collaboration by depicting EU's toughness as a psychology of "keeping up with the Joneses."[55] But the nightmare did not end when the negotiations with the three trading powers on market access were completed. China still had to solve the outstanding issues with the USA and the EU, on a bilateral basis. In addition, China had to finish its negotiations with the remaining demanding members before the final approval procedure was initiated. During the talks on the outstanding issue of agricultural subsidies with the USA, China insisted that its status be identified as a developing nation entitled to maintain 10% subsidies as opposed to 5% for the developed nations. After tough bargaining during the APEC meeting in Shanghai in June 2001, China reached agreement with the USA, setting 8.5% as the capped rate of agricultural subsidy. The EU accepted this result without dissents. To China's complete surprise, the WTO accession was nearly blocked by Mexico and Switzerland in the remaining bilateral talks. As a developing country and signatory of the North American Free Trade Agreement (NAFTA), Mexico was deeply worried about the NAFTA-incurred trade creation being undermined by China's cheap exports. Hence, it insisted on maintaining extensive anti-dumping mechanisms against Chinese products. Switzerland raised demands on chemicals and pharmaceuticals, which were its particular concern. China had no other choice but to cave in. It was not until December 11, 2001, that China's membership was eventually confirmed in Doha by the signing of the Protocol on the Accession and the Working Party Report.

The WTO Entry: A Big Gamble for China?

The accession talks were conducted strictly on commercial terms. China's agreements with the USA and the EU formed the cornerstone of the final accession protocol of the WTO (all the agreements concluded on bilateral and multilateral bases will hereafter be called the WTO deal or WTO agreement). What is the WTO deal all about? Like all other new entrants, China gained institutionalized wider access to the global markets. Yet under the terms of the WTO agreement, China was identified as a non-market economy for 15 years, a clause that no other WTO members accepted. This contrasted starkly with Russia, which took longer to join the WTO but whose market economy status was fully recognized by the USA and the EU, despite the fact that its marketization level was far below that of China. Such a discriminatory provision left the Chinese products vulnerable to the arbitrary anti-dumping and countervailing measures of its major trading partners.[56] Two WTO plus provisions were also imposed on China: one was the so-called transitional product-specific safeguard that allowed other members to impose restrictions on Chinese exports under softer conditions than those spelled out in the Uruguay Round agreements for 12 years after China joined the WTO.[57]

The other was the "textile safeguard" mechanism that allowed other members to impose quotas on Chinese textiles until December 31, 2008. China became the only country to be subjected to such restrictions on textile exports for four years after the Multi-fiber Agreement (MFA), which set quotas on textiles and clothing for the developing world, was phased out by the end of 2004.[58] These three WTO plus provisions, according to Nicholas Lardy of the Brookings Institution, violated the "most basic principle of the WTO."[59]

In contrast to the unfree "freer" trade abroad, China opened its door much wider. Depicting the WTO deal as an "unequal treaty" imposed on China,[60] Lardy dismissed the substantial tariff concessions China made as overstated, arguing that tariff reductions and exemptions used to be a normal practice in many parts of China in the past decade. Thus, the drastic nominal tariff cuts would not inflict extra impacts on the local firms.[61] Chinese WTO negotiators expressed similar views on the domestic media.[62] This line of argument overlooked the fact that the domestic firms had already been severely impaired thanks to China's radical import liberalization prior to the WTO accession.[63] More importantly, the reduced tariff rates would be capped upon accession institutionally so that China would not be able to increase in case of need.[64]

The real crux lies in the fact that "the deal clearing Chinese entry into the WTO is more about liberalizing foreign investment and ownership than liberalizing trade."[65] China promised to enforce TRIMs and TRIPs upon accession with no grace period as had been allowed for all other WTO members including the developed nations.[66] These two multilateral agreements were the product of techno-nationalism of the advanced countries that forced the codification of "protection of [their] technological advantages" in the Uruguay Round,[67] which "entrenched the position of the advanced countries" having "a lead in high-technology industries."[68] To be more specific, the TRIMs were designed primarily to discourage import substitution of the developing nations by means of outlawing their imposition of local content, export performance and trade balancing requirements on foreign investors. Aimed at stronger protection of intellectual property, the TRIPs not only "restricts reverse engineering, imitation and mandatory licensing"[69] but also "requires countries to provide patent protection for both processes and products, in all fields of technology."[70] These three "capstone agreements," with GATS included, institutionalized "protectionism of the strong" at the expense of the poor nations.[71]

What made China's entry terms particularly unique was not merely its promise to enforce TRIMs and TRIPs upon accession but also a TRIMs-plus concession it made specifically to the USA in the bilateral talks—to relinquish its rights to impose technology transfer on the American investors—a concession to be enjoyed by investors all over the world according to the principle of MFN. This was startling since even under TRIMs, coercing foreign investors into transferring technology remained the legitimate sovereign right for all the member states.[72] Moreover, in the final accession protocol, China, in the capacity of a developing nation, expressly promised to "initiate negotiations" on the WTO's plurilateral Agreement on Government Procurement (GPA) "as soon as possible"[73] and, more specifically, to no longer sponsor the state-owned enterprises (SOEs).[74] In a nutshell, the extensive commitments on market access China made for WTO membership were far more detailed than those accepted by India,[75] making China the most open developing country and even one of the most open economies in the world. Its openness was even greater than some of the OECD countries.[76]

Lardy rightly explained how the Chinese leadership expected to use the accession to leverage increased foreign competition to accelerate domestic economic reform. He contended that by transforming the inefficient state banks and the SOEs, China's WTO membership would eventually contribute to higher living standards of the people and continued economic growth.[77] Peter Nolan held a contrarian view. He juxtaposed China's WTO entry with the country's opening up after the Opium Wars one and a half centuries earlier.[78] He used a metaphor—"battle of the giants or defeat of the pygmy"—to question the viability of the Chinese firms in the wake of the WTO entry. He argued that the global business and information technology (IT) revolutions, also known as the Third Industrial Revolution, in the 1980s and 1990s, had equipped the Western multinational corporations (MNCs) with "a global brand, a global market, and a global procurement system" (*3-globals*), making them extremely competitive in the entrenched world system of oligopolistic capitalism. Although China had produced not a small achievement in *absolute* terms in the last two decades through carrying out Japanese-style industrial policies, enabling it to avoid the "industrial collapse of the former USSR,"[79] these industrial progresses had failed to foster China's leading firms into truly competitive global players prior to the WTO accession.[80] After carefully comparing the performance of Chinese and the global firms in the last two decades, Nolan found that "the competitive capability of China's large firms after two decades of reform are still extremely weak in relation to the global giants" across all industrial sectors.[81] The gap was huge and had even widened since "China's leading firms are further behind the global leaders than they were when the industrial policies began almost two decades ago."[82] Based on these findings, Nolan predicted that joining the WTO would present the large SOEs with "immense difficulties on the 'global level playing field' which is about to arrive in China." The US firms will "take the lead in the defeat of China's large corporations." The Chinese pygmies "are not in position to compete with the world's leading firms" on its own market.[83] Nolan concluded that in the age of globalization (oligopolistic capitalism), catching up with the West had become "highly unrealistic" for China with or without the WTO membership.

Whether Nolan's projections would turn out to be reliable or not, the arguments he made about China's then industrial position were deeply persuasive. Similarly, China's two top-class academic institutions, all affiliated with the highest authority of the party state, produced two research reports in 2005 on the country's industrial development. The contents of both reports were even more revealing, which nicely complemented Nolan's analysis. One was issued by the Modernization Research Centre (MRC) of the Chinese Academy of Sciences (CAS); the other was jointly issued by the CAS and the Chinese Academy of Engineering (CAE). Both reports happened to use 2001 or 2002 as the year of enquiry to review the level of modernization China had achieved. The MRC's report claimed that

> China ranked 69th among the 108 countries around the world in terms of comprehensive modernization index. Up until 2002, China remained an economically underdeveloped country. The gap between China and the advanced economies was huge. In 2002, *China was just in the middle stage of industrialization*; its general level of economic modernization was lower

> than that of world average … if per capita GDP and economic structure were taken as the chronicle difference with the advanced economies, China's level of modernization in 2002 could only match that of Britain in 1858, the U.S. in 1892, Japan in 1957, and South Korea in 1976.[84]

Thus, the economic transformation of China was far from completed despite having experienced two decades of sustained high economic growth.

The second report (hereafter called CAS-CAE report or the Report) argued that in 2001 *China was still in the primary stage of industrialization* if only measured by two commonly used indicators: per capita GDP and employment structure. Such way of assessing China's phase of industrialization could have underrated the country's actual level of development, the Report claimed. If more weight were given to the industrial value-added and manufacturing in their respective proportion to GDP, China should have arrived at the middle stage of industrialization that took on the following features. *Firstly*, rapid industrial growth was overshadowed by low per capita GDP and low productivity. In 2001, China's per capita GDP was only US $908.8 in exchange rate terms, far lower than the world average of US $4890. The average return on asset, per capita profitability and sales revenue of China's top 500 industrial enterprises were equivalent to only 24.62%, 12.31%, and 9.51%, respectively, of the global 500 in 1998. Even the performance of China's top 100 industrial giants was slightly better on average with their average return on asset, per capita profitability and sales revenue being 26.4%, 17.6% and 12.7% of the global 500, respectively. In 2001, the average return on asset of all the SOEs and the non-SOEs was only 3.5%.

Secondly, China's key production technologies remained far backward compared with those of the advanced economies. A state survey carried out by the State Economic and Trade Commission (SETC) on 15 industrial sectors like the steel, non-ferrous industry, petrochemical industry and electricity, and so on reveals that the technological gap between China and the NDCs was 10–15 years, and the gap in key technologies was even wider. For instance, on the part of China's capital goods production (in Chinese phraseology "equipment manufacturing"), the most cutting-edge industrial sector, only one-third was relatively advanced in techno-economic performance; nearly one-fifth was obsolete; and more than 40% were overdue for replacement. Machine building was China's core capital goods sector. Only 12% of it was technologically advanced, nearly 30% was outdated even in China's home market. *Thirdly*, China's tertiary industry developed quite slowly relative to the seemingly rapid industrialization. *Fourthly*, China's rapid industrialization, which had been fueled by state planning, did not bring forth rapid urbanization. In 2001, China's rural employment accounted for 78.7% of all workforce even though the industrial output had risen to 78.5% of the national economy.[85]

Authored by China's most prominent scientist-/engineer-academicians, and edited by Zhu Gaofeng, Vice-President of CAE, the Report assessing then China's industrial position was authoritatively reliable. Acknowledging the country's economic backwardness prior to the WTO accession, the Report, different from Nolan's pessimistic projection, viewed globalization as the solution to speeding up the country's industrialization. In the Report's recommendation section, the authors highlighted the importance of industrial policy, advocating for setting up "development innovation fund" and "venture fund"; promoting cooperation on joint research and development (R&D) between the local firms, universities, and research institutions; and lastly but most vaguely, creating an innovation-friendly environment.[86] This was merely a repetition of the useless clichés uttered by the Chinese economists a decade ago.[87] The Report made no mention of the shrinking policy place following China's WTO accession nonetheless. Instead, it placed high expectations on the FDI, hoping that increased competition would prompt the foreign investors to adopt the most advanced technologies to be transferred to China using greater market access as quid pro quo. This was essentially a refreshed version of "exchanging for technology with market access" (ETMA)[88]—meaning "I give you market, you give me technology," a strategy MOFTEC had carried out from 1992 onward. Largely unsuccessful as it turned out to be, the ETMA had all along aroused great controversy within China's industrial community. In the eyes of the authors, however, it was the lack of *effective competition* that caused the failure of ETMA. To make competition work, they suggested that China build up stronger national firms as well as create a perfect "level playing field." For that matter, they suggested that the "ultra-national treatment" preferential policies accorded to foreign firms that discriminated against the domestic firms be abolished.[89]

This piece of recommendation raises a set of paradoxes. *Firstly*, building stronger national firms entails proactive industrial policies, many of which had been precisely delegitimized by China's own liberalization commitments, especially those pertaining to TRIMs (and TRIMs-plus) and TRIPs. *Secondly*, unlike the 1980s in which investment from the Chinese diasporas formed the mainstay of FDI, the 1990s saw the dominance of MNCs from the industrial West that took greater interest in market seeking than in exploiting China's cheap labor force for export. They were much less cost-sensitive to those preferential policies than the investors from Hong Kong, Macau and Taiwan (HKMT) that were overwhelmingly export-oriented, low-tech, labor-intensive original equipment manufacturers (OEMs). For Western MNCs, the removal of the preferential policies was more than compensated for by China's wider market access destined for the establishment of the "global level playing field," which ironically posed a greater menace to the local firms. *Thirdly*, utilizing advanced technologies by the MNCs' affiliates, an internalized form of transfer of technology, "may hold back deeper learning processes and spillovers into the local economy."[90] Those market-seeking MNCs were indeed more inclined to adopt the newest technologies. Yet in targeting the local firms as their rivals, the MNCs had every incentive to prevent technology leakage. As the Report correctly noted, "retaining core technology is the *rational* choice of foreign investors." This had been substantiated by the fact that the technologies transferred to Chinese firms in the past decades were mostly suitable ones that had been outdated in the MNCs' home markets.[91] What further held back the technology spillover effect of FDI was the change in ownership structure of FDI from 1992 onward when the MNCs set up wholly owned subsidiaries (WOS), which swiftly exceeded the joint ventures (JVs) in both numbers (1997) and amounts (2000). WOS was the preferred form of ownership, beneficial to foreign firms in protecting their technological know-how. This, along with the enforcement of TRIMs that banned coercive technology transfer, made China's access to the most advanced technologies much more difficult.

Strictly toeing the party's neoliberal line of deep integration, the CAS-CAE report made the revelation of the truth about China's industrial weakness not a liability but an asset in political terms. Ironically, severe impact had taken place at the very moment when the Report was released some four years after China joined the WTO. In contrast to the official rhetoric of the post-entry China "having made a great feat,"[92] two high-ranking central government officials supervising China's large-sized SOEs acknowledged in their internal reports that the domestic firms had suffered enormous impact from foreign competition, a situation that was far more serious than expected.[93] Their depiction of the situation was unquestionably authentic. Even the strongly neoliberal-oriented Ministry of Commerce (MOFCOM, successor of MOFTEC from 2003) issued the "Report on Transnational Corporations in China 2004" in early 2005. In this report, the MNCs were found to have captured more than one-third of the market share in areas of light industry, chemical industry, pharmaceuticals, and mechanical and electronic industries.[94] More than one year later, a far more detailed report was released by the Development Research Centre (DRC) of the State Council, the second largest official think tank, which was also strongly neoliberal-oriented. The revelation of this report was even more stunning. It claimed that in China's major industrial sectors opened up to FDI, almost all the top five players in each sector were either owned or controlled by the MNCs. Of the country's 28 major industrial sectors, 21 were under the de facto control of the MNCs. For instance:

- of the 60-strong beer manufacturers, all but two were MNC-controlled JVs using foreign brands;
- the largest five glassmakers were all JVs;
- the largest five elevator manufacturers in China were controlled by the MNCs;
- the cosmetics industry was controlled by 150 MNCs;
- 20% of the pharmaceuticals were controlled by MNCs;
- of China's auto industry, foreign brands accounted for 90% sales revenues.[95]

Such an outcome was by no means completely unpredictable given China's sharply shrinking policy space in the context of the greatly strengthened oligopolistic capitalism, though the severity of impact might have been grossly underestimated. Back to the juncture when China had just joined the WTO, Nolan's caveats were deliberately ignored both in China and in the West.[96] This was understandable from the position of the Chinese regime determined to gain WTO membership at all costs. The real problem, however, was that no effective and serious preparations had been made on the part of the domestic firms prior to and even after China joined the WTO. This was particularly pronounced during the so-called transition period that more or less gave Chinese firms some breathing space in the initial post-entry years.[97] Behind this strange phenomenon are a series of abnormal state behaviors. First of all, the regime imposed upon the nation a self-fulfilling teleology: the WTO entry stood for the right course of China's modernization through fully integrating into the global economy; increased competition arising from the accession would help restructure the SOEs, raise the efficiency of resource allocation and ultimately achieve wealth and strength of the nation.[98] Such an assertion justified the authoritarian regime's suppression of dissenting views skeptical of the hasty accession. Secondly, although Premier Zhu Rongji did more than once call on the domestic firms to brace for the impact, he only paid lip service and took no meaningful actions. Conversely, not only did he eschew consultation with the domestic firms and the line ministries with a view to working out first and second best options before the accession talks, but he also precluded their participation in the negotiation process. He even kept them, except MOFTEC, in the dark as to what Chinese negotiators had committed after the deal was made. These conducts rendered the domestic firms mentally disarmed, placing them in a state of blind optimism. Let me elaborate on this.

On a visit to Beijing prior to China's accession, the WTO Director General Renato Ruggiero highlighted the benefits to be extended to China by referring to all the advantages that had been negotiated among the 130 WTO members. He told the Beijing University audience, "China is entitled to export its products and services to the markets of other WTO members at the rates and duty and levels of commitments negotiated in the Uruguay Round," according to the WTO's two cardinal principles of

MFN and non-discrimination.[99] Such an ahistorical and biased account about the WTO,[100] uttered by a "respected foreigner,"[101] was widely quoted by the domestic media to justify the party's decision on deep integration. With China approaching the WTO entry, the CCP's propaganda department banned virtually all open debates. At the same time, it developed a nuanced approach to shaping public opinion through exaggerating the goodies of globalization but downplaying its adverse effect to vindicate the abovementioned self-fulfilling WTO teleology, which was abbreviated as "short-term pains, long-term gains."[102] The teleological inclination of some Western left-wing's scholars, such as Nicholas Lardy as mentioned earlier, paradoxically fit squarely into the party's propaganda.[103]

As part of the well-orchestrated propaganda campaign, a good number of central government advisors serving in the Chinese universities and official think tanks spared no effort to expound the great historical significance of the WTO accession in one way or another. The most fanatic advocate was Zhang Hanlin, advisor to MOFTEC and Professor of International Economics from the University of International Business and Economics (UIBE), a key national university owned and financially sponsored by MOFTEC. Immediately after the signing of the bilateral Sino-US agreement in November 1999, he spoke in a most authoritative tone that China's accession to the WTO stood for "an important strategic choice of China's integration into the world economy ... [It is] the inevitable choice of China's opening to the outside world ... therefore [it] is the path destined to lead China to a strong nation in the twenty-first century."[104]

Previously trained in the West, Yu Yongding and Zheng Bingwen, senior research fellows at CASS whose mission was to strictly follow the dictates of and advise to the top leadership, produced the most comprehensive review report on the *pros and cons* of China's WTO accession in December 1999, just one month after the Sino-US agreement was concluded. They listed five major advantages and five major disadvantages of the WTO accession on the basis of industry-specific analysis. The five advantages were:

1. The accession would be a "triple-win" endgame for China, the USA and the WTO. A WTO "without the participation of China" would

be incomplete and without universality. China as the world's seventh largest economy and tenth biggest trading power would exert more influence on the world economy. The USA would be able to have its huge trade deficits with China incrementally corrected due to the former's wider market access.

2. The accession would usher in a new era of China's reform and opening. China could borrow the power of FDI and external driving forces to forge ahead the deadlocked reform at home.
3. The accession would enable China to partake in the rule setting in international economic institutions, thereby enhancing her position in the community of nations. The accession would also increase the bargaining position of the developing nations as a whole and as a result speed up their integration into the "mainstream of the world economy."
4. The allocation of resources would be significantly improved by adhering to the law of comparative advantage.
5. The accession would prompt a heavy influx of FDI, hence stimulating the domestic demand.

The five disadvantages were:

1. China's indigenous firms and existing economic system would suffer from external impacts.
2. Increasing dependence on global markets would render the Chinese economy volatile, thus making it more difficult for the central government to institute macroeconomic control and readjustment.
3. A large number of unemployed rural and urban labor force would have to be relocated.
4. Income disparity between the urban and rural areas would grow due to external impact on China's uncompetitive agriculture.
5. The enforcement of TRIPs would kill a great number of the indigenous firms.

Echoing the teleological official rhetoric of "short-term pains, long-terms gains" the WTO accession would necessarily engender, the report eschewed answering the crucial question of how to overcome those disadvantages but rather argued for viewing the accession with "a positive attitude." The two authors urged domestic players to "seek advantages and avoid disadvantages" through making full use of the opportunities brought by the WTO entry while at the same time minimizing the damages to the Chinese economy. For that purpose, they suggested that "in-depth studies" about the WTO be made.[105] Painting a rosy picture, the authors concluded that the great significance of China's WTO accession lied in the long-term prospect that the country's huge domestic market, the potentially largest one in the world, would not only be exploited by China itself but also be "opened to the world with conditions and jointly exploited by all countries of the world."[106]

Feebly arguing about the potential mechanism to enable the transforming of "pains" into "gains," this "most authoritative [official] report" inadvertently exposed an astounding "state secret": up until the eve of the country's WTO accession, "in-depth studies" about the WTO were virtually non-existent. As one senior official at the State Council privately complained, few serious studies had been carried out with regard to the relevant laws on foreign trade and investment under the WTO agreement with a view to facilitating the local firms' "understanding their obligations."[107] This demonstrated that excessive concessions had been made even without a proper knowledge of the WTO on the part of the negotiators and the senior leaders in charge! Without an accurate, unbiased understanding of the WTO and its whole set of rules in the first place, how could the domestic players ready themselves for the pending impact? Throughout the year 2000, Premier Zhu Rongji did repeatedly urge the SOEs to have a sense of urgency as the economic restructuring moved forward and China approached entering the WTO.[108] He called again for "losing no time in preparing for the entry" in March 2001.[109] But as always, he did not elaborate on what the government would do to awaken the SOEs to brace for the prospective life-or-death struggle.[110] On the day following China's entry to the WTO on November 10, 2001, the *People's Daily* issued an editorial, hailing this great event as being of historic significance in the course of China's modernization drive. Praising the party's "appropriate and insightful strategic decision making," the editorial painted a rosy picture of the forthcoming great rejuvenation of the Chinese nation under the party's strong leadership *on the condition* that "we are *mentally unified, sufficiently prepared and assisted by proper measures*."[111] Yet even until this critical moment, according to an internal survey, an acute lack of knowledge of the WTO was prevalent among the bureaucrats and the SOEs' managers.[112]

Lacking in-depth studies and sufficient preparations made China's WTO accession look like a big gamble. This, at least on the surface, went against the risk-averse political instinct of the technocratic leadership that fully took over when Deng Xiaoping passed away in early 1997. It was acknowledged that it was Premier Zhu Rongji who had played the key role in reassuring his Politburo comrades that the pending impact would be "neither economically nor politically disruptive." His confidence seemed to be derived from the advice of the visiting US Chairman of the Federal Reserve, Alan Greenspan, who told the Premier to the effect: "China should not be frightened by the challenges that competition would bring for its still rather protected industries and financial sectors. Rather, the WTO membership would create new jobs in the wake of closures of SOEs."[113] According to the account of Laurence Brahm, political economy analyst based in Beijing and the Premier's personal friend, Zhu resold this idea to his Politburo colleagues, who gave him the decisive backing for the simple reason that the idea was from "a highly respected foreigner."[114]

One prevailing view regarded China's quest for the WTO membership as the "reformers' attempt to lock in market reform policy."[115] Brahm highly commended China's "managed marketization" reform throughout the 1990s under the auspices of Zhu as a great success. The reform, as he saw it, "had brought China to the brink of a full-blown market economy"; competition was the only thing that was missing from the reform agenda. Time had now ripened to make the "managed marketization" complete by fully integrating China into the global economy.[116] In other words, it was the successful market reform in the 1990s that naturally led to China's deep integration. Was it true? Ironically, the Chinese Premier held an entirely different view. Just three months after China joined the WTO, he had a straight talk with Stephen Roach, chief economist of Morgan Stanley in March 2002. He said, "If China did not join the WTO, it would be impossible to restructure and sustain economic growth."[117] Such straightforward utterance did not give the impression that the reform in the past decades had been successful. Had the reform been a success, why would China have had such a need for a WTO deal on such extremely harsh terms just in order to "lock in the reform"? Wasn't the price unnecessarily too high? Why did the sustained rapid economic growth not seem to have lent China increased bargaining power but rather brought China an "unequal treaty"?[118]

Nevertheless, Zhu's "straight talk" had revealed precisely the true motive of the Chinese regime in securing the WTO membership at all costs: using deep integration to forge ahead the deadlocked reform at home and repower the economic growth. But excessive concessions the authoritarian regime made on market access seem to suggest that it was deliberately sacrificing China's autonomous development for an export-led strong growth. For the Chinese Premier, influenced by neoliberal gurus like Alan Greenspan or not, he did have reason to believe that, thanks to his personal experience, opening to global competition would work to "transform challenges into opportunities, and pressure into motivation."[119] A case study based on the fieldwork carried out by Professor Peter Nolan of the University of Cambridge whom I assisted in early 2002 deserves mention to illustrate how the Premier was eager to address the thorny issue of SOEs' restructuring through radical trade and investment liberalization, a typical Washington Consensus approach that he believed had worked in practice!

Case Study: The '98 Agreement

In 1998, Premier Zhu Rongji decided to reach an agreement with the Kodak Corporation of the USA on setting up JVs nationwide to bail out China's debt-laden photographic film industry. Zhu's intention was to confer a large part of the domestic market to Kodak to exchange for the latter's injection of capital and technology transfer. According to the so-called '98 Agreement concluded by the Chinese government and Kodak, three of the seven major Chinese firms would set up JVs with Kodak, which held the controlling share. The other three Chinese firms would be forbidden from partnering with other foreign investors within three years of Kodak's acquisition of the former three. Lucky, as the largest and sole profit-making domestic filmmaker and the banner of China's film-making sector, would not participate in the big-bang industrial restructuring.[120]

During his visit to the USA on April 13, 1999, Zhu Rongji summarized the '98 Agreement in a banquet in New York, "I can tell you a story. When I met Dr. George Fisher, chairman of Kodak and asked him to come to China for cooperation two years ago, I was labeled by a person in power as a traitor for the second time. But after two years of heavy investment by Kodak in China, Kodak had fostered the development of China's film-making industry. So that gentleman cursing me a traitor approached me recently, saying he was wrong in the past. I believe from now on, I will not be labeled a traitor any more. Thus, I think this kind of [market access] *concessions* were beneficial to both China and the U.S. Foreign companies, including Kodak had a much better record in paying taxes than our state-owned enterprises. … *I believe only through competition will we be able to run our SOEs well.*"[121]

Nevertheless, Zhu Rongji did not explain how "Kodak fostered the development of China's film-making industry." According to a report by the liberal-oriented newspaper *Twenty-First Century Business Herald* (*21 shiji jingji daobao*) based in Guangzhou, the rapid expansion of Kodak in China did not lead to Lucky losing market share. Rather, Lucky had achieved substantial increase in sales revenue.[122] This shortly turned out to be just a temporary phenomenon. Lucky's good days did not last long. Kodak dramatically increased its market share from less than 30% before the '98 Agreement in 1997 to 63% in 2001 after massive consolidation of its China business from 1998. With Japan's Fuji taking away 20% of market share, Lucky was backed into a corner due to its small scale of production, reliance on key intermediary products that could not be produced domestically, outdated technical equipment imported in the 1980s and weak R&D capabilities. From 2001 onward, Lucky experienced a successive decline in performance. Unable to compete with the two global giants, Kodak and Fuji, Lucky had to come to terms with Kodak on setting up a JV, in which Kodak acquired over 20% of Lucky's equity in 2003.[123] The Lucky myth evaporated. Kodak overtook Fuji to become the market leader of China's film-making industry (Table 2.1).

Table 2.1 Lucky's financial indicators from 2000 to 2004[124] (unit: RMB yuan)

Year	Revenue	Post-tax profits	Assets	Equity	Earnings/ share
2000	758,946,417	215,350,881	1,109,517,285	967,175,564	0.756
2001	638,148,275	139,866,344	1,156,977,070	1,107,041,908	0.409
2002	592,958,900	124,183,669	1,173,027,261	1,094,425,578	0.363
2003	564,279,072	80,021,348	1,124,527,645	1,046,602,343	0.234
2004	618,997,507	78,035,840	1,032,739,491	953,236,180	0.228

Source: China Securities Regulatory Commission

What about those Chinese firms entering into JVs with Kodak in 1998? Take the Gongyuan Plant (Shantou, Guangdong) as an example. The JV scheme did bring immediate tax increase, debt repayment and relocation of employees (2000 staff members) from the Gongyuan Plant to the JV controlled by Kodak. Yet the Plant itself was left in the cold after the asset reorganization was completed. All the Plant's young and capable technical staff were transferred to the high-paying JV nearby. Therefore, the Plant completely lost the ability to innovate. What it could produce was the black-and-white films. Since the specific market for black-and-white films was too small, the wages received by the remaining less-skilled workers were too low to support their subsistence. The Plant had no other choice but to rent out redundant workshops and used the revenue as the funding source of the payroll.[125] Similar results befell the other two Chinese firms. Those "opportunities" or "motivation" existed only in the imagination of the actual decision-maker. He stepped down as Premier in March 2003. Failure to foresee the endgame after his retirement—that the erstwhile industrial capability of Chinese firms in the photographic film industry was virtually destroyed—did not affect the Premier's goodwill for an industrial reinvigoration through further caving in to the systemic pressure for liberalization of trade and investment on an unprecedented scale.

However, it is still oversimplified to assume from the above isolated case that as the Premier of the world's most populous country, he was so naive as to be easily misguided by foreign neoliberal gurus about the omnipotence of competition. His true thoughts about the perils of China's excessive market access might never be known. But there was strong evidence to suggest that he was deeply worried about the possibility that China's national industrial and economic system would disintegrate under fierce foreign competition. Wu Jinglian, one of the most famous economists and one of Zhu's most trusted economic advisors, unwillingly explained the decision-makers' motivation to join the WTO on a semi-open occasion in November 1999, "We have used up all means to restructure those big SOEs and big state banks but have no way [to succeed]. Those big SOEs and state banks remain entirely uncompetitive. I personally support China's accession to the WTO; otherwise, we cannot move on with the restructuring (*shizai gaibudong*) at all." He acknowledged frankly in the end that the impact on the domestic enterprises after the accession would be enormous. "To be honest, we could not exclude the [worst] possibility that the Chinese economy could backslide to pre-Liberation (1949) situation,"[126]—a euphemism for utter foreign domination of the Chinese economy.

On open occasions, however, Premier Zhu only admitted his anxiety with the agriculture.[127] He virtually never made any reference to the second and third industries, as if they did not really merit worry.[128] China's agriculture characterized by small plots of land of each household and the primitive method of production was, predictably, in no way to compete with agribusiness giants from the USA, Canada and Australia, and was thus regarded as the sector to be hardest hit.[129] Zhu's motive for "entirely opening up all chains of operation, including R&D, production, distribution, storage, and trade" of Chinese agriculture to foreign competition was "essentially to exchange for access to the developed countries' markets for the industrial products."[130] This would further exacerbate the developmental quandary of the rural areas caused by the central state's urban-biased policies throughout the 1990s. Wen Tiejun, a prominent rural expert and civil servant of the PRC's Ministry of Agriculture (MOA), openly expressed his deep uneasiness about the post-entry impact on China's agriculture. He received harsh warning from Premier Zhu personally who reprimanded the indocile Mr. Wen for "not doing the rightful things" (*bugan zhengshi*).[131]

Nevertheless, trading off Chinese agriculture for industry does not mean that Premier Zhu was at ease that enough jobs would be created to more than compensate for the job losses as a result of the closure of the

SOEs. Several times in the 1990s, he briefed the senior cadres that the intrusion of one foreign firm may lead to the closure of ten local firms.[132] Realistic as he used to be, the Premier might place some hope on the "transition period," during which the domestic firms would rise up to the challenge and become strong enough to face up to global competition when the market was fully opened a few years later. The problem was that even in the so-called transition period, the impact could be enormous anyway. Kerstin Leitner, the United Nations Development Programme (UNDP's) China Representative, predicted in early 2002 that the "stricture of WTO membership" would cost China 40 million jobs,[133] a figure far greater than that estimated by most Chinese and foreign institutions.[134]

Well informed of all sorts of negative feedback before and after the WTO accession, Zhu Rongji, not allowing China's quest for WTO membership to be derailed, had to respond to the widely held suspicions within the party in certain way. His tactics were twofold. Firstly, concomitant to his half-hearted appeals for making preparations, he tried to water down the potency of the WTO rules by creating a misconception that the rules could be easily ignored after China joined the WTO. He was once quoted as saying in private that "never mind those rules; we will go ahead with our own,"[135] hinting that China had never intended to implement the WTO agreement; thus, there was no need to worry about the impact. His wording was clearly aimed to placate the WTO skeptics within the party. He never meant business anyway for the simple reason that China's "globalization plus" approach had subjected the country to profound administrative and legal changes at home in order to ensure her full compliance with the WTO agreement. In fact, even before the accession, the Chinese regime had set out to amend and abolish huge amount of existing laws and regulations according to its WTO commitments.[136] The Supreme Court ruled that where the domestic laws contradicted the WTO statutes, the latter would take precedence.[137] MOFTEC Deputy Minister and chief negotiator Long Yongtu told the audience during his visit to Hong Kong in December 2000, "The WTO framework consists of internationally recognized practices. If China really wants to be part of the world, it must follow the same rules. We are telling our people, *you will have to follow the [international] rules, not your own rules.*"[138] These words and deeds were the hard evidence of China's embrace for globalization in an institutionally irreversible way.[139]

In additional to legal compliance at home, the institutional bondage of the WTO itself and those reviewing mechanisms of major powers also made any breach of the specific obligations China had promised to honor extremely difficult under the transparency regime of the WTO. I hereby quote an extract from Barshefsky interview with Jim Lehrer on PBS News Hour.[140]

JIM LEHRER: There are a lot of people who are skeptical that China won't follow the rules once they get in the WTO.

CHARLENE BARSHEFSKY (US Trade Representative and chief negotiator): I think that we have put in place a package of very stringent enforcement mechanisms, unlike any other accession, including the two special remedies I've already mentioned, the special safeguard, as well as the dumping remedy. And I think further, *the more specific the obligations under which China operates, the more likely compliance and implementation; and one of the reasons that we negotiated very hard for a very long time was to ensure that the obligations China was undertaking in every sector and in every sub-sector of its economy were as specific, as delineated, as precise as possible, so there would be no question in China's mind what it was obligated to do at each and every step of the way.*

Secondly, fearing that keeping the domestic firms well informed would derail the accession,[141] Zhu Rongji kept the stakeholders, particularly the large SOEs and the bureaucracy except MOFTEC away from the negotiation process. Either prior consultation with or participation of the large SOEs and the line ministries was intentionally eschewed for this sake. On one occasion, when chief negotiator Long Yongtu was briefing the doubtful SOEs' managers someday in 1999, he was questioned as to why internal consultation was precluded. Long retorted angrily, "We need not discuss with anyone. When Chairman Mao and Premier Zhou decided to open the door for Sino-U.S. relations, whom did they discuss with?!"[142] In the end, except MOFTEC, neither the industrial community nor the line ministries were clear about what China had committed in the negotiations,[143] not to mention the fact that convincing arguments for the radical deep integration were lacking all the time.[144] Even more bizarrely, the National People's Congress (NPC), the rubber stamp of the

CCP, that enacted the Legislation Law in 2000, openly breached the PRC's Constitution in November 2001 by illegally authorizing MOFTEC to submit the Approval Text issued by the Chinese government to the WTO.[145] All these undemocratic proceedings were intentionally ignored by both the Chinese and the Western media.[146] Misguided otherwise by the "win–win" illusion created by the party-state propaganda machine, not just ordinary Chinese citizens but also a great many central and local government officials were immersed in a euphoric atmosphere, sincerely believing in the teleological myth of the so-called short-term pains, long-term gains.[147] Blindly optimistic about the post-accession prospect, many domestic firms did not take the "WTO-wolf" seriously and thus were largely ill-prepared for the impending impact.[148]

With China already inside the WTO, transparency first and foremost became the testing stone of whether the Chinese government would honor its words of playing by global rules to operate in the open rather than in the black box. Nonetheless, the WTO entry did not bring the transparency that many people had been yearning for. In the first instance, the central government turned a deaf ear to mounting appeals for disclosing the full texts of the WTO agreement in the wake of the accession. MOFTEC used to be the most ardent advocate for WTO entry, asserting that joining the WTO would necessarily contribute to China's rapid economic development, increased transparency and high efficiency of public administration. Yet it was the same MOFTEC that was obstinately resistant to the reasonable demands of the general public for making available full texts of the WTO agreement as quickly as possible. It was not until December 10, 2001, that MOFTEC released the English-language text on its website, three months after China had completed all the bilateral negotiations and one month after it finalized the multilateral negotiations. The Chinese version agreements were made available online only at the end of December 2001. Absurdly, MOFTEC issued a verdict that only the English versions of WTO accession documents have legal bindings.[149] MOFTEC legal advisor Zhao Weitian told the *Twenty-First Century Business Herald* that the Chinese version was just for reference; only the English, French and Spanish versions were legally binding. He explained that the PRC's Constitution made no stipulation as to how to transform international treaties concluded by the Chinese government into domestic laws, and there was only one stipulation in the General Rules of Civil Law that in case of conflict between the international treaties and domestic laws, the former should take precedence. Zhao fell short of explaining what this implied if there were no relevant laws at home: would Chinese lawyers have to litigate by citing the English text of the WTO agreements, or would the court verdict be written in English? Zhao admitted that the quality of Chinese judges was not good enough. Thus, to transform the WTO agreements into domestic laws, China needed a great many professional judges, lawyers, legal advisors, scholars and experts. And, for that purpose, Zhao claimed that related disciplines be set up in Chinese universities.[150]

Gu Haibing, professor of law at the Renmin University of China (RUC), was infuriated by MOFTEC's verdict nullifying the validity of Chinese version of the WTO agreements. He posted an article on the Internet harshly critical of the MOFTEC verdict. He raised three sets of professional questions. *Firstly*, why did the Chinese version not have a legal binding? If not, was it still necessary for the NPC to publicize the notice of approval? Would all the forthcoming laws and regulations related to the WTO be invalid? Was it still necessary for the NPC and the State Council to release those "illegal" documents in Chinese? *Secondly*, why on earth did the MOFTEC not disclose the Chinese version ahead of the English one? If only the English version was legally valid, was it the case that MOFTEC negotiators reported their duties to the top leaders in English rather than in Chinese? Were all the decisions concerning the WTO accession made in accordance with the English clauses? *Thirdly*, was it reasonable for the MOFTEC to monopolize the translation of the accession documents and designate its preferred publishing house to sell the three-volume documents in huge numbers at extremely high price? Was it not a deliberate act of the MOFTEC to try to prevent Chinese citizens from accessing the public information that was supposed to be made available in a timely and convenient way and free of charge? Professor Gu hereby alluded to the corruption of the MOFTEC that abused its prerogative to enrich itself. He pointed out in the end that the ad hoc way the MOFTEC disclosed China's WTO accession documents was illegal since it breached the PRC's Legislation Law enacted on March 15, 2000.[151]

If Gu's attack on MOFTEC debunked the hypocrisy of the "rule by law" rhetoric of the party state, the misbehavior of the Supreme Court in the wake of the WTO accession, from a professional perspective, called the regime's institutional capacity to cope with the impact into serious question. The Supreme Court, the judiciary branch of the PRC, was a neutral government institution that had neither economic stake in the WTO nor affiliation with the special interests. To the surprise of all, the Supreme Court was utterly unclear about the legal status of the WTO agreement even one year after China had joined the WTO, the period during which all the legal documents had been made available online or through publication. On a visit to the USA in 2002, one senior judge of the Supreme Court answered the "legal status" question in a self-complacent and arrogant tone, "We need to organize hundreds of Chinese law experts to study this legal status issue." One famous Chinese-born political economy analyst residing in the USA was outraged. He wrote a harsh comment on his webpage to rebut this senior judge's response. He argued that the WTO agreements were so important as to be influencing the interests and destiny of billions of the Chinese people. Was it not absurd that the legal status of such fatal agreements was still uncertain in the eyes of the senior judges at the Supreme Court? If the agreement's legal status was uncertain, how did the Supreme Court dare to dictate to annul or clear up so great an amount of existing legal documents to ensure their conformity to the legally "unsettled" WTO agreements?[152]

It was not merely malfeasance but, perhaps more importantly, a severe lack of professionalism that lay behind the senior judge's ignorance. Institutional incompetence, however, was not just limited to the Supreme Court but rather permeated the entire bureaucracy. This not only made the widely anticipated "rule of law" far out of reach but also made the "rule by law," aimed simply at making the authoritarian rule more efficient, problematic. As shown from the above analysis, this sort of institutional deficiency was by no means part of a sophisticated unified approach of which the party state was deliberately taking advantage to circumvent the neoliberal framework of the WTO in a bid to enforce neo-mercantilist policies after the WTO accession. On the contrary, it characterized the nature of the Chinese party state as being still semi-modern at the turn of the new millennium. The leadership's tactics of organized deceit against the people and the bureaucracy interacted with the "bad" institutions to plunge the nation into a state of blind optimism before and even after China joined the WTO, perpetuating rather than alleviating the country's extant industrial disadvantages as specified in the CASS report of 1999. The WTO deal was a fateful gamble in both form and substance!

Attitude of Intellectual Elites and Independent Social Activists

Narrowly defined as researchers and scholars engaging in social science research, the Chinese intellectuals as a whole were overwhelmingly in favor of China's accession to the WTO. Opponents were mostly left-wing intellectuals, particularly the old leftists within the regime. The new leftists were not in a monolithic alliance with the old leftists against globalization. Those new leftists who were against China's WTO accession drew intellectual inspirations primarily from the dependency theory, contending that the WTO entry would solidify China's position as an exploited periphery of the metropolitan core of Western capitalism in the international division of labor. Han Deqiang, a famous young New Left political economist in the late 1990s, wrote a great deal of articles to deconstruct the competition myth and the pitfalls of the neoliberal development approach. His true identity was blurred in ideological terms as he increasingly affiliated himself with Maoist utopian socialism. This distinguished him from intra-party ultra-leftists, known as the old leftists who were critical of the Cultural Revolution nonetheless. But Han also distanced himself from radical neo-Marxists in the West such as Andre Gunder Frank who advocated a thorough delinking from the capitalist world system to get rid of dependency. Han instead allied himself with the liberal reformist strand of dependency theorists like Raul Prebisch in the recognition that a thorough delinking was unrealistic in practical terms, despite the fact that an ideological delinking must be adhered to. Regarding the prevailing view that labeled all non-neoliberal alternatives as trade-exclusive "close-doorism," a Chinese political phrase referring to excess protectionism bound for economic backwardness, Han dismissed this sort of thinking as sheer nonsense. Citing the case of the USA, a great power that emerged behind a century-long high tariff protection, Han argued that big countries could afford trade exclusion through "sufficient domestic competition," despite the fact that he had fiercely attacked the "blind faith" held by the neoclassical economists in the omnipotence of competition.[153]

Another New Left scholar Wang Shaoguang took a neutral position. He made two basic points: "I should indicate to those against the globalization that more openness could possibly benefit the Chinese economy on the whole; but at the same time I would remind those who have a superstitious belief in globalization that more openness would not necessarily benefit the Chinese economy on the whole." Wang contended that China had benefited from the incrementally deepening external integration in the last three decades in at least three respects: (1) international trade enabled China to adjust structure in accordance with its comparative advantage, thereby increasing the whole efficiency of the allocation of resources; (2) all China's industries benefited from the spillover of knowledge from FDI and other forms of foreign interactions and enhanced their technology efficiency; and (3) competition with foreign firms forced the Chinese firms to improve their product quality and to develop new management skills, thereby increasing the macro-level productivity. Wang concluded that no one doubted the effectiveness of openness, whose advantages had outweighed its disadvantages in the last two decades. "We hope and have reason to believe that further openness will lead to the same outcome."[154] Wang's pro-globalization stance made him less like a typical new leftist and more like a market liberal. Nonetheless, arguing that the reform and opening in the past six or seven years had increasingly become a "zero-sum game" in which only a small number of people reaped the gains of economic growth while many others "became losers in absolute terms," Wang emphasized the role of the state in realizing distributive justice—an orthodox leftist view. He argued that those people who had suffered in the past could possibly refuse to endorse and even openly oppose the existing reform and opening policies against the backdrop of mounting uncertainties in the wake of China's accession to the WTO. Therefore, the central state should play an important role in readjusting its redistribution policies to mitigate the distributive conflicts.[155]

At the time of China's WTO entry, the Chinese nationalists were not entirely clear whether globalization would be beneficial to the modernization of China.[156] A few years later, they all of a sudden became proponents of free trade no less fanatical than those "Chicago boys" all over the world. This contrasts sharply with the 1990s in which they were out-and-out economic nationalists. Wang Xiaodong, the nationalist "godfather," wrote an influential article in 1995 denouncing the neoclassical logic of comparative advantage.[157] This article was absorbed into his new book published in 1999, coauthored by himself together with Song Qiang, Fang Ning and Han Deqiang, the latter two being staunch left-wing economic nationalists. The new book titled *The Chinese Road under the Shadow of Globalization* and the coauthorship made his affiliation with economic nationalism self-explanatory. Yet in year 2005, the "shadow of globalization" changed its meaning completely since Wang was increasingly of the belief that it was not that China was unable to compete with the industrial West under free trade conditions but that the jealous Westerners were reluctant to accommodate a rising China within the existing international system.[158] Taking bandwagoning with the liberal international order for granted and short of convincing economic and industry analyses, Wang attributed the country's economic miracle to the laboriousness of the Chinese people. Regardless of increasing evidence of China's dependent development after joining the WTO, Wang asserted that it was now the USA that, fearful of the irresistible rise of China, was frequently breaching its free trade commitment. Thus, strong actions should be taken by China to retaliate against the "mischievous anti-dumping practices" of the developed countries against Chinese exports to "force them to maintain free trade with China."[159] Given China's globalized economic and trade interests, and deeply convinced of the inevitability of conflicts with the West in the not-too-distant future, Wang called for massive rearmament and a tit-for-tat strategy against the West in Chinese foreign policy. Toeing the official line of deep integration, the tough nationalist made his version of nationalism a strange hodgepodge of old-fashioned power politics and economic liberalism.

Except a small number of new left-oriented economists who either kept silent or joined hands with Han Deqiang in issuing a petition letter to the NPC in open protest against the WTO accession such as CASS scholars Yang Fan and Zuo Dapei,[160] the great majority of the Chinese economists were market liberals in favor of China's WTO entry. They were economic internationalists resentful of any notion associated with economic nationalism such as "infant industry protection." Few took interest in Friedrich List, the nineteenth-century German political economist, and his seminal work, *The National System of Political Economy*. Misreading David Ricardo's theory of comparative advantage and disregarding the three preconditions he set in particular,[161] they shared Long Yongtu's deep contempt for protectionism. Long was quoted as saying that it was a good thing for China to keep working like the servant of the developed countries for many decades ahead.[162] He even asserted that protectionism only led to underdevelopment; only by opening up the domestic market would China's national industries be able to develop.[163] Echoing Long's neoliberal rhetoric, official think-tank researchers and scholars in the profession of economics and international business in some universities went further in rejecting economic nationalism. They were a small number of elites in economics circle capable of influencing the central state's economic policymaking. They supported radical liberalization of trade and investment. As they saw it, such notions as "national industry" (*minzu gongye*), "national enterprises or firms" (*minzu qiye*), and so on were outdated and no longer applicable in the age of globalization; all foreign firms investing in China were "Chinese firms" because they were under the jurisdiction of the Chinese courts. Therefore, distinguishing national enterprises from foreign enterprises did not make any sense.[164] Turning a blind eye to the explosive growth of market power of the MNCs on Chinese market and the domestic firms' increasing dependence on key parts and components and manufacturing equipment from foreign sources in the initial years after the WTO accession,[165] some economists even called for redefining the notion of "Assembled in China" as being equal to "Made in China."[166]

Among the liberal arguments in favor of China's WTO accession, Justin Yifu Lin's "comparative advantage strategy" (CAS) thesis provided the most systematic explanation of what drove China's deepening external integration in the reform era. Lin argued that the catch-up strategy usually led to various market distortions and rent-seeking, which exacerbated the "disadvantage of backwardness" of the developing nations. The "advantage of backwardness" would function only if developing nations abandoned nationalist catch-up and took full advantage of their factor endowment having comparative advantage. He contended that "the success of China's economic reform is based on the premise that China abandons the catch-up development strategy. For the planning system to be transformed into a market system, the most crucial factor is to develop the economy in accordance with China's comparative advantage by fully exploiting her abundant cheap labor to develop the labor-intensive industries."[167] Positing nonetheless that uninterrupted technological upgrading was the key to maintaining a long-run growth, Lin deemed the existence of a technological gap between the late developer and the West—the driver of technological upgrading. His argument went that "the technological gap between China and the developed nations in 1978 is far greater than that of Japan and the East Asian Tigers with the West. It is this sort of gap that had prompted a forty-year-long high growth rate of Japan and the Tigers from the 1950s and 1960s onwards respectively. Thus, the larger technological gap between China and the West could keep the Chinese economy growing rapidly for nearly fifty years. … And China will be able to overtake the U.S. to be the world's largest economy as late as 2030." Lin concluded that only by carrying out the CAS would China's advantage of backwardness be brought into full play so that China's industrial structure could be speedily elevated to the level close to that of the developed nations.[168]

Yu Zuyao, a moderately liberal economist at Tsinghua University, argued that the most severely impacted sector after China's WTO entry would not be the weak domestic industries but China's basic economic and political system. Perhaps shocked by the rumored editorial of *The Economist* claiming that the WTO accession ran the bell for Chinese Communism,[169] Yu contended that the Chinese socialist system must be upheld. Taking little heed of the economic implications of the WTO accession, Yu as an economist paid greater attention to high politics. He argued that economic globalization was still in the process of evolution.

China must not overlook reverse trends of worldwide anti-globalization and regionalization. Interpreting political globalization not as "an increasing trend toward multilateralism ... toward an emerging 'transnational state apparatus,' and toward the emergence of national and international nongovernmental organizations,"[170] but as an inevitable trend toward multipolarity in international politics, Yu asserted, "Even if we have identified ourselves with 'economic globalization,' we must face squarely the irresistible trends and pattern of international politics characterized by 'political multipolarization,' and at the same time adamantly oppose unipolarization"—the synonym of US hegemony.[171]

Like many liberals in the West, Chinese liberal intellectuals other than the economists had a deep-seated belief in the spillover of economic change on the party state's political superstructure. Their way of thinking was to a huge extent shaped by the decades-long ideological education of the CCP after 1949. Many of them were unaware that they were still thinking in the way Marxists did. They placed high hopes on China's accession to the WTO, deeming it an effective way of forcing China's convergence with the West economically and politically. Some radical liberals were so optimistic about the prospect of the democratic transformation of China as to believe that entry to the WTO would prompt the authoritarian regime to establish the rule of law. Liu Junning, political scientist at CASS, claimed that joining the WTO would structurally eliminate corruption since the USA and Western firms, once they entered the Chinese market, would transplant their codes of conduct at home to China and press the Chinese government to combat corruption.[172]

He Qinglian made serious objections to such a view. As one of the most famous sociologists with profound knowledge of economics, she shared the leftists' concern about the impact of globalization on the Chinese economy. She agreed with the leftists that in addition to China's weak high-technology industries, the small household-based rural economy could by no means rival the US modern agriculture. Regarding the prevailing thought that joining the WTO could create an extra ten million jobs, she countered, "But how many more jobs will disappear because of the accession?" She argued that the world economic pattern had little relevance to China's WTO entry simply because the world market had been carved up; China would have to compete with the other developing nations for the export markets of low-tech consumer goods. In this sense, it was not so much that China needed the WTO as that the developed nations needed the emerging market of China. Yet she supported China's accession to the WTO anyway, although on entirely different grounds. She dismissed Lin Junning's viewpoint as "totally groundless" since there was abundance of evidence to suggest otherwise: Many corrupt regimes in the developing world, particularly those in Latin America, were members of the WTO; and China per se had, in a variety of ways, exhibited the symptom of "Latin Americanization," which arguably had made China a "failed state." She contended that the Chinese regime was using strong growth precisely as the excuse for putting off the political reform to an indefinite future. But it could be the worsening of social conflicts caused by the accession rather than the power of the WTO rules that sooner or later would force the desired political change in China.[173] An Zhiwen—the son of the liberal-minded party veteran An Ziwen—who had close ties with the deposed General Secretary Zhao Ziyang, held a similar view in this respect.[174]

Similar to the liberal intellectuals in China, the great majority of Chinese intellectuals living abroad "staunchly" supported China's entry to the WTO, as Su Shaozhi observed. Su was a foremost Marxist theorist at CASS in the 1980s. He was forced into exile after his expulsion from the party in 1987. Su argued that the overseas Chinese intellectuals were of the firm belief that China's accession to the WTO would "force the Chinese regime to combine economic reform and political progress, thereby furthering the rule of law and democracy." Su anticipated that so long as the authoritarian regime duly honored its commitments, it would have to "deepen and quicken up economic reform, separate the party from state affairs and business, renounce the party state's monopoly of and intervention in the economy, privatize the SOEs, etc. … The eventual establishment of a market economy system will seriously undermine the economic foundation of the Communist Party's one-party dictatorship."[175] Mr. Su's opmitimism regarding the political prospects of China's deep integration after the WTO accession was the most representative among the liberal intellectuals, although he admitted that "impact could be enormous in the short run."[176] Cui Zhiyuan, a well-known New Left political scientist at the Massachusetts Institute of Technology (MIT), voiced objection to China's hasty accession to the WTO. He argued that entry to the WTO was not an urgent task for China as the benefits of the entry were "hugely uncertain," whereas the costs that China would have to bear were "absolutely certain."[177] He suggested that the Chinese government look inward to stimulate consumption at home as an alternative to the WTO accession.[178]

Interestingly, some exiled dissident leaders also objected to China's WTO accession. *The Chinese Workers' Movement* Chairman Han Dongfang raised concerns that the hardship of Chinese workers would become even worse after the accession and that the workers' rights would continue to be ignored. Another famous dissident leader Wei Jingsheng held that the closer trade ties between China and the West after the accession could only strengthen the power of the Chinese autocratic regime and make workers' lives more miserable. Yan Jiaqi, an outstanding exiled political scientist of CASS and the protégé of the then General Secretary Zhao Ziyang in the 1980s, argued that in absence of fully fledged privatization, legal system building, and perfection of social security network in the first place, accession to the WTO could only reinforce the polarization between the rich and poor, thereby making China the new semi-colony of foreign capitalism.[179]

Yang Xiaokai differed from both the leftists arguing that China would repeat the tragedy of the semi-peripheral Latin American countries to be exploited by the Global North and the market liberals' view asserting that the accession would facilitate the deepening of reform in China. He contended that since the interests of Chinese private enterprises were not represented in the course of the negotiations, the transplanting of the WTO agreements into China's existing system would generate the rules of the game unfair to private entrepreneurs. As he saw it, China's accession to the WTO could give rise to two likely outcomes: (1) Private businesspeople might demand the same rules of the game to be applied to all investors within the Chinese territory. This would generate powerful dynamics of institutional change. (2) As the Chinese regime held on to state opportunism and applied different standards to foreign private firms, this would create tensions between the WTO's rules and the party-state institutions, which would eventually set China on a path of lopsided economic development.[180]

In general, despite a few skeptics from various intellectual affiliations, the overwhelming majority of the Chinese intellectuals were liberal-oriented in full support of the WTO accession. Their uncritical embrace of globalization distinguished them from not only the quite many intellectuals in both the Global South and the Global North debating fiercely about globalization, but also their predecessors in the Republican era (1927–1949) who were overwhelmingly economic nationalists no matter their value preferences. The distinction was particularly pronounced against the backdrop that it was the major economic crisis, namely, severe stagflation within the Global North in the late 1970s and the debt crisis in 1982 following the perceived failure of ISI in Latin America that prompted the neoliberal counterrevolution. China, in contrast, had not encountered a crisis of similar magnitude by the late 1990s. Rather, it was widely perceived as having achieved huge success in both market reform and export-oriented industrialization (EOI). Its foreign currency reserve registered a new historical record in 2001. However, the country's questionable integration did not arouse any suspicion on the part of the intellectuals. Information blockade imposed by the regime was part of the reason, although negligible. For most Chinese intellectuals, the WTO's neoliberal rules of the game or whether globalization would inhibit China's autonomous modernization was neither their specialism academically nor their point of interest politically. Even if some scholars who had a good command of economics such as He Qinglian spoke of the adverse economic effect, they refrained from pointing their finger at global capitalism, lest that be used by the regime to eschew the desired democratic transformation.

As mentioned earlier, the way of thinking of many Chinese intellectuals remained largely Marxian—economic determinism, for instance. Ironically, their understanding of economics and global political economy was shaped by the liberal economists working closely with the regime and the regime's ad hoc "world outlook." This was reinforced by the fact that the intellectuals themselves became new vested interests as a result of the commercialization reform of public education in the late 1990s. The reform was part and parcel of the regime's strategy of co-opting the intellectuals in a bid to consolidate the regime through the building of a triple alliance between the political, business and the intellectual elites. The co-option strategy paid off as evidenced by many intellectuals becoming collaborators of the regime.

For the majority of the Chinese intellectuals, their concern with China's WTO entry was political rather than economic. As they understood it, China's accession to the WTO was quintessentially the Chinese *government's accession to the WTO* (*zhengfu rushi*). In other words, it was the communist authoritarian regime rather than the domestic enterprises that would bear the brunt of the impact in the sense that the enforcement of international rules would sooner or later force the regime to wage political reform. For this sake, they not only unconditionally supported China's questionable integration, but also turned a blind eye to the blatantly undemocratic or even unconstitutional way the authoritarian regime made the WTO deal. For the opportunistic communist authoritarian regime, the intellectuals' wholehearted endorsement of the WTO accession served as a no better public relations promotion on behalf of the regime. Their "secret" political agenda in terms of attempting to rein in the regime by virtue of "foreign forces" only exposed their political naivety and enduring role of being merely a group of "useful idiots" to the communist rulers.[181]

The Role of Jiang Zemin

Joining the WTO at all costs was a momentous decision made by China's "collective Napoleons"—the seven members of the CCP's Politburo Standing Committee (PSC)—in accordance with the Leninist principle of democratic centralism. It was barely adopted by not even a simple majority. Of the seven decision-makers, only three voted in favor of the accession, three against, and one abstained.[182] Although General Secretary and State President Jiang Zemin was designated by Deng Xiaoping as the core of the third-generation leadership in 1992, he did not have the legitimate authority to impose his will upon his PSC colleagues. In fact, none of them, including the three *ayes*, were genuinely optimistic about the prospect of China's deep integration. Despite the consensus among them regarding the necessity of the WTO entry, though on different grounds, major divisions over the terms of accession remained until the last minute. Brahm's account on the "decisive backing" Zhu Rongji secured from his PSC comrades was not well grounded.

Foreign observers and China studies scholars tended to view the perceived differences among Chinese leaders as the evidence of a recurring power struggle between the reformers and the conservatives. They classified Jiang and Zhu as reformers, determined to further the reform by fully integrating China into the global economy, whereas leaders such as Li Peng, former Premier, now Chairman of the Standing Committee of the NPC, were portrayed as conservatives hostile to market economy and dedicated to rescuing the moribund planning economy and the SOEs. Such a dichotomous conservative–reformist divide oversimplified the complexity of Chinese politics. In the first instance, all senior leaders were intransigent in preserving the one-party dictatorship, thus without exception being die-hard "conservatives" in political and ideological terms. They all agreed to embed market into the socialist system, despite disagreement over a number of concrete issues, such as more market or more state control, shallow integration or deep integration, and so on. Fundamentalist leftists, known as the ultra-leftists (old leftists) and Maoists, were not factionally allied with the "Napoleons" in the PSC. They completely dropped out of the political arena in the wake of the 14th National CCP's Congress in September 1992, an unexpected outcome of Deng Xiaoping's making. In this sense, the CCP's propaganda machine was not overexaggerating when it said that the third-generation leadership led by Jiang was "uniformly composed of reformers" (*qingyise de gaigepai*) in non-political-ideological terms.[183] Regarding the decision-making over the WTO accession, only Jiang Zemin, Zhu Rongji and Li Lanqing, first Deputy Premier and Jiang's protégé and close ally, voted *in favor of* entry to the WTO on harsh terms; Vice-President Hu Jintao, Jiang's heir apparent designated nonetheless by Deng Xiaoping in 1992 as Jiang's successor, abstained; Li Peng was joined by Wei Jianxing and Li Ruihuan to vote *against* the WTO deal.[184] Li Ruihuan was then Chairman of the Chinese People's Political Consultative Committee (CPPCC); and Wei Jianxing was head of the CCP's Central Disciplinary and Inspection Committee (CDIC). Both were well-known reformers within the CCP and staunch supporters of Deng's economic reform.

Long Yongtu explained in an interview with China's Central Television (CCTV) right after the Sino-US agreement was signed that the conclusion of the agreement "genuinely reflects the courage and resolution of our leadership in adhering to the 'reform and opening.'"[185] Long hinted on another occasion that joining the WTO was a *political* decision made by the top leadership.[186] He vaguely mentioned the role Zhu and Jiang had co-played in the accession talks. Yet by making public the "political decision," Long made his meaning no more intelligible: it is not Premier Zhu but President Jiang that played the most important role in making the fatal accession decision, despite the fact that the president had been heavily influenced and assisted by the Premier during the entire process of negotiations.

Hui Feng argued that the administrative reform in 1998 shortly after Zhu assumed the Premiership in March drastically enhanced the authority of the streamlined central government. He thought of this as the key reason why the Premier was able to overcome resistance of the conservative bureaucrats.[187] In fact, the administrative reform that Feng commented on so positively was strongly boycotted by the bureaucracy and quickly aborted. Although Zhu was entitled to exercise veto power in executive decision-making according to the PRC's Constitution, the composition of the State Council was the result of intense bargaining between different factions within the party. Except the financial sector under his immediate mandate, he was even unable to appoint the cabinet ministers, not to mention deputy premiers, at his own will. Many positions were filled by those having nepotistic ties with various intra-party factions. Lacking a solid power base in central government and provinces, Zhu turned out a weak premier. In addition, his presumptuous personality and harsh working style alienated some of the potential reform-minded allies, which placed him in an extremely isolated position within the Politburo.[188] His position as the No. 3 figure within the party was further weakened by his failed trip to the USA and the ensuing US bombing of the Chinese embassy in Belgrade. Therefore, the Premier had neither the moral authority nor the practical capacity to circumvent the suspicious bureaucracy.

Without the strong backing of Jiang Zemin, Zhu was even incapable of reining in some of the cabinet ministers linked with ad hoc factions inside the party.[189] Jiang offered Zhu the crucial backing considering the Premier's indispensable role in carrying out the most difficult economic reform since the second half of the 1990s. He declined Zhu's resignation after the Beidaihe Conference in the summer of 1999 during which Zhu was fiercely attacked.[190] Jiang shrewdly made use of his positional authority to keep the unruly bureaucracy at bay in the last sprint to the WTO accession. It was he rather than Premier Zhu that made a series of significant decisions from behind the scene, including the much greater concessions made to the EU after the Sino-US agreement was concluded in November 1999.[191] They cooperated closely in a sophisticated division of labor. Jiang diplomatized the WTO issue, while Zhu technically supervised the negotiations. It has been the legacy of Mao Zedong and Zhou Enlai that diplomatic issues were not subject to open debate. Hence, foreign policy decision-making remains highly centralized in the hands of the top leadership, with few people involved.[192] As head of the Central Foreign Affairs Leading Group (CFALG), President Jiang was the final decision-maker in Chinese foreign policy. Although the growing importance of economics had involved more actors other than the Ministry of Foreign Affairs (MFA), such as the industrial ministries and large-sized SOEs, into the policy consulting process of the country's economic diplomacy, Jiang and Zhu joined hands to make the WTO accession a highly sensitive *high politics* issue, using it as the best excuse for black-box decision-making.

Jiang Zemin was a typical Soviet-style technocratic leader with a good engineering background. Except for the brief career interruption during the Cultural Revolution (1966–1976), he had long been an experienced practitioner in China's automobile and electronics industries from the 1950s till the 1980s. He had also been in charge of overseeing China's international trade for a brief period in the early 1980s. With these qualifications, Jiang was clearly aware of the complexity and sophistication of modern industry, particularly the hardship of technological development and the sensitivity of technology in international politics. For one thing, he once seriously warned the attendants in a national conference on science and technology in 1995, "You should bear in mind, [anticipating] purchasing the most advanced technologies [from the advanced countries] is totally out of the question."[193] This clearly shows that the well-educated president was by no means so easily misguided by the prevailing neoliberal cliché assuming that autonomous technological capability building is costless economically and insignificant politically. Jiang was not alone in this respect. Sharing the president's concern, Zhu Lilan, Minister of Science and Technology (MOST), openly ridiculed the notion of exchange for technology with market access (ETMA) advocated by Wu Yi, former Minister of MOFTEC, now State Councilor (equivalent to Vice-Premier) in charge of foreign trade and inbound and outbound FDI, and Li Lanqing, former Minister of MOFTEC before Wu Yi.[194] Madame Zhu Lilan was famous for her exquisite professionalism as an outstanding technology expert and her daring outspokenness in making open debates in particular.[195] As cool-headed as Madame Zhu, a good number of high-ranking officials in central government ministries were nonetheless disgruntled with the way Zhu Rongji excluded them from the WTO talks and even kept them virtually in the dark as to what had been committed to by MOFTEC negotiators, who only followed the Premier's instructions—with Jiang's backing though—to make one grave concession after another.[196,197]

Jiang and Zhu did so because they enjoyed broad domestic support. Han Deqiang noted that cadres at all levels of administration, especially those in central government and rich coastal areas, white-collar employees in foreign subsidiaries in China, and a proportion of the intellectuals, were the main backers of the WTO accession, since "developing the outward-oriented economy is not only the logical result of the reform and opening, but also compatible with their individual interests."[198] Han's finding was largely accurate, although he may have underrated the no-less-potent forces against the hasty accession within the party. In light of huge differences within the party and bureaucracy, Jiang, in the capacity of paramount leader, could have shelved the contentious issue of WTO accession and instead sought broader consultation and consensus building in the first place. Yet he made no attempt to reconcile the internal differences. Rather, he manifested no less eagerness than Premier Zhu Rongji in embracing globalization!

As noted by foreign observers, Jiang was a leader who "lacked vision."[199] His overriding concern was to ensure that any sort of economic *perestroika* would strengthen rather than undermine the communist party's absolute monopoly of power. For the opportunistic president and the party leadership as a whole, *glasnost* (openess) and democratization, which had led to the collapse of the Soviet Union, were not an option and would not be so in the foreseeable future.[200] Now that the *short-term* gains of the accession, namely, export-led, FDI-led growth by fully utilizing China's comparative advantage in cheap labor, were "absolutely certain," whereas the long-term gains of an alternative internal integration approach predicated upon a managed democratic transformation were "hugely uncertain," assuming the latter approach had been seriously contemplated and "secretly" assessed by the president, the kind of choice he would make to address the legitimacy crisis was self-evident. In fact, deep anxiety over the regime's performance-based legitimacy caused by the declining economic momentum compelled Jiang to swiftly decide on the particular approach of economic development on the party's behalf amid the spiraling socioeconomic crisis at the turn of the century. Fortunately enough, the president's power base in Shanghai played a crucial role in strengthening his resolve in deep integration. This went against Hui Feng's account that played down the part of the local state in influencing the PSC's final decision-making.[201]

Shanghai was the PRC's largest metropolitan industrial hub. Thriving in the "treaty-port" years (1842–1943), Shanghai established a wide range of international connections. Selected as one of the 14 open coastal cities in 1984, Shanghai benefited considerably from the "privileged" external integration, thus having a greater incentive to embrace globalization. Jiang's protégé—Huang Ju—the party boss of the Shanghai municipality, secretly initiated a special WTO-related research project at the sensitive juncture when NATO's bombing of the Chinese embassy in Belgrade had sparked nationwide backlash against not only the "imperialist" West but also the soft Chinese foreign policy and even the "pro-Western" president himself. This neoliberal-oriented report that enumerated "ten great economic advantages" the WTO membership would provide Shanghai was first submitted to Vice-President Zeng Qinghong, member of Politburo and Jiang's "Shanghai-gang" close ally. Zeng was greatly inspired by the report and passed it on to "Comrade [Jiang] Zemin" without delay.[202] With solid backing from his power base in the locality and the close collaboration of Zhu Rongji and Li Lanqing in the PSC, Jiang took advantage of his opponents' inability to furnish alternatives to impose the final accession decision.

Jiang's gambling of the country's deep integration was also driven by an untold personal ambition—that is, to use his distinct contribution to

China's WTO membership to enhance his standing in history.[203] Obsessed by the greatly mythologized "reform and opening" discourse to which he himself had contributed enormously throughout the 1990s, Jiang wished to be juxtaposed with Deng Xiaoping, who in the spring of 1992 made capitalism (market economy) legitimate in China. Jiang intended to go further to ally China's communist capitalism with global capitalism with a view to securitizing the country's economic development permanently while preserving the regime's absolute monopoly of power on a more solid basis. Different from Deng nonetheless, who in a sense viewed the Western-dominated international system with suspicion in both high politics and low politics terms, judging that the "two big issues" of peace and development were far from resolved,[204] Jiang and the entire communist leadership seemed to have been caught up in a pacifist idealism, believing that the US-led liberal order, once China joined it, would no longer pose a menace to Chinese state security, hence regime security.[205] This ideational shift was in large part a manifestation of China's deepening dependence on the advanced countries' markets and technology as far as the leadership's Marxist way of thinking was concerned. Such impalpable subconscious submissiveness was openly embodied in the leaders' increasing conviction of commercial liberalism that economic interdependence fosters peace. In Long Yongtu's words, "the more open the economy, the safer the country."[206] Jiang was delighted to see his gamble pay off shortly after China joined the WTO. In late 2002, the newly formed fourth-generation leadership headed by Hu Jintao fully endorsed Jiang's approach of liberal globalization at the 16th National CCP's Congress, rating it as the only correct way of building "a socialism *of* (instead of '*with*') Chinese characteristics."[207] Ceasing to oppose "hegemonism"—a synonym for US-led liberal hegemonic order, the new leadership further viewed full integration into the international system of global capitalism one year later as a guaranteed way to realize the peaceful rise of China.[208] From then on, accession to the WTO became not only the personal legacy of Jiang, but far more importantly an institutionalized legacy of the CCP—a political correctness—which his successors, like it or not, must inherit politically and ideologically.

Joining the WTO at all costs was not because of China's successful market reform and industrialization in the last two decades but because of the severe economic plight by the late 1990s, which radicalized the communist regime's quest for WTO membership. Overcommitments to trade-and-investment liberalization and acute ill-preparedness of the local firms rendered China's deep integration approach questionable. After all, the momentous accession decision made by the top leadership—Jiang Zemin in particular—was politically, rather than economically, motivated in a bid to address their overriding concern for legitimacy through achieving strong Ricardian growth even at the expense of China's autonomous development. As internal integration had never been identified as an option in the eyes of the decision-makers, deeper external integration became the only "correct" path of development in the age of liberal globalization. Why did China's reform and opening end up in such an "inevitability"? Since the reform and opening exhibit strong path-dependence under the authoritarian framework, the following chapters will examine the institutional origins of China's "external orientation" from the perspectives of both domestic politics and international politics in the reform era.

Notes

1. Cited from Cheng (2015), "Capitalism Making and Its Political Consequences: A Comparative Political Economy of China's Communist Capitalism."
2. V. I. Lenin (1956), *The Development of Capitalism in Russia*, Moscow: Foreign Languages Publishing House, p. 44; Robert Gilpin (2001), *Global Political Economy: Understanding the International Economic Order*, NJ: Princeton University Press, p. 346; Also Hugo Radice (2015), "National Decline, Capitalist Success," in *Global Capitalism: Selected Essays*, Oxon: Routledge, p. 93.
3. Shi Guangsheng (2009), "A Review of Negotiations on China's 'Reentry' into the GATT and Accession to the WTO," *Hundred-Year Tide (Bainianchao)*, No. 7.
4. Li Lanqing (2008), *Breaking the Siege: Days when the Door Started to Open*, zhongyang wenxian chubanshe, p. 332.
5. Li Lanqing (2008), *Breaking the Siege*, p. 336.

6. Shi Guangsheng (2009), "A Review of Negotiations on China's 'Reentry' into the GATT and Accession to the WTO," *Hundred-Year Tide (Bainianchao)*, No. 7.
7. Li Lanqing (2008), *Breaking the Siege*, pp. 333–334.
8. MOFTEC and State Council senior officials Sun Zhenyu and Xu Binjin gave detailed accounts of the two talks, Shenzhen, 21/12/1992.
9. Sun Zhenyu talked about 1992 Sino-US deal on market access, Shenzhen, 21/12/1992.
10. MOFTEC official Long Yongtu talked about China's GATT negotiations, Shenzhen, 21/12/1992.
11. Wang Yi (2006), *In the Days of Negotiating China's Entry into GATT/WTO*, Beijing: zhonggong zhongyang dangxiao chubanshe, p. 150.
12. Japanese Foreign Minister Yoriko Kawaguchi stated in her address for the Asean-Japan Commemorative Summit, that "during the Asian financial crisis of 1997, Japan provided assistance of some 80 billion US dollars to the countries of Asean, demonstrating unequivocally the intensity of Japan's commitment to the region. Such striking commitment is a result of thirty years of increasingly close cooperation in trade, development, political and security relations," 10/12/2003. http://www.ph.emb-japan.go.jp/pressreleases/press-64.htm
13. Reinhard Drifte (2003), *Japan's Security Relations with China since 1989: From balancing to bandwagoning?* (The Nissan Institute/Routledgecurzon Japanese Studies) (1st ed.), Oxon: Routledge, pp. 154–155.
14. A Record of Zhu Rongji's Remarks (hereafter "Zhu's Remarks") (2011), vol. 3, Beijing: renmin chubanshe, p. 63.
15. Manuscript of Willem E.C. van Kemenade (1999), "China and the World Trade Organization."
16. *The People's Daily*, 27/11/1998.
17. Manuscript of Willem E.C. van Kemenade (1999), "China and the World Trade Organization."
18. *Xinhua News Agency*, Beijing, 15/03/1999.
19. Ibid.
20. Ibid.
21. Laurence Brahm (2002), *Zhu Rongji & the Transformation of Modern China*, Singapore: John Wiley & Sons (Asia) Pte Ltd., p. 267.
22. China and the World (online) (http://www.zgysj.com), No. 5, 1999. This website was created in 1996 and no longer exists.
23. *Xinhua*, Beijing, 15/03/1999.

24. Brahm (2002), pp. 267–268.
25. Kemenade public lecture in China Europe International Business School (CEIBS), Shanghai, June 1999.
26. China and the World (online), No. 5, 1999.
27. Conversation with an internal source, 2/11/2001.
28. China and the World (online). No. 5, 1999.
29. "Special Interview with Long Yongtu: The Accession Negotiations were Accomplished This Way," (*tanpan shi zheyang wancheng de*) *Caijing*, 14/11/2001. http://finance.sina.cim.cn/g/20011114/129329.html
30. According to an informed source, 12/08/2005.
31. Zhou Xisheng, "zhu zongli fangmei shenming dayi (Premier Zhu Visit the US to Declare Righteous Cause)," *The Outlook (liaowang)*, No. 17, 26/04/1999.
32. Shen Jiru (1999), "Several Thinkings on the Kosovo Question," *World Economics and Politics*, No. 7. This article was actually written on April 24, two weeks ahead of the embassy bombing.
33. Interview with an informed source, 16/12/1999.
34. Interview with an informed source, 22/01/2002.
35. Wan Ming (2007), "The United Stated States, Japan, and the European Union: Comparing Political Economy Approaches to China," *The Pacific Review*, 20:3, pp. 397–421 (p. 401).
36. Drifte (2003), p. 33.
37. Wan (2007), p. 400.
38. Algieri (2002); Shambaugh (1996).
39. Stokes (1999): 180. Sources of Stokes, Algieri Shambough and Lapres are indirectly cited from Wan Ming's essay (2007).
40. Raj Bhala (2000), *Enter the Dragon: An Essay on China's WTO Accession Saga*, pp. 1469, 1489, 1496. https://law.drupal.ku.edu/sites/law.drupal.ku.edu/files/docs/resources/library/IntlTradeLaw/Enter%20the%20Dragon%20PDF.pdf
41. Wan (2007), p. 401.
42. Brahm (2003), p. 269.
43. *Phoenix Panorama*, 9/01/2013. http://phtv.ifeng.com/program/fhdsy/detail_2013_01/09/20995008_1.shtml
44. Shi Guangsheng (2009), "A Review of Negotiations on China's 'Reentry' into the GATT and Accession to the WTO," *Hundred-Year Tide (Bainianchao)*, No. 7.
45. Di Yinqing (1999), "A Critique on Sino-U.S. Agreement on China's WTO Accession," *China and the World (e-journal)*, No. 41, December. http://www.zgysj.com/99/zs9912a.htm#2

46. Editorial of the *People's Daily*, 16/11/1999.
47. Mark O'neill, "US and China Sign WTO Deal," *South China Morning Post (SCMP)*, 16/11/1999.
48. *People's Daily* editorial, 16/11/1999.
49. Lapres 2000:8, cited from Wan (2007).
50. Sheel Kohli, "EU Refuses to Rush Agreement," *SCMP*, 23/02/2000.
51. Manuscript of Willem E.C. van Kemenade (1999), "China and the World Trade Organization."
52. Mark O'Neill, "Beijing, Europe Sign WTO Deal," *SCMP*, 20/05/2000.
53. Lapres 2000: 8–14; 2001: 507, cited from Wan (2007).
54. "Beijing Reveals in WTO Achievement," *Reuters in Beijing*, 20/05/2000.
55. Shi Guangsheng (2009), *Hundred-Year Tide (Bainianchao)*, No. 7.
56. Agreement on Market Access between the People's Republic China and the United States of America, 15/11/1999. Released by USTR on 14/03/2000.
57. Nicholas Lardy, "China and the World Trade Organization: Problems on the Road to Liberalization," http://unpan1.un.org/intradoc/groups/public/documents/apcity/unpan003154.pdf
58. Ibid.
59. "WTO Accords Not Without Dangers," *SCMP*, 22/05/2002.
60. Ibid.
61. Nicholas Lardy (2002), *Integrating China into the Global Economy*, Washington: Brookings Institution Press, p. 27.
62. Long Yongtu, "Entry into WTO Is Not Equal to Full Open-Up," *Guangdong Information Daily* (Hong Kong), 12/11/1999.
63. Di Yingqing (1999), "A Critique on Long Yongtu's Article 'Entry into WTO Is Not Equal to Full Open-Up,'" *China and the World*, December. http://www.zgysj.com/99/zs9912a.htm; "WTO Entry Will Put 40 m Chinese Out of Work," *Guardian*, 27/01/2001. https://www.theguardian.com/business/2002/jan/27/theobserver.observerbusiness1
64. China and the World (online), No. 5, 1999. http://www.zgysj.com
65. Robin Hahnel, "China to Join the WTO: What Does It Mean?" http://www.zmag.org/ZSustainers/ZDaily/1999-12/14landau.htm
66. Peter Nolan (2001), *China and Global Economy: National Champions, Industrial Policy, and the Big Business Revolution*, New York: Palgrave, pp. 196–197; Nolan (2002), "China and the Global Business Revolution," *Cambridge Journal of Economics*, 26:1, pp. 119–137; Shadlen, K (2005), "Exchanging Development for Market Access? Deep Integration and Industrial Policy under Multilateral and Regional-Bilateral Trade Agreements," *Review of International Political Economy*, 12:5, pp. 750–775.

67. Andrew Walter and Gautam Sen (2003), *Analyzing the Global Political Economy*, NJ: Princeton University Press, p. 53.
68. Ibid., p. 57.
69. UNCTAD (2009), *The Least Developed Countries Report 2009: The State and Development Governance*, New York and Geneva, p. 151. http://unctad.org/en/docs/ldc2009_en.pdf; Also Shadlen (2005).
70. WTO and the TRIPs Agreement. http://www.who.int/medicines/areas/policy/wto_trips/en/
71. Wade (2003), introduction: p. xliv; Peter Nolan (2001), *China and Global Economy: National Champions, Industrial Policy, and the Big Business Revolution*, New York: Palgrave, p. 152.
72. China agreed to eliminate and cease "enforcement of trade and foreign exchange balancing requirements, local content and export performance offsets and technology transfer requirements made effective through laws, regulations or other measures." Accession of the People's Republic of China Decision of 10 November 2001, Annex 1A III 8 (a): Trade-Related Investment Measures (to be noticed to the Committee on Trade-Related Investment Measures). Also Shadlen (2005).
73. WTO, Report of the WTO Working Party on the Accession of China (1 October 2001), WT/ACC/CHN/49, at paragraphs 337, 341.
74. "All laws, regulations and measures relating to the procurement by state-owned and state-invested enterprises of goods and services for commercial sale, production of goods or supply of services for commercial sale, or for non-governmental purposes would not be considered to be laws, regulations and measures relating to government procurement. Thus, such purchases or sales would be subject to the provisions of Articles II, XVI and XVII of the GATS and Article III of the GATT 1994." Ibid., paragraph 47. This refers mainly to China's commitment to stop protecting the large-sized SOEs through trade and investment liberalization and acceding to the GPA.
75. Nolan (2001), "China, the US and the WTO: Battle of the Giants or Defeat of the Pigmies," (manuscript).
76. China's economic openness ranked the ninth. The preceding eight countries of higher openness than China: Ireland, Belgium, the Netherlands, Austria, South Korea, Sweden, Finland and Canada. *Deloitte Research* (UK), 2005.
77. Lardy (2002), p. 20.
78. Peter Nolan (2002), "China and the Global Business Revolution," *Cambridge Journal of Economics*, 26:1, pp. 119–137.

79. Peter Nolan (1995), *China's Rise, Russia's Fall: Politics, Economics and Planning in the Transition from Stalinism*, NY: St. Martin's Press; Nolan (2001) (manuscript). For "3-globals," see Peter Nolan (2004), *Transforming China: Globalization, Transition and Development*, London: Anthem Press, p. 238.
80. Nolan listed the achievement as below: the SOEs have "grown rapidly in terms of value of sales; absorbed a great deal of modern technology; learned how to compete in the marketplace; substantially upgraded the technical level of their employees; learned wide-ranging new managerial skills; gained substantial understanding of international financial markets; become sought-after partners for multinational companies." Nolan (2001) (manuscript).
81. Ibid.
82. Nolan's finding of China's weak competitive capability was so important as to deserve being quoted in full. He pointed out, "This is extremely marked in the high-technology sectors, such as aerospace, complex equipment such as power plants, pharmaceuticals, as well as in 'mid-technology' sectors such as integrated oil and petrochemicals and auto components; ... even in sectors with apparently less advanced technology, such as steel and coal, there is significant gap with leading global companies in the high value-added segments of the market." Ibid. Also Nolan (2002), pp. 119–139, with the conclusion that "in these fundamental senses, China's industrial policy of the past two decades must be judged a failure."
83. Nolan (2001) (manuscript).
84. The Chinese Academy of Sciences, "The Report on China's Modernization 2005," 18/02/2005.
85. Zhu Gaofeng et al., (ed.) (2003), *China's Manufacturing in the Age of Globalization* (Chap. 9), Beijing: shehui kexue wenxian chubanshe.
86. Ibid., pp. 15–19; 351–352.
87. Ibid. The book's "references" are clearly suggestive of the influence of liberal economists on these authors.
88. ETMA first appeared in the 1980s when the severe shortage of hard currency forced the Chinese government to open up certain segments of domestic market to foreign investors to exchange for the latter's technology transfer. It became part and parcel China's national development strategy from 1992.
89. See the Report, pp. 17, 312.

90. UNCTAD (2001), "Transfer of Technology—UNCTAD Series on Issues in International Investment Agreements," p. 15. http://unctad.org/en/docs/psiteiitd28.en.pdf
91. The Report (2003), p. 310; Chen Man (2001), "A Comprehensive Analysis on the Effect of FDI on Chinese Economy," *Strategy and Management*, No. 3.
92. In December 2004, China Central Television (CCTV), the largest state television station controlled by the party's powerful Propaganda Department and professionally guided by the State General Administration of Broadcasting and Television (SRABT) under the Ministry of Culture, launched an all-out propaganda offensive on the great achievements of China's economic development three years after it joined the WTO. In a CCTV's interview with Wu Jinglian. He, on the one hand, admitted the huge impact had taken effect, placing domestic enterprises in a difficult situation; but on the other hand, asserted that the domestic enterprises fared better after the WTO entry by citing the example of the Number One Auto Corporation based in Changchun. In 2011, ten years after China joined the WTO, Wu defended ETMA in the auto industry, asserting that without substantial market opening, the rapid development of China's auto industry was unlikely. *Nanfang Daily*, 19/08/2011. http://www.chinanews.com/auto/2011/08-19/3269919.shtml
93. Internal remarks of Li Rongrong, Minister of the SASAC and Wang Zhongming, director of the research center of the State Asset Supervision and Administration Commission (SASAC). Cited from Peter Nolan's public lecture at LSE's *China Week* in mid-February 2005.
94. He Bi, "Excess Opening Brought Political and Economic Crisis to China," http://www.wyzxwyzx.com/Article/Class4/200706/19776.html; also http://finance.sina.com.cn/j/20050228/13451389655.shtml
95. Shi Weigan, *Re-examining the Role of FDI: of 28 Major Industries, 21 Controlled by the MNCs*, Guangzhou: nanfengchuang, 28/08/2006.
96. Private conversation with Peter Nolan in January 2002.
97. As a matter of fact, the "transitional period" was partially terminated by the Wen Jiabao administration after Zhu Rongji stepped down in March 2003 that went beyond the WTO deal to further liberalize foreign investment in industrial certain sector. See report "Cars: Driving Ambitions?" (David Murphy), *Far Eastern Economic Review*, 27/05/2004.

98. Chinese newspapers and magazines before and after China joined the WTO were deluged with such an account.
99. "China and the World Trading System," speech delivered by WTO Director General Renato Ruggiero at Beijing University, 21/04/1997. http://www.wto.org/french/news_f/sprr_f/china_f/htm
100. The so-called universal MFN principle was imposed by the USA with a view to scraping the European imperial trading blocs; while non-discrimination or reciprocity made free trade less free by restricting developing nations' access to advanced countries' market. Walter and Gautam (2003), *Analyzing the Global Political Economy*, pp. 31–32.
101. Brahm (2003), p. 264.
102. This was evidenced by an internal party document issued in late 2001. There were altogether 48 clauses on 32 pages specifying how the *pros* and *cons* of China's WTO deal should be reported by the domestic media under the tight control of the party (He 2006, 83). A typical example of this was the analytical article on Beijing Youth Daily. It emphasized the expected benefits China was hoping so enthusiastically to reap from the enlarged global markets in the first place; then admitted the certain pains that the country's deep integration would incur to those industries where China was being in a remarkable comparative and/or competitive disadvantage, such as agriculture, automobiles, chemicals, pharmaceuticals, banking and insurance. *Beijing Youth Daily*, 16/11/1999.
103. Lardy (2002), p. 20.
104. Zhang Hanlin (1999), *A Guiding Book on the World Trade Organization*, Beijing: duiwai jingji maoyi daxue chubanshe. http://www.cctv.com/oriental/dfzz/jmnr/20021219/20.html
105. Yu Yongding and Zheng Bingwen (2000), "The Research Report On China's Entry Into WTO: The Analysis of the China's Industries," Beijing: shehui kexue wenxian chubanshe, Beijing, January 1. Main points can be found at: http://www.bjtextile.com/members/discussion/wto/wto2002-1.htm
106. Ibid.
107. Wang Xiangwei, "WTO Barrier Falls to Cheers and Warnings," *SCMP*, 21/09/2000.
108. Julia Han, "Zhu Urges Faster Implementation of Social Security," *SCMP*, 20/11/2000.

109. Zhu Rongji told audience at the press conference upon the closing of the National People's Congress on March 5th, "our entry into the WTO will bring us a number of new problems, we are facing many arduous tasks … we should lose no time in preparing for China's entry into the WTO and fulfilling our tasks in the transitional period." Zhu Rongji spoke at the NPC on 5/03/2001, *People's Daily*, 6/03/2001.
110. Wu Jinglian thought the accession a life-or-death struggle for Chinese enterprises, especially the SOEs (more on footnote 257).
111. *People's Daily* (editorial), 11/11/2001.
112. According to a Chinese scholar involved in the policy consulting of the WTO accession, the central government randomly sent out 5075 questionnaires to investigate to what extent government officials and managers of SOEs knew about the WTO and relevant rules. The result was astounding. Less than 30% of the respondents could tell clearly what the WTO was; and less than 10% could answer the rules-related questions. Source: internal lecture in Shenzhen by Professor Hou Tieshan of Dalian Polytechnic University in 2001. Therefore, the Chinese government decided to launch programs to train professionals in WTO rules among the bureaucrats and SOE managers. However, the contents of the training programs were biased and misleading and strictly conformed to the party's propaganda.
113. Brahm (2002), p. 264.
114. Ibid.
115. Wing Thye Woo (2001), "Recent Claims of China's Economic Exceptionalism—Reflections Inspired by WTO Accession," *China Business Review*, 12:2/3, pp. 107–136.
116. Brahm (2002), p. 279.
117. Stephen Roach (at China Development Forum in Beijing), "China: Straight Talk from Zhu," 27/03/2002. www.morganstanley.com/GEFdata/digests/20020327-wed.html (This hyperlink no longer exists).
118. Peter Nolan viewed China's WTO entry an event of historic significance, comparable to the country's opening up after the Opium Wars. Nolan (2001) (manuscript).
119. Brahm (2003), p. 280.
120. *quanqiu qiyejia* (*Global Entrepreneurs*), April issue 2004.
121. "Lucky, Kodak and Fuji: Life-or-Death Struggle vs. Co-Prosperity through Competitive Cooperation," *21st Century Business Herald*, 28/05/2001.

122. Ibid.
123. Interestingly, Kodak's JV initiative was not aimed at controlling Lucky in the first place, but blocking its main rival Fuji reaching a JV agreement with Lucky. "Is Kodak the Santa Claus?" *Caijing*, No. 23, 5/11/2003.
124. http://www.csrc.gov.cn/cms/uploadFiles/600135_2003_n.77093521328.pdf; http://www.csrc.gov.cn/cms/uploadFiles/600135_2002_0.1061046629140.pdf; http://www.csrc.gov.cn/cms/uploadFiles/600135_2004_n.94182234944.pdf
125. A fieldwork carried out by Peter Nolan and Wang Xiaoqiang in which I was involved in Gongyuan Film-making Plant in January 2001.
126. Wu Jinglian made this remark in one of his serial lectures to the China Europe International Business School (CEIBS) in November 1999.
127. Press Conference 15/03/2001. *People's Daily*, 16/03/2001.
128. *Zhu Rongji's Answers to Journalists' Questions*, p. 105, Beijing: renmin chubanshe, 2009. Wang Xiangwei, "Mainland Stands at the End of WTO Struggle," *SCMP*, 17/09/2001.
129. Wen Tiejun (2004), "Impact of WTO Entry on Chinese Peasants, Agriculture, and Rural Development," http://www.moa.gov.cn/fwllm/jjps/200405/t20040509_201786.htm. A good example is the import surge of soybeans after China joined the WTO. See report "*The Fall of Soybeans* (dadou lunxian)," 14/12/2006, Twentieth-first Century Economic Report. http://finance.sina.com.cn/g/20061214/10363164364.shtml
130. "'Floor,' 'Ceiling,' and China's Food Security Dilemma," *Pengpai News*, 22/08/2015. http://www.thepaper.cn/newsDetail_forward_1365998
131. According to an informed source, 16/04/2000.
132. Zhu's Remarks (2011), v.2, p. 375; v.3, p. 184; v.4, p. 197.
133. Nick Mathiaso, "WTO Entry Will Put 40 m Chinese Out of Work," *The Observer*, 27/01/2002. http://observer.guardian.co.uk/business/story/0,,639832,00.html; Salomon Smith Barney (investment bank) estimated that "within five years after the WTO entry, China will have 40 million people unemployed, 5–10 million rural workers, 10 million laid-off SOE workers, and 20 million non-SOE workers (Far East Economic Review, 5 October 2000)." See S. M. Shafaeddin (2002), "Some Implications of Accession to WTO for China's Economy," *International Journal of Development Issues*, 1:2, pp. 93–128. http://unctad.org/en/docs/osgrs80_en.pdf
134. Most estimates put the figure of unemployment caused by China's WTO accession in the initial years around 10 million. http://unpan1.

un.org/intradoc/groups/public/documents/apcity/unpan011943.pdf; http://news.creaders.net/society/2001/11/01/356820.html; http://business.sohu.com/result.html; A.S. Bhalla, Shufang Qiu (2004), *The Employment Impact of China's WTO Accession*, London and NY: RoutledgeCurzon, pp. 66–69.

135. This remark made by Zhu in private appeared on Chinese website but was removed very shortly.
136. Vivien Pik-Kwan Chan, "NPC Prepares Laws for Entry into Trade Body," *SCMP*, 21/11/1999; William Kazer, "Rush to Adjust Laws for WTO," *SCMP*, 15/06/2000; Mark O'Neill and Reuters, "Long Haul Starts on Law Revision," *SCMP*, 4/07/2000; *Xinhua*, 23/04/2001.
137. *Yangcheng Evening News*, 29/10/2000.
138. Edith Terry, "One Very Positive Big Deal," *SCMP*, 19/09/2001.
139. Enoch Yiu, "Officials Hold Key to Success of Law Changes," *SCMP*, 2/07/2001.
140. "Online Newshour: Trade Dealer," 18/11/1999. http://www.pbs.org/newshour/bb/white_house/july-dec99/barshefsky_11-18.html
141. Mark O'Neill, "Textile City Prepares for Big WTO Windfall," *SCMP*, 22/11/1999.
142. Interview with managers of a large-sized SOE in Shanghai in May 1999.
143. Ibid. and interviews with some central government officials in June/July 2005.
144. In 2001, Chinese vice foreign minister Li Zhaoxing went to Nankai University in Tianjin to make a speech on China's WTO accession. He claimed that many of the developing countries had fallen victims to the economic globalization, but China would surely benefit from the globalization. Logical links were invisible in his speech on how China would become a winner in the end. Interview with a professor in political science at Nankai University.
145. Zhang Naigen (2011), "On the Changes of Chinese Legal System for Implementing the WTO Laws," *The Legist (faxuejia)*, Issue (1), pp. 9–18. http://article.chinalawinfo.com/ArticleHtml/Article_59681.shtml
146. Protests by a handful of New-Left scholars against China's WTO accession were ignored by all domestic and most international media.
147. One economically backward coastal city deputy-mayor, when interviewed by the party's mouthpiece, trumpeted the great historical significance of the WTO accession and the "historical opportunity" the

accession would bring to the city. Her reasoning was exactly the same as the party's cliché of "short-term pains but long-term gains." Up until today, the city remains the most backward among the dozen cities within the province.

148. Wang Xiangwei, "WTO Barriers Falls to Cheers and Warnings," *SCMP*, 21/09/2000. Long Yongtu said in a special interview on October 22, 2001, less than one month before China entered the WTO, "It is inappropriate for such a lot many people not having much knowledge of the WTO accession to talk about what preparations need to be done." An abstract of speech by vice-minister of Moftec Long Yongtu on the international trade forum at the 90th Guangzhou Export Fair, *Chinese Entrepreneurs* (*zhongguo qiyejia*), No. 11, 2001.
149. Gu Haibing, "Three Questions with MOFTEC," 18/01/2002. http://www.dajun.com.cn/rushisanwen.html (this hyperlink no longer exists); China's protocol of accession to the World Trade Organization (Chinese translation): http://www.people.com.cn/GB/jinji/31/179/20020125/656050.html; "MOFTEC Enriching Itself from Translating WTO Documents," https://www.secretchina.com/news/gb/2002/01/22/10590.html.%E4%B8%96%E8%B4%B8%E6%96%87%E4%BB%B6%E4%B8%AD%E8%AF%91%E6%9C%AC%E7%88%86%E5%87%BA%E4%B8%AD%E5%9B%BD%E5%A4%96%E7%BB%8F%E8%B4%B8%E9%83%A8%E4%BB%8E%E4%B8%AD%E7%89%9F%E5%88%A9.html; Liu Jingdong (2007), "An Interpretation of the 'Judicial Review Clause' of the Accession Protocol of the People's Republic of China," http://www.iolaw.org.cn/showArticle.aspx?id=2133
150. Twenty-First Century Business Herald, 17/12/2001.
151. Gu Haibing, "Three Questions with MOFTEC," 18/01/2002. http://www.dajun.com.cn/rushisanwen.html
152. Caoan Jushi, "Who Can Be So Shameless?" Caoan Jushi argued that under such untransparent arrangements, neither domestic enterprises nor the government was able to ready themselves for the fatal impacts. https://www.peacehall.com/news/gb/pubvp/2002/12/200212170446.shtml
153. Han Deqiang (2000), *Collision—The Pitfall of Globalization and China's Realistic Choice* (Chap. 1), Beijing: jingji guanli chubanshe.
154. Wang Shaoguang (2002), "When the Pie Is Made Bigger…," *Dushu* (Beijing), No. 2.
155. Ibid.

156. The nationalists were the least explicit in terms of their stance over the CCP's decision to join the WTO.
157. Shi Zhong (Wang Xiaodong) (1995), "The Logic of Comparative Advantage should not be Pushed to the Extreme," *Strategy and Management*, No. 3. This article was absorbed into his book published in 1999, titled *The Chinese Road under the Shadow of Globalization*, Beijing: zhongguo shehui kexue chubanshe, 1999. This book was the third influential work on Chinese nationalism after *China Can Say No* (1996) and *Behind the Demonizing of China* (1996) in the 1990s.
158. Wang Xiaodong, "Chinese Nationalism under the Shadow of Globalization," 7/02/2005. http://www.lse.ac.uk/collections/asiaResearchCentre/pdf/Transcript/WANGXiaodongFinalTranscriptEnglish.pdf
159. http://blog.dwnews.com/?p=21740&cpage=1
160. http://economist.icxo.com/htmlnews/2008/10/14/1321401_1.htm
161. The three conditions are: "full employment, capital immobility and similar capacities to produce goods for the world market." Ray Kiely (2006), *New Political Economy of Development: Globalization, Imperialism, Hegemony*, Oxon: Palgrave, p. 14.
162. "Traitor Long Yongtu in the Twenty-First Century" (*ershiyi shiji hanjian zhilongYongtu*).http://www.wyzxsx.com/Article/Class22/200807/45136.html
163. Long Yongtu claimed, "It is a completely out-of-date mentality that a country's industry will be able to develop if only it is protected by the state. Facts have proved that the industry can develop only in an open environment," *Zaobao*, 2/12/2001.
164. For instance, Xue Rongjiu, Professor at UIBE and the Chairman of China's WTO research council, stated that the concept of "national industry" was unsuitable since it was no longer the age of "semi-feudal, semi-colonial" society, as it was before 1949. There is a great change in connotation of this concept. In light of the spirit of WTO, continued use of this concept is inappropriate. He proposed using a new concept, "domestic industry," which covers all enterprises in operation within the Chinese border, including not only the SOEs, but the collectively owned and private firms, as well as the wholly owned foreign firms and JVs that are making contributions to China's economic development ("Council Chairman says, The Concept of 'National Industry' is Out-Of-Date," *Guangzhou Daily*, 6/12/1999). Liu Shijin, Director of

Industry Department of the State Council's Development and Research Centre, contended that conflicts of interest between Chinese and foreign investors should not be mixed together. He agreed with Xue Rongjiu in arguing that Chinese auto enterprises, whether local or foreign firms, are Chinese enterprises ("Two Important Understandings of China's Auto Industry," 2/09/2002). However, there are quite a number of scholars who, though they endorsed the open policy, held contrarian views in the big debate regarding the redefinition of national industry in 1996. Their views, however, fell on deaf ears in practical policy dimensions (Qianxian, No. 7, 1997).

165. George Gilboy (2004), "The Myth of China's Miracle," *Foreign Affairs*, 83:4, pp. 33–48.
166. Interview with Ding Li, senior research fellow at Guangdong Academy of Social Sciences, 25/07/2007.
167. Ma Guochuan (2008), *A Collection of Interviews with Chinese Economists (fengyujiancheng: zhongguo zhuming jingjixuejia fangtanlu)*, Beijing: SDX Joint Publishing House, p. 189.
168. Ibid.
169. The source of the rumor was the US-based ejournal "China and the World" run by a group of overseas Taiwanese Maoists. Actually, the long article that appeared on *The Economist* three days after the signing of China–US deal was overwhelmingly about economics and made virtually no mention of political impact. See "The Real Leap Forward," *The Economist*, 18/11/1999. http://www.economist.com/node/259987
170. Valentine M Moghadam (2005), *Globalizing Women: Transnational Feminist Networks*, Baltimore, MD: The Johns Hopkins University Press, p. 35.
171. Yu Zuyao, "Still Impoverished behind Prosperity," *China Economic Times*, 4/03/2002.
172. Liu Junning, "The Political Significance of China's Accession to the WTO," http://www.jiuding.org/Article/Class8/plwz/200509/210.html
173. He Qinglian, "What Is the Goodness of Joining the WTO?" *Duowei News*, 2/04/2000.
174. Zong Fengming (2007), *Zhao Ziyang: Captive Conversation*, Hong Kong: Open Press, p. 295.
175. Su Shaozhi (2006), *Democracy Cannot Wait*, Hong Kong: Greenfield Bookstore, p. 196.

176. Ibid.
177. Cui Zhiyuan, "Joining the WTO Is Not China's Pressing Task," *Zaobao*, 6/07/1999.
178. Cui Zhiyuan (1999), "Stimulating Domestic Demand Is a Revolution," *Review of International Economics* (Beijing: guoji jingi pinglun), No. 5–6.
179. Su (2006), *Democracy Cannot Wait*, pp. 196–197.
180. Yang Xiaokai, "The Two Possible Outcomes of China's Accession to the WTO," http://www.boxun.com/hero/yangxk/45_1shtml
181. It is an open secret that the Chinese communist officials deeply despise the intellectuals. Interview with an informed source, 07/08/2005.
182. According to a well-informed source.
183. CCTV documentary EP. 1–12: "Deng Xiaoping," 1997. http://tv.cntv.cn/videoset/C14817; http://list.youku.com/albumlist/show/id_1375329.html?&ascending=0
184. According to a well-informed source.
185. Di Yinqing (1999), "A Critique on Sino-US Agreement on China's WTO Accession," *China and the World (e-journal)*, No. 41, December, see webpage: http://www.zgysj.com/99/zs9912a.htm#2
186. Long Yongtu, "Talks were Accomplished this Way," *Caijing*, 5/11/2011. http://magazine.caijing.com.cn/20011105/111966.shtml
187. Hui Feng (2006), *The Politics of China's Accession to the WTO*, New York: Routledge, p. 6.
188. It is said that Tian Jiyun, a former ally of Zhao Ziyang and famous reformist leader in the Politburo, was rather displeased with Zhu's "minefield" rhetoric, since such wording was a reminder of Zhu's heroism alone with all others being barriers to his reform. Conversation with an informed source in May 1999.
189. Wu Jichuan, Minister of Information Industry (MII), openly opposed Zhu's market access commitments on China's sensitive infant information industries, arguing that the liberalization would seriously endanger China's national security. Wu was bold enough to challenge Zhu because he had the backing of his mentor, former Premier Li Peng, now the Chairman of China's legislature, the National People's Congress. However, Jiang intervened and warned Wu not to oppose the WTO deal. Wu had to give in. According to an informed source.
190. Interview with Wang Xiaoqiang, 2/02/2001.

191. Long Yongtu, "Talks were Accomplished this Way," *Caijing*, 5/11/2011. http://magazine.caijing.com.cn/20011105/111966.shtml
192. Diplomacy has always been a taboo that precludes open debates and defiance from within or outside the bureaucracy since the late Premier Zhou Enlai made two iron rules for compliance: there is nothing in diplomacy that is unimportant; and there is limited empowerment in diplomacy. These two rules inherited from Zhou centralized the power of foreign policymaking in the hands of top leaders, particularly the General Secretary. During the WTO talks, Jiang's trusted aide, PSE member and First Deputy-Premier Li Lanqing suggested mimicking the way border treaty negotiations were conducted most secretly by keeping the party and the country unknown "until the last minute of the signing of the agreement." See report on *Twenty-First Century Business Herald*, 19/11/2011. http://s.21so.com/index.php?r=qlinks/index&id=201111_c9f64cd5b41c04778171a6493df71dd6
193. "Jiang Zemin's Speech at the National Conference on Science and Technology," 26/05/1995. http://news.xinhuanet.com/st/2006-1/07/content_4021964.htm
194. CCTV-jiaodianfangtan (focus), March 1999.
195. http://baike.baidu.com/view/303969.htm
196. Fan Hengshan, head of a Department of the System Reform Office of the State Council, complained that even many of the central government ministers were kept unknown of the details of the WTO agreements. "Dialogue between Famous Economists and Entrepreneurs on WTO," http://finance.sina.com.cn/g/20011106/125923.html
197. When state bank managers demanded MOFTEC negotiators not to make excessive concessions in some sensitive fields, the latter pretended to agree but did the opposite according to the directives of Zhu Rongji without further notifying the former. Interview in a Southern Province with a senior state bank manager, July 20, 2006.
198. Han Deqiang, "The Pros and Cons of China's Accession to the WTO, Dynamics and Debates," a speech addressed to the European Parliament, 26/06/2001. http://www.wyzxsx.com/Article/Class17/200411/845.html
199. John Pomfret, "Experts: Chinese Leadership Lacks Vision," *Washington Post*, 28/10/1999.
200. Zong (2007), citing then General Secretary Jiang Zemin's chief political adviser Liu Ji's words, p. 116.
201. Hui Feng (2006), pp. 240–241.

202. Huang Qifan told the audience at China Europe International Business School (CEIBS) on November 16, 1999.
203. Some comments even attributed it to the private need of President Jiang Zemin "to increase his standing in China and China's standing in the world." David Roche, "Euphoria will Wear off when the Fed Raises Rates," *SCMP*, 16/11/1999.
204. *Selected Works of Deng Xiaoping* (hereafter "Deng's Works") (1993), vol. 3, Beijing: renmin chubanshe, pp. 353 (in year 1990), 383 (in year 1992).
205. According to Liang Shoude, Deng viewed US hegemonic order as both the source of prosperity and the source of instability. Thus, the CCP remained committed to "maintain world peace and oppose hegemonism" until 2002 when the CCP held the 16th National Party's Congress in November. Viewing "the possibly of a new world war [is] not 'less likely,' but 'totally unlikely in the foreseeable future,'" the CCP eschewed mention of "opposing hegemonism" and rephrased its world outlook into "maintain world peace, and promote common development," Seminar on Chinese Foreign Policy and Grand Strategy, 16–17/10/2003, Peking University. Jiang's Reports in 1997 and 2002: http://cpc.people.com.cn/GB/64162/64168/64568/65445/4526290.html (Jiang Zemin's Political Report addressed to the 15th National Party's Congress: Part 9: Foreign Policy, 12/09/1997); http://cpc.people.com.cn/GB/64162/64168/64569/65444/4429116.html (Jiang Zemin's Political Report addressed to the 16th National Party's Congress: Part 9: Foreign Policy, 8/11/2002).
206. "Long Yongtu: The More Open the Economy, the Safer the Country," *New Beijing Daily* (*Xinjinbao*), 10/12/2006. http://finance.qq.com/a/20061210/000064.htm
207. According to multiple internal sources.
208. "Peaceful Rise: China Faces the World as a 'Friendly Elephant,'" *Xinhua*, 24/04/2004. http://www.china.com.cn/chinese/zhuanti/boao/551888.htm

3

Chinese Reform and Development in the 1980s

The onset of China's economic reform in the late 1970s coincided with the decline of the USSR-led socialist Second World, which was losing an economic warfare with the capitalist First World in the Cold War. Behind the upcoming crisis besetting the Soviet Bloc was the socialist industrial economies' inability to compete globally given their ever-enlarging technological gap with the West, which highlighted the inadequacy of state socialism—long on input-driven extensive growth, but short on total factor productivity (TFP)-driven intensive growth. Compared with the reform in the Soviet Bloc, the reform in China was driven predominantly by the pressing need to lift the country out of the extreme poverty caused by Mao's utopian socialism, particularly the catastrophic Cultural Revolution.[1] This had become a high consensus among the post-Mao leadership eager to bail out the party state mired in deep crisis. Rejecting Maoist extremism, nonetheless the reform in the 1980s was not aimed at renouncing socialism but was aimed at the self-perfection of socialism. This stands for the idealist pursuit of the ruling and intellectual elites who held the belief throughout most of the 1980s that the Chinese Communist system was reformable. For Deng Xiaoping, keeping the party in power permanently was what motivated his reform initiatives. As he saw it, a far-reaching reform was essential to the modernization of China, hence the survival of the regime.

J. Yue, *China's Rise in the Age of Globalization*, Palgrave Studies in Economic History, https://doi.org/10.1007/978-3-319-63997-0_3

Deng was a flexible pragmatist. The rapid success of the decollectivization reform in the early 1980s turned him into a convinced market liberal. Yet, as a veteran communist, he knew the limits the communist dogma and institutions would set on his reform project. His distinct approach of *perestroika without glasnost* enabled the market-oriented reform to make headway without being stymied by die-hard ideologues. But it also contributed to the deconstruction of communism as a belief system. The ensuing collapse of reform consensus on the vague vision of socialist self-perfection made him a sheer Machiavellian who did not care about the means so long as the regime would be consolidated no matter what "ism" was actually at work. This did not imply that Deng as the paramount leader was capable of forcing ahead the market-oriented reform at will. Strongly checked by the economic tsar Chen Yun, another veteran communist and political heavyweight, he could not even match either Yuri Andropov or Mikhail Gorbachev in overwhelming opponents. Eschewing glasnost and lacking ideological vindications instead rendered his reform difficult to rival Chen Yun's approach, known as the "birdcage," in overruling the market through strengthening of central planning.

The story of the 1980s was not a merely economic reform story. The regime's decision to focus industrial investment on consumer goods rather than capital goods dramatically enhanced the people's livelihood, a correct decision that had little to do with but paradoxically added to the credibility of the market-oriented reform.[2] Without a major overhaul of state socialism characterized by public ownership and central planning, nonetheless, the consumption-led prosperity diminished by the end of the 1980s. Contrary to conventional wisdom that the Chinese reform in the 1980s was a huge success, Deng's patchwork reform in urban China achieved only limited success. It did not go much beyond Soviet economist Evsei Liberman's ideas raised in the 1950s and Hungary's market socialist experiments from the late 1950s until the early 1980s in terms of more material incentive, increased price flexibility, and greater enterprise autonomy. Meanwhile, the leadership's acute myopia in devising a proper development strategy and the Chinese Communist Party (CCP) strict ban on open factionalism left little room for consensus building between the market reformers and the central planners on an alternative pathway of development sponsored by a revamped central planning apparatus in concert with the market forces. As the de facto chief architect of China's economic reform, Deng's protégé—Premier Zhao Ziyang—decentralized fiscal power to the provinces and outlined a coastal development strategy, which effectively undermined the planning system, paving the way for its eventual breaking apart in the early 1990s. Endorsed ironically by both Deng and Chen Yun, Zhao's methods paid off in forging ahead the market reform but at the expense of national economic reintegration, and henceforth the country's autonomous development well into the 1990s and beyond.

Mao's Legacies and China's Transition to Post-totalitarianism

Shortly after the end of the Cultural Revolution in 1976, how to inherit the legacies of Mao Zedong became a thorny issue facing the post-Mao leadership. The devastation of the Cultural Revolution made reform a necessity. The new leadership following the arrest of the Gang of Four was determined to get China back on the right track of modernization. However, in the wake of harsh intra-party backlash against Mao's political purges after 1949, Deng Xiaoping brought the denouncement of Mao to a sudden halt, lest further exposure of Mao's "mistakes" lead to the self-denial of communist totalitarianism from its very institutional origin. Deng's circumscription on de-Maoification in political-ideological domains underlined the fact that the impending reform process would be strongly path dependent. Aimed at the "self-perfection of socialism," the idealist-oriented reform in the 1980s was intended to make the Chinese socialism more efficient and effective both economically and administratively, thereby consolidating the CCP's one-party leadership.

Legitimized by the Maoist ideology,[3] the CCP's adherence to the absolute monopoly of power had deep Stalinist roots, which can be further traced back to Marxism and Leninism. Communism, as Marx reasoned, is an alternative and superior form of modernity to that of liberal democracy based on market capitalism. The Marxist theory of social development informs that the development of industrial capitalism sows the seeds of its replacement of socialism on a global scale, though not necessarily through revolutionary means. Lenin's, and later Stalin's, contribution was to skip the stage of capitalistic development and instill socialism in a backward agrarian society by making communism a modernization project. The Marxian notion of "proletarian dictatorship" and Lenin's "vanguard of the proletariat" justified the Russian Bolsheviks' establishment of a one-party political system on the basis of which a centrally planned economic system was forged as the mobilizing tool for implementing a Gerschenkronian "catch-up" strategy to achieve modernity. In Lenin's words, "Communism is Soviet power plus the electrification of the whole country."[4] Inheriting Lenin's party state institutions and political deterministic logic, and by instituting "revolution from above," Stalin discarded Lenin's NEP and radicalized Leninism into brutal totalitarianism to accommodate the state-led heavy industrialization on the basis of massive renationalization of the economy.

The CCP was the creation of the Soviet Russian-controlled Communist International (Comintern) in the early 1920s. Its final victory was heavily indebted to Soviet military sponsorship in the Civil War (1946–1949) after World War Two. Yet the CCP's decision to "lean to one side"—the side of the USSR-led socialist camp—declared by Mao on June 30, 1949, was not purely on ideological grounds. In fact, the CCP had developed cordial relations with the USA from 1943 until 1947 just in order to avoid excessive dependence on Stalin's Russia. The American–Soviet rivalry in China against the backdrop of the intensifying Cold War eventually led Mao to side with the USSR against the USA. In June 1949, three months before the founding of the PRC, Stalin, to prevent New China from staying neutral after seizing power, promised to aid China's postwar modernization program on an unprecedented scale.[5] The USA's belated olive branch extended for roughly the same time as a Far East-version Marshall Plan aid to China, albeit not to Mao's full knowledge, could no longer change Mao's mind to ally with the Soviets.[6] Nevertheless, the door was not entirely shut between the PRC and the USA, despite Beijing's forged strategic alliance with Moscow in January 1950. It was not until China's intervention in the Korean War in June, particularly Mao's rejection of the UN's appeal for a ceasefire in the early phase of the war that the last chance of normalization of relations between China and the USA was kicked away. This largely self-imposed isolation made China a pariah state for the next two decades. The Sino-USA escalating enmity during the Korean War (1950–1953) dramatically radicalized Chinese politics, perpetuating its comprehensive economic and political Stalinization.[7] Having no other access to technology and management expertise, the PRC could only emulate the Soviet model of industrialization in its quest for modernity. Large-scale Soviet assistance ensued as a reward for China's intervention in the Korean War, as Mao had rightly anticipated.[8] Under massive Soviet sponsorship, the first Five-Year Plan (1953–1957) and the 156 heavy industrial projects were carried out with huge success, which laid the foundation for China's socialist industrialization.

Nikita Khrushchev's secret speech in February 1956 denouncing Stalin's cult of personality and "grave abuse of power" three years after Stalin's death in 1953 opened the door for reforming totalitarian communism. The huge impact that the Khrushchev Thaw engendered across the world compelled Mao to accept some degrees of de-Stalinization within his party in the same year. But he quickly struck back to "recapture his influence the following year and afterwards, to roll back [political] de-Stalinization in China."[9] Ironically, the Khrushchev Thaw, allowing diversity in building socialism, enabled Mao to pursue a "Stalinist road to socialism" in a more radical way.[10] Mao's vision was to surpass the Soviet "big brother" to become the new overlord of the communist world through faster industrialization. Discerning a number of fatal flaws in the Stalinist model, however, such as over-investment in heavy industry and over-centralization of power that held back local initiatives, Mao developed his new thinking epitomized in his report delivered to the CCP's Politburo in April 1956, titled "On the Ten-Pair Grand Relations." In it, Mao in the first instance dismissed the Stalinist heavy industrialization at the expense of light industry as a "fundamental mistake" that China had fortunately avoided. A higher ratio of state investment, Mao claimed, should flow to light industry and agriculture. Highlighting the importance of intersectoral balance, Mao ironically drew his proposition closer to that of Bukharin and Maslov—Stalin's enemies—in the 1920s' Red Russia.[11] However, such a realistic view was swiftly forsaken by Mao himself with the onset of the Second Five-Year

Plan (1958–1962), also known as the Great Leap Forward (GLF), during which the Stalinist approach of accelerating heavy industrialization was pursued in a much more irrational way, leading to a stunning economic disaster—the Great Famine—that cost dozens of millions of innocent lives in rural China.

Another "invention" of Mao was decentralizing power to the localities. He put the idea into practice in 1958 with an extra intention to spur on the GLF. Yet he was preceded by Khrushchev, who decentralized economic management in 1957 on similar grounds that "top-down decision-making did not provide incentives for initiative and innovation."[12] Motivated by different end goals, decentralization ended up in "total chaos"—economic anarchy—in both countries, as well as the Great Famine in China. This kind of administrative decentralization stood no chance of success for it had disrupted the vertically integrated supply chains across regions that only tight central planning could have managed through a top-down command system under state socialism. Forced to recentralize the economy, China and the Soviet Union stepped on different paths of "self-perfection of socialism." Abandoning the rather limited experiments of market socialism in the 1960s, the Soviet reformers such as Alexei Kosygin resorted to material incentives and strove for computerized "optimal" planning through the installation of "automated management systems" in the 1970s, though were largely unsuccessful in the end.[13] Mao's China, by contrast, clung to the Stalinist "crude planning method," despite having adopted some NEP-like liberal policies in the ensuing few years when the Great Famine was coming to an end in 1962, to cope with the "much less technologically complex" industrial activities characterizing the early-stage socialist industrialization.[14] The recurrent ossification of the planning system, however, prompted Mao to decentralize again in 1970 during the heyday of the Cultural Revolution. This time, Mao was using decentralization as an incentive to foster provincial autarky (self-sufficiency) in preparation for the perceived large-scale war with the two superpowers, the USSR in particular.[15]

Provincial autarky became institutionalized even after the war threat from the USSR evaporated in the wake of the Sino-US rapprochement from the early 1970s onward. As an unprecedentedly strong state in Chinese history, Mao's China dwarfed the pre-1949 Nationalist regime in achieving genuine unification of the country politically, thereby making national economic reintegration a reality.[16] Fragmenting the national market, nonetheless, the building of intranational autarky rendered Mao's revolutionary strong state inadequate in terms of its normative role in sponsoring national development first and foremost through generation of economies of scale in an empire-sized unified national market. Needless to say, market integration is crucial to any type of modern economy—market-based, planning-based or a mixture of both. The American industrialization in the late nineteenth century succeeded to a large extent, thanks to the country's huge domestic market in which state governments were not entitled to "regulate inter-state commerce."[17] The European Single Market (ESM) was even more integrated than that of the USA, and "the most economically integrated."[18] As the most advanced socialist economy in the Second World, East Germany adopted a vertical integration approach, the "Kombinat," under tight central planning, which operated highly efficiently on the back of the vast markets of not only the Soviet-led Council for Mutual Economic Assistance (COMECON) but also the ESM to which the East German industrial products were given privileged access.[19] Prone to diseconomies of scale arising from market segmentation, Mao's provincial autarky made little economic sense. By fusing economic feudalism and crude planning at the center, Mao fostered the worst blending of two most inefficient institutions in his futile attempt to transcend the Soviet Union's advanced socialism.

Until his death in 1976, Mao left behind him a diversified economy. This was a rare feat many developing nations had failed to attain at comparable stage of development. Having established a heavy industrial base, Mao's China achieved a preliminary industrialization but paid a dreadful price for that. The GLF cost tens of millions of lives in peacetime. The vast countryside remained extremely impoverished as a result of "internal colonization," an approach of "socialist primitive accumulation," by which the urban kept extracting surplus from the rural through a so-called scissor-pricing mechanism to fund the industrialization. City dwellers did not live a significantly better life either.[20] Rampant goods shortages kept the savings rate artificially high, which also financed the industrialization. Despite these forced accumulation policies, the industrial workforce barely increased and peaked around 70 million. Behind the "frozen" industrial employment was the negative technological contribution to TFP (–1.2% per annum), implying paradoxically that a large portion of state investment had been wasted.[21]

In a nutshell, Mao's industrial revolution made little headway in both poverty reduction and catch-up. Despite having achieved a relatively high rate of economic growth, China's share in world gross national product (GNP) did not increase but declined from 4.7% in 1955 to 1% in 1978,[22] even lower than that of Qing China at its nadir (17%).[23] A large portion of the population lived in extreme poverty.[24] Except for a handful of military-related industries, the country's civilian sectors were rather primitive and backward technologically and lagged far behind most of its Second World socialist counterparts, not to mention the advanced market economies of the USA, Western Europe, and Japan. It could not even match South Korea and Taiwan in both people's standard of living and technological development.[25] This contrasted sharply with Stalin's Russia in the 1920s and 1930s whose rapid industrialization not only made the USSR a recognized industrial power but also politically dwarfed the industrial West being plagued by the Great Depression (1929–1933), thereby making Soviet communism an appealingly potent alternative to the capitalist modernity.[26] Failing to generate profound economic transformation, Mao's approach to industrialization did not make China the Soviet-type advanced socialism, but rather made it an economically and technologically backward "agrarian socialism," as coined by Wang Xiaoqiang.[27]

Such an outcome was the corollary of developmental Maoism. But for the fanatically idealistic Mao, drawing wrong lessons in the aftermath of the GLF, retrospectively speaking, ideological purity was much preferred to modernity, at least in the short run. As he saw it, economic backwardness would be easily overcome by arousing the initiatives of the people—the so-called spiritual atomic bomb. What deserved serious concern was the "changing of color" of the Chinese socialist regime due to state capture by the intra-party revisionist power-holder, "the capitalist roaders," such that the CCP would probably be transformed into a fascist party someday in the future.[28] Those revisionists' quest for modernity would not likely be a genuine modernization built on the basis of self-reliance as well, but one of comprador capitalism characterized by the country's inextricable dependency on and subordination to the imperialist powers economically and politically.[29] The Cultural Revolution, as Mao saw it, was exactly meant to kick-start an enduring sociopolitical revolution with a view to transforming human nature (*dousi*) on the one hand, and the periodic purging of the nomenclatura, especially hidden intra-party capitalist roaders (*pixiu*) by virtue of the so-called great democracy (*da minzhu*)—a type of totalitarian democracy—in the form of "dictatorship by the masses" (*qunzhong zhuanzheng*) on the other.

Conceivably, Mao's utopian approach to purifying socialism was doomed from the very outset given the impracticality of both goals (dousi, pixiu), not to mention the fact that he had never intended to destroy the highly disciplined communist party that was crucial to the vibrancy of the totalitarian party state, replacing it with a Chinese "Paris Commune" even on a parochial basis.[30] The so-called *qunzhong zhuanzheng* existed only in the first two years of the Cultural Revolution, ending up in the "revolutionary rebels" (*zaofanpai*) being brutally suppressed by the bureaucrats still in power with Mao's explicit endorsement.[31] Mao's betrayal highlighted the instrumental and hypocritical essence of the "great democracy" and the limits of his seemingly omnipotent authority. Before he passed away in September 1976, he had been acutely aware of the ultimate failure of his last revolution.[32] A full-blown resurrection of the bureaucracy after his death had become utterly unavoidable. Yet he helplessly bet his legacy on an illusion, as Zhang Chunqiao, his bona fide follower and key member of the Gang of Four, claimed afterward, that the "Mao Zedong thoughtified revolutionary masses" would slavishly follow his ideological dictates to rise up sooner or later to rebel against the capitalist roaders by dint of their "civil rights"— enshrined in PRC's constitution in 1975, also known as the Four Great Freedoms, namely, "speaking out freely, airing views fully, holding great debates, and writing big-character posters."[33]

Mao's tragedy lies in the fact that the anti-law nature of totalitarianism rendered the masses' constitutional rights uninstitutionalizable. More importantly, he did not realize that his era of revolutionary extremism was gone forever and was forgone by the increasingly enlightened Chinese people, who as human beings were naturally inclined to pursue wealth and freedom, and by the bureaucracy that had been traumatized so much by the Cultural Revolution, particularly the "great democracy." As a matter of fact, the Cultural Revolution began to alienate itself in the immediate aftermath of the Lin Biao Incident in September 1971. Quite a number of urban middle-school and college students, known as the "educated youth" (*zhishi qingnian*) who were initially used by Mao to purge the revisionists, then sent to the countryside to eschew massive unemployment in the urban areas under the pretext of "receiving re-education from the peasants," were shocked by the incredibly extreme poverty of the socialist countryside. Those intellectually *avant garde* began questioning Mao's utopian socialism. Their rethinking of Maoism was inspired by the Lin Biao Incident and deepened by accessing not only the original works of Marx and Lenin but also a good deal of translated foreign books forbidden to the general public but allowed to circulate among the intra-party senior cadres in the pre-Cultural Revolution years. One such an inspiring book was *New Class: Analysis of Communist System* written by the exiled veteran Yugoslavian communist Milovan Djilas.[34] From then on, their faith in the infallibility of Maoism, though not necessarily by extension the entire communist system, was severely shaken.

For the post-Mao leadership in the wake of the fall of the Gang of Four, change became inevitable. Kornai argued that change in socialist states "that moves away from the classical system in some direction is compelled by the accumulated tensions and contradictions." There are four groups of symptoms of inducement to change: *accumulation of economic difficulties, public dissatisfaction, loss of confidence by those in power*, and *outside example*.[35] In 1976, China exhibited all of these symptoms, overshadowed nonetheless by one extra and more intractable challenge in its own right: poverty—a symptom which sufficed to delegitimize the Communist regime as per classical Marxism and Leninism.[36] However, these symptoms were not entirely the products of the Cultural Revolution. One unintended consequence of the Cultural Revolution was that the very need for its self-justification from the outset had entailed a thoroughgoing revelation of a myriad of dark sides of the old regime (1949–1966). Thus, the havoc the Cultural Revolution wrought on the party state and the resultant "crisis of belief" across the nation made any attempt of prospective rulers to resume the harsh rule of the old totalitarian regime virtually impossible. Lenin once argued that a revolutionary situation emerges when "it is impossible for the ruling classes to maintain their rule without any change" and when "'the lower classes [do] not want' to live in the old way."[37] The Cultural Revolution, whose devastation led to its eventual self-denial, though, was launched ironically on the basis of discrediting the pre-Cultural Revolution old regime. No longer able to rule "in the old way," the rehabilitated bureaucratic elites, resentful of any prospective sociopolitical revolutions ever since, were left with only one option with regard to the regime's self-help: reform and opening.

As a matter of fact, many of the beneficiaries of Mao's Cultural Revolution within the Politburo—barring the Gang of Four—such as Vice-Premier Ji Dengkui, had realized even before Mao's death that China must change.[38] This strong consensus, cemented by their common pragmatism in addressing Mao's utopian debacle, was in the first place driven by the need to justify the de facto coup led by Mao's handpicked successor Hua Guofeng, internal security chief Wang Dongxing, and Marshal Ye Jianying—all being beneficiaries and trusted by Mao—against the Gang of Four through denouncing the Cultural Revolution as a national disaster. The Gang of Four rather than their mastermind Mao were conveniently held to account. Hua Guofeng was among the first senior leaders to declare that the national economy by the end of the Cultural Revolution was almost "on the verge of collapse." He told the NPC deputies in his Government Work Report in February 1978 that sabotage of the Cultural Revolution had cost total industrial output at 100 billion yuan, steel output 28 million tons, and fiscal revenue 40 billion yuan in the years between 1974 and 1976.[39] Vice-Premier Li Xiannian estimated at the National Planning Conference in December 1977 that the Cultural Revolution had caused losses to national income at 500 billion yuan, equivalent to 80% of China's capital construction, which was greater than the total fixed-asset investments in the three decades since 1949. Li declared that during the ten-year Cultural Revolution, five years recorded economic growth of less than 4%, three years for negative at -5.7% for 1967, -4.1% for 1968, and -1.6% for 1976, respectively.[40]

The "verge of collapse" thesis became an indisputable standard narrative ever since, which, from a strictly analytical perspective, overstated

China's economic plight in 1976.[41] Yet for the post-Mao leadership headed by Hua at the juncture, such a narrative was conducive to dispelling widespread global suspicions of an impending campaign of de-Maoification, the legend of which the arrest of the Gang of Four had naturally engendered.[42] Bringing down the Gang of Four, however, did not strengthen the authority of Hua, but rather put him in an increasingly difficult position for the simple reason that the *coup* had created a power vacuum to be justifiably filled by the revisionists "purged" by the Gang of Four (not Mao), Deng Xiaoping in particular, whose return to the power center became hard to resist, thereby shifting the power balance increasingly in his disfavor. Under such circumstances, Hua's removal was just a matter of time. Paradoxically, nonetheless, contrary to the ex post official evaluation imposed on Hua, his political demise was caused not by his alleged economic and political conservatism that made him an anachronism but his pragmatism and weak-willed personality. Had he truly followed the "Two-Whatevers" in practical terms,[43] there would have been little chance of Deng's re-rise in such a short span of time. In fact, it was Hua who first called for shifting the priority of the party to speeding up China's modernization, as early as December 1976. He also gave his explicit support, without Deng's involvement in any way, for expanding importing technologies from the capitalist First World in June 1978. It was Hua rather than Deng that gave first support to the creation of China's first Special Economic Zone (SEZ) in Shenzhen.[44] As Mao's handpicked successor, Hua did have little incentive to initiate de-Maoification at least in the short run. But he was by no means the stumbling block to China's post-totalitarian transition in the early post-Mao years.[45] Ironically, it was Deng rather than Hua who forcefully brought the embryonic intra-party intellectual backlash against Mao to a sudden halt in early 1979.[46]

Deng's defense of Mao was out of necessity, in that unlike Stalin in the Soviet Union, "Mao is both [China's] Lenin and Stalin."[47] He himself had remained a staunch Maoist until the early 1960s.[48] In the face of the spontaneous intra-party "mental emancipation" (*sixiang jiefang*) drive that Deng had been involved in and encouraged proactively at the very beginning, such as the widely noted acclaim he gave to the Democracy Wall Movement in late 1978,[49] he swiftly sensed the danger that an unbridled de-Maoification would eventually backfire not only on himself and the entire leadership but also on the communist totalitarianism per se. Thus, Deng forcefully put a break on the *sixiang jiefang* initiative by imposing the "Four Cardinal Principles," namely, upholding the socialist path, the people's democratic dictatorship, the leadership of the CCP, and Marxism–Leninism and Mao Zedong Thought, in March 1979, the hard core of which was unequivocally the CCP's absolute monopoly of power. Following this was the merciless crackdown on the Democracy Wall activists. Deng's entrenched power position vis-á-vis Hua was allegedly responsible for his authoritarian "turn." As Chen Yan put it, Deng's embrace for *sixiang jiefang* only served the purpose of "power seizure" (from Hua) rather than "power consolidation."[50] However, the "turn" was just superficial. Deng's strongly authoritarian personality had been consistent and cemented by his deep-seated conviction that a disorderly and chaotic society typified as a "dish of loose sand" characterizing the pre-1949 old China that would derail the national objective of modernization. The Cultural Revolution, as Deng saw it, was precisely such a tragedy of historical repetition. Therefore, the erstwhile highly disciplined CCP, which was deemed by Deng as being crucial to China's modernization drive, must be reconsolidated to restore law and order.

Deng's obsession with power and authority did not suggest that he desired to become a Mao-type absolutist ruler. He had neither the kind of authority or charisma, nor the thought-making capability to rival Mao. Although an indisputable strongman in the post-Mao era, Deng knew his own limitations quite well and sought instead the willing collaboration of the bureaucracy. The party elders, having drawn painful lessons from the Cultural Revolution, would not tolerate the rise of a new totalitarian dictator either. Thus, in the wake of Hua's removal, collective leadership was reasserted in line with the Leninist principle of "democratic centralism." Despite being overshadowed by informal politics by which the eight revolutionary veterans (*balao*) wielded immense power from within the party state institutions, including the CCP's highest decision-making body, the PSC, this sort of "intra-party democracy" that existed only at the top of the pyramid of power did erect some types of checks and balances among the septuagenarian political heavyweights—all of Mao's generation—particularly between Deng Xiaoping and Chen Yun.

Chen Yun was another revolutionary veteran and one of the founding fathers of the PRC with even "slightly greater seniority"[51] than Deng. Concomitant with the rebuilding of collective leadership was the removal from the PRC's constitution of the Four Great Freedoms in the year of 1982, signifying that by outlawing the so-called *qunzhong zhuanzheng*, the "dictatorship by the bureaucracy" was reinstituted. Nevertheless, partly as compensation, and partly feeling somewhat guilty to the Chinese people for its past misdeeds,[52] the Communist regime incrementally relaxed social control to allow greater room for social organizations to grow and thrive, albeit under the party's tight surveillance, and greater tolerance for free expression. Similar to post-Stalin Russia, the Chinese rulers also adopted a similar approach akin to the "social contract" by setting out to deliver prosperity in exchange for people's political obedience.

The CCP's post-totalitarian turn, driven by the bureaucratic entrenchment notwithstanding, to some sort of benign authoritarianism was received with much gratitude among the people, especially those persecuted intellectuals who had just been rehabilitated by Deng Xiaoping's close aide, Hu Yaobang, an upright veteran communist, who was then in charge of the CCP's powerful Central Organization Department (COD). Political de-Maoification in the limited sense of ending the harsh class struggle thus sparked hope and faith of making Chinese socialism more humane. Against such a backdrop, the forfeit of "constitutional rights"—the Four Great Freedoms—did not significantly upset the Chinese people, who were not even touched by Deng's crackdown of the Democracy Wall Movement. Deng was as popular as ever before among the people. The deeper reason was that during the initial years after the Cultural Revolution, memories remained alive for quite many people of the turbulence and massive violence brought by the "great democracy" during the Cultural Revolution. They feared and resented intuitively any prospective uncertainty a national disorder under whatever pretext would bring to make their lives miserable again. For the vast majority of the Chinese people, their overriding aspiration was the coming back of the kind of perceived "moderate communism" in the 1950s in lieu of the brutal Maoism.[53] As they hoped for it, order and better life were far more important than and henceforth preferred to freedom and democracy. They trusted Deng Xiaoping and regarded him as the new hope of China.

The 1980s, its first half in particular, was the happiest moment Chinese intellectuals had experienced since 1949. Their social status and influence grew rapidly. This was in large part to do with the indispensable role they were expected to play in the relaunched modernization drive presided over by Deng Xiaoping. They were deeply grateful to Deng personally, who not only freed them from the humiliation and disgrace imposed by anti-intellectualist Maoism but also reclassified them as the constituent part of the "working class"—the leading class in the PRC's constitution. Deng's appeals for "respect for knowledge and talents" further resurrected the once-dormant imperial tradition of absorbing the intellectuals into the establishment in exchange for their collaboration. The ensuing state-rebuilding, with a view to normalizing and modernizing the state in lieu of Mao's half-modern revolutionary state,[54] that entailed professionalization of the bureaucracy drove massive expansion of the bureaucracy staffed by a vast number of new college graduates. Such modernity-oriented state-rebuilding thus provided unprecedented chances for upward social mobility, regardless of class affiliation of the elite candidates. Benefiting from these revolutionary changes, many intellectuals were truly captivated by the vision of a vibrant socialism that could be self-perfected through reform.

The 1980s was such an exciting moment as the intellectuals had never been so close to the power center before since 1949. Upon returning to Beijing from the countryside, a group of ambitious educated youth, mainly the princelings and their kindred spirits, engaged in intense socialization with a clear aim to change China in a most efficient way through helping the CCP "scientify" (*kexuehua*) its decision making based on innovative ideas. Backed by strong blood ties with the party elders, they managed to break through the maze of bureaucratic rules to build quasi-dialogue links with the highest authority. The creation of the State System Reform Institute (SSRI) in 1984 stood for the formalization of such a nexus into a regular official *danwei* (work unit) that served as the de facto "general staff" of the State Council to directly aid Premier Zhao Ziyang in designing concrete reform scenarios. Unlikely to be replicated a second time, notwithstanding, the extraordinary success they had achieved in securing condescending collaboration of the state reinforced their previous belief that the communist system was reformable and could be reformed from within by highly gifted people like them.[55] Their success story emboldened a great number of like-minded young intellectuals from different family backgrounds to join the regime. However, their vision for a self-perfected Chinese socialism shortly fell apart, thanks to the paradox generated by Deng's distinct approach of "perestroika without glasnost." Short of ideological justifications, such an approach based on sheer pragmatism only hardened the Deng–Chen dichotomy regarding the role of the market within the confines of state socialism, thus rendering any market-based socialist-oriented alternative virtually unlikely.

Deng's Pragmatism: The Sole Solution?

Hua Guofeng's removal in 1981 ushered in the new era of Deng Xiaoping who had become the de facto "leading core" in the Third Session of the CCP's Eleventh Central Committee in December 1978.[56] Deng promoted two of his henchmen in 1980–1981 as his helpers, Hu Yaobang as the General Secretary (the nominal paramount leader of the CCP) and Zhao Ziyang as the Premier. He himself controlled the People's Liberation Army (PLA) under the title of the Chairman of the Central Military Commission (CMC) of the CCP. Staffed mainly by the *balao* and their close aides, the new Politburo leadership agreed that Mao's *backward socialism* must be reformed. This dwarfed the Soviet Union in the first half of the 1980s where senior leaders preceding Gorbachev were even reluctant to mention the term "reform" for its being reminiscent of the Prague Spring put down by Soviet tanks in 1968.[57] Fortunately for the Chinese, it was precisely the devastation of the Cultural Revolution that made the reform in China relatively easy, at least ideationally, despite economic de-Maoification in whatever way: optimizing central planning, emulating market socialism, remained an outstanding issue in practical terms. Following the successful rural reform in the first half of the 1980s, the economic reform that ensued in urban areas became the focus of controversy, which swiftly evolved into intensifying power struggle between the market faction led by Deng Xiaoping and the planning faction led by Chen Yun.

Deng's rapid rehabilitation in less than a year after the end of the Cultural Revolution was almost entirely attributed to the strong support of Chen Yun and Ye Jianying,[58] who deemed Deng the right statesman after Mao to lead China toward national revival. With collective leadership put in place, Chen Yun seized control of the Central Disciplinary and Inspection Committee (CDIC) and the COD, both of which were key organs of the CCP's nomenclatura system. These political resources, added to his revolutionary career and prestige, made him a heavyweight capable of counterbalancing Deng in the post-Mao era. As the CCP's most renowned economic expert, Chen Yun was entrusted to tackle macroeconomic adjustment from 1979 until 1981. Hua Guofeng was made the scapegoat for having pursued an over-ambitious modernization agenda, nicknamed "import-financed Great Leap Forward" (*yang yuejin*). Regardless of national fiscal constraints, the *yang yuejin* resulted in acute structural imbalances and economic overheating. Ironically, the no less significant role Deng had played in encouraging the *yang yuejin* was intentionally ignored as he was then politically allied with Chen Yun in plotting to bring down Hua. Admitting the irreplaceable role Chen Yun had been playing in stabilizing the Chinese economy since 1949, Deng agreed that Chen Yun should have the final say in economics.[59]

This obviously did not imply that from then on the strong-minded Deng voluntarily relinquished the economic reform initiatives. On the contrary, he regained the initiative in 1984,[60] the year he made his first tour to Shenzhen, one of the four Special Economic Zones (SEZs) and the most economically dynamic area neighboring Hong Kong. He forcefully rolled back attacks on his open-door policies, especially on Shenzhen from the intra-party ideologues and the central planners, both having Chen Yun's blessings, who thought that Deng's reform had gone too far toward capitalism. The subsequent tug of war over China's reform agenda seemed to suggest further that the Deng–Chen divide during the 1980s was that between a pro-market reformer and an anti-market conservative. Such a long-held cliché in the first instance misconstrued the different role-plays of both people in economic statecraft. As the economic tsar, Chen Yun played a role similar to that of the executive vice-chairman of the board of directors (BOD) in a big firm, who, strangely though, also held the post of chief financial officer (CFO) committed to the principle of financial prudence. Deng in contrast played a role similar to that of a non-executive chairman, whose overriding concern was achieving visible gains instantly so as to please the stockholders. Aging yet still energetic, Deng was eager to see swift transformation of the economy and society. His fanatic zeal for high growth rate was mingled with and to a great extent contributed to his radical thinking on economic reform. This drove him to being at loggerheads with Chen Yun in general terms.

In reality, the Deng–Chen division over economic reform was not about overhauling China's state socialism but about the pace of reform and how to handle the market-planning relationship within the state socialist framework. The terms "market faction" and "planning faction" were hereby used only to highlight the relative emphasis on the role of the market given by each side in exploring a feasible reform agenda. Deng and Chen were both reformers not contented with the calamitous practice of developmental Maoism. They had developed a good working relationship in the early 1960s to jointly grapple with the GLF. As pragmatic practitioners, they both believed in "seeking truth from facts." After the Cultural Revolution, they converged on unleashing market forces to reinvigorate the moribund socialist economy and on importing foreign technology to accelerate China's modernization. In a nutshell, their difference was that between a radical and a moderate reformer.[61] As a matter of fact, the first mention of "[developing] market economy" was made not by Deng Xiaoping but by Chen Yun in early 1979; Deng expressed a similar view later that year,[62] despite the fact that the term "market economy" was used to refer merely to its dispensable yet subservient role to central planning.[63] In addition, Chen Yun, along with Deng Liqun, a party veteran subsequently labeled by the liberal intellectuals as an anti-reform ultra-leftist heavyweight, preceded Deng in the late 1970s and early 1980s in unambivalent support of decollectivizing the rural economy while Deng, like the majority of the party elders, was initially opposed to it.[64]

Although not a born market believer bent on embracing a market-oriented economic reform from the very outset, Deng was the kind of revolutionary well known for his toughness, flexibility and pragmatism.[65]

Strong-willed as he was, Deng would do resolutely as he saw fit. A notable example was his swift turning to support the rural decollectivization, which led to a sweeping nationwide dismantling of the commune system, a most daring measure of de-Maoification under his sponsorship. Deng's rupture with Chen Yun began to intensify from 1984 onward when China's economic reform was shifted away from the rural to the urban. Throughout the 1980s, nonetheless, Deng never objected to Chen Yun's insistence on the centrality of central planning. He did so not merely out of expediency given the political correctness Chen Yun's view embodied, but more importantly due to ideational limitations, henceforth lack of alternatives. As a veteran communist leader, Deng knew quite well the limits the communist dogma and institutions set on his reform initiatives. Yet, as an unconventional statesman, he also knew most profoundly the vital importance of overruling dogma rather than being overruled by it.

Not constrained by any dogma, Deng was by no means a devout believer of the planning economy. He was once put in charge of economic rectification in 1974–1975 and was to certain extent aware of the deficiency of the planning system. In addition, he did not have a personal stake in the PRC's first Five-Year Plan (1953–1957) as Chen Yun did, thus having little historical burden and incentive to cling to it. For Chen Yun, nonetheless, the planning economy was what characterized the socialist system and made socialism superior to capitalism both theoretically and practically, as most convincingly evidenced by the successful industrialization of the Soviet Union. Vowing to perfect central planning whereby the Chinese socialism would be consolidated economically and politically, Chen Yun viewed economic stability based on intersectoral balance and moderate growth rate as the top priority. Unsympathetic to over-centralization though, Chen Yun's adherence to central planning was also in part to do with the impact of political crisis in Poland where the Solidarity Movement led by Lech Walesa arose out of the country's economic plight. Among the senior leaders who were all shocked and upset by the Polish crisis, Chen Yun paid particular attention to the economic origin of the crisis. Identifying economics and propaganda as the two main triggers for regime collapse[66]—the former in particular—Chen Yun believed more firmly than ever that a tighter control of the economy through strengthening state planning was imperative. This particular belief made up his most famous "birdcage" theory: liberal market forces must be contained within the framework of state socialism characterized by public ownership and central planning; in other words, planning rules the market.[67]

Caging the market, a "moderate Leninist approach"[68] invented by Chen Yun, was essentially a revised version of the NEP, in the sense that it did not seem to be a "*temporary* retreat to state capitalism"[69] as Lenin had envisioned in the 1920s when the Gosplan (State Planning Committee) was just created and was far from becoming entrenched. It was rather a highly institutionalized way of utilizing and restricting, if not transforming, the forces of capitalism under state socialism.[70] Theoretically traceable to Leninism, Chen Yun's "birdcage" thesis was congruent with the vague intra-party consensus on the necessity of reform along *socialist* lines. By maintaining ideological coherence in such a way, the prudent economic tsar made himself the ardent defender of Chinese socialism. This in turn not only rendered him immune to criticism politically but also bolstered his position within the party. Deng instead conceived the "cage" in a different way. As he saw it, the "cage" was a political rather than an economic one which could be made bigger. Market forces should be given a greater role to play without having to worry about the consequences as long as the party's absolute monopoly of power remained uneroded. As Zhao Ziyang later recounted in his house arrest, "in Deng's eyes, as long as the political power was tightly held in the hands (of the CCP), he did not care about any method in economics (socialist or capitalist)."[71]

Inclining himself to political determinism made Deng resemble Lenin in this regard. This did not however prevent him from choosing to be a Marxist by holding to economic determinism, believing that economic success was the panacea for everything. After all, theses of Lenin's "temporary retreat" and Chen Yun's "birdcage"—"either as a temporary measure in the transition from capitalism to socialism, or as [a] characteristic of socialism itself,"[72]—did not radically depart from classical socialism.[73] But would Chinese socialism still be kept in place politically by way of embracing market capitalism in an economically unconstrained way, as Deng perceived it? That did not seem to haunt Deng at all who, as always, was obsessed with his most famous "Cat Theory": *a cat is a good cat so long as he catches the mouse.* He even openly suggested to a visiting African leader "not [to] do socialism; ... So long as it helps to improve the people's standard of living, you may call it whatever 'ism' as you wish later on."[74] Understandably, Deng's politically incorrect remarks were unlikely to be made public to the party members, as they completely removed the ideological cloak of the social contract, pointing to a deeply embarrassing fact: like Leonid Brezhnev (1906–1982)—General Secretary of the Communist Party of the Soviet Union (CPSU)—in his late years, Deng as the paramount communist leader in the 1980s' China was losing faith in communism. Their difference lay in the fact that Brezhnev regarded communism as a "deceptive nonsense"[75] in an already advanced socialist society; whereas Deng dismissed communism as no longer relevant to China both as an end goal and as a modernization project.

Deng's ultimate concern was unequivocally non-ideological: the CCP's permanent monopoly of power rather than ideological purity in any sense. His ideological apathy might in the first instance arise as an ironic reaction against the "not-insignificant role" he had played in leading the *absurd* Great Debate with the Soviet Union over ideological purity in the early 1960s.[76] In contrast to Chen Yun who maintained good relations with the Soviets after 1949 and admired the Soviet system in its entirety,[77] Deng resented the Soviet way ever since largely due to his personal experience. His continued aloofness toward Soviet communism in the reform era was reinforced by the unexpected huge success of the rural reform and the "outside model" of capitalist modernity in particular. Keeping a watchful eye on global development against the backdrop of the ongoing Cold War, Deng shrewdly sensed the decline of the socialist East in the prolonged economic warfare with the capitalist West after World War Two. The amazing prosperity of the Global North he witnessed during his visits to Japan, Singapore and the USA in 1978 and 1979 convinced him of the efficacy of the market. Now that socialism had become something of which nobody within the party could give a clear-cut definition,[78] anything conducive to creating prosperity, his pragmatic intuition informed, could be done under the banner of socialism.

Deng's Machiavellian pragmatism irrespective of ideological implications, however, by no means implies that he could do whatever he wanted. First of all, since all theories about market-based solutions would have to be imported from the capitalist West, Deng was unable to resort to Marxist or Leninist orthodoxy to theorize and vindicate those market-oriented reform practices that presumably went beyond either Lenin's NEP or Chen Yun's "birdcage," even if the overarching institutional framework of state socialism remained untouched. His thesis of the so-called preliminary stage of socialism (PSS) propounded at the Thirteenth National Party's Congress in October 1987 only highlighted the awkward opportunism of his reformist camp in a futile attempt to justify his pro-capitalist experiments. This rendered him defenseless to constant attacks, though in an indirect way, from the ideologues and central planners who used the "Four Cardinal Principles" he had invented to oppose his backslide to capitalism. Deng was no match for Mao, incapable of either imposing his will upon the suspicious party still imbued with the communist dogma, or vanquishing his rivals, Chen Yun in particular, by virtue of a bitter "line struggle." Rather, he had to count on the support of the nomenclatura and consensus building with the party elders. As nothing could justify his market reform except instant economic success, Deng, as a political strategist, was adamant to take actions and was ready to retreat if necessary, sometimes even at the expense of political ethics.[79]

Politically tactful and resourceful as he was, Deng did figure out a distinct way of getting things done: "eschewing controversy" (*bu zhenglun*), on the one hand, and verbally upholding socialism on the other. By so doing, Deng did manage to muddle though. Yet such a blatant ideological insincerity, coupled with the deconstructive power of the market-oriented reform per se, fundamentally eroded communism both as a belief system and the ideological foundation of the Communist regime. This exacerbated the belief crisis that had been ameliorated in the early reform years and discredited the reform consensus on the self-perfection of Chinese socialism within and outside of the party. Deng's intuitive fear of social disturbance reinforced his resolve to tighten control. Meanwhile, his unswerving determination to preserve the one-party dictatorship at all costs[80] led him, from 1983 onward, to join hands with the party elders, for or against his market reform, to suppress the liberal intellectuals. This led to the fall of his implicit grand alliance with the intellectuals, the majority of whom had once been the natural supporters of his market-oriented reform and modernization project in the early reform era. Alienating the intellectuals, though, Deng's inveterate political conservatism helped to cement intra-party unity in an increasingly turbulent environment.

In contrast to Gorbachev's indecision, Deng had never been hesitant to pursue his approach of "perestroika without glasnost," despite the fact that such approach was making him increasingly a lonesome reformer. Deng was acutely aware that the impediments to his market-oriented reform were not just ideational and ideological, but, far more importantly, they were institutional. Hence, starting from 1986, Deng called for a "political system reform" (*zhengzhi tizhi gaige*) several times. Deng's ultimate motivation, however, was not introducing checks and balances with a view to building the rule of law and even democracy in China, but rather optimizing the existing communist nomenclatura system by making it more efficient.[81] His staunchest reformist ally and protégé Zhao Ziyang later recalled that nobody within the CCP except Deng could rival the all-powerful Leninist party state institutions to effect a democratic transition by means of a *political [rather than a political system] reform* (zhengzhi gaige). Zhao, purposefully or not, overrated Deng's actual power, in that even the God-like Mao, who was far less circumscribed than Deng, failed miserably in the end in his futile attempt to rein in the intractable bureaucracy. In fact, Zhao was not really interested in a constitutional transition at an ostensibly improper moment. Rather, increasingly obsessed with the notion of so-called neo-authoritarianism by the late 1980s, he was anxiously longing to become a powerful "enlightened dictator" himself, comparable to Chiang Ching-kuo of Taiwan or Park Chung-hee of South Korea.[82] In this regard, despite some pro-democratic rhetoric,[83] he did not make himself markedly different from his mentor Deng Xiaoping by holding the identical belief that "China is a huge county with enormous complexities; thus, centralization of power is definitely imperative to [China's] economic development in the first place."[84]

Sandwiched by the mutually radicalizing forces of intra-party ideologues and central planners from the left and liberal intellectuals from the right, Deng, despite remaining the indisputable "leading core," was compelled to see his market reform increasingly stuck in a dilemma. What would be the next step? To re-Stalinize or Gorbachevize China? Or was there a third way in the sense of keeping the current approach of "perestroika without glasnost" going but in a different way? This seeming dilemma effectively pointed to the second major challenge facing Deng, which was much harder to address in China's ad hoc political and institutional settings: lack of talent for statecraft. Inheriting Mao's half-modern institutions hostile to technocracy, Deng fell victim to the severe paucity of statesmanlike technocratic elites to exercise exquisite statecraft in carrying out a well-defined reform and modernization strategy. Both his two protégés Hu Yaobang and Zhao Ziyang, whose respective statesmanships were not up to his expectations, were by no means the ideal candidates for their positions. In fact, Deng soon regretted their appointment as early as the 1980s[85] but could find no better replacement. There was no Chinese Dr. Hjalmar Schacht or Dr. Ludwig Erhard available from within the existing nomenclatura system to supervise economic development on his behalf. Nor were there a good number of reform-minded, consensually unified political and bureaucratic elites comparable to those in the late-nineteenth-century Meiji Japan. Having no clear idea of "what is to be done" himself, Deng did not have a well-articulated roadmap on how to modernize the economy, and through what kind of reform. His only way out seemed to be sheer pragmatism; in his own words, to "feel the stone to cross the river."[86]

Not knowing exactly how far and where he should go by feeling the stone to cross the river, nonetheless, Deng was also circumscribed institutionally by the party state discipline which, in accordance with the Leninist principle of "democratic centralism," forbade open factionalism so as to avert intra-party rupture. As a matter of fact, as an open-minded leader, Deng, despite his enduring distrust of, if not hostility to Western democracy, had once "very seriously" contemplated the possibility of "expanding intra-party democracy." Deng's vision was to reinvigorate the increasingly ossified party through regularizing intra-party competition by emulating Japan's Liberal Democratic Party (LDP). He shortly gave up for fear that the legitimized factional rivalry would cause the CCP to fall apart from within.[87] This abortive reform had a negative impact on China's development in the long term, in the sense that it institutionally forestalled a strategic compromise struck between the two major factions in terms of seeking an alternative market-based pathway of development sponsored and regulated by a reinvented "Gosplan"—a socialist developmental state with Chinese characteristics. Fighting instead under the table with no transparent rules to follow,[88] the Deng and Chen factions radicalized each other by means of solidifying a perceived planning–market dichotomy, which as a consequence, prompted Zhao's neoliberal turn in economic thinking in the late 1980s. For Deng who assumed final responsibility for the intra-party unity, his respect of Chen Yun's final say in economics was embodied in his ultimate dependence on the latter's experience to stabilize the national economy. Serving as the last resort, such dependence further reinforced Chen Yun's role in Chinese economics and politics, which ironically threw Deng himself into the "birdcage" of the economic tsar.

The 1980s: Limited Success of Reforms and Unsustained Prosperity

Portrayed by the CCP as the "chief architect" of China's economic reform after 1992, Deng Xiaoping eclipsed his erstwhile close aide Zhao Ziyang who as State Premier and the General Secretary of the CCP throughout the 1980s was the de facto chief architect. Joined by Hu Yaobang, the CCP's General Secretary from 1980 until January 1987, the so-called Deng-Hu-Zhao triad formed the backbone of the market faction within the CCP. Throughout the 1980s, Zhao had the strong backing of Deng on virtually all reform scenarios. His room for maneuver, however, was tightly circumscribed by the way Deng handled his relations with the other party elders. The formidable ideological constraints and the balance of power between Deng and Chen Yun forced Deng to compromise from time to time by deferring the agenda of reform and opening that he desired until an appropriate moment.[89] Being a long-time practitioner, nonetheless, Zhao, despite being patronized by Deng politically, sometimes distinguished himself from his mentor Deng as well as General Secretary Hu Yaobang by focusing on the actual quality of economic growth rather than mere growth rate. Utterly ignorant of economics, Deng and Hu simplistically took high growth as the symbol of economic success. Therefore, although the hard-core member of the market faction, Zhao drew himself closer to Chen Yun than to Deng in the sense of pursuing realistic economic targets, as evidenced by his implicit endorsement for Chen Yun's rationale on economic adjustment at the turn of the 1980s.[90] Being a convinced socialist, Zhao paid particular attention to the social implications of a moderate but balanced growth. He stressed steady growth (but favored high growth rate in the 1990s after being put under house arrest; see Zong (2007), p. 244), sound economic performance, and more *actual benefits* (shihui) to the people.[91] He was among the few senior leaders within the Communist leadership that gave equal weight to social justice.[92] As an idealist reformer, Zhao had a deep-seated faith in the reformability of the communist system.[93]

The 1980s ushered in an unprecedented economic boom after 1949. It was explicitly accredited by Deng Xiaoping during his famous Southern Tour in early 1992 to the efficacy of his "reform and opening" policies.[94] This is partly true. However, the economic reform in the 1980s' China was not much dissimilar to the Kosygin reform in 1965 and the "market socialist" reform in Hungary from the 1960s until the early 1980s in general. What made China unique was its extraordinary success in the rural reform and the greater stride it had made in "opening up" as compared with its Second World counterparts. The Chinese decision-makers kick-started the reform in the urban by de-overcentralizing the economy through expanding enterprise autonomy of the SOEs in 1980.[95] This was the only scenario accepted by all factions within the CCP including the most conservative State Planning Commission (SPC)—China's Gosplan.[96] In the wake of the abortive system-wide reform attempt at the macro-level in late 1986,[97] China's economic reform became deadlocked ever since.

By contrast, "opening up" was progressing relatively smoothly as it was by no means meant for the overhaul of state socialism but rather served the simple purpose of importing advanced technologies and management expertise from the capitalist West. Unlike Gorbachev's USSR until the late 1980s where efforts to open up the "advanced" socialist economy, particularly to liberalize trade and investment to even very limited extent were met with strong resistance from within and outside of the party both ideationally and practically,[98] "opening-up" had been broadly accepted in China as a necessity dating back to the late 1970s, precisely on account of the country's acute economic backwardness. Although delinked from economic reform at the outset, "opening up" incrementally exposed the country to a greater external influence than did the Soviet Union in the 1980s. A striking example was the vigorous appointment of Werner Gerich (1919–2003), a technology expert from West Germany as General Manager of the Wuhan Diesel Engine Works who served from 1984 until 1986. His overhaul effort in the image of Western capitalist firms revolutionized the way many Chinese practitioners, either enlightened officials like Zhu Rongji or SOEs' managers, understood modern corporate management.[99] Greater openness, nonetheless, was driven by the unintended consequence of technology imports at the turn of the 1980s when import surge quickly drained China's foreign currency reserve, exacerbating the central state's fiscal quandary. Deficits soared and drove up consumer prices, which alerted both Zhao and Chen Yun. Against such a backdrop, setting up joint ventures (JVs) with foreign investors was encouraged in lieu of pure technological imports with a view to ameliorating the central state's fiscal difficulty and introducing management expertise to the badly disciplined SOEs in a practically more convenient way.[100]

Despite mounting interplay of "reform and opening" toward the end of the 1980s, the main driver of China's economic reform was decidedly internal rather than external. Within the "birdcage" of state socialism, reinvigorating the SOEs was deemed to be the centerpiece of reform and the key to making market socialism work. Drawing inspirations from the rural reform, Chinese leaders developed a distinct way to expand enterprise autonomy of the SOEs by attempting to transplant the contract responsibility system (CRS) from the rural to the urban in 1983.[101] Emboldened by the instant success of the rural reform, radical reform-minded leaders aspired to repeat the success in urban industrial enterprises in one stroke. The most enthusiastic advocates were Hu Yaobang[102] and his protégé Hu Qili, a new political star who allied with Zhao Ziyang after Hu's ousting in January 1987.[103] They as party leaders grossly underestimated the complexities of economic reform in urban areas that, unlike the socially costless rural reform, involved taking on powerful vested interests of both the cadres and the industrial workers. The SOEs workers' "organized dependency" on the omnipotent party state came into being in the Mao era,[104] which nonetheless made them de facto "middle class" in the Chinese society. Despite low average nominal wages, their guaranteed access to the socialist welfare in terms of job security, free medicare, pensions, and so on constituted both the source of consumption and the institutional barrier to the deepening of market reform in the 1980s.

The nationwide CRS reform in urban areas worked for a while and came to a standstill in 1986 due to the irreconcilable conflict of interests between the state and the SOEs' managers. Under the inborn "soft budget constraints,"[105] the SOEs' managers were tempted to profit themselves as well as the workers to the maximum through over-investment to expand production without even calculating depreciation expenses. Ridiculed as "divide all, and eat up all" (*fenguang chijin*) though, this failed reform did not prevent the leadership from launching a second-round CRS reform in December 1986 to further expand enterprise autonomy. Unable to move toward ownership restructuring of the SOEs, the market reformers headed by Deng and Zhao had no other option but to see the economic reform turn into a stalemate. A compromise was reached on the eve of the Thirteenth National Party's Congress in October 1987 when Zhao Ziyang, acting General Secretary who succeeded his deposed predecessor Hu Yaobang, drafted the political report setting the tone for the Congress regarding China's economic reform: "state regulates market, market guides enterprises" (*guojia tiaokong shichang, shichang yindao qiye*). Not highlighting the centrality of planning, Zhao's carefully nuanced words were "unopposed" by all factions, including Chen Yun-led central planners.[106]

Convinced that a far-reaching market-oriented reform was crucial to the country's long-term growth on a self-sustaining basis, the market reformers, not much different from the planning faction—the conservative reformers led by Chen Yun—seemed to be not fully aware that the reform was merely a necessary condition for development. Of no less significance was an insightful and well-organized developmental strategy under the sponsorship of a strong state. As afore-mentioned, Deng had no roadmap for economic reform. His largest contribution was approving reform scenarios proposed by his close aide Zhao and sponsoring bottom-up reform initiatives.[107] Identifying himself as a great reformer, nonetheless, Deng was eager to achieve prosperity whereby to opportunistically justify his reform still in progress. Fingers crossed, similar to the Soviet economy in the 1950s that "experienced a genuine flourishing,"[108] prosperity was attained during the 1980s in China without much difficulty, thanks to the demand-side policies involving dramatic wage increases in the urban and the radical diversion of state investments from heavy industry to light industry.

It was not Deng alone—all the senior leaders in the aftermath of the Cultural Revolution agreed that compensating the people, or urban *danwei* (work unit) staff in the narrow sense, by constantly raising their wages even at the expense of state fiscal health was not only moral[109] but also necessary politically for winning the hearts and minds of the people who had lived under conditions of pervasive poverty for decades. Consumption soared due to consecutive wage rises in conjunction with the urban CRS reform without effective restructuring of the SOEs. With very few SOEs being permitted to go bankrupt under state socialism for the sake of "welfare for stability" (*huaqian mai wending*), the central state's fiscal position rapidly eroded,[110] exacerbated by the massive fiscal decentralization that Premier Zhao Ziyang vigorously promoted in 1980. These demand-side policies that caused the economy to prosper were made possible ironically on the back of the high accumulation policies in the Mao era. As Kueh rightly put it, "Without the material foundation laid by Mao, it would have been very difficult for Deng to launch his reform and open-door policy starting in 1979."[111] Throughout the 1980s, political opportunism in economic policy making permeated in the minds of not just Deng but all the senior leaders.[112] Their myopic impulse was prone to compromise China's industrialization drive by deviating from the normative objective of national development, a notion conceptualized by Wallerstein as "catching up."[113] As Zhao Ziyang recalled, Deng did not have a mature plan for China's industrial development in mind. What dominated his mindset was how to get rid of poverty as quickly as possible. It was his conviction that getting rich through whatever means must be the top priority; and only after becoming wealthy enough would China be better able to develop high-tech industries.[114]

Deng, given his pro-Ricardian propensity, utterly overlooked China's extant advantage of already being diversified economically, and of being preeminent in, though, a small number of military-related high-tech sectors. The country's vast pool of human resources composed predominantly of high-literacy urban workers, and a large science community also had shaped its potential dynamic comparative advantage. In addition, compared with the Soviet Union in the 1980s, China had a less "heavy" industrial structure in terms of capital goods in relation to consumer goods and a far less entrenched Gosplan. Therefore, normatively speaking, China was in a better position to catch up by exploiting its relative advantage of backwardness through proper industrial policies, especially uninterrupted human-capital investment, albeit time-consuming, in technical education in conjunction with the market forces. Strongly resentful of Mao's utopian communism, nonetheless, Deng held a dichotomous view with regard to "opening up" versus self-reliance whereby he simplistically dismissed the latter as the source of economic backwardness. His personal revenge against the Gang of Four after the Cultural Revolution even led him to the decision to quit the Y-10 Big-plane project that had made considerable headway by the middle of the 1980s.[115]

Deng's opportunistic pragmatism, albeit not entirely his alone, in seeking immediate benefits and success gave rise to two fatal decisions with regard to China's national development in the 1980s. One was readjusting industrial structure by diverting heavy investment from heavy industry to light industry to address the consumer goods shortage. This was also in part to do with the economic adjustment presided over by Chen Yun to rectify the "import-based Great Leap forward" (*yang yuejin*) in which over-investment in capital goods had generated huge fiscal deficits. Focusing on investing in consumer goods—an intra-party consensus involving the entire leadership—made enormous economic and political sense,[116] resulting in not merely intersectoral balance but also a domestic demand-led economic boom. This contrasted starkly with Gorbachev's ill-conceived "strategy of acceleration" (1985–1986), which continued to pour huge amounts of money into the already over-invested capital goods, mainly the machine-tool industry. By so doing, Deng dwarfed Gorbachev in terms of gaining time and credibility for the precarious reform unfolding thereafter.[117] However, China paid a high price for the nationwide "heavy-to-light" diversion as it had disrupted the technology accumulation of the country's still-backward capital goods sector.[118] The second fatal decision was entirely made by Deng, which involved transforming a good number of China's defense industry enterprises into consumer goods producers—known as the "military-to-civilian diversion" (*junzhuanmin*)—symbolizing a role change precipitated by Deng's momentous decision on disarmament announced in November 1984. With drastic cuts on defense spending, many a defense industry enterprise was restructured into low-tech producer of civilian consumer goods. For instance, some high-tech aircraft engine plants located in the country's hinterland were changed into low-tech refrigerator plants. The *junzhuanmin* drive caused a vast outflow of engineers and technicians from China's most cutting-edge industrial sectors, leading to an abrupt derailment of their technological development.

The two downgrading diversions were relatively technologically simple and economically attractive, which resulted in a triple-win: state fiscal burden alleviated, SOEs' profits and workers' income increased. Everybody was happy and cared little about the adverse effect of an artificial deindustrialization of the capital goods sector, particularly the brain-drain, would incur on China's industrial development in the long term. This was an entirely predictable consequence that had upset quite some engineers and government think tank researchers at the time.[119] Nevertheless, it was still too much for Deng to personally bear the full curse in that there was not a proper market system in the early reform years to enable commercialization of military technologies to become military–civilian dual-use technologies. In addition, the dwindling state capacity due to Zhao's fiscal decentralization rendered the central state unable to finance the defense industries in their entirety. Anyway, such situational logic should in no sense obscure the fact that the two diversions fostered not the upgrading but rather the downgrading of China's industrial structure. Thus, the prime mover of prosperity in the 1980s was not so much the country's rapid industrialization as the reversal of Mao's policy of "high accumulation, low consumption." In other words, it was primarily the two diversions that powered the input-driven extensive growth and thereby brought prosperity to China's shortage economy when the people's propensity to consume was extremely high in the first reform decade of the 1980s.

In fact, Deng's perception of a diminishing war threat, henceforth, rising expectation of a long peace in China's periphery, also drove the diversions in important ways. Since the Sino-US rapprochement in the early 1970s, China had become a de facto ally of the USA to strategically contain the Soviet Union. The ending of the Cold War more than a decade earlier in the Far East created a prolonged peaceful environment favorable for China's modernization drive. The perceived economic success of the late-comer industrializers, particularly the NIEs in East Asia, convinced Deng that forging friendly ties with, as well as opening up domestic economy to, the USA was the key to the "wealth of the nation."[120] That belief prompted China to join the international system of global capitalism in exchange for Western sponsorship of its reform and opening. Against such a backdrop, the CCP silently abandoned the old Leninist notion of "imperialism," replacing it with "hegemonism," aimed chiefly at the USSR. In addition, China distanced itself from the Third World by cutting aids and practically ceasing support for the "Southern Challenge." Like Yoshida Shigeru (1878–1967) in post-WWII Japan,[121] Deng viewed a proactive bandwagoning with the liberal order under American sponsorship the feasible shortcut to achieving "a rich nation and strong army." However, unlike Yoshida, Deng was by no means a mercantilist realist. As a dedicated believer of power politics, he was attempting to achieve a realist ends through liberal means. At the Opening Session of the Twelfth CCP's National Congress in September 1982, Deng warned the metropolitan West "never to expect China to become their *vassal state*."[122]—an exploited periphery in the capitalist world system. Such nationalist rhetoric did not draw him any closer to the Third-World dependency theorists skeptical of the world system. His vigilance against Western capitalism was more political and ideological than economic, as evidenced by his merciless crackdown on "bourgeois liberalism" influenced by "hostile foreign forces"—namely Western values and political systems.

Deng was demonstrably unaware that as China opened the door wider, his embrace of global capitalism exposed the country's startling backwardness—from "material" to "essence"—with the capitalist West to Chinese citizens. This gave rise to a deep sense of inferiority—a social psychology called "worship the foreign" (*chongyang meiwai*), which permeated across the country involving both the elites (mainly the bureaucrats and SOEs' managers) and the ordinary people. The Chinese lost their national pride and admired virtually everything foreign, and from the West in particular. Many SOEs' managers deemed it fashionable to enter into joint ventures with foreign investors regardless of whether the new business was technologically advanced or not. Misguided by economists, state media, and even senior leaders like Hu Yaobang who spared no effort to incite excessive consumption in the mid-1980s,[123] many people were amazed by the mass consumption of Western post-industrial societies. Their obsession with consumerism led them to despise industriousness and to treat "trading goods" (*zuoshengyi*) rather than "producing goods" (*zuoshiye*) as the vogue. Now that "getting rich is glorious,"[124] as taught by Deng, that justified all means; "getting rich" (*zhifu*) rather than "catching up" (*ganchao*) became the country's new development paradigm. The pervasive dire quest for making big and quick money across society thus severely deteriorated China's traditional (and socialist) work ethic including traits such as hard work, honesty, personal integrity, responsibility, and, all in all, making sacrifices for the nation. This contrasted strongly with the East Asian developmental states, for example, Japan and Taiwan, at comparable stages of economic development where their Listian pursuit of modernity through catching up was well suited to "Confucian capitalism."[125]

Zhao Ziyang as "Chief Architect"

There is no evidence to suggest that Zhao Ziyang was any different than Deng Xiaoping in adopting the above policy options. As a "frontline" practitioner, he was put in charge of concrete economic policy and reform scenarios. Many preliminary ideas concerning the market-oriented reform can be attributed to Zhao. Deng was behind the scene, shielding Zhao from assault by the political opponents. Though inept at economics, Deng was adept at making judgments and decisions by following his political intuition. Thus, although it was Zhao rather than Deng that was the de facto "chief architect" of China's economic reform,[126] it is inappropriate to downplay the role of Deng given the symbiotic relationship between the two leaders. Without the patronage of Deng, carrying forward the market-oriented reform by Zhao alone would be totally out of the question. Holding only a high school degree, Zhao was widely acknowledged as a capable leader having a remarkably better understanding and judgment of modern economics and economic policy than his peers.[127] Yet as a communist reformer, Zhao turned out to be neither an economic statist nor an economic nationalist. He put into practice fiscal decentralization in 1980 and coastal development strategy in 1988, both being his unique contributions to China's reform and opening, with an explicit liberal orientation. With the reform stuck in a quagmire in the late 1980s, he became increasingly obsessed with the neoliberal paradigm.

Supported by both Deng Xiaoping and Chen Yun, Zhao decentralized fiscal power to the provinces in 1980 in a bid to inspire local initiatives. Chen Yun gave backing to the reform as he also opposed over-centralization that stymied economic dynamism. Far beyond his expectation, however, the fiscal reform paradoxically impaired his effort to optimize central planning by following the "scientific Soviet way." With provincial autarky remaining intact, the reform transformed the provinces into powerful allocators of resources within their own spheres of influence. For the "local lords," especially those in some (not all) coastal areas like Guangdong permitted to retain most of the revenues, letting market forces function dramatically increased government revenues, thereby enabling them to invest more freely and extensively and to enrich themselves. Becoming new vested interests, many of them tended to increasingly associate themselves, though implicitly, with the market reformers at the center rather than with the central planners. The rise of the "local lords" as *intra-provincial* resource allocators in conjunction with their entitlement to regulate *inter-provincial* commerce, therefore, practically compromised the effectiveness of central planning in regulating a normatively vertically integrated national economy. Laying the institutional foundation for the eventual disintegration of the planning system in the 1990s, Zhao's fiscal reform ironically highlighted the path dependency of developmental Maoism characterized by de-centered planning and provincial autarky. Contented with this reform that facilitated market forces within the state socialist "birdcage" in a creative way,[128] after 1989, Zhao and his successors never contemplated abolishing provincial autarky to create a highly integrated national market through further institutional reform. Reinforcing path-dependent economic federalism in the Mao era, Zhao's reform paradoxically blended itself with increasing economic openness by fostering *intranational autarky* at home and renouncing *national autarky* abroad. Such a blending naturally inclined the leadership to eschew the option of a refreshingly defined pathway of market-based self-reliance premised upon, first and foremost, domestic market integration, and to move toward "outward orientation."

Zhao was an enlightened leader receptive to new ideas. He was advised mainly by the SSRI staffed by a group of physically energetic, mentally shrewd, and hard-working young researchers. They put forward reform scenarios and presented Zhao with the policy options available. They were the staunchest supporters of China's market-oriented reform and made extensive studies and in-depth enquiries at home and abroad. In early 1987, the DRC under the State Council submitted to Zhao a brief report, authored by Wu Jinglian,[129] introducing Japan's industrial policy. SSRI researchers also noticed the role of industry financing in which China and Japan shared certain similarity. This finding aroused their interest. They decided to make a visit to Japan to see what China could learn from Japan's experience. Funded by the George Soros Foundation, they made the trip to Japan in June 1987, during which they carefully investigated how MITI (Ministry of International Trade and Industry) and *Keiretsu* fostered local firms into globally competitive national champions. After returning to China, they issued a report, later developed into a book titled *The Inspirations of the Japanese Model* in early 1988. One of the authors and key investigators Cheng Xiaonong argued that for China to emulate Japan, the SPC—China's "Gosplan"—must first be reinvented into a sort of MITI, bestowing new functions in "serving" rather than "controlling" the national enterprises. His appeal for redefining the state–business relationship in the image of Japan's developmental state entailed substantial curtailment of the SPC. When he briefed Zhao on his finding after returning from Japan, Zhao just listened and made no comments, because he was being vexed by the thorny issue of price reform, an enduring headache for all reformers in the socialist states.[130]

Zhao's non-committal response signaled his inability to revamp the SPC, in that even if he was not impressed by the proposal of constructing a Chinese developmental state, unfolding a market-oriented reform entailed overhauling the SPC in a significant way. In the face of the institutional barrier to reaching a "strategic compromise" between the two factions headed by Deng and Chen Yun, as mentioned earlier, the "front-line practitioners" feud between Zhao and the central planners became a life-or-death power struggle in which each side attempted to crush the other decisively. Despite the fact that fiscal decentralization had created potential supporters for his market reform in the localities, Zhao, under the shadow of the party elders including his mentor Deng, was not in a position to factionally ally with the "local lords," who nonetheless dared not openly take sides given the party's discipline banning open factionalism. The obscure power struggle at the top also deterred them from getting involved—not to mention the fact that the nomenclatura system of appointments was firmly controlled by the Chen Yun faction. Zhao's promotion to acting General Secretary in early 1987 shortly after Hu Yaobang's downfall, albeit to his personal disliking, was the decision of Deng who resisted Chen Yun's nomination of Deng Liqun as the new chief party boss. Such an arrangement, however, did not make Zhao potentially stronger but weaker politically against the backdrop of an unfolding "political system reform" (*zhengzhi tizhi gaige*).

October 1987 ushered in the Thirteenth National Party's Congress, during which the blueprint for a "political system reform" was unfurled. According to the new party rule of separating party from government (*dangzhengfenkai*) decided at this Congress, Zhao, entrusted to design the "political system reform" scenario before the Congress, must abandon Premiership after being formally elected the General Secretary. Two of his allies within the Politburo, Wan Li and Tian Jiyun, were vetoed by the party elders as nominees for the Premiership. Li Peng became the acting Premier with the support of Chen Yun and Li Xiannian two months later. He was the son of a revolutionary martyr and adopted son of late Premier Zhou Enlai. He was previously a hydro-electric engineer who was sent by the CCP to study in the Soviet Union in the 1950s. He became a rising political star under the sponsorship of Deng Yingchao, widow of Zhou Enlai and one of the *balao*. Deng Xiaoping was a bit worried about Li's pro-Soviet proclivity. Yet he had no better candidates from his own camp and had to accept Li Peng. Li knew little about economics. He relied instead on the first Vice-Premier Yao Yilin who also headed the powerful SPC. Yao Yilin was a hard-core central planner and a dedicated disciple of Chen Yun. Although Zhao as chief party boss continued to head the CCP's Leading Group for Financial and Economic Affairs (LGFEA), losing the Premiership meant the substantial weakening of his authority in economic decision-making. Thus, the market reformers' "tentative victory" at the Congress was swiftly eclipsed by the central planners' firmer grip on economics.

As a matter of fact, after ousting Hu Yaobang in January 1987, Deng's opponents were plotting to bring down Zhao, in an attempt to isolate Deng completely from the economic reform agenda. Under such circumstances, Zhao's political survival was increasingly at stake. Zhao knew clearly that his reform had infuriated the ideologues and the central planners. One such a figure was President Li Xiannian, Politburo member and one of the *balao* allied with Chen Yun. Li was one of the few senior leaders not purged by Mao during the Cultural Revolution but instead was promoted to Vice-Premier in charge of economic management. For complicated reasons, he viewed Zhao's market reform with deep hatred,[131] warning, "[Zhao] Ziyang has learned too much of foreign things. We must tell him this cannot be done and must be discontinued."[132] Deng Liqun recalled, "Li Xiannian once asked Chen Yun ... 'Comrade Chen Yun, does Zhao Ziyang look like a capitalist-roader?' Chen replied, 'it's not a question of '*like or not*.' He definitely is a capitalist-roader. His ideas, his life and his political views, have proved he is an outright capitalist-roader.'"[133] Trusted by Deng, nonetheless, Zhao was not as soft as his predecessor Hu Yaobang. With Deng's backing, he struck back in the capacity of acting General Secretary by dissolving the Central Secretariat's Research Office headed by Deng Liqun in July 1987, a step that tremendously emboldened the market reformers and the liberal intellectuals who regarded Deng Liqun as China's *Andrei Zhdanov* (1896–1948), Stalin's ideological watchdog.[134]

Nevertheless, like Deng, Zhao had to vindicate his market-oriented reform through keeping the economy robust. Inspired by the perceived "generally sound economic performance" in the wake of the Thirteenth National Party's Congress,[135] Zhao attempted to break the reform deadlock in a roundabout way. The export boom in southeastern coastal provinces motivated him to ponder China's development strategy, whereby pro-market institutions, as he hoped for it, would grow out of the old regime. This constituted his second major contribution, known as the Coastal Development Strategy (CDS). The idea, however, was not based on his prescient constructivist vision, but rather a reflection of what had actually happened in those parts of China where the overseas investors predominantly from HKMT processed imported parts and components into end products to be re-exported to global markets by tapping into China's vast cheap labor force—a perceived East Asian Tigers' approach of export-oriented industrialization (EOI) in the 1970s and 1980s. In Zhao's view, although these investments did not bring advanced technologies, they contributed to China's trade and foreign exchange balancing, export growth and, most important of all, job creation, and therefore income growth for the migrant workers.

Zhao's ideas about CDS ripened in late 1987, which signifies his ultimate determination to renounce the country's traditional import substitution strategy of economic development.[136] He argued that China had a population of 100–200 million residing in the coastal areas slated for external integration. He believed that these areas should take full advantage of the "rare opportunity" of ongoing structural adjustment of the world economy to accelerate their economic development. The main points of the strategy were as below:

1. Developing outward-oriented labor-intensive industries;
2. Delinking from hinterland markets by *importing* raw materials from and *exporting* end products to overseas markets, commonly known as "two ends abroad," *on a large-scale* (*liangtou zaiwai, dajin dachu*);
3. Mobilizing the initiatives of non-SOEs, mainly village and township enterprises; and
4. Holding these enterprises accountable for their profits and losses and further delegating foreign trading power to qualified enterprises.[137]

Containing a hidden reform agenda, Zhao's strategy of parochial external economic integration was fully endorsed by the LGFEA and the State Council and by Deng Xiaoping who encouraged him to seize the day and implement it "resolutely and boldly."[138] Approved by the Politburo in February 1988,[139] the CDS also received positive feedback from the coastal provinces involved. However, skepticism remained and was not limited to conservative reformers. Li Peng and Yao Yilin were worried about the inflation that would be fueled by the acceleration of development of the coastal areas at a time when the national economy was already overheating. Not utterly opposed to Zhao's strategy, Chen Yun was concerned about a foreign exchange imbalance in the case of failure to massively export as anticipated. Some researchers from line Ministries doubted the feasibility of "*liangtou zaiwai*," which, as they saw it, was only suitable for small economies like the Tigers, but not necessarily so for superlarge economies such as that of China. Yang Xiaokai, a former educated youth and famous political economy scholar studying abroad at the time, managed to deliver a letter of dissent to Zhao in January 1989. In it, Yang argued that given the size of China's population, massive integration of its coastal areas into the global economy would cause global imbalance and shortages of resources, thereby incurring unfavorable changes in international politics.[140] Zhao ignored all of these caveats!

By pushing the socialist economy, though not entirely, into the capitalist world system, Zhao was basing his strategy on a substantial misunderstanding of the East Asian model of development. First and foremost, his strategy did not contain a technology policy to facilitate a higher-stage import-substituting industrialization (ISI). It had been rumored that his idea of CDS was influenced by the policy recommendation of Wang Jian, who was then a young research fellow of the SPC. Concurring with Zhao's vision of "[China] becoming part of the world economy," he advocated for "adopting a correct long-term development strategy" in an internal report submitted to the decision makers, to the effect that China should develop export-oriented labor-intensive industries whereby huge export earnings would be generated to import capital goods as the basis for implementing the second-stage import substitution of heavy and chemical industries.[141] Wang was ostensibly illustrating a typical EOI approach that the East Asian NIEs, bar the city-state of Hong Kong, had successfully carried out in the 1970s and 1980s. Zhao clarified his view a decade later that the idea of CDS was entirely his, which diverged from that of Wang Jian.[142]

Zhao's clarification, along with his fiscal decentralization reform that had significantly weakened state capacity, clearly demonstrates that he was neither an economic nationalist nor an economic statist. In lieu of *general trade*, the thriving *processing trade*[143] to be given further impetus by the CDS in coastal provinces, by definition, had little positive impact on the domestic economy, either regionally or nationally. Far more importantly, the implementation of CDS would curtail nationwide inter-sectoral linkages between China's most economically dynamic coastal areas, mainly the Pearl River Delta and the Yangtze River Delta, and other parts of the country, prompting superfluous economic diversification within the hinterland provinces,[144] thereby further fostering provincial autarky that had been reinforced by Zhao's reform of fiscal decentralization. Consequently, the two distinct contributions Zhao made to China's reform and opening, despite their efficacy in undermining central planning in important ways, severely eroded internal integration and therefore the economic and institutional foundations for China's autonomous development. Singapore's Prime Minister Lee Kuan Yew cautioned in the early 1990s, to the effect, that, for such a big country as China, the best [developmental] option was to focus on its vast domestic market to sustain long-term development.[145]

Having a limited effect on the national economy, except for powering the rapid export-led growth of some coastal areas, mainly the SEZs, Zhao's CDS was quickly eclipsed by the worsening economic situation and the failed price reform later in the year. Earlier reform efforts such as fiscal decentralization and the CRS, and the two diversions drove unprecedented prosperity from a low starting point, which was ironically made possible by Mao's policies of high accumulation in previous decades. These dividends were depleted by the late 1980s, symbolized by the failure of the SOEs to upgrade in the wake of market saturation. The SOEs' continued overproduction of consumer durables highlighted their inability to supply higher-quality, multi-variety new products to meet the consumers' changing needs, which as a consequence began to drive the economy downward. With prosperity fading, inflation set in, driven by the half-way price reform introduced in March 1985, known as the dual-pricing (*shuangguizhi*) system. Under "dual-pricing," the SOEs were allowed to sell extra-quota products on the markets at much higher market prices than those within-quota products whose prices were set or regulated by the state. Responding to price signals as such, the SOEs were tempted to expand extra-planning (quota) production for the purpose of profit maximization through speculating between the two prices. Consumer prices went up due to the slackening of central planning. With more and more SOEs suffering losses, fiscal subsidies to the SOEs, and the urban dwellers increased dramatically, which accounted for 30% of China's total fiscal revenues in 1988. The central state was forced to print money to finance public deficits, thereby further driving up inflation. The peril of stagflation, thus, radicalized both factions over how to address the dual-pricing, which became the focal point of the new price reform.

Public dissatisfaction with the negative effect of dual-pricing, such as the increasingly disordered market and corruption, was what motivated the price reform in the first place. In March 1988, Li Tieying, Director General of State Economic Restructuring Commission (SERC), argued for complete price decontrol.[146] Economist Wu Jinglian of the DRC made a similar suggestion the following month.[147] Such a shock therapy-like scenario immediately aroused the interest of Deng Xiaoping who was so impatient with the reform deadlock as to give his full backing without consulting Chen Yun and even his protégé Zhao Ziyang. Unopposed to the price reform in general whereby deficits would be reduced, Chen Yun insisted that the reform be carried out in a prudent and gradual way. Yet there has been no strong evidence to the present day to demonstrate that he had expressly objected to the rash approach to price reform.[148] On the contrary, having foreseen runaway inflation, he instructed Yao Yilin to secretly prepare for restoring full price control and re-imposing comprehensive economic regulation in advance.[149]

According to some accounts, Zhao was initially lukewarm to such a radical scenario but was forced to execute Deng's order. The lessons of price reforms in other socialist states reminded him that without overhauling the Gosplan—the hard core of the macro-control economic regime—and the SOEs in the first place, a mere price decontrol could only result in wave after wave of price hikes.[150] Zhao recounted later during his house arrest that the particular way the price reform unfolded in 1988 was simply raising ex-plant prices by the central government instead of having prices determined by the market in a manageably incremental way; such a "planning" approach stood no chance of succeeding even if it did not cause hyperinflation.[151] Nevertheless, he defended the dual-pricing system for its utility in eroding central planning, deeming it the "necessary" price given the complexities of Chinese politics.[152] Back to the summer of 1988, Zhao might have preferred continuing dual-pricing, at least temporarily, for the sake of economic stability without Deng's intervention. But time was not on his side in the face of the latter's growing impatience and simmering social grievances against dual-pricing, which had become an increasingly sensitive political issue by the late 1980s as far as its sociopolitical implications were concerned. Opening up unprecedented space for rent-seeking, dual-pricing was taken advantage of first and foremost by the princelings and the relatives of power holders at all levels of administration to enrich themselves at minimal cost. They became "the first people to get rich first"—the greatest beneficiaries of the Chinese "socialism at preliminary stage." Senior leaders, for or against Deng's reform, turned a blind eye to their families amassing huge wealth through the power-money nexus. The fact that myriads of "red families" including Zhao's and Hu Yaobang's were implicated in such self-enriching scandals[153] exposed the hypocrisy of the Communist regime's "preliminary-stage" socialist promise of "letting some people get rich first through their honest labor and legal business operations" before "common prosperity" was eventually attained.[154] Socialism was thus betrayed by the entire Communist leadership renouncing egalitarianism in its initial sense.

As the target of social resentment himself, Zhao met his Waterloo in August 1988 when the price reform caused a nationwide buying spree and hyperinflation, which seriously destabilized the economy. He brought the two-week reform to an abrupt halt and declared implementation of the "rectification of economic environment and improvement of economic order" (*zhili zhengdun*) in September. Not admitting to his own fault, Deng retreated behind the scene and acquiesced to the Chen Yun faction holding Zhao accountable for the trouble he made and re-imposing price control as the remedy. Zhao's position as nominal paramount party leader was severely weakened. His removal was just a matter of time, despite Deng's continued patronage thereafter. Deep setbacks inclined Zhao toward Milton Friedman's neoliberal notions accompanied by his growing interest in neo-authoritarianism; his younger advisers at SSRI, as Luo Xiaopeng recalled later on, were preparing privatization plans, akin to Jeffrey Sachs' shock therapy approach to be set in motion.[155] Whether

Zhao would become China's Boris Yeltsin or Chiang Ching-kuo, assuming that he emerged victorious from the subsequent Tiananmen Incident, remains an interesting counterfactual. In fact, thanks to the *zhili zhengdun*, all economic reforms were frozen up until August 1989. As such, the dual-pricing system remained unscathed.[156] Being still the hotbed of corruption and not properly addressed in a timely fashion, the dual-pricing kept discrediting the socialist promise and fueling public anger, driving the country toward the Tiananmen tragedy in the summer of 1989. Paradoxically, it was the strong-positioned central planners after Tiananmen that decided to phase out dual-pricing, replacing it with an explicitly market-oriented single pricing regime in November 1989.[157]

The 1980s was the decade of hope and despair for the Chinese. The regime's post-totalitarian turn and modern state-rebuilding, as entailed by the CCP's *Modernization Relaunch* after the Cultural Revolution gave rise to unfulfilled nationwide expectation of building an advanced socialism with a human face. Aiming at the "self-perfection of socialism," the modernity-oriented reform served the ultimate purpose of consolidating the Communist regime rather than undermining it. Thus, Deng Xiaoping's approach of "perestroika without glasnost" was demonstrably path dependent. His feud with Chen Yun was more about the pace and extent of the market-oriented reform than about its necessity within the "birdcage" of state socialism. Achieving only limited success in the 1980s, market reform gained its reputation mainly through the unprecedented prosperity driven by the demand-side policies as well as certain extent of deindustrialization in capital goods sector, both being made possible by the material foundation laid in the Mao era. This contrasts starkly with the post-Stalin Soviet economy in the 1950s that "experienced genuine flourishing" and remarkable scientific and technological leapfrogging. Lacking talents of economic statecraft, the CCP was also burdened by its ad hoc factional politics that left little room institutionally for strategic compromise between the market reformers and the central planners, thereby making it virtually unlikely to construct a socialist developmental state. Both factions had seriously ignored the country's extant advantages, particularly the vital importance of national economic reintegration. Their myopia was no more pronounced than in the way they inherited Mao's legacies in terms of decentralizing fiscal power without ending provincial autarky, and in the way they endorsed Zhao's Coastal Development Strategy. These attempts severely eroded China's internal integration and inclined the socialist economy toward "external orientation" in a largely irreversible way.

Stepping away from self-reliance, China bet its economic future on good relations with the capitalist West. The arrival of the West, however, served as a double-edged sword: opening the eyes of the Chinese and adding to their loss of national pride. The country's backwardness that had become more apparent by the late 1980s was now linked to Deng's "perestroika without glasnost." The impact of an *outside model* of both the advanced economies and its Second World counterparts undergoing profound changes, particularly glasnost and democratization in the USSR and the introduction of a multiparty system in Hungary, thus dramatically radicalized the way many intellectuals and even nomenclatura elites thought about China's future along anti-socialist (liberal democratic) lines. Nonetheless, the regime's hypocrisy in betraying socialism under the cloak of defending socialism via such "reform" measures as dual-pricing, drove China to the brink of a revolutionary turmoil. With Zhao's ousting in the wake of the Tiananmen Incident in the summer of 1989, the central planners achieved a crushing victory. But like market reformers, their victory was tentative, as the market-oriented economic reform had silently taken roots precisely on account of Zhao's distinct contributions, ironically also endorsed by the central planners, who never contemplated their corrections by committing themselves to economic nationalism and economic statism simultaneously.

1989 was the turning point for China. Harshly putting down pro-democracy demonstration did not usher in a full-blown socialist restoration, but rather the betrayal of socialism in a more thoroughgoing way, an astounding process of Chinese post-Communist transition that few inside and outside China then had correctly predicted.[158]

Notes

1. Yang Jisheng (2004), *The Political Struggle in the Era of Reform*, Hong Kong: Excellent Cultural Press, p. 17; Yang Jisheng (2015), "How China Dealt with Mao's Legacies after the Cultural Revolution?"—

Speech at the seminar on "Maoism: Perspectives half a Century later" at Keio University (Tokyo, Japan), 27/12/2015. http://yangjs001.jigsy.com/entries/general/%E6%9D%A8%E7%BB%A7%E7%BB%B3%EF%BC%9A%E6%96%87%E9%9D%A9%E5%90%8E%E4%B8%AD%E5%9B%BD%E6%80%8E%E6%A0%B7%E5%AF%B9%E5%BE%85%E6%AF%9B%E6%B3%BD%E4%B8%9C%E7%9A%84%E2%80%9C%E9%81%97%E4%BA%A7%E2%80%9D

2. This dwarfed Gorbachev's inappropriate "acceleration (uskoreniie) strategy" that eroded the credibility of perestroika. Marshall I. Goldman (1992), *What Went Wrong with Perestroika* (updated), NY: Norton, pp. 88, 94.
3. Mao's opening remarks at the First Session of the First NPC on 15/09/1954. *People's Daily*, 16/09/1954.
4. Vladimir. I. Lenin (1920), "Our Foreign and Domestic Position and Party Tasks," speech delivered to the Moscow Gubernia conference of the R.C.P.(B.), 21/11/1920. *Lenin's Collected Works* (4th English Edition), Moscow: Progress Publishers, V. 31, pp. 408–426.
5. Shen Zhihua (2009), "From Xibaipo to Moscow: Mao Declared 'Leaning to One Side,'" *Journal of Chinese Communist Party History Studies*, No. 4. http://military.china.com/history4/62/20100805/16063530.html
6. "Inside Story: US 5-billion-$ Aid to China in Case of No 'Leaning to One Side,'" *renminwang*, 21/06/2010. http://news.ifeng.com/history/special/chubingjiazhi/detail_2010_06/21/1648724_0.shtml; also http://news.ifeng.com/history/zhongguojindaishi/detail_2011_02/05/4564965_0.shtml
7. Li Hua-yu (2001), "The Political Stalinization of China: The Establishment of One-Party Constitutionalism, 1948–54," *Journal of Cold War Studies*, 3:2, pp. 28–47. Thomas P. Bernstein and Hua-yu Li (ed.) (2010), "Instilling Stalinism in Chinese Party Members: Absorbing Stalin's Short Course," in *China Learns from the Soviet Union, 1949–Present*, Plymouth: Lexington Books.
8. Xu Zerong (2000), "China's Role in the Korean War," *Modern China Studies*, No. 1.
9. Bernstein, T and Li, H (ed.) (2010), *China Learns from the Soviet Union, 1949–Present*, p. 29.
10. According to Li Hua-Yu, Stalin acquiesced to Mao's radical economic Stalinization in exchange for his political obedience. Li, H (2006), *Mao and the Economic Stalinization of China, 1948–1953*, Lanham, MD: Rowman & Littlefield, p. 134.

11. Amlan Datta (1973), *Perspectives of Economic Development*, London and Basingstoke: Macmillan, p. 104.
12. Slava Gerovitch (2008), "InterNyet: Why the Soviet Union did not Build a Nationwide Computer Network," *History and Technology*, 24:4, pp. 335–350.
13. Ibid.
14. Allin Cottrell and W. Paul Cockshott (1993), "Socialist Planning after the Collapse of the Soviet Union," Prepared for conference on The Socialist Calculation Debate after the Upheavals in Eastern Europe, Centre d''etudes interdisciplinaires Walras–Pareto, Universit'e de Lausanne, December 11–12, 1992. Published in Revue europ'eene des sciences sociales, tome XXXI, no. 96, 1993, 167–185. Martin Cave (1980), *Computers and Economic Planning: The Soviet Experience*, Cambridge: Cambridge University Press, p. 178.
15. Liu Yia-ling (1999), "The Segmentation of China's Domestic Market—The Institutional Legacy of the Planning Economy," *Journal of Sociology of NCCU*, No. 29, October, pp. 1–32.
16. Susan L. Shirk (1993), *The Political Logic of Economic Reform in China*, Berkeley: University of California Press, p. 160.
17. Richard F. Bensel (2000), *The Political Economy of American Industrialization, 1877–1900*, Cambridge: Cambridge University Press, p. 7.
18. Neil Fligstein (2008), *Euroclash: The EU, European Identity, and the Future of Europe*, Oxford: Oxford University Press, p. 87.
19. Marshall Goldman (1992), *What Went Wrong with Perestroika*, p. 57.
20. Salaries for urban dwellers did not increase for 20 years following 1957. The average wage per annum declined from 624 yuan in 1957 to 575 yuan in 1976. Rationing was rampant due to severe shortages of consumer goods, and housing conditions were rather difficult for many of the urban families especially in big cities like Shanghai. Cao Pu, "The Historic Origins of China's Reform and Opening," *xuexi shibao*, 18/10/2008.
21. Kent Deng (2012), *China's Political Economy in Modern Times: Changes and Economic Consequences, 1800–2000*, Oxon: Routledge, p. 123.
22. Li Lanqing (2008), *Breaking the Siege*, p. 17.
23. "In 1820, the Qing dynasty had about 33 percent of the world's total GDP, a share that had never been achieved in China's history … Within a period of 50 years, from 1820 to 1870. China's GDP share to the

world total dropped sharply from 33 percent to about 17 percent." Rongxing Guo (2017), *An Economic Inquiry into the Nonlinear Behaviors of Nations: Dynamic Developments and the Origins of Civilizations*, London: Palgrave Macmillan, p. 194.

24. In 1978, the CCP admitted that there are as many as 250 million people living in extreme poverty. The World Bank estimated the figure (on $1/day) at 490 million in 1981, more than half of the population. http://web.worldbank.org/archive/website00819C/WEB/PDF/CHINA_-4.PDF
25. Cao Pu, "The Historic Origins of China's Reform and Opening," *Study Times (xuexi shibao)*, 18/10/2008. http://www.ce.cn/xwzx/gnsz/gdxw/200810/12/t20081012_17038696.shtml
26. Marshall I. Goldman (1983), *USSR in Crisis—The Failure of an Economic System*, NY: Norton, p. 21.
27. Cited from Chen Yan (2006), *China's Awakening: An Evolution of Chinese Thoughts after the Cultural Revolution (1976–2002)*, HK: Tianyuan Publishing House, pp. 101. Original source: Wang Xiaoqiang (1980), "A Critique of Agrarian Socialism," *Problems of Rural Economy*, No. 2.
28. Yang Jisheng (2003), "In Remembrance of Li Shenzhi," http://www.cssm.gov.cn/view.php?id=29924; Mao's written instructions, 9/05/1963. http://cpc.people.com.cn/GB/64184/64186/66671/4493614.html
29. "The Chinese People must Oppose Slavish Comprador Philosophy," editorial of *Hongqi* (Red Flag), No. 4, 1976. http://www.360doc.cn/article/94763_7164027.html
30. Yan Changgui (2005), *The Inside Story about the Use and Annulment of the Appellation of "Shanghai Commune*," Beijing: bainianchao, No. 8, p. 44. http://www.hprc.org.cn/pdf/BNCH200508008.pdf
31. Hu Ping (2017), "A Review of Yang Jisheng's New Book on the History of the Cultural Revolution," *China Human Rights Bi-weekly*, No. 201. http://www.hrichina.org/chs/zhong-guo-ren-quan-shuang-zhou-kan/hu-ping-da-li-tui-jian-yang-ji-sheng-xian-sheng-xin-zhu-tian-di
32. Jin Chongji (2011), *The Biography of Mao Zedong* (Vol. 6), Beijing: zhongyang wenxian chubanshe, p. 2750. http://www.people.com.cn/GB/historic/0615/1957.html
33. Zhang Chunqiao's warnings after his imprisonment were deeply embarrassing to Deng Xiaoping and Chen Yun in jail. Gao Wenqian (2003), *Zhou Enlai in His Late Years*, NY: Mirrorbooks, p. 550.

34. Song Yongyi and Sun Dajin (ed.) (1999), *The Cultural Revolution and Its Heresies* (online) (part 4). http://tttan.com/HT/xanc/groups/GROUP_4/history/M1123881232/M1150763546/M.1136511915.A.html
35. Kornai Janos (1992), *The Socialist System: The Political Economy of Communism*, Oxford: Clarendon Press, pp. 383–386.
36. Wan Li, http://www.reformdata.org/index.do?m=wap&a=show&catid=301&typeid=&id=5014
37. V. I. Lenin, "The Collapse of the Second International," *Collected Works*, V. 21: August 1914–December 1915 (Moscow: Progress Publishers, 1964), pp. 213–214.
38. Debate on "New Democracy": Zhang Musheng's view, a panel discussion chaired by Lu Yuegang, released by ChinaSunTV (yangguang weishi) on 18/08/2011. https://www.youtube.com/watch?v=KGzQi4rGSjw&list=PL064A9B9FF2FAFA85
39. Cao Pu, "The Historic Origins of China's Reform and Opening," *xuexi shibao*, 18/10/2008. http://www.ce.cn/xwzx/gnsz/gdxw/200810/12/t20081012_17038696.shtml
40. Zhongyang caijing lingdao xiaozu bangongshi: "zhongguo jingji fazhan wushinian dashiji," Beijing 1999.
41. Chen Donglin (1997), "A Realistic Critique of the Economic Construction during the Cultural Revolution," *Studies on Chinese Economic History*, No. 4.
42. Han Gang article on Hua Guofeng. http://www.yhcqw.com/html/qsp/2011/212/KH15.html; http://www.rfa.org/mandarin/zhuanlan/yehuazhongnanhai/gx-02252014123900.html
43. Hua Guofeng then held three key positions: party chairman, premier and chairman of the central military commission.
44. Fang Mao (2016), "Hua Guofeng and China's Open-Door," *yanhuang chunqiu*, No. 5. http://www.yhcqw.com/html/qsp/2016/513/16513213014J3AC10163J58J1514E70A59I.html
45. Still there were political prisoners, like Li Jiulian, Zhong Haiyuan, and Wang Xinyou, being executed at least until 1980 by the Hua Guofeng administration even after the fall of the Gang of Four.
46. Wu Yong (2004): "The Ideological Battle between 1978 and 1988," *Modern China Studies*, No. 3. http://www.modernchinastudies.org/cn/issues/past-issues/85-mcs-2004-issue-3/875-19781988.html
47. Roderick MacFarquhar and Michael Schoenhals (2006), *Mao's Last Revolution*, Cambridge: Belknap Harvard, Mao's Last Revolution, p. 457.

48. Gao Wenqian (2016), "Mao's Cultural Revolution Legacy and Xi Jinping's Statecraft," an essay delivered to the academic seminar on the fiftieth anniversary of the start of the Cultural Revolution, VOA, 6/05/2016. https://www.voachinese.com/a/gao-wenqian-cultural-revolution-part1-20160505/3317245.html
49. Chen Yan (2006), "The Democracy Wall Movement and Its Historical Status," *Modern China Studies*, No. 2. http://www.modernchinastudies.org/cn/issues/past-issues/92-mcs-2006-issue-2/956-2012-01-05-15-35-10.html
50. Chen Yan (2006), *China Awakening*, p. 25.
51. "Chen Yun, Who Slowed China's Shift to Market, Dies at 89," *The New York Times*, 12/04/1995. http://www.nytimes.com/1995/04/12/obituaries/chen-yun-who-slowed-china-s-shift-to-market-dies-at-89.html?pagewanted=all
52. On December 26, 1977, Deng told a visiting foreign communist delegation, "How to embody the superiority of socialism? Is the decline rather than improvement of people's standard of living the proof of the superiority of socialism? If that kind of thing can be called 'superiority,' we prefer rejecting this sort of socialism." On another occasion, when inspecting Northeastern provinces in September 1978, Deng said, "We are too impoverished, too backward. Honestly speaking, we feel sorry for our people … If socialism is demonstrated by persistent poverty after more than twenty years. What's the use of socialism?" See Xie Minggan (2010), "Before and after 'the Decision to Reform' was Made," September. http://www.reformdata.org/index.do?m=wap&a=show&catid=301&typeid=&id=5014
53. Chen Yan (2006), "The Democracy Wall Movement and its Historical Status," *Modern China Studies*, No. 2.
54. During Mao's reign, the Complete Book of Six Codes (《六法全书》) promulgated in the Republican era was completely abolished. Only two legal codes, namely, the PRC's Constitution and the Marriage Law, were allowed to exist. Mao's socialist state building was anti-modern. Pei Yiran (2015), *The Disillusion of Utopia*, Taipei: Independent & Unique, p. 161.
55. He Weilin (2015), *Unfinished Manuscripts*, HK: Strong Wind Press, p. 14.
56. Hu Sheng (ed.) (1991), *Seventy Years of the CCP*, Beijing: zhongyang dangshi chubanshe, p. 566.
57. Zubok's lecture at London School of Economics on CPSU's history, 28/02/2017.

58. Marshal Ye is one of the *balao*. He was the key figure that allied with Hua and Wang Dongxing (internal security chief) in the coup that overthrew the Gang of Four in October 1976.
59. Conversation with Cheng Xiaonong, 14/10/2016.
60. Interview with Cheng Xiaonong, 16/10/2010.
61. The author agrees with He Weilin in rejecting the inaccurate and simplistic dichotomy of reformist-conservative divide. He Weilin (2015), *Unfinished Manuscripts*, p. 88.
62. "(If some people) says the market economy only existed in capitalist societies, (this) is definitely incorrect. Why can't socialism have market economy? This (market economy) cannot be labeled as capitalism." Li Lanqing (2008), *Break the Siege*, pp. 173–174.
63. Wei Xinghua (2010), "Chen Yun's Thought on Planning vs. Market is the Forerunner of China's Economic Reform," *Social Sciences Journal of Universities in Shanxi*, 22:9, September, pp. 1–5. http://www.nssd.org/articles/article_detail.aspx?id=35324464; Deng's original remarks (26/11/1979), "Ours is Planned Economy Supplemented by Market Economy," http://zg.people.com.cn/BIG5/33839/34943/34944/34946/2617351.html; Given the term's extreme sensitivity ideologically then for being synonymous with capitalism, Deng's speech was kept confidential until after 1992, the year "market economy" was eventually legalized.
64. Deng's Works, vol. 2 (1983), Beijing: renmin chubanshe, p. 315.
65. Mao had two incisive comments on Deng, the once designated successor after State President Liu Shaoqi. One comment was made in the 1950s when Deng followed closely Mao's line: "an iron fist in a velvet glove" (*mianli cangzhen*). The other was made in the 1970s when Deng was suspended his post and ousted the second time by Mao for his stubborn adherence to revisionism: "(he) rhetorically vows not to reverse the verdict (of being a capitalist-roader) against him… (His promise) was untenable; in fact (he) always clings to his 'Cat Theory.'"
66. A Chronicle of Chen Yun (*Chen Yun nianpu*) (2000), vol. 3. Beijing: zhonggong zhongyang wenxian yanjiushi, p. 262.
67. *Selected Works of Chen Yun* (1995), vol. 3, Beijing: renmin chubanshe, p. 320.
68. Cheng Chen (2007), *The Prospects for Liberal Nationalism in Post-Leninist States*, University Park: Pennsylvania State University Press, p. 114.

69. Donald C. Hodges (1981), *The Bureaucratization of Socialism*, Amherst: University of Massachusetts Press, p. 84.
70. https://www.revolvy.com/topic/State%20socialism&item_type=topic
71. Zong Fengming (2007), p. 74.
72. http://englishdictionary.education/en/state-socialist
73. "Classical socialism was a movement to replace the unplanned and exploitative institutions of capitalism with national planning, public ownership, and distribution according to human need rather than by the arbitrary capriciousness of the market." T.A. Burczak (2006), *Socialism after Hayek*, Ann Arbor, MI: Michigan University Press, p. 2.
74. For understandable reasons, these sensitive words were not included in the *Selected Works of Deng Xiaoping*. Du Daozheng, "How to Look on Deng Xiaoping Today?" *Caijing*, 05/12/2008.
75. "The CPSU's General Secretary: Communism is a 'Deceptive Nonsense,'" http://history.dwnews.com/news/2015-10-03/59685843.html
76. Li Jingxian (2008), *Deng Xiaoping's Meeting with Gorbachev Remembered*, Beijing: bainianchao, No. 3. Deng told Gorbachev outspokenly on May 16, 1989, that both sides had uttered "many empty words" and that "[now] we do not believe that our side was absolutely correct then after more than twenty years of practice." http://cpc.people.com.cn/GB/85037/85038/7407132.html
77. "Ezra Vogel: Six Key Figures in the Deng Xiaoping Era," *The Paper* (pengpai xinwen), 13/08/2014. http://www.thepaper.cn/newsDetail_forward_1261111
78. Deng's Works, vol. 3, p. 63; Zong (2007), p. 125.
79. In 1986, when China started to experiment stock market trading, it was immediately under the attack from the conservatives who accused it of being "capitalist." Deng was in support of the stock market development, especially its financing function to China's capital-devoid economy. Deng rebuffed the opponents' view simply by stating, "just close it down [in case of big problems]." This example vividly describes Deng's flexible but opportunistic political character. The negative side of Deng's opportunism was later reflected in his attitudinal change toward the price reform in 1988. Deng threw out Premier Zhao Ziyang as his scapegoat to moderate backlashes of the planning faction bureaucrats headed by Chen Yun so as to keep himself intact (see Cheng Xiaonong's article on the price reform in 1988).

80. According to Yang Jisheng (2004), p. 18, Chinese veteran economist Yu Guangyuan concluded as early as the late 1970s, "Hoping the CCP to undertake political reform (which is meant to end its monopoly of power) is like 'asking a tiger for its skin' (*yu hu mopi*)."
81. Zhao Ziyang (2009), *The Secret Journal*, Hong Kong: New Century Press, p. 278; Wu Wei, "Two Different Roadmaps of Political Reform between Deng Xiaoping and Zhao Ziyang," *The New York Times* (Chinese online), 15/12/2014. https://cn.nytimes.com/china/20141215/cc15wuwei41/
82. Zhao had a candid talk with Deng in the year of 1988, briefing him on the new notion of "neo-authoritarianism." Deng replied: "This is what I have been for. But better not use this term." Yang Jisheng (2004), p. 565.
83. Zhao's perception of democracy at the time was rather vague, which included no more than greater political participation of the "democratic parties"—sneered as the "vase parties" (*huapingdang*)—under the CCP's tight control, greater intra-party democracy, and the rule of law. Zhao (2009), pp. 294–295.
84. Zong (2007), pp. 84, 121, 286.
85. He Weilin (2015), pp. 370–371.
86. "The History of the 'Stone Theory,'" *Guangming Daily*, 9/04/2014. http://epaper.gmw.cn/gmrb/html/2014-04/09/nw.D110000gmrb_20140409_3-14.htm; Han Zhenfeng, "Who First Raised the 'Stone Theory' as a Reform Method?" *Guangming Daily*, 6/01/2015. It is Chen Yun rather than Deng Xiaoping that first raised the "stone theory." http://history.people.com.cn/n/2015/0106/c372327-26335792.html
87. Su Shaozhi (1999), "Theory and Practice of Political System Reform in the Deng Xiaoping Era," *Modern China Studies*, No. 3. http://www.modernchinastudies.org/us/issues/past-issues/66-mcs-1999-issue-3/503-2012-01-01-10-06-23.html
88. For instance, in the policy-making process, Deng, more often than not, intentionally prevented Chen Yun's involvement in the Politburo Standing Committee discussions on reform policies; Chen retaliated by blocking Deng's policies through his protégés in the powerful central planning bureaucracy. This irregular authoritarian politics put Zhao Ziyang in an awkward position. Yang (2004), pp. 24–25; Zong (2007), p. 153.

89. The opening of Yangpu Development Zone in Hainan, with Deng's backing notwithstanding, was dubbed as a traitorous behavior in the year of 1988 when the province of Hainan was just created. The decision to open up Yangpu was made by the State Council only on March 9, 1992, in the aftermath of Deng Xiaoping's southern tour early in the year.
90. Conversation with Cheng Xiaonong, 14/10/2016.
91. Zhao (2009), p. 126.
92. "Cheng Xiaonong: The Economic Reform without Zhao Ziyang was Led Astray," *Epoch Times*, 27/01/2005. http://www.epochtimes.com/gb/5/1/27/n795482.htm
93. In this sense, Zhao remained a "Traditional Communist" even until quite late during his captivity, as Zhang Boshu portrayed him. Zhang Boshu (ed.) (2011), *Zhao Ziyang's Road*, HK: Morningbell Press, p. 5.
94. Excerpts from Actual Talks by Deng Xiaoping in Wuhan, Shenzhen, Zhuhai and Shanghai (18/1–21/2, 1992). http://zg.people.com.cn/GB/33839/34943/34944/34947/2617452.html
95. This initial reform scenario was agreed by both Deng Xiaoping and Chen Yun, as well as the SPC and the Ministry of Finance, which was "not an easy matter at the time." http://www.reformdata.org/content/20080305/20835.html
96. "China's Reform and Opening Meets No End—An Interview with Xu Jing'an," *China Economic Herald*, 12/12/2008.
97. "The Price-Fiscal-Taxation Comprehensive Reform Scenario Approved (in August 1986)," which was, nonetheless, abandoned in October. http://www.reformdata.org/special/270/about.html; Also, Jia Kang's article on *Caijing*, 30/08/2010. http://www.caijing.com.cn/2010-08-30/110508381.html
98. Marshall Goldman (1992), *What Went Wrong with Perestroika?* pp. 117; 162–169.
99. "The Most Influential Foreign Experts in the 60-year History of New China," *People's Daily*, 23/10/2009. http://world.people.com.cn/GB/8212/171502/10248026.html
100. During the initial seven years of reform, FDI in China was just US $6.06 billion (1979–1985) in all, in which the year 1985 saw FDI inflow at US $1.96 billion. FDI rose from US $2.24 billion to US $11 billion in 1991 in another six years.
101. The reform experiment began in 1981.

102. He Weilin (2015), p. 337.
103. Wu Jingling's lecture at CEIBS, November 1999; "SOEs' Reform: 30 Years in Retrospect," 2/12/2011. http://www.chinareform.org.cn/economy/Enterprise/practice/201112/t20111202_129053.htm
104. Andrew G. Walder (1983), "Organized Dependency and Cultures of. Authority in Chinese Industry," *The Journal of Asian Studies*, 43:1, pp. 51–76.
105. János Kornai (1979), "Resource-Constrained Versus Demand-Constrained Systems," *Econometrica*, 47:4, pp. 801–819.
106. Zhao (2009), p. 135.
107. Ibid: Epilogue by Roderick MacFarquhar, pp. 301–310.
108. Girsh I. Khanin (2003), "The 1950s: The Triumph of the Soviet Economy," *Europe-Asia Studies*, 55:8, pp. 1187–1211.
109. In September 1978, Deng openly repented the party's former wrongdoing for having kept the people persistently poor over the past decades. "Deng Xiaoping Say Sorry to the People," *Study Times*, 25/12/2012. http://history.people.com.cn/n/2012/1225/c198865-20005852.html
110. China's fiscal revenue as a percentage of GDP dropped from 33.8% in 1978 to only 10.8% in 1995.
111. Y.Y. Kueh (2008), *China's New Industrialization Strategy: Was Chairman Mao Really Necessary?* Cheltenham: Edward Elgar Publishing Limited, vii.
112. This is clearly reflected in Deng Liqun (2006), *Twelve Springs and Autumns*, HK: Strong Wind Press.
113. Immanuel Wallerstein (1992), "The Concept of National Development," *The American Behavioral Scientist*, 35:4, pp. 517–529.
114. "Knocking the Door at Fuqiang Lane No. 6 to Interview Zhao Ziyang in Summer 2004," HK: Qianshao, No. 3, 2005; Wang Xiaodong, "China's Nationalism under the Shadow of Globalization," public lecture delivered at the London School of Economics, 7/02/2005.
115. A Chronicle of Deng Xiaoping (Deng Xiaoping nianpu, 1975–1997) Part One (2004), Beijing: zhongyang wenxian chubanshe, p. 616.
116. "China's Reform and Opening Meets No End—An Interview with Xu Jing'an," *China Economic Times*, 12/12/2008.
117. Marshall Goldman (1992), *What Went Wrong with Perestroika?* p. 88.
118. Liu Liqun (1992), "The Transformation of China's Economic Development Strategy and Its Problems," The State Council's Development and Research Centre (DRC) internal report: No. 43, 25/09/1992.
119. Liu Liqun, for instance. Interview with Liu in Beijing, 26/08/2005.

120. Li Shenzhi (2002), "The PRC's Foreign Policy," March. http://paper.usc.cuhk.edu.hk/Details.aspx?id=2200; Yuan Ming (2005), "The U.S. Factor in the Process of China's Modernization," *Diplomatic Review*, No. 3. http://www.aisixiang.com/data/12185.html
121. Kenneth Pyle (2008), *Japan Rising: The Resurgence of Japanese Power and Purpose*, NY: PublicAffairs
122. Deng's Works (1993), vol. 3, p. 3.
123. On August 20, 1983, liberal economist Zhang Weiying, then an MSc student in economics, published a hugely controversial article titled "To Make Money is not Wrong" (*weiqian zhengming*) on the *China Youth Daily*, a liberal-oriented newspaper affiliated with the Communist Youth League (CYL). Guangzhou: nanfang renwu zhoukan, 6/07/2007. http://news.qq.com/a/20070706/003155.htm; http://www.xzbu.com/5/view-1203578.htm; During the mid-1980s, the *China Youth Daily* initiated discussions on "what is modern life style?," pointing to the thriving consumerism in China. http://women.sohu.com/g-xinzhoukan/consume.html; other newspapers and periodicals, such as *Chinese Women*, *Pursuit*, and so on, also organized open discussions on modern life style. See Youth Digest: first half-month (1985), No. 4. http://www.ifreetxt.com/forum.php?mod=viewthread&tid=195273&extra=page%3D1
124. Deng Xiaoping had never made such utterances in any abstract way. Rather, the vague mention he made was accompanied by the commitment of pursuing common wealth as the end goal and of disallowing income inequality, or in his own words, "never will we allow a new bourgeoisie to emerge." See "Answering Michael Wallace (60 Minutes)," 2/09/1986. http://zg.people.com.cn/BIG5/33839/34943/34944/34947/2617792.html
125. Ronald P. Dore (1987), *Taking Japan Seriously: A Confucian Perspective on Leading Economic Issues*, Redwood: Stanford University Press; Douglass Smith (1991), *The Confucian Continuum: Educational Modernization in Taiwan*, NY: Praeger; Ruth Hayhoe (1992), "Book Review: The Confucian Ethic and the Spirit of Capitalism," *Curriculum Inquiry*, 22:4, pp. 425–431.
126. The Secret Journal of Zhao Ziyang (2009), Epilogue by MacFarquhar, p. 304.
127. Cheng Xiaonong (1995), "Decision and Miscarriage: Radical Price Reform in the Summer of 1988," in *Decision-Making in Deng's China: Perspectives from Insiders*, ed. Carol Lee Hamrin and Suisheng Zhao, Armonk, NY: M. E. Sharpe, pp. 189–206.

128. Recent research indicated that Zhao's "creative" fiscal decentralization could be traced back to 1971 when similar measures had been adopted, though under experiment.
129. "Wu Jinglian Talks about Industrial Policy," Dameisha Forum (Shenzhen), 04/11/2016. http://economy.caijing.com.cn/20161104/4195056.shtml
130. Interview with Cheng Xiaonong, 12/11/2009.
131. Yao Jianfu, "Li Xiannian Masterminded the Coup against Zhao Ziyang," http://www.chinainperspective.com/ArtShow.aspx?AID=10026
132. Zhao (2009), p. 264.
133. Deng Liqun (2006), "Twelve Springs and Autumns," p. 529.
134. Yang Jisheng (2004), p. 27.
135. Zhao Ziyang (2009), p. 241.
136. According to Hao Yufan, the notion of "export orientation" in lieu of ISI had dominated Chinese leaders (he did not mention concrete names) in the years 1985 and 1986, who were convinced of the necessity of making Chinese economy part of the global economy through joining so-called international economic cycling (*guoji jingji da xunhuan*). Hao Yufan (2007), "China's Foreign Economic Policy in the Past Fifty Years," *Review of Foreign Affairs* (Beijing: waijiao pinglun), No. 5, pp. 57–63. http://www.xueshu.com/wjpl/200705/24020684.html
137. Zhao (2009), pp. 163–164.
138. Tian Jiyun (2015), "The Formation and Implementation of the Coastal Development Strategy," *yanhuang chunqiu*, No. 3. http://www.yhcqw.com/html/cqb/2015/39/15391919259H8E597782DI69GEE3384DKC.html
139. Zhao (2009), p. 173; also Ibid. Zhao hidden reform agenda was illustrated in the *People's Daily* editorial dated 19/05/1988, titled "An Event of Historical Significance—On the Coastal Economic Development Strategy."
140. Li Xianglu (2016), "A Forerunner of Reform Remembered (*huiyi yiwei zhanzai gaige qianyan de zhangzhe*)," *yanhuang chunqiu*, No. 2. http://www.yhcqw.com/html/hyp/2016/29/1629152821DIF7810084A898K0F55BJ8G4A.html
141. Wang Jian's report was first printed in *dongtai qingyang*, an internal publication of the Xinhua Agency on November 1, 1987. It was openly published on *Economic Daily* on January 5, 1988.
142. Zhao clarified later that the coastal development strategy was completely his making, Zhao (2009), p. 168.

143. General trade refers to import of foreign goods and export of Chinese-made products with overwhelmingly local contents. General-trade exportation, given its external demand-pull mechanism, has a direct impact on the domestic economy and serves as the engine of economic growth.
144. Li Changli (1989), "An Externally-Oriented Strategy Should Not Be The General Development Strategy of China as a Big Country," *jingji lilun yu jingji guanli (Economic Theory and Economic Management)*, No. 5.
145. http://www.cuhk.edu.hk/ics/21c/supplem/essay/0409009.htm (this hyperlink no longer exists)
146. Cheng, X (1995), "Decision and Miscarriage: Radical Price Reform in the Summer of 1988," pp. 189–206.
147. Wu Wei (2015), "Decision Making behind the 1988 Price Reform," *yanhuang chunqiu*, No. 12. http://www.yhcqw.com/html/cqb/2015/129/15129181313AIJ1410032B9DBK8329E88IGJ.html
148. Before and After the Rash Price Reform in 1988, *yanhuang chunqiu*, No. 10, 2005. http://www.yhcqw.com/html/psz/2008/417/084171020487KHIH14944D7BE6BFJJAE3A8.html; Wu Wei (2015), "Decision Making behind the 1988 Price Reform," *yanhuang chunqiu*, No. 12.
149. Cheng, X (1995), "Decision and Miscarriage: Radical Price Reform in the Summer of 1988," pp. 189–206.
150. Ibid.
151. Zhao (2009), pp. 145–146.
152. Zong (2007), p. 88.
153. Luo Yu (2015), *Farewell to the General Staff*, HK: Open Press, pp. 120, 241–244. Yu Jie's commentary article, 3/12/2015. http://www.rfa.org/mandarin/zhuanlan/wenyitiandi-cite/yj1-12032015162442.html; about corruption scandal implicating Hu Yaobang's family: an informed source referred to Liu Hu, Hu's second son (October 2016).
154. "Let Part of the People, Part of the Country to Get Rich First," 17/02/2009. http://cpc.people.com.cn/GB/64162/82819/143371/8818525.html
155. Yu Meisun (2007), "In Memory of Milton Friedman and Zhao Ziyang," http://www.open.com.hk/old_version/0702p27.html; Regarding Luo Xiaopeng's accounts, see Hu Ping's article, "Reinterpreting 'China Model,'" *China Human-Rights Biweekly*, 8–21/02/2013. http://biweeklyarchive.hrichina.org/article/4883.html
156. Guo Shuqing (1992), "Three-Year Rectification and Improvement and China's Economic Reform (sannian zhili zhengdun yu zhongguo jingji gaige)," *shengchanli yanjiu (Productivity Research)*, No. 5, pp. 18–32.

157. The CCP's decision to further *zhili zhengdun*, 9/11/1989. http://www.people.com.cn/GB/shizheng/252/5089/5105/5188/20010429/455917.html
158. Dr. Chen Kuide at Princeton was among the first few people to discern the rightward transformation of Chinese communist dictatorship in early 1992. http://www.rfa.org/mandarin/pinglun/125754-20040114.html

4

From Tiananmen to Shenzhen: Transition to Capitalism

1989 was a turning point in human history: the Tiananmen Incident, the collapse of communism in Central-Eastern Europe, and the end of the Cold War. These big events that changed the course of history are described by the historians as "The Global 1989." The year 1989 saw a great divergence in the communist world in which regimes within the Warsaw Pact collapsed one after another following the fall of the Berlin Wall on November 9. Thanks to Gorbachev's policy of non-intervention, the democratic transition of these socialist states to market capitalism was accomplished in a largely peaceful way. In China, by contrast, Deng Xiaoping ordered the People's Liberation Army (PLA) to quell the demonstrators in Tiananmen on June 3rd and saved the regime from collapse. The bloody crackdown, however, did not block Communist China's subsequent transition to capitalism but rather accelerated its non-democratic transition to a bureaucratic capitalism. Different from that of Putin's Russia, the Chinese system of post-communist kleptocracy was cloaked in market Leninism, under which the party state's simultaneous embrace of global capitalism from 1992 had bred a "crony-comprador capitalism."

Conventional wisdom holds that the tough way Deng Xiaoping dealt with the Tiananmen revolt made China's democratic transformation entirely impossible. Such a narrative is over-simplistic. The Kwangju

J. Yue, *China's Rise in the Age of Globalization*, Palgrave Studies in Economic History, https://doi.org/10.1007/978-3-319-63997-0_4

Uprising in 1980 was brutally put down by the South Korean army with the connivance of its ally, the USA. Yet the crackdown did not prevent pro-democracy regime change seven years later due to the relentless fight against dictatorship of the "self-identified middle class" dedicated to the belief that "We should promote human rights even if it delays economic growth."[1] Like the Tiananmen revolt, the Kwangju Uprising was caused by an economic meltdown and was followed by massive economic liberalization. The ensuing export-led prosperity in both countries, however, resulted in divergent developmental and political outcomes. As opposed to South Korea's successful industrialization that led to profound economic transformation and created a thriving middle class demanding democracy, China's flagging industrialization, eclipsed by robust export-led growth throughout the 1990s, was accompanied by omnipresent cynicism among the rulers and the ruled, and by the docility of a pseudo-middle class.[2] Many former democracy fighters, particularly the liberal intellectuals, became active collaborators of the regime. Committed to self-enrichment rather than developmental goals in the first place, the "softened" party state became highly predatory and repressive at the turn of the century, only a decade later after Tiananmen. As *New York Times* wrote amidst the Chinese Communist Party (CCP) Sixteenth National Party's Congress on November 10, 2002, "After a 20-year transition, the world's last major *left-wing dictatorship*, the Communist Party of China, has transformed itself. It is now, arguably, the world's last major *right-wing dictatorship*."[3]

Why transition in such a way? Was it inevitable?

After Tiananmen: Death of Reform?

Back to the summer of 1989, the Tiananmen tragedy seemed inevitable, thanks to so-called dam-stalemate (*daba jiangju*) effect, as Li Shenzhi termed it. Li was a liberal-minded veteran communist who joined the CCP in the Yan'an era (1940s) and worked in the capacity of foreign affairs secretary for late Premier Zhou Enlai in the 1950s. He accompanied Deng Xiaoping on the historic visit to the USA in January 1979. According to him, the "structural rigidity" of the communist system (dam) made the desired mutual concessions between the regime and the demonstrators unlikely.[4] Wang Lixiong shared Li's judgment. As one of China's most famous dissident scholars, Wang argued that it was the decades-long totalitarian rule of the CCP that was responsible for the non-compromise of both sides whose mindsets had been shaped by Mao's "struggle philosophy." For the vast majority of the people, notions such as the "you-die-I-live" class struggle and the way mass movement was organized were what they were familiar with. Wang risked offending those democracy fighters in 1989, contending that there were actually limited democratic elements within the pro-democracy movement itself except for some slogans calling for "reason, compromise, and respect for law."[5] Unreservedly critical of the Communist regime for the Tiananmen bloodshed, both scholars had no incentive to defend the regime on any dubious grounds. But what could have made the "inevitability" thesis more convincing was Deng's real motivation behind his decision of using force to disperse the protestors. Worried about instability of the PLA, Deng sent in large numbers of heavily equipped troops to Beijing with the dominant purpose of preventing a civil war.[6] It has been recognized shortly after the crackdown that without Deng and his effective control of the army, the CCP regime would have been at stake.[7]

The regime survived amidst global condemnation; its legitimacy based on the communist ideology was severely eroded. Deng Xiaoping had a foreboding in the immediate aftermath of Tiananmen that backlash from the ultra-leftist ideologues against his market-oriented reform was unavoidable. Addressing the high-ranking PLA officers executing the martial law on June 9, Deng warned that the party's basic line laid out at the Third Plenary Session of the Eleventh Central Committee (1978) was not wrong and must be continued.[8] The tenet of this particular address was in actuality not so much to justify his crackdown decision as to defend his "reform and opening." Nevertheless, this crucially important message that he conveyed to the outside world went virtually unnoticed at home and abroad. In the face of consecutive fall of communist regimes in the Soviet Bloc, especially the disintegration of the Soviet Union two years later, the CCP leadership were having an incredibly hard time that even ordinary Chinese citizens could discern without difficulty. Deng's reform and opening was left in jeopardy. On the one hand, the ultra-leftist ideologues waged a massive ideological crusade against his reform and open-door policy, though in an implicit way. With central planners fully taking charge, a good number of reform measures were frozen, postponed, or even abolished. On the other hand, led by the USA, the Western world imposed economic sanctions and an arms embargo against China. Washington also suspended its economic, cultural, and military exchanges with Beijing. The integration of China, which was thrown into isolation again, into global capitalism seemed to have been reversed.

Confronted with unimaginable domestic and international challenges, Deng was in full control. Still, his experience, insight and capability were indispensable to the survival of the regime. As a pragmatic leader, he silently accepted the demise of communism and the termination of Sino-US strategic partnership with the ending of the Cold War. Therefore, he vetoed the ideologues' appeal for waging a meaningless ideological battle with the moribund Communist Party of the Soviet Union (CPSU), prior to the August Coup in 1991. He admonished the party to base the country's foreign policy on national interest rather than on defunct ideology. Opposing China "claiming leadership" on global affairs, as suggested by some Third World leaders, Deng thought the idea counterproductive and infeasible given China's rather weak national strength vis-à-vis the West.[9] What China should do was to take a defensive posture strategically, or in his words: "observe calmly; secure our position; cope with affairs calmly; hide our capacities and bide our time; be good at maintaining a low profile; and never claim leadership; make some contributions," later known as the "24-character strategy."[10] Stressing the importance of "hiding our capacities and biding our time" through "maintaining a low profile" (*taoguangyanghui*) diplomatically, Deng believed that after several years China would definitely become "truly more powerful politically," thereby having a greater say in international affairs.[11] Nevertheless, since China was a great power that ought to play its role in some way, one great contribution it could make at the current moment, Deng argued, was promoting the creation of a New International Political and Economic Order (NIPEO)[12]—a Chinese equivalent of the New International Economic Order (NIEO) as espoused by the Third World countries in the 1970s. Focusing on the "domestic"[13] at the critical juncture of the Global 1989, Deng claimed that China was a big country; so long as it maintained stability under the strong leadership of the CCP, "nobody can crush us."[14]

Was Deng hinting at breaking with the international system of global capitalism and instead moving China to some market-based self-reliance, given the new realities after the Cold War? As a matter of fact, prior to his enunciation of "24-character strategy," Deng reiterated his earlier warnings (1980) on June 16, 1989, less than two weeks after the crackdown, and made his view more explicit:

> "The whole imperialist Western world has been attempting to force all socialist countries to abandon socialist road and *integrate them into the orbit of international capitalism*. We must resist this adverse trend. … If we do not uphold socialism, China will be nothing but a dependent state, not to mention that *development is not that easy because world market has become saturated, making it less easy for us to squeeze into*."

As such, he concluded that, "Only socialism can save China and only socialism can develop China."[15] Still, Deng fell short of giving a clear-cut definition of what socialism is; neither did he explain what he meant by NIPEO. Claiming China to be a developing country but refusing to "claim leadership," Deng was ostensibly eschewing direct confrontation with the West, politically and economically. This sufficed to render his reference to NIPEO, which by definition stands for a collective collaboration between the developing nations, pointless, not to mention that he was probably ignorant of the failed NIEO, also known as the "Southern Challenge" that was long gone and gave way to neoliberalism almost a decade earlier in the wake of the 1982 debt crisis. In addition, by "big country," Deng seemed to be underscoring the importance of stabilizing China politically rather than referring to its being a potentially huge market poised to underpin China's self-reliance in lieu of "external orientation," whereby the country's being integrated "into the orbit of international capitalism" could be avoided.

In fact, there is no evidence to suggest that Deng's preference regarding external orientation ever changed. On the same day, when he cautioned against the peril of "squeezing into" the already saturated overseas markets, he urged Li Peng and Yao Yilin to carry out reform and opening courageously, especially "to do something in opening-up, for instance, attracting foreign investment and building more development zones so as to convince the outside world that China's reform and open-door policy is not changed and will be furthered."[16] What's more, to make his commitment and dedication to reform and opening more palpable, Deng resorted to great power diplomacy. He briefed Brent Scowcroft, special envoy of President George Bush and US national security advisor on a secret visit to Beijing in late 1989 that Sino-US relations "should *after all* make a turn for the better."[17] Clearly enough, the perceived peril of China becoming "a dependent state" was, in Deng's eyes, not economic but political, and could be addressed by maintaining tighter control at home. He seemed to believe that "external orientation" was economically costless; the only cost China had to pay was *the political*: no opposing US hegemonic new world order in *practical* terms. Hence, with self-reliance being precluded, China's continued bandwagoning with the liberal order would and could only be achieved through *APPEASING* the West!

Domestically, like their market-faction counterparts, the central planners, after gaining the upper hand in economics, must vindicate their own approach with sound economic performance. Their victory, nonetheless, was tentative for failing to entrench central planning through alternative economic and institutional reforms. For one thing, after crippling Deng's price reform in 1988, they kept the dual pricing system in place even after the Tiananmen Incident while allowing continued existence of expanded enterprise autonomy. This created internal tensions within the planning system, in that for planning to work, "double pricing" and enterprise autonomy must be abolished. Although the party's control over the state-owned enterprises (SOEs) had been reasserted through instituting the so-called manager's responsibility system under the leadership of the party's committee (*dangwei lingdaoxia de changzhang fuzezhi*), the central planners were unable to prevent speculation by increasingly market-conscious SOEs' managers to continue profiting from dual pricing. As a result, the "within-planning" product shortages and market disorder continued as usual. Meanwhile, not reversing fiscal decentralization, the central planners kept provincial autarky intact. Therefore, Zhao's key legacies were inherited paradoxically by the central planners who, willingly or not, were beginning to adapt themselves to ever-growing market forces.

As a matter of fact, as practitioners, the central planners were not utterly anti-market. During the three-year stabilization (1989–1992), despite requisite policy reversals in the early post-Tiananmen days, the market reform was slowly resumed nonetheless. In the first instance, the dual pricing was, phased out in November 1989, just five months after the Tiananmen Incident, by the central planners in favor of "single pricing." Mandatory planning continued to shrink from 1990, leading to further lessening in price control, which nearly vanished in some coastal provinces.[18] Pilot areas, not limited to the coastal provinces, were singled out by the State Council dominated by the central planners for carrying out pension and medicare reforms in 1990 and 1991,[19] with a notable (neo)liberal orientation.[20]

The biggest success the central planners achieved was bringing down the inflation from 17.8% in 1989 to 2.1% in 1990 and 2.9% in 1991. Accordingly, the economic growth slowed down to 4.3% in 1989 and further down to 3.0% in 1990, thanks to stringent austerity measures. Sluggish demand eroded the profit margins of the SOEs. Overproduction of the SOEs, however, was not caused by sheer economic reasons. Almost immediately after Tiananmen, the regime took draconian measures to limit private businesses, in an attempt to purify the economic foundation of socialism on ideological grounds. To the surprise of the Chinese leadership, these measures dealt a heavy blow to the SOEs as well given the interdependent intersectoral linkages established between the SOEs and private businesses in the 1980s. Although most bank loans flowed to the SOEs in 1990, their financial plight kept deteriorating, and the economy remained sluggish. Hence, these economic Stalinist measures were soon silently abandoned. In April 1991, Zhu Rongji was promoted by Deng Xiaoping from the party boss of Shanghai to Vice-Premier. Zhu was a former central planner whose expertise, capability and "strong state" propensity gained him the trust of both Deng Xiaoping and Chen Yun. Upon assuming office, he was put in charge of bailing out the SOEs in the northeastern provinces from debt crisis. Zhu accomplished his first mission efficiently and effectively.[21] This to a certain extent drove the economy to take a turn for the better. Thanks to continuous credit expansion in 1991, industrial production increased, and as a result, economic growth accelerated and reached 8%. These were nonetheless driven mainly by the non-state sectors.[22]

Lessons Drawn from Tiananmen

By the end of 1991, it had become evidently clear that the central planners, after three years of *zhili zhengdun*, proved unable to provide an alternative approach to delivering a self-sustaining prosperity within the state socialist "birdcage." It was time for Deng to strike back. The huge impact of the Global 1989 and his eagerness to institutionalize his legacy prompted him to launch radical market reform without further bargaining with the central planners. "Development is the hard truth!" That is the greatest lesson Deng drew from the collapse of communism. As he saw it, "Gorbachev is an idiot,"[23] whose glasnost and democratization not only brought down the regime but also destroyed the Soviet Union as a nation-state. Yet merely rejecting democracy without creating prosperity would not necessarily save the communist regime from implosion either, as evidenced by the overthrow of Romania's Stalinist regime under Nicolae Ceausescu in December 1989. Thus, bringing China back to Maoism, though logically sound in ideological terms, would be disastrous in political and practical terms. For Deng, any retreat to Maoism was tantamount to acknowledging total failure of his economic reform, not to mention that the ultra-leftists were using the "Mao Zedong fever" permeating the Chinese society from early 1990 in protest of the Tiananmen crackdown in a bid to discredit Deng's reform and open-door policy. Deng was thus faced with an urgent task of defending his reform, on the one hand, and of justifying the Tiananmen crackdown on the other. As he saw it, it was the reform and opening that brought prosperity to the people, and it was the crackdown that prevented China from repeating the fate of the USSR. Deng made his intentions crystal clear in his famous southern tour (*nanxun*) remarks in early 1992, "Without the achievements of reform and opening, we could not pass the June 4th. Had we failed to pass, there would have been chaos and civil war."[24] Therefore, the only way to address his legacy concern was establishing a link between the two and making China more prosperous.

Indeed, economic reform in the 1980s had benefited the great majority of the population. With his "perestroika without glasnost" stuck in a quagmire from the mid-1980s, Deng's popularity declined precipitously.

Yet in the summer of 1989, he still enjoyed sympathy from a vast number of the people, especially peasants who, similar to the "silent majority" of the Soviet citizens sympathetic to the August Coup putsch organizers,[25] simply refrained from taking to the streets. Many onlookers shared his uneasiness about prospective anarchy reminiscent of the not-far-away chaos of the "Great Democracy" during the Cultural Revolution. Those getting involved sided with the students on multiple grounds. Behind the superficial pro-democracy movement, as Wang Lixiong most convincingly argued,[26] was a hidden popular psychology of wanting capitalist wealth and socialist egalitarianism simultaneously. That was an impossible mission for either Deng or Gorbachev, whose reforms had likewise raised such unrealistic expectations in their respective countries. Unlike the humanist socialist Gorbachev, Deng Xiaoping was a communist revolutionary never hesitating to use violence to restore law and order. Silencing the people whose defiance disappeared almost overnight, Deng and the Communist leadership were convinced that social unrest in China would pose no serious threat to the regime so long as the latter remained assertive enough.[27] The fact that not all people were grateful to him and the benign post-Mao regime even if they had benefited from his reform and lived a much better life under him than under Mao also reinforced Deng's firmness in not appeasing the people any longer.

In a nutshell, Deng Xiaoping drew three major lessons from Tiananmen: no democracy, no appeasing the people, and appeasing the West. Following the *nanxun* in early 1992 that symbolized his crushing victory over the central planners, Deng was poised to radicalize his approach of "perestroika with glasnost" by abandoning state socialism and self-reliance in a thoroughgoing way. To the benefit of Deng and the post-Tiananmen regime, the demise of communism and the "shock and awe" effect of brutal repression inadvertently eliminated the ideological and institutional barriers to the unfolding market Leninist reform. In the absence of a new belief system, and guided instead by "an ideology of no ideology,"[28] the reform served the simple and straightforward purpose of strengthening the party state's absolute monopoly on power. This implies that through tighter control, first and foremost by "killing the bud in its infancy," stability would be guaranteed whereby the regime would be able to devote itself to wealth creation through whatever means. Deng believed more firmly than ever before that, as mentioned earlier, economic success was the panacea. Borrowing a metaphor from Deng himself (from the 1980s), so long as the economy kept growing, "[even with no democracy,] horse-racing will go on as usual; and dancing ball [will be] hot as always (*ma zhaopao, wu zhaotiao*)."[29]

The Princelings' Report

An interlude in the year of 1991 between the August Coup and Deng's *nanxun* deserves to be highlighted. In the name of the Theory and Ideology Group of the official *China Youth Daily*, a mouthpiece of the CCP associated with the Communist Youth League (CYL) Central Committee, a group of princelings and their kindred spirit co-authored a startling article titled "China's Realistic Response and Strategic Choice after the Dramatic Change in the USSR."[30] The article (hereafter called "the Report") was completed on September 9, some three weeks after the August Coup in the Soviet Union. It was instantly delivered to the highest authority and attracted serious attention.

In this Report, the authors did not hesitate to acknowledge the reality that the regime's legitimacy based on the communist ideology was being depleted against the backdrop of the Global 1989. Therefore, continuing to impose it upon the people could only invite resentment. As such, the CCP should give a "creative reinterpretation" of the regime's two sources of legitimacy—Marxism and *Sinicized* Marxism—by focusing on the latter, highlighting the "Chinese characteristics," a populous backward country that had made socialism a necessity. But that was not enough. Traditional values of the Chinese culture in lieu of the outdated ideology, they argued, should be embraced and blended with patriotism (nationalism) as the new source of political legitimacy. They suggested the CCP to transform itself from a revolutionary party to a ruling party concentrating on the construction of modernization. They rejected economic and political radicalism, either left-leaning or right-leaning. They defended the decollectivization reform in the rural and advocated for a gradualist approach in the urban under the auspices of a recentralized government. They warned the decision makers against the forward and excess consumption (*chaoqian xiaofei*) as it would make the economic growth hard to sustain. They envisioned a disordered post-Cold War world that would turn against China, despite the fact that the East Asian region would probably remain "relatively stable." With the mega-trend of global multipolarity that began from the late 1980s continuing, so long as China managed to maintain stability for 20 years, a positive change in China's favor would definitely emerge. Thus, national interest rather than "morality" (ideology) should dominate Chinese foreign policy.

Knowing perfectly well that the top concern of the CCP rulers was staying in power permanently, the princelings included in the Report some nuanced recommendations. For instance, in addition to holding tight on the "barrel of the gun," they suggested that lessons be drawn from the fall of the CPSU in terms of directly assigning state assets to party officials so that they became the stockholders (*caichan jingji*) rather than the administrators that merely supervised the economy on the party's behalf. As such, *dangzheng fenkai* had to be reduced to the minimum so as to transform the CCP into the most powerful "interest entity" (*liyi zhuti*) having a strong incentive to maintain political dominance and stability. Meanwhile, those politically insignificant loss-making small- and medium-sized SOEs could be privatized for the sake of efficiency. As good mind readers, they specifically warned the top leadership against enlisting popular support for the economic reform by excessively raising people's expectations of it, which was dangerous politically. The party should, they argued, abandon the policy of "appeasing the people" (*jiaomin zhengce*) and not hesitate to impose discipline and order heavy-handedly.

Having grown up in the Mao era, the princelings, this Report's authors included, naturally thought of themselves as future leaders of the country whose top mission was inheriting power from their fathers. However divergent their views on Tiananmen demonstrators, they resented power-sharing and were united behind the party elders headed by Deng who ordered the crackdown. It was widely rumored that Chen Yun told Deng Xiaoping in the immediate aftermath of Tiananmen: "After all, only our kids are reliable!"[31] An unwritten intra-party rule shortly came into force, to the effect that at least one child of each Red Family be promoted to central government minister. Meanwhile, members of New Class families were allowed again to "swim in the sea," a synonym for doing business. This violated the CCP's previous interdicts during the 1980s, especially the most recent one issued in an unprecedentedly harsh tone on July 28, 1989.[32] The institutionalization of collective heredity and chartered wealth grabbing through a money–power nexus thus created large numbers of crony capitalists from within the New Class. Like what they did through dual pricing in the 1980s, the princelings took the lead again in amassing wealth. Trusted by the Old Guards as diehard defenders of Chinese socialism, nonetheless the princelings, though not all of them, were scared by the fall of Communism and its global implications. Their deep fear of a sudden collapse of the CCP drove their unprecedented greed and thirst for wealth. Chinese economist Luo Xiaopeng recounted in 2012 that Deng Zhifang, the younger son of Deng Xiaoping, once confided to one of his inner-circle friends shortly after Tiananmen, "Previously, we never thought of making big money (*gaoqian*) for ourselves. Now we must think about it very seriously."[33]

Thus, under the surface of "socialist resurrection" after the Tiananmen Incident, socialism was betrayed even further. With regard to the Princelings' Report, it is hard to gauge to what extent this Report had influenced Chinese rulers. Yet the Report was in any sense extremely important as their recommendations coincided, to a considerable extent, with China's political and economic changes in the coming decade. There were nonetheless variations. First of all, economic radicalism predominated from 1992 onward. The marketization reform in the urban areas was implemented in an extremely radical way. Secondly, rather than state assets being assigned directly to nomenclatura, managers of a great number of the SOEs conspired with local officials to transfer huge amounts of stolen assets into their pockets. Tens of millions of urban workers in the SOEs were sacked without receiving proper compensation. Thirdly, contrary to the authors' prediction of souring relations between China and the West, reconciliation materialized in 1992, only three years after the Tiananmen. In addition, in the ensuing debate between a US-trained economist Justin Yifu Lin, and Wang Xiaodong, one of the authors of the Report, Dr. Lin achieved a landslide victory whose neoclassical thesis of comparative advantage has underpinned China's development strategy ever since. Wang lost favor with the regime, which was turning increasingly "pro-Western" despite its nationalist rhetoric. Generally speaking, nonetheless, the utterly blatant Machiavellianism of this suggestive Report bolstered the confidence of the regime in dealing with its own people in a more intransigent way, thereby fostering its subsequent transformation from "the world's last major left-wing dictatorship" to "the world's last major right-wing dictatorship."

Turning Point in 1992: Socialist Market or Market Leninism?

> If we do not adhere to socialism, if we do not carry out reform and opening, if we do not develop the economy and improve people's standard of living, it will definitely lead [China] to a dead end.[34]—Deng Xiaoping in 1992

Given his age, eagerness to make his reform legacy irreversible and to retrieve his reputation spoiled by the crackdown[35] drove Deng to make a showdown with his opponents. From mid-January until the end of February 1992, Deng, who had formally retired in November 1989, made his journeys to a handful of key economic provinces where he addressed local officials on the justification of a socialist market. Like Mao, Deng adopted similar "back thrust" tactics by touring the southern provinces in an attempt to mobilize support among the "local lords." During his southern tour (*nanxun*) to Zhuhai, one of the four SEZs, Deng chaired a special meeting in which senior PLA generals participated and vowed their allegiance. In his last stop in Shanghai, Deng even refused to meet with Chen Yun who was enjoying a winter holiday, as usual, in China's largest industrial city and template of the planning economy. Learning that Deng had secured strong backing from the PLA, Chen Yun knew that objection was futile; he decided to quit.[36]

What messages did Deng convey during his *nanxun*? First and foremost, he contended that market and planning existed in both the capitalist and the socialist economic systems. More elements of market or more elements of planning were not what distinguished socialism from capitalism. He said, "*Planning economy is not equal to socialism.* Capitalism also has planning;

Market economy is not equal to capitalism. Socialism also has market. Planning and market are both economic means."[37] Admitting frankly that nobody within the CCP, Mao and himself included, could furnish a clear-cut definition of "socialism, Marxism, and capitalism,"[38] he uncharacteristically attempted to give a new definition to socialism. Not mentioning a single word about Communism, Deng instead defined socialism in an opportunistic way by spelling out three criteria for socialism.[39] Socialism, according to him, was such a thing *as long as* it "increases the productive force, improves people's standard of living, and enhances China's comprehensive national strength."[40] But still, he fell short of explaining the "fundamental difference between capitalism and socialism." Rather, he continued to repeat the old dogma that "only socialism can save China; and only socialism can develop China."[41] In this way, Deng paradoxically took socialism as both a means and an end. To reconcile his ideological insincerity and blatant pragmatism, Deng asserted that a high economic growth was of absolute necessity; a low growth was tantamount to failure in politics as it would lead people to question the validity of socialism after comparing China's economic performance with that of the other nations, especially its neighbors.[42] This is the first time that Deng linked high growth with political legitimacy. And he called for developing an outward-oriented economy.[43]

Deng's "back thrust" tactics paid off. His remarks evoked nationwide repercussions, especially in the coastal areas in Southeastern China that had achieved rapid export-led growth since the late 1970s. As anticipated, Deng's popularity was back again among the ordinary Chinese and the disgruntled intellectuals who, for different reasons, were happy to see the revival of the reform. General Secretary Jiang Zemin initially remained ambivalent. On March 14th and 23rd, the military ignored their boss twice to openly express support for Deng and his reform and open-door policy.[44] On May 22nd, Deng made an inspection tour to the Capital Iron and Steel Complex (*Shougang*), where he allegedly charged Jiang for being aloof to his *nanxun* "remarks."[45] Sensing Deng's unprecedented heavy-handedness in imposing his reform agenda, Jiang stopped vacillating. On June 9th, he gave a keynote speech at the Central Party School where he, for the first time, propounded the notion of a socialist market economy.[46] Deng was satisfied and forgave the wavering General

Secretary. Under such circumstances, the entire situation changed substantially. The Fourteenth National Party's Congress held in October 1992 enshrined Deng's new thinking on socialist market into the party constitution. His "theory on building a socialism with Chinese characteristics," as enunciated by the Congress, was further written into the PRC's constitution the following year, which was later touted as so-called Deng Xiaoping Theory. The planning faction suffered a fundamental debacle. Except Premier Li Peng, all followers of Chen Yun were driven out of the Politburo Standing Committee (PSC). The dust finally settled when the leftists, mainly the ideologues and the central planners, dropped out almost completely from the power center, a phenomenon unprecedented in the history of the Chinese Communist Party (CCP).[47]

Ostensibly, Deng's crushing victory was enabled by the situational logic: the impact of the Global 1989, and by his political stratagem to a lesser extent, rather than by the theoretical power of his "theory" per se. Amidst the Party's Congress, a Peking University professor of political economy jumped out of his office window to kill himself in protest of what he perceived to be the CCP's ultimate betrayal of socialism.[48] Having failed politically, the ideologues headed by Deng Liqun and his cohort Duan Ruofei refused to endorse Deng's "theory" and were biding time to strike back. From 1995 onward, prior to Deng's death in February 1997, they issued 10,000-word-long letters of petition to the Central Committee almost year by year, condemning Deng's capitalist-oriented reforms.[49] In reality, even by the end of the 1990s, not merely Deng, but no one else within and outside the party could convincingly explain what was meant by a "socialist market economy" and "socialism with Chinese characteristics."[50] Whether intentionally or not, Deng had confused *economic planning* (if any) under capitalism with the *planning economy* under socialism, which is incomparably different. Blurring the boundary between modern capitalism and state socialism, nonetheless, Deng was forced to redefine socialism in order to justify "market economy" in China. The paradox is, from his definition (including three "*as-long-as*"), all the now-developed countries (NDCs) were socialist states and had long been so by every measure. Recalling the conversation between Deng and a visiting African leader in the 1980s, he had been so outspoken about socialism that his utterance deserves to be quoted again, "I suggest you not [to] do socialism; … So long as it helps improve the people's standard of living, you may call it whatever 'ism' as you wish later on."[51] If the "whatever 'ism' of anything but socialism was now defined as socialism, what would make socialism 'socialism'?"

There is no denying that Deng's victory did not make the argument of his "theory" slightly more cogent. As Wang Lixiong vividly put it, "He is a chief-architect needless to design anything; he has a so-called Deng Xiaoping Theory without 'any theory' at all."[52] Lacking theoretical capacity, Deng was simply unleashing market forces by stimulating people's desire for materialism. His argument about socialism, therefore, made sense of the reverse logic: only a thriving economy could keep the party in power and consolidate its rule, thereby saving Chinese "socialism." In other words, "It's the economy, stupid."[53] And "it is (only) the economy (that is important)." That slogan suited Deng perfectly well whose top concern was regime legitimacy after Tiananmen. As a matter of fact, the third-generation leadership led by Jiang had explored and experimented numerous ways to increase regime legitimacy by other means like neo-Confucianism, patriotism or nationalism,[54] but largely in vain due to their incompatibility with either the Communist ideology or practical policy objectives. Thus, the Chinese rulers, after trying various solutions, eventually recognized that economic growth was the only reliable source of legitimacy of the Communist regime. Therefore, an efficiency-biased marketization reform was necessary.

Under communist institutions and culture, once something was justified by necessity, it became a political correctness that nobody could challenge in the foreseeable future. The CCP's forceful justification of "market economy" not only reshaped China's path-dependent reform process, prompting its transition from that of market socialism in the 1980s to that of market Leninism after 1992, but also created a near-superstitious belief in market fundamentalism across the nation. Such a neoliberal turn necessarily entailed a Washington Consensus-type reform agenda at the expense of social justice, leading to the betrayal of socialism in an institutionally thoroughgoing way. Pragmatic as he was, Deng was after all a veteran revolutionary whose remnant belief in socialism led him to believe that the strong party state would remain uneroded in the long distant future; he was committed to promoting "common prosperity" through income redistribution[55]—Deng's socialist promise. He seemed deeply naive in this respect for failing to realize that, as individuals, he and his successor could in no way rival institutions or reverse the institutional change his reform had evoked. Moreover, with the demise of Communism, what could hold the nomenclatura together and maintain their political loyalty was nothing but material interests. They as technocratic elites were far more opportunistic than Deng in embracing capitalism. Committed to an "ideology of no ideology," as coined by Lin Chun, they were bound to become the largest beneficiaries of the market Leninist reform, henceforth the largest special interests poised to capture the state for further self-enrichment.

Such a trajectory is not what Deng had intended or anticipated. Nor was it the corollary of Tiananmen. From a historical and comparative perspective, it is ostensibly not the Tiananmen crackdown per se, but the particular way Deng Xiaoping drew lessons from the Tiananmen that changed China profoundly in the direction that few could foresee accurately.

Notes

1. Georgy Katsiaficas (2006), "Neoliberalism and the Gwangju Uprising," http://www.eroseffect.com/articles/neoliberalismgwangju.htm
2. He Qinglian (2015), "An Academic Myth: The Rise of the Middle Class will Promote Democracy," 17/11/2005. http://heqinglian.net/2005/11/17/%E4%B8%AD%E5%9B%BD%E5%A4%A7%E9%99%86%E4%B8%BA%E4%BB%80%E4%B9%88%E6%9A%B4%E5%8A%9B%E8%94%93%E5%BB%B6%EF%BC%9F-56-48-21/
3. Joseph Kahn, "The Nation: Party of the Rich; China's Congress of Crony Capitalists," *The New York Times*, 10/11/2002.
4. Zhu Xueqin (2003), "Common Sense or Pride?" http://www.edubridge.com/erxiantang/l2/zhuxueqin_lishenzhi.htm
5. Wang Lixiong (2000), "The Mao Zedong Mentality and Its Undercurrents," *Modern China Studies*, No. 3.
6. Interview with Wang Lixiong in September 2003. Zhao Ziyang also acknowledged the existence of such an element. Zong (2007), p. 201.
7. After June 4, all work units were ordered to rethink the "turmoil and counter-revolutionary rebellion." The audience was told that without

those old comrades, especially Deng Xiaoping, it was difficult to define the nature of the turmoil.

8. *People's Daily*, 10/06/1989. Deng's Works, vol. 3, p. 324.
9. Deng's speech in December 1990. Deng Xiaoping nianpu (Part II) (2004), Beijing: zhonggong zhongyang wenxian yanjiushi, p. 1346. http://theory.people.com.cn/n/2012/1028/c350803-19412863.html
10. "Chen Junhong on Deng's Strategy," *renminwang*, 28/10/2012. http://theory.people.com.cn/n/2012/1028/c350803-19412863.html; About "Deng Xiaoping's '24-Character Strategy,'" http://www.globalsecurity.org/military/world/china/24-character.htm
11. Deng's speech in April 1992. http://theory.people.com.cn/n/2012/1028/c350803-19412863.html
12. Deng's speech in December 1990. http://theory.people.com.cn/n/2012/1028/c350803-19412863.html
13. *Beijing Daily*, 7/04/2010. http://news.xinhuanet.com/politics/2010-04/07/c_1220556.htm
14. Deng Xiaoping nianpu (II) (2004), p. 1289. http://news.china.com/history/all/11025807/20120301/17066016.html
15. Deng's Works, vol. 3, p. 311.
16. Deng's Works, vol. 3, pp. 311–313.
17. Ibid., pp. 350–351, 10/12/1989.
18. Han Shaogong and Wang Yao (2002), "Societal Cracks and Rebuilding," November, Suzhou. http://boxun.com/news/gb/pubvp/2014/07/201407070559.shtml#.WWUA5VUrLIU; Zhou Qiren (2008), "What did Deng Xiaoping Do Correctly?" An address delivered to "Seminar on China's Reform: 30 Years Anniversary," Chicago University. *Economic Observer Daily*, 28/07/2008. http://zhouqiren.org/archives/655.html
19. A Chronology of China's Pension Reform. http://www.reformdata.org/index.do?m=wap&a=show&catid=301&typeid=&id=28415; China's Medicare Reform. http://www.reformdata.org/special/57/about.html
20. Aiqun Hu (2012), "The Global Spread of Neo-Liberalism and China's Pension Reform since 1978," *Journal of World History*, 23:3, pp. 609–638.
21. China Enterprise Management Annual 1993. http://www.reformdata.org/content/19930101/9533.html
22. Wu Jinglian (1999), *Studies on China's Economic Development*, Shanghai: yuandong chubanshe, pp. 387–388.
23. Chris Miller (2016), "Could Mikhail Gorbachev Have Saved the Soviet Union?" *Foreign Policy*, 21/12/2016. http://foreignpolicy.com/2016/12/21/could-mikhail-gorbachev-have-saved-the-soviet-union/

24. Deng's Works, vol. 3, pp. 370–371.
25. Robert Strayer (1998), *Why did the Soviet Union Collapse? Understanding Historical Change*, Oxon: Routledge, pp. 191–193.
26. Wang Lixiong (2000), "Mao Zedong Mentality and Its Undercurrents," *Modern China Studies*, No. 3.
27. Politburo member Qiao Shi led a CCP delegation on a visit to Romanian and Bulgaria to exchange experience on suppressing the demonstrators. http://www.standoffattiananmen.com/2015/06/people-of-1989-qiao-shi.html
28. Chun Lin (2008), "China: Changing the Rules of the Game," *Soundings*, 39:1, pp. 7–19.
29. http://nf.nfdaily.cn/nanfangdaily/zt/nshiz/60jg/200909010001.asp
30. Cited by *China Spring*, No. 1, 1992. http://non-violentes.blogspot.co.uk/2014/06/blog-post.html
31. Cheng Xiang (2014), "How the CCP's Crony Capitalism Came into Being?" HK: ejinsight, 29/05/2014. http://forum.hkej.com/node/113277
32. On July 28, 1989, the CCP's Central Committee and the State Council made decisions with regard to addressing "the masses' concerns." http://cpc.people.com.cn/GB/64162/64165/67447/68007/4640256.html
33. Luo Xiaopeng (2012), "The Premier's Dilemma under the Party's Heaven," *Century China*, 24/8. http://www.chinainperspective.com/ArtShow.aspx?AID=17301
34. Deng' Works, vol. 3, p. 370.
35. Zong (2007), p. 42.
36. Hu Ping (2016), "Zhuhai Meeting and the Role of the PLA in CCP's Internal Strife," 1/07/2016. http://www.rfa.org/mandarin/pinglun/hup-ing/huping-07012016100604.html; cited from Ezra Vogel (2013), *Deng Xiaoping and the Transformation of China* (Chinese edition), HK: CUHK Press, pp. 591–596.
37. Deng's Works, vol. 3, p. 373.
38. "Deng Xiaoping's Southern Tour Remarks [Original]," *zhongwai guanli*, 19/07/2016. http://cj.sina.com.cn/article/detail/1790671321/31346?column=china&ch=9
39. In the 1980s, Deng did not even hide his suspicion of socialism, which he had once conveyed to a visiting African leader. For understandable reasons, those sensitive words were not included into the *Selected Works of Deng Xiaoping*. Du Daozheng (2008), "How to Look on Deng Xiaoping Today?" *Caijing*, 05/12/2008.

40. Deng's Works, vol. 3, p. 372.
41. *Selected Works of Deng Xiaoping*, vol. 3, p. 311.
42. *Selected Works of Deng Xiaoping*, vol. 3, p. 375.
43. *Selected Works of Deng Xiaoping*, vol. 3, p. 375.
44. *China Daily*, 16/01/2013. http://dailynews.sina.com/bg/news/int/int/chinesedaily/20130116/06004162368.html; Hu Ping (2016) on the role of PLA. http://www.rfa.org/mandarin/pinglun/huping/huping-07012016100604.html
45. http://www.people.com.cn/GB/historic/0522/1680.html; Zhou Ruijin, "I and Huangpu Ping," http://xwjz.eastday.com/eastday/xwjz/node358630/node358631/u1a4624446.html; http://www.shtong.gov.cn/node2/node2245/node4522/node5661/node5686/node63733/userobject1ai8825.html; http://3g.ifeng.com/news/history/lszt/deng/news?aid=29910392&mid=1477658816538_6mq57i5450&rt=1&p=10(&11)
46. Jiang Zemin's Remarks at the Central Party School, 9/06/1992. http://www.scio.gov.cn/ztk/xwfb/36/10/Document/929008/929008.htm
47. Wang Lixiong (2000), *Modern China Studies*, No. 2.
48. Ma Licheng and Lin Zhijun (1998), *Cross Sword (jiaofeng)*, Beijing: Today's China Press, pp. 205–209.
49. "How did Jiang Zemin handle the 'ten-thousand-word' petition letter from mid-1990s onwards?" http://news.ifeng.com/a/20140508/40201801_0.shtml
50. Even until the late 1990s, few economists including the most ardent neoliberal economists such as Wu Jinglian could tell what "socialist market economy" meant. There was wide special coverage of the discussion on this topic on the domestic media.
51. For understandable reasons, these sensitive words were not included into the Selected Works of Deng Xiaoping. Du Daozheng, "How to Look on Deng Xiaoping Today?" *Caijing*, 05/12/2008.
52. Wang Lixiong (2000), *Modern China Studies*, No. 2.
53. "If Voters Don't Believe that 'It's the Economy, Stupid', We're All Doomed," *The Telegraph*, 1/04/2015. http://www.telegraph.co.uk/finance/comment/jeremy-warner/11509865/If-voters-dont-believe-that-its-the-economy-stupid-were-all-doomed.html
54. For instance, nationalism was promoted after 1989 in a bid to head off Western ideological crusade and "American hegemonism." This, however, by no means implied that Chinese leaders would act in a realist

manner in foreign relations. They used nationalism merely for the purpose of mobilizing public support, but would never allow it to derail China's low-profile foreign policy. Nor were they to commit themselves to economic nationalism in any meaningful way.

55. Deng's Works, vol. 3, pp. 373–374.

5

The 1990s: Washington Consensus in China?

The 1990s, in the wake of Deng Xiaoping's Southern tour in early 1992, saw the resurgence of "economic radicalism" that the princelings had warned against one year earlier, despite themselves ironically being no less radical with regard to some common issues, such as privatization. Contrary to conventional wisdom, a near-shock therapy price liberalization was accomplished within two years (1993–1994) in the first place.[1] In addition, from 1993 onward, large numbers of small and medium-sized state-owned enterprises (SOEs) were privatized in the localities with the connivance of the central state. In the absence of proper compensation and a sound nationwide safety net, massive layoffs of urban industrial workers dramatically drove up levels of income inequality, leading to persistent underconsumption ever since. Aimed at "asset stripping" rather than "wealth creation," and manipulated by the SOEs' insiders in complicity with local officials, this sort of nomenclatura privatization did not make the Chinese economy more efficient at both macro and micro levels. The relative decline of the SOEs, nonetheless, was offset by an export boom and soaring FDI from 1992, which kept Chinese economy growing robustly, thereby enabling China to avoid "transitional decline" characterizing post-Communist transition economies in the former Soviet

J. Yue, *China's Rise in the Age of Globalization*, Palgrave Studies in Economic History, https://doi.org/10.1007/978-3-319-63997-0_5

Bloc. However, different from the East Asian developmental states, the Chinese decision makers blended export promotion with unprecedented market opening rather than with a higher stage of import substitution, which further weakened the SOEs. By the late 1990s, underconsumption and flagging industrialization rendered China's high GDP growth difficult to sustain. The country's inexorable dependence on exports and FDI therefore prompted the Chinese regime to resort to "WTO plus" deep integration in a bid to reverse the declining economic momentum and to address its overriding concern for legitimacy.

Radicalizing "Reform and Opening" as Political Correctness

The two key issues of the SOEs' reform and the liberalization of trade and investment dominated China's reform and opening agenda after 1992. As the centerpiece of the market Leninist reform, restructuring of ownership (*gaizhi*) was considered to be the key to transforming the SOEs into "genuine firms."[2] The *gaizhi* became a pressing issue from 1993 given the fact that although the SOEs absorbed the largest share of state financial resources, their contribution to China's employment and economic growth kept declining[3] as compared with the non-SOEs, including village and township enterprises (VTEs) and the foreign-invested enterprises (FIEs). Subsidizing loss-making SOEs had become a heavy burden to state finance.[4] The deeper reason for underperformance of the SOEs is that until the mid-1990s, the SOEs failed to achieve remarkable technological progress despite the fact that various reform and reinvigoration scenarios had been tried.[5] The SOEs had little incentive to improve product quality even in the face of a "buyers' market" when the consumption-led prosperity came to an end in the late 1980s. Rather, under the "soft budget constraint," they had a strong impulse to expand production regardless of boom or bust. Since the bulk of FDI was from Hong Kong, Macau and Taiwan (HKMT) engaging in processing trade and not thus encroaching on the domestic market, the declining performance of the SOEs was ostensibly not the result of external competition but the unsuccessful restructuring per se.

For the Chinese regime, the SOEs' restructuring remained a thorny issue. On the one hand, it had to prop up the SOEs for the sake of political stability; on the other hand, it had to keep the country financially healthy by reducing subsidies to SOEs, and for this purpose, laying off redundant workers became a prerequisite for making the SOEs' efficient players capable of operating and assuming budget responsibility autonomously.[6] At the Fourteenth National Party's Congress held in October 1992, Zhu Rongji was further elevated to Politburo Standing Committee member in full charge of the economy. As the new economic tsar, Zhu, in November 1993, embarked on the SOEs' ownership restructuring (*gaizhi*) in terms of introducing multiple forms of ownership and whereby to establish the so-called modern enterprise system (corporate governance) in the image of Western firms within the SOEs. Zhu's genuine interest, however, was corporatizing the large-sized SOEs, while leaving the small- and medium-sized SOEs at the disposal of local governments. This left the door open for spontaneous privatization in the localities.[7] Zhu Rongji was expressly opposed to blatant privatization of local state-owned SMEs, arguing that doing so would "render socialism non-existent."[8] But he was just paying lip service. With more and more SOEs, especially the locally affiliated small- and medium-sized SOEs, continuing to suffer losses on a larger scale, he changed his mind and was unopposed to "selling some small SOEs to individuals."[9] In November 1995, the Chinese Communist Party (CCP) decided to initiate further reform titled "Grasp the big, let go [of] the small" (*zhuada fangxiao*),[10] which means to foster large-sized SOEs into "bigger and stronger players" at all costs while withdrawing state sponsorship of the SMEs.

The scenario was allegedly based on the fact that "the big" were empirically less susceptible to losing money than "the small."[11] The prevailing theoretical foundation for the *gaizhi* at the time was that the SOEs were inherently inefficient, thanks to the widely dispersed ownership of the SOEs, although nominally held "by the whole people," that demotivated the management. Thus, the best way out was "concentrated ownership" held by the SOEs' insiders through management buyout (MBO); otherwise, the SOEs would sooner or later "melt" into bankruptcy. This is the so-called popsicle theory (*binggun lilun*) advocated by people such as Professors Li Yining and Zhang Weiying, neoliberal economists at Peking University.[12] Carrying out *zhuada fangxiao* on such a basis is theoretically illogical since the ownership structure of the SOEs, small or big, was exactly the same. In addition, sheer privatization of "the small" was by no means the only solution to the underperformance of the SOEs in practical terms. For one thing, the prevalent property theory was more than falsified by Japan's mixed ownership that helped to build Japan into an economic superpower. In addition, privatization did not necessarily lead to efficiency improvement, as international experience had shown. The latest UNDP report (2015) concluded that "first, 'no model of ownership (public, private or mixed) is intrinsically more efficient than the others'; and second, that 'efficiency of service provision under all ownership models depends on factors like competition, regulation, autonomy and wider issues of institutional development.'"[13]

Thus, the crux of China's SOEs' restructuring does not lie in whether privatization is necessary or not, but that as one of the options of *gaizhi*, the way in which privatization was to be carried out in China's ad hoc political and institutional settings mattered more than the necessity of privatization per se. In fact, the peril of "insider control" was looming large after some ten years of contract responsibility system (CRS) reform in the urban since the early 1980s. Vowing to "kill the bud in its infancy" in the aftermath of Global 1989, the Chinese regime was more tough-minded in banning all forms of independent unionization. This rendered the urban industrial workers easy prey to the asset pillaging of SOEs' insiders. Sponsored by the "reformist" sub-national administrations, the nomenclatura privatization went on smoothly and was met with little resistance from the workers despite massive layoffs and inappropriate compensation. Such privatization was much more unjust than the *voucher privatization,* at least in the initial phase in the post-Communist Russia where national wealth was evenly distributed among all citizens. It should also be pointed out that the peasants lived no better a life from the early 1990s. Their living standards virtually stagnated due to the urban-biased policies the central state had carried out from 1988 at the expense of rural development.[14] The immiserization of workers and peasants dramatically heightened income inequality between the rich and the poor and between the rural and the urban. Contrasting this reality with Deng's old vision, "If reform results in income polarization, it is a failed reform,"[15] the CCP had thus engineered a successful "anti-socialist" reform project in the 1990s.

Prior to the *gaizhi*, the Chinese regime had started to implement trade and investment liberalization since late 1992 in the wake of Deng's southern tour. What drove China's wider market access was the leadership's eagerness to promote external-oriented economic development in accordance with Deng's instructions by imitating the perceived East Asian model. For that purpose, China needed to get the Western-imposed economic sanctions removed as early as possible. China's "low-profile" foreign policy paid off. By abstaining from the UN Security Council vote on armed intervention in Iraq in 1990, and by making substantial concessions on issues of intellectual property rights (IPR) and market access to the USA in 1992, China secured US retention of most-favored-nation (MFN) trading status and the lifting of sanctions by the West altogether.

Unlike the typical EOI approach of successful late-industrializers in East Asia that blended export promotion with import substitution on the back of an insulated domestic market, China seemed contented with the neoliberal notion of so-called indiscriminate market access, in the hope of promoting export of labor-intensive products by fully exploiting its comparative advantage of cheap labor on the one hand, while opening up its vast domestic market in exchange for technology transfer from the global firms, a strategy called "exchange for technology with market access" (ETMA), on the other. The ETMA-centered development strategy differed from Zhao Ziyang's Coastal Development Strategy (CDS) in important ways. Targeting mainly the HKMT investors, Zhao's CDS was parochially based whose "two ends abroad" (*liangtouzaiwai*) approach did not encroach on the domestic market, at least in theoretical terms. By contrast, the new strategy under the auspices of Zhu Rongji targeted predominantly the market-seeking investors from Organization for Economic Co-operation and Development (OECD) countries. Its intention was not so much increasing export earnings as securing technology transfer by liberalizing trade and investment as a quid pro quo. Such a strange combination of export promotion with market access ran counter to either "embedded liberalism" that enabled Western economies to prosper in the long postwar decades by liberalizing trade while restricting capital movements, or the developmental-state approach of the East Asian newly-industrialized economies (NIEs) restricting both imports and FDI.

The radicalization of China's reform and opening after 1992, apart from the Deng Xiaoping factor, was not so much the result of lack of experience or ignorance of the policy makers as their deliberate decisions. Foresight had never been scant from the regime's "insiders." For one thing, warnings were issued from 1990 to 1992 from inside the regime against insider-manipulated privatization and excessive opening but were ignored.[16] Moreover, a rarely known significant policy debate about whether "comparative advantage" should underpin China's development strategy in the early 1990s ended up in the opposing "catching-up" side being severely penalized.[17] From 1994 until 1996, another round of policy debate broke out between economist Justin Yifu Lin, on one side, and nationalist Wang Xiaodong and Liu Liqun (DRC research fellow) on the other regarding which development strategy should take precedence: comparative advantage or catching-up. The debate aroused little attention within academic and policy communities,[18] despite powerful counterarguments made by the latter. Prior to this debate, Lin's view had become official policy.

As a matter of fact, from late 1992 onward, skeptics of China's market Leninist reform and excessive opening were increasingly prone to being implicitly labeled by the CCP's propaganda organs as "leftists" who "opposed the party's reform and opening policies."[19] Deng's caveats during his *nanxun* in 1992 against "perils from the Left" lent weight to the third-generation leadership, now composed of "all reformers alike," as depicted by the CCP's mouthpiece,[20] who mythologized reform and opening into unchallengeable political correctness. By so doing, the Chinese leadership eschewed the embarrassment caused by the "'socialist market economy' without socialism" in ideological terms. Yet, as a deliberate political strategy, mythologizing reform and opening only fueled further radicalism. And by silencing all dissenting opinions by maximizing abstraction of the reform and opening, simplifying it as "the more marketized, the more externally integrated, the better and correct politically," the Chinese decision makers confined their policy options to a very narrow range.

The Statecraft of Zhu Rongji

In contrast to Zhao Ziyang whose reform initiatives were hampered by the central planners in the 1980s, forcing him into neoliberal solutions, the new leadership under Jiang Zemin and Zhu Rongji had more options in 1992. With "market economy" being justified, they got the staunch support of both Deng Xiaoping and Chen Yun in terms of strengthening central government authority. Zhu, himself being a central planner in the past, had close links with China's Gosplan, whose role, as he saw it, remained indispensable to China's macroeconomic stability. After becoming a Politburo Standing Committee (PSC) member in October 1992, Zhu was appointed First Vice-Premier in April 1993, taking full charge of economic reform and development. These developments imply that institutional barriers to internal integration had decreased significantly after 1992. Trusted by both Deng and Chen politically, Zhu had greater flexibility than Zhao did in devising his own roadmap of reform and development.

One big problem confronting Zhu was that the vacuum left over by the scrapping of the planning system after 1992 was not automatically filled by a functioning market but by a dual system in which a chaotic market and state socialist institutions coexisted. Zhu was a statist, believing that a strong state was indispensable to an orderly economic development of China. This was what Deng Xiaoping and Chen Yun both agreed. As a former central planner, Zhu supported the creation of a market system in lieu of central planning. Yet he was skeptical about the efficacy of mere legal and economic means to regulate the Chinese market still in chaos.[21] His preference for administrative means, nonetheless, made him infamous in 1993 and 1994 when he strove to correct rampant market disorders, hyperinflation and economic overheating caused by Deng's *nanxun* in 1992.[22] He was cursed by many SOEs' managers and government officials, especially those in the coastal provinces, as "a planner at heart" (*guzili de jihuapai*), a derogative word equal to "opposing reform" in political terms. Benefiting enormously from Deng's reform in the 1980s, vested interests in these areas who were emboldened by Deng's *nanxun* remarks became market fundamentalists almost overnight. They sincerely believed in *unfettered* market, *unconditional* decentralization, and *free trade*. Any attempt to "regulate the market" and to recentralize power from the localities, as they saw it, was tantamount to opposing Deng's reform and opening, hence restoring the planning economy.[23] In the face of wide-ranging resentment, and risking being labeled as an "anti-reformer," Zhu was unswayed by these attacks. Fortunately, Deng gave him the green light to address the trouble he made.

Heavily influenced by Chen Yun's "birdcage" theory, Zhu placed great emphasis on the "general equilibrium" of the national economy and the primacy of the state in even market-based economic development. His long-time career as a practitioner in China's Gosplan (State Planning Commission; SPC) and the State Economic Commission (SEC) gave him a broad view of how the socialist economy was organized. Du Runsheng, one of the most distinguished economists, commented on the three economic leaders after Hua Guofeng this way, "Zhao Ziyang knew a bit of market economy, Li Peng knew nothing of economics, Zhu Rongji knew a bit of planning economy."[24] It was roughly true that Zhu knew more about planning than about market, as informed by his past experience. His understanding of market economy was no more than artificially creating an equilibrium between supply and demand through *administrative* means.[25] His ostensibly "non-market" propensity to manage the "socialist market economy" made him somewhat similar to the 1960s' Soviet reformers obsessed with building a "computerized socialist utopia."[26] In addition, Zhu despised private enterprises, including the state-owned SMEs, ignoring their greater role in innovation and job creation. Instead, he attached great importance to large-sized SOEs, viewing them as the primary sources of innovation and the agents of industrialization. His ways to reinvigorate the SOEs were threefold: injecting technical renovation funds, closing redundant production lines, and selecting "good cadres" for management[27]—a typical central planner's solution.

Before his promotion in April 1991 as Vice-Premier, Zhu as the mayor and party boss of Shanghai was widely regarded as China's "Gorbachev," given his perceived moderate attitude toward the city's demonstrators in 1989. It was not so much his Gorbachevite humanism as the "shock and awe" effect of the Tiananmen bloodshed that rendered massive use of force in Shanghai unnecessary. In fact, Zhu was no less tough than his counterparts in Beijing in restoring order in Shanghai, although in an intelligent way.[28] This, along with his rare talent in economics, gained him the full trust of Deng Xiaoping who ignored intra-party suspicions. It must be pointed out that the CCP after the Global 1989 took the collapse of the Soviet Union very seriously and would not allow China's "Gorbachev" to rise from within the nomenclatura; Zhu was no different than other leaders in reaching identical conclusions.[29] He had neither the vision of nor the commitment to building a democratic socialism in China. His approach of managed marketization thus diverged entirely from the social market economy that West Germany and France created after World War Two under democracy. After taking office in Beijing in 1991, his strong-willed personality and preference for tighter control of the economy earned him the nickname "economic tsar." But like other leaders, he had no intention to establish the rule of law for the sake of social justice. His image, style, and inner world suggested that he was no more than a clean official within the Communist Leviathan, who anticipated that the despotic institutions would function efficiently under his reign.

In contrast to Zhao Ziyang in the 1980s who gave due consideration to social justice when promoting market-oriented reform, Zhu, upon assuming Vice-Premiership, was determined to promote an efficiency-biased marketization reform by repudiating socialist welfare in the first place. His rule of "no appeasing the people" was no more pronounced than in his first initiative, the so-called "breaking the three irons" (iron wage, iron rice bowl and iron management position) (*za santie*) campaign in 1991. As is known, only the first "two irons" were broken in the years that ensued; interests of the SOEs' management were well protected as they were part of the nomenclatura. The *zhuada fangxiao* reform that began from 1995 saw massive layoffs among SOEs' workers. Between 1995 and 2002, around 30 million SOEs' workers lost their jobs.[30] After he assumed Premiership in March 1998, three de-socialist reforms abolishing free medicare, education and housing were carried out under his auspices, which further exacerbated the immiserization of the unemployed workers as well as the peasants in the rural areas. Not such a committed Communist as Gorbachev,[31] Zhu experienced great attitude change in the past decade (1989–1998), during which he, as mayor of Shanghai in 1989, objected to wage differentials between staff in the

SOEs and the FIEs; yet in 1998 he favored greater wage differentials between the managers and the workers, so long as the SOEs would "make money and pay taxes."[32]

Radical price liberalization (1993–1994) and privatization of the SOEs made Zhu a fellow traveler if not a devout disciple of the neoliberal Washington Consensus (WC). As a statist, Zhu re-regulated more than de-regulated the economy through a wide range of government interventions with a view to building an orderly and competitive market. In this respect, to his great embarrassment, many of the interventions were rendered ineffectual by the corrupt party state institutions. Yet, in general, his strong interventionism enabled privatization and trade and investment liberalization—the two key ingredients of the WC—to be undertaken in a hugely efficient way. For one thing, upon taking office as Premier in March 1998, he initiated institutional reform and abolished the State Asset Administration Bureau (SAAB), created a decade ago by his predecessor Li Peng to supervise the SOEs nationwide, so as to facilitate and give a further impetus to the "let go [of] the small" in the localities.[33] Back to the year 1992, Zhu in the capacity of Vice-Premier was directly involved in the market access talks between China and the USA, during which China made extensive concessions to open the door much wider than in the 1980s. From then on, he seemed more and more convinced that only "reciprocal opening" (*shuangxiang kaifang*) made sense for China's reform and opening, and doing so would prompt the US business community to lobby on China's behalf, thereby "favoring China's development much more than do the Americans."[34] Paradoxically, Zhu seemed genuinely upset by the harm excessive influx of FDI had done on the SOEs. At least twice between 1996 and 1998, he warned the "local lords" that their introduction of one foreign firm normally led to the closing down of several SOEs in other provinces, and that this was uneconomical.[35] But the displacement effect of FDI on the SOEs did not deter him from seeking further liberalization of trade and investment as to the extent of embracing the "WTO plus" deep integration in 1999.[36]

Being neither a socialist nor an economic nationalist naturally inclined Zhu for "external orientation" to underpin China's development strategy. His endorsement of ETMA highlighted his neoclassical faith in "indiscriminate market access." His former work experience in Shanghai also provided justification for his embrace of globalization. The period (1987–1991) when he served as the mayor and party boss of Shanghai saw the decline of China's planning system. The withering of mandatory planning and increasing scope of indicative planning undermined the SPC's ability to transfer goods and materials from one place to another. Fiscal decentralization introduced by Zhao Ziyang from the early 1980s prompted the less-developed areas, especially resource-rich hinterland provinces to establish their own high value-added downstream industries ("processing industries" in the jargon). Their drive for economic diversification curtailed intersectoral linkages across the nation, leading to not only diminishing demand for industrial goods from Shanghai but also tighter restrictions on resource outflow to the latter. As one of the "local lords," Zhu was vexed by the national economic feudalism that put the economy of Shanghai at stake. Aware that he could no longer count on the weak central state for solutions, Zhu arrived at the conclusion that the acute resource bottlenecks of Shanghai could only be addressed through external orientation, that is, increasing exports to earn as many hard currencies as possible for importing the needed raw materials.[37] He made it! Nevertheless, success in Shanghai did not seem to have prompted him to ponder carrying out institutional change to overcome economic feudalism whereby to create a unified national market on which the economic future of all parts of China—Shanghai, in particular—hinged in the long term. Rather, convinced by the efficacy of liberal globalization, he seemed to have arrived at an entirely different conclusion: deepening China's external integration. He applied his liberal globalization approach nationwide after becoming the "economic tsar."

Vowing to increase state capacity to cope with the mounting financial difficulties, Zhu as a statist reversed Zhao's policy and recentralized fiscal power from the provinces through tax-sharing reform in 1994. His fiscal recentralization without market integration nonetheless only fostered the "local lords" to strengthen provincial autarky by expanding economic diversification locally to overachieve the preset target of "forced growth" of the Communist regime that based its legitimacy on high GDP growth. The party state's evaluation mechanism linking officials' careers to GDP further amplified this ad hoc institutional legacy of both the traditional socialist system and Deng Xiaoping. Although displeased with Deng's frenetic quest for high growth from a technocratic perspective,[38] Zhu was in no position to rival the powerful "growth-forcing" institutions that had become even more intractable than in the pre-reform era. The "local lords," who were trapped in a race to the bottom in terms of either competing for FDI or blocking "free trade" within China, dedicated themselves to high GDP growth at all costs. With "shortage economy" ending in 1996, diseconomies of scale arising from nationwide industry isomorphism[39] led to across-the-board industrial decline.[40] Having limited means to regulate intra-provincial economies, Zhu's "strong" state was virtually powerless to deter the unstoppable diversification drive of the provinces.[41] Unable to count on corrupt Customs authorities, one of the key central government institutions, Zhu was even forced to plead with the local lords not to smuggle raw materials awash in glut domestically.[42]

Ostensibly, Zhu was in no sense Chinese Ludwig Erhard (1897–1977) who dedicated himself to blending socialism and the market. Despite having more options at least in theoretical terms from the outset, his neoliberal inclination led him to eschew socialism and internal integration to set China onto an alternative market-based self-reliance pathway of development. Rather, his "managed marketization" and radical external integration not only made the SOEs more difficult (to be analyzed below) but also created more formidable barriers to internal integration institutionally. Captivated by the reform and opening myth, which he himself helped to create in order to justify his neoliberal approach, nonetheless, Zhu left himself with only one option: greater external integration. And by so doing, he set China on a different path in an institutionally irreversible way, epitomized by his dire quest for WTO membership, thereby making the politically correct reform and opening a self-fulfilling prophecy.

Reform and Opening: Interacting the Wrong Way?

After signing the memorandum of understanding on IPR with the USA on January 17, 1992, China honored its commitments by revising its patent and trademark laws and enacting the anti-monopoly law in the second half of 1992.[43] In the same year, after nine rounds of hard bargaining, China and the USA concluded the memorandum of understanding on market access on October 10th. China agreed to remove most trade restrictions in the next few years. Meanwhile, at the "request" of the USA,[44] "China promised that it would *not subject any products to import substitution measures* in the future while stating that it had eliminated all import substitution regulations, guidance, and policies."[45] Despite enduring suspicions on the part of the US administration and business community on whether the promise would be honored then, and there seemed to be evidence suggesting Chinese default in a number of cases afterward,[46] the Chinese leaders took their commitment seriously in general as they had developed a new strategy to encourage industrialization, a strategy they believed would dwarf import substitution to bring technological leapfrogging for China, the so-called *yi shichang huan jishu* or exchange for technology with market access (ETMA). The intellectual origin of the ETMA can be traced back to the middle of the 1980s when the acute hard currency shortfall forced the Chinese government to enter into joint ventures (JVs) with the foreign businesses in the auto industry.[47] No longer limited to the auto industry, the ETMA took on a new meaning in 1992 in the sense that acquiring advanced technologies through "reciprocal opening" had become China's national development strategy. Targeting the OECD countries, especially the Triad (the USA, Japan, and the EU) where technologically advanced multinational corporations (MNCs) were concentrated, the ETMA closely served China's foreign policy goal of "appeasing the West" set by Deng Xiaoping after the Global 1989.

FDI, especially MNCs from the West, soared from 1992 as a result of the ETMA strategy. In 1992 alone, FDI reached $27.5 billion and more than doubled the previous year, which exceeded the total amounts of FDI in the entire 1980s. From 1993 until 1997, China ranked among the largest FDI destinations globally, next only to the USA and was the largest recipient of FDI among the developing nations. Its share in total fixed-asset investment rose from 7.5% in 1991 to peak at 17% in 1994 and stayed at more than 10% in the years that followed. Exports by the foreign-invested enterprises (FIEs) rose from 1.88% in 1986 to 20.44% in 1992 and further to 50.06% in 2001.[48] Their shares in China's indus-

Table 5.1 FDI in Chinese economy (1991–2001)

Year	Industrial output (%)	Share in GDP (%)	Tax contribution (%)
1991	5.29	1.96	–
1992	7.09	2.71	4.25
1993	9.14	3.67	5.71
1994	11.25	4.55	8.51
1995	14.31	5.87	10.96
1996	15.14	6.26	11.87
1997	18.57	7.74	13.16
1998	24.34	9.81	14.38
1999	27.75	11.10	15.99
2000	31.29	12.63	17.5
2001	27.98	11.12	19.01

Sources: Websites of Ministry of Commerce (MOFCOM) and State Bureau of Statistics (Stats)

trial value added and taxation also rose exponentially throughout the 1990s (Table 5.1). The influx of FDI was one of the prime drivers of China's prosperity in the first half of the 1990s.[49] Its role was even more salient against the backdrop of the harsh austerity measures taken by Zhu Rongji from 1993 to curb inflation.[50] FDI had contributed enormously to the "soft landing" of the Chinese economy in 1996 when the SOEs kept declining and the risk of deflation was looming large.

Taiwanese development economist Wan-wen Chu regarded ETMA as China's unique approach to enforcing import substitution in a flexible way through setting up JVs.[51] As analyzed in Chap. 2, the MNCs' technology spillovers on local firms were rather limited given their reluctance to transfer advanced technologies. The wholly owned subsidiaries (WOS) of the MNCs swiftly overtook the JVs in both numbers (1997) and amounts (2000) to become the dominant form of ownership, making it even more difficult for Chinese firms to access to the "core technologies" of the MNCs. In fact, the notion of ETMA highlighted the lack of will to develop among Chinese decision makers who renounced self-reliance on neoliberal grounds. Except in very limited sectors in which industrial policies such as local contents were attempted,[52] China failed to devise an appropriate strategy to facilitate the absorption, assimilation and upgrading of the imported technologies by the nationally owned enterprises (NOEs), either the SOEs or the private firms. More broadly, the Chinese state had never set forth a whole package of mutually reinforcing and well-coordinated Listian-type trade, industrial and technology policies to direct the country's industrialization.[53] The only industrial policy promulgated in 1994 was sectorally confined within the auto industry, known as the Automotive Industrial Policy (AIP). Yet even this sole industrial policy did not encourage the efforts of autonomous innovation of the domestic firms. Rather, the AIP placed heavy emphasis on technology imports and placed high hopes of industrial upgrading on entering into JVs with the global firms. This, as Chu argued, contrasted sharply with the practice of the East Asian developmental states that stiffly resisted being brought into partnership with the global firms, while sparing no effort to foster independent innovation capabilities of the local firms.[54]

Excessive dependence on technology imports is not a phenomenon unique to the auto industry. As the main carrier of technology imports, China's medium and large-sized SOEs across the country's industrial sectors attached little importance to the assimilation and absorption of imported technologies. As late as 2003, for instance, the ratio of funds invested by China's medium and large-sized industrial enterprises in technology imports and those invested in assimilation/absorption was just 1:0.07. In contrast, the ratios of both Japan's and South Korea's enterprises were kept around 1:10.[55] By the same token, Chinese policy makers were so short-sighted during the 1990s as to utterly ignore the vital importance of investing in technical education with a view to building up a large pool of highly skilled labor force for subsequent technological upgrading.[56] These developments severely impaired Chinese firms' innovation capability, rendering them inextricably dependent on technology imports from the advanced economies.

The ETMA ended up in failure by the end of the 1990s.[57] As a matter of fact, FDI was a double-edged sword. Although having driven the Chinese economy to grow rapidly, FDI did not lead to the substantial technological progress of the SOEs.[58] Unlike HKMT investors, the influx of market-seeking MNCs from the industrial West had a tremendous impact on the SOEs. Attracted by China's wider market access in the aftermath of Sino-US deals, FDI from the Triad rose sharply from US $1.46 billion in 1992 to US $11.74 billion in 1997, a sevenfold increase in just five years. It only slightly declined in 1998 to US $11.28 billion and has risen again ever since (Table 5.2). This ran counter to the pessi-

Table 5.2 FDI from HKMT and Triad (USA, Japan, EU) (1991–2001) (unit: US $100 million)

Year	GDP (%)	FDI (total)	HKMT	(%)	Triad	(%)
1991	9.2	43.6634	28.7166	65.77	11.0132	25.22
1992	14.2	110.0751	85.5757	77.74	14.6385	13.30
1993	13.5	275.1495	204.1334	74.19	40.5846	14.75
1994	12.6	337.6650	230.5648	68.28	61.0378	18.08
1995	10.5	375.2053	232.2192	61.89	83.2278	22.18
1996	9.6	417.2552	241.5216	57.88	98.5974	23.63
1997	8.8	452.5704	239.2139	52.86	117.3677	25.93
1998	7.8	454.6275	214.2357	47.12	112.7749	24.81
1999	7.1	403.1871	189.6175	47.03	116.68	28.94
2000	8.0	407.1481	177.9626	43.71	117.7792	28.93

Source: www.fdi.gov.cn

Table 5.3 Trade balance of FDI (1986; 1991–2000; 2005) (unit: US $100 million)

Year	Imp. (total)	(%)	Exp. (total)	(%)	Balance
1986	24.03	5.60	5.82	1.88	−18.21
1991	169.08	26.51	120.47	16.75	−48.61
1992	263.87	32.74	173.60	20.44	−90.27
1993	418.33	40.24	252.37	27.51	−165.96
1994	529.34	45.78	347.13	28.69	−182.21
1995	629.43	47.66	468.76	31.51	−160.67
1996	756.04	54.45	615.06	40.71	−140.98
1997	777.20	54.59	749.00	41.00	−28.2
1998	767.17	54.73	809.62	44.06	**42.45**
1999	858.84	51.83	886.28	45.47	27.44
2000	1172.73	52.10	1194.41	47.93	21.68
2001	1258.63	51.67	1332.35	50.06	73.72
2005	3875.13	58.70	4442.09	58.29	**566.96**

Source: www.fdi.gov.cn

mistic projection that the decline of the SOEs would dampen domestic demand, thereby making the Chinese market less appealing to the MNCs.[59] Rather, gaining a strong foothold on the domestic market in the year of 1998, as evidenced by the trade balance of FDI that turned into surplus and kept increasing ever since (most notably from 2005 onward), the MNCs began shifting to production increasingly for global markets and boosting exports from China by integrating it into their global supply chain (Table 5.3).[60]

However, the "political correctness" of the regime's logic of opening up and, as mentioned earlier, the party state's evaluation system linking the officials' chances of promotion to growth performance prompted all subnational administrations to scramble for FDI. Numerous policy preferences, such as arbitrary tax concessions and free use of land, were accorded by the local lords to foreign investors even at the expense of the NOEs, including the SOEs. The institutionalized nationwide discriminations against the NOEs, in taxation, for instance,[61] added to the predicament of the SOEs. Against such a backdrop, the *zhuada fangxiao* that began in 1995 further weakened the SOEs in their entirety. The so-called *zhuada fangxiao* was in large part a hidden Washington Consensus approach to reforming the ailing SOEs in the mid-1990s. The idea was to reinvigorate a small number of extra large-sized SOEs through entrusting them with monopolistic or oligopolistic power at the upper stream of economic activities and at the same time to withdraw state sponsorship of the large number of loss-making SMEs. Such a reform scenario highlighted the compromise between the regime's political rationale and its economic needs in that bailing out the SOEs in their entirety was financially unviable, whereas the large-sized SOEs located in key industrial sectors needed to be preserved at all costs as they controlled key economic resources crucial to the survival of the regime. The state-owned SMEs were, in contrast, much less important economically and politically. Privatizing them to offload fiscal burden without using the name of privatization was feasible given the "shock and awe" of Tiananmen and the mystifying of reform and opening as political correctness after Deng Xiaoping's *nanxun* in 1992. The concomitance of removing state sponsorship of the bulk of the SOEs and liberalizing trade and investment led China's reform and opening to interact under the worst conditions to the detriment of the NOEs, resulting in the SOEs being driven out of the market in huge numbers.

The extra large-sized SOEs kept expanding in size under massive state sponsorship. Nonetheless, under the institutional constraints of "forced growth" and the selection of senior managers of the SOEs based on political criteria (*dang guan rencai* or "party controls talents") rather than the candidates' professional expertise, the SOEs had very little incentive to innovate as usual. Thus, although becoming bigger in size under massive state sponsorship, they remained uncompetitive as a whole.[62] The FIEs in contrast achieved an overwhelming advantage over the NOEs. By the late 1990s, they had become the market leaders by dominating China's high-tech sectors and international trade.[63] The privately owned enterprises (POEs), though more dynamic than the SOEs, were largely backward technologically and poorly managed in relative terms. Most of their industrial operations could not be classified as regular manufacturing.[64] Thus, the SOEs, despite their inherent inefficiencies caused by the Communist institutions, made up the backbone of China's regular manufacturing. Their relative decline throughout the 1990s paradoxically eroded the country's foundation of autonomous national development.

1996 was a turning point. The SOEs across all industries for the first time posted net losses and thus were forced to lay off workers in huge numbers. Meanwhile, the non-performing loans (NPLs) of the four big state banks accumulated by the loss-making SOEs were so great as to place the nation's financial system at stake. Therefore, the Chinese regime had no other choice but to acquiesce in massive spontaneous privatization of the SOEs in the localities. China's Communist authoritarian system, which by definition was no different from Mao's totalitarianism in the sense of seeking absolute monopoly on power, was uncompromisingly intolerant of free association, particularly the independent unionization reminiscent of the 1970–1980s' Solidarity Movement in Poland. In such an institutional and political setting, the spontaneous privatization naturally evolved into the sort of nomenclatura privatization, benefiting only the insiders of the SOEs with whom corrupt local officials conspired. Economists at the World Bank found that China's "restructuring effort itself did not seem to improve the efficiency of firms per se," that "experienced a reduction in profitability and efficiency."[65]

Massive layoff of SOEs' workers and rampant corruption contributed to the quickly enlarging income gap between the rich and poor. By 1999, the Gini Coefficient reached 0.457, ranking China among the most unequal societies in the world.[66] The unbridled crony capitalism institutionalized unfair wealth redistribution to the disadvantage of the great majority of people, whose interest the party proclaimed to represent.

Such an endgame significantly dampened domestic demand and further evoked an enduring challenge to China's economic development well into the twenty-first century: underconsumption. The institutionalized demand shortfall led to an export-dependent economy that has persisted ever since. What's more, the displacement effect of FDI on the SOEs led to a deterioration of the country's industrial and employment structure, reinforcing its dependence on FDI. The double dependence on export and FDI highlighted not the strength but rather the substantial structural weakness of the Chinese economy. Nolan contended that it was the remarkable industrial progress that the SOEs achieved in the 1990s that made China the second largest recipient of FDI in the world.[67] That was partly true. The SOEs' total output did keep growing rapidly throughout the 1990s, but their industrial value added as a percentage of GDP kept going down. This was also compounded by the fact that a great number of the SOEs continued to build up unwanted products despite the heavy-handed state-led industrial restructuring.[68] In contrast, the share of industrial value added of the FIEs rose swiftly during the same period. The relative decline of the SOEs, therefore, caused China's industrialization to essentially stagnate (Table 5.4).[69] By 1998 and 1999, devastated by underconsumption and floods at home and the financial crisis in East Asia, the Chinese economy was sliding rapidly to the verge of recession.

Table 5.4 China's industrial value added by ownership and industrialization rate in the 1990s (unit: %)

Year	A (FIEs)	B (extractive and raw material industries)	C (SOEs)	D (private and collective enterprises)	E (industrialization rate)
1992	5.5	26.9	42.1	25.5	18.4
1994	8.5	26.6	40.8	24.1	20.4
1996	9.8	21.5	30.7	38.0	17.4
1998	12.2	20.1	25.9	41.8	16.2
2000	15.4	22.3	26.5	35.8	18.5

E = (A + C)/GDP
Source: Cheng, X (2003), p. 39

Table 5.5 GDP growth rate, FDI, and capital flight (unit: US $100 million)

Year	1992	1993	1994	1995	1996	1997	1998	1999	2000
GDP (%)	14.2	13.5	12.7	10.5	9.6	8.8	7.8	7.1	8.0
FDI	110.07	275.15	337.67	375.21	417.26	452.57	454.63	403.19	407.72
Capital flight	–	–	–	–	–	364.74	386.37	238.3	480

Source: China State Statistics Bureau, MOFTEC (Ministry of Foreign Trade and Economic Cooperation), and MOF (Ministry of Finance) web database

FDI, for the first time since China's opening up in 1978, declined drastically given the country's gloomy economic prospects (Table 5.5).

The Chinese regime was extremely sensitive to the FDI shrinkage[70] and was more or less aware of the necessity of an economic transition. A great deal of effort had been made to boost consumption but to no avail. The Keynesian approach under Chinese institutions only led to the crowding out of POEs' investment,[71] more corruption and wasteful investments.[72] To the opportunistic third-generation leadership, the only way out seemed to be further "external orientation" by means of institutionalizing wider access to overseas markets and attracting as much FDI as possible through joining the WTO. Chinese leaders did have good reason to believe in the neoliberal logic of globalization, since it was paradoxically the export boom and huge influx of FDI from the early 1990s onward that had kept the Chinese economy growing fast even under the shadow of deflation and massive capital flight (Table 5.5). These positive effects of globalization thus spurred on the Chinese Communist leadership to deepen the country's integration into the global economy as the only way to resume the economic momentum, thereby addressing their overriding concern for legitimacy. That was the political rationale of China's WTO accession. In other words, it was not economic success in the 1990s that naturally led to China's deep integration but rather the predicament in the country's neoliberal reform and development that forced China to further liberalize the economy.

In conclusion, the 1990s saw radicalization of reform and opening along neoliberal lines. Chinese new rulers, composed of technocratic elites, had neither the vision nor the statecraft to manage the country's post-Communist transitions, economically and politically, and their relationship with global capitalism in an extraordinarily insightful way. Abandoning socialism and self-reliance has instead led the market Leninist regime to embrace crony capitalism and global capitalism, which as a logical consequence, set the country on a dependent path of development at the turn of the millennium.

Notes

1. http://zhouqiren.org/archives/655.html; Zhu's Remarks, vol. 2, p. 67.
2. Nancy Liu, Lawrence R. Sullivan and Wu Jinglian (1995), "On the Establishment of a Modern Enterprise System: Selections from 'Reform in Large-Scale and Medium-Size Enterprises,'" *International Journal of Political Economy*, 25:1, pp. 7–45.
3. SOEs' share in China's fixed-asset investment declined from 81.9% (1980) to 52.2% (1999); industrial output from 77.6% (1978) to 28.2% (1999); retail from 54.6% (1978) to 23.3 (1999); tax contribution from 86.9% (1978) to 71.1% (1995). Source: China Statistics Almanac.
4. Subsidies to loss-making SOEs were 41,129 million yuan and 36,633 million yuan in 1993 and 1994, respectively, which accounted for 9.46% and 7.02% of state fiscal revenues. Fiscal revenues accounted for 11.7% and 10.5% of China's GDP in 1993 and 1994. http://news.sohu.com/s2016/dianji-1866/
5. Hu Peizhao (1994), "Impediments of Reverse Growth of China's Modern Enterprise System," *jingji yanjiu (Economic Research)*, No. 7.
6. Zhu's Shanghai Remarks, vol. 1, p. 120.
7. He Qinglian (2003), *The Pitfall of Modernization* (updated), Sunnydale: Broad Press, pp. 65–77.
8. Zhu's Remarks, vol. 2, p. 56.
9. Zhu's Remarks, vol. 2, p. 244.
10. Zhu's Remarks, vol. 2, pp. 226, 243, 467.
11. "The SOEs' Restructuring in 1995," 17/12/2008. http://www.china.com.cn/news/zhuanti/zgztk/2008-12/17/content_16961083.htm
12. The "popsicle theory:" http://baike.baidu.com/item/%E5%86%B0%E6%A3%8D%E7%90%86%E8%AE%BA/6723664
13. "Is the Private Sector more Efficient? A Cautionary Tale" 2015 by UNDP Global Centre for Public Service Excellence (GCPSE).

14. Qiu Xiaohua and Du Yu (1994), "zhongguo nongcun shichang de fazhan qianli ji kaifa silu (The Potential and Development Thinking on China's Rural Market)," *jingji yanjiu (Economic Research)* (Beijing), No. 8.
15. Deng's Works, vol. 3, pp. 110–111, 123, 139. http://wap.eastday.com/node2/node3/n461/u1ai557220_t72.html. Before he passed away in 1997, he openly expressed deep anxiety about unfair distribution (income inequality) that had made the consequence of development even more serious than underdevelopment. See "Deng Xiaoping Reflects on China's Development in His Late Years: The Challenge of Redistribution," http://history.sina.com.cn/bk/ggkfs/2014-03-10/172284860.shtml
16. http://blog.sina.com.cn/s/blog_53a7ac510100028i.html; The article titled "Why has Socialism Suffered Setbacks?" was the most representative. It was written by Wang Xiaodong, pen-named Shi Zhong. This article was published in "Inside Reference (*neibu canyue*)" May 25, 1991, an unopened publication subservient to the *People's Daily*.
17. Wang Xiaodong, who was involved in the internal debate about China's development strategy then, opposed pushing the logic of comparative advantage to the extreme, but he was unfairly treated for his view and removed the post from his work unit (interview with Wang Xiaodong, February 8, 2005).
18. Yang Ping: The Charms of Ideas: some important debates revisited. http://intermargins.net/intermargins/TCulturalWorkshop/academia/intellectual%20field/if06.htm
19. This has become increasingly commonplace and ordinary people's "basic common sense" ever since even until the present day.
20. CCTV documentary: *Deng Xiaoping*, January 1997.
21. Zhu' Shanghai Remarks, pp. 479–480.
22. A raft of Hong Kong media reports about Zhu's so-called economic conservatism in the early months of 1993, especially January and February.
23. The author was then working in a large-sized SOE in Shenzhen and heard lots of such accusations.
24. Interview with Cheng Xiaonong, 12/11/2009.
25. Zhu's Remarks, vol. 3, pp. 166–167.
26. Vladislav Zubok (2009), *Zhivago's Children*, Cambridge, MA: Harvard University Press, p. 276.
27. Zhu Rongji Remarks, vol. 3, p. 167.
28. Gao Xin and He Ping (1993), *Biography of Zhu Rongji* (Chap. 7), Taipei: The Journalist, pp. 155–183.

29. Assuming Premiership in March 1998, Zhu stated at the first press conference held on March 19th: "During the past years, our party has made the correct conclusion [with regard to the Tiananmen Incident] in all major conferences. This conclusion will not be reversed. I was then [in 1989] working in Shanghai and held the same view with that of the party center," *People Daily*, 20/03/1998.
30. China Labor Bulletin (September 2005), Report on Chinese Workers' Movement (2000–2004), Hong Kong. http://www.clb.org.hk/sites/default/files/archive/en/File/No.4%20labourmovement%28S%29.pdf
31. Joseph Masih and Robert Krikorian (1999), *Armenia At the Crossroads*, Oxon: Routledge, p. 1.
32. Zhu's Shanghai Remarks, p. 323; Zhu's Remarks, vol. 3, p. 168.
33. Cheng Xiaonong (2016), "China Model: The Communist Capitalism," *China HR Bi-weekly*, 22/06, No. 185. http://www.hrichina.org/chs/zhong-guo-ren-quan-shuang-zhou-kan/cheng-xiao-nong-zhong-guo-mo-shi-gong-chan-dang-zi-ben-zhu-yi
34. Zhu's Remarks, vol. 2, p. 299.
35. Ibid., vol. 2, p. 375; vol. 3, p. 184.
36. Even in 2001 when China committed to not impose local contents as seen in the Sino-US deal reached in 1999, Zhu pretended to be economically nationalistic, claiming: "If we allowed the FIEs to sell their products on our domestic market, how is it possible for our SOEs to compete with them?" Zhu's Remarks, vol. 4, p. 197.
37. Zhu's Shanghai Remarks, pp. 439–440.
38. Zhu's Remarks, vol. 1, p. 408 (1993); vol. 2, p. 150.
39. In 1996, the industry similarity between the coastal and the central provinces was 0.935, while the figure between the central and the western provinces was as high as 0.979. *People's Daily*, 4/12/1996. Also see Zhu's Remarks, vol. 2, p. 187.
40. *People's Daily*, 23/01/1997.
41. Zhu's Remarks, vol. 3, p. 166.
42. Ling Zhijun (2011), "Zhu Rongji and the Hearts and Minds of the People—A Record of China 1990–2002," 14/7. http://book.ifeng.com/shuzhai/detail_2011_07/14/7690430_9.shtml
43. "Sino-US Talks on IPR Revisited," http://www.sipo.gov.cn/ztzl/zxhd/ggkf/bdpl/hg/200812/t20081218_430588.html
44. Internal seminar the author joined in Shenzhen, 12–13/12/1992.
45. Ibid., MOFTEC official Sun Zhenyu's detailed account of Sino-US talks, 12/12/1992.

46. Scott Kennedy (2002), *China Cross Talk: The American Debate over China Policy since Normalization*, Lanham: Rowman & Littlefield Publishers, p. 247.
47. The ETMA as a tentative economic policy was first applied in the auto industry in the mid-1980s when the state was running short of foreign currency reserve to be used to import technologies from the West on a large scale. Thus, China's economic leaders decided to set up JVs in anticipation of acquiring technologies from foreign partners. ChinaAuto article: http://www.chinaauto.net/huiyi/200621510456/news/2006215182938.htm
48. Fan Baichuan and Zhou Guiyuan (2011), *Coordinating Domestic Development and International Integration (tongchou guonei fazhan he duiwai kaifang)*, Beijing: zhongguo caizheng jingji chubanshe, p. 27.
49. Kong Qingjiang (2002), *China and the World Trade Organization: A Legal Perspective*, Singapore: World Scientific Publishing Co Pte Ltd., p. 33.
50. Chen Man (2001), "An Analysis of FDI," *Strategy and Management* (Beijing), No. 3, pp. 93–103.
51. Wan-wen Chu (2009), "The Chinese Model of Industrial Policy under Catch-Up Consensus: The Case of the Automobile Industry," *China Economic Quarterly*, 8:2, pp. 501–532.
52. Kong Qingjiang (2002), *China and the World Trade Organization: A Legal Perspective*, p. 33.
53. Yue Jianyong (2013), *Behind the WTO Entry—The Neoliberal Logic of China's Developmentalism*, HK: Twenty-first Century, June, pp. 83–94.
54. Chu, W. (2009), *China Economic Quarterly*, 8:2, pp. 501–532.
55. "The EMAT in China's Auto Industry," ChinaAuto.Net article. http://www.chinaauto.net/huiyi/200621510456/news/2006215182938.htm
56. "Who Are Willing To Be The Skilled Workers Tomorrow?" *China Business Daily (zhonghua gongshang shibao)*, September 1995. Shortage of skilled workers became more acute at the turn of the century when some knowledge- and technology-intensive enterprises in China's most dynamic coastal areas were unable to recruit sufficient numbers of skilled labors.
57. Chen Man and Yue Jianyong (2002), "Exchange Market Share for Technology? An Analysis of China's Strategy in Absorbing FDI," *Modern China Studies*, No. 4, pp. 93–100.
58. Cheng Xiaonong (1996), "Where did Prosperity Come from?" *Modern China Studies*, No. 3.

59. Ibid.
60. Yue Jianyong (2004), "The Dim Prospect of China's Industrialization," *Dushu* (Beijing), No. 7, pp. 140–144.
61. Income tax for SOEs was set at 55% and FIEs at 33% (15% in SEZs). It was not until 2007 that uniform taxation was carried out.
62. Yue Jianyong (2011), "The Myth of the Chinese Model," *Leaders* (Hong Kong), No. 40, June, pp. 11–27.
63. Ibid. and Yue (2004), *Dushu*, pp. 140–144.
64. Cheng Xiaonong (2003), "Reinterpreting China's Miracle: Dynamism and Consequences of Economic Growth," *Modern China Studies*, No. 1, pp. 25–46.
65. Sharid Yusuf et al. (2007), *Under New Ownership: Privatizing China's State-owned Enterprises*, Stanford: The World Bank and Stanford University Press, pp. 207–8, 115.
66. Sun, Liping (2004), *Transition and Fracture: Structural Changes of the Chinese Society in the Reform Era*, Beijing: Tsinghua University Press, p. 272.
67. Nolan, P (2001), "China, the US and the WTO: Battle of the Giants or Defeat of the Pygmies?" (manuscript).
68. Zhu Rongji in the capacity of Vice-Premier in charge of restructuring and development complained repeatedly about the inefficiency of the SOEs in his numerous internal speeches. See Zhu's Remarks, vol. 1–3.
69. Cheng, X (2003), pp. 25–46.
70. Zhu's Remarks, vol. 3, p. 379.
71. Yue, J (2001), "FDI and China's Economic Growth—Roots of China's Integration into the Global Economy," *Strategy and Management* (Beijing), No. 4, pp. 70–77.
72. *Southern Weekend*, 8/03/2003. http://news.eastday.com/epublish/gb/paper148/20030308/class014800018/hwz899803.htm

6

USA, Global Capitalism and "Drawing China Out"

Sino-US rapprochement in 1971–1972 created favorable conditions for China's reform and opening in the late 1970s. It is arguable that without Mao's decision to engage the USA, China's reform and opening in the Deng Xiaoping era would have been extremely difficult if not entirely impossible.[1] This line of argument might have overstated the role that Mao had played in re-setting China onto the path to modernity in the "long 1970s."[2] In fact, in virtually all communist states, bar the dynastic North Korea, the death of an incumbent leader staying in power for long, iron-fisted or even mediocre, is prone to dramatic changes due to the accumulated contradictions. Both the death of Joseph Stalin in 1953 and the death of Leonid Brezhnev in 1982 were accompanied by sea changes in the USSR's domestic and/or foreign policies. Prior to Mao's death in 1976, pressures for change were building up in the tightly controlled society and even within the CCP. Deng Xiaoping, after his return to the power center under Mao's auspices in 1974, had become increasingly wary of his mentor's autarkic self-reliance, which, as he saw it, made China extremely backward economically. Even Mao's hand-picked successor Hua Guofeng was pushing for radical changes after the arrest of the Gang of Four in October 1976,

J. Yue, *China's Rise in the Age of Globalization*, Palgrave Studies in Economic History, https://doi.org/10.1007/978-3-319-63997-0_6

less than one month after Mao's death. Thus, change is inevitable and will happen any way with or without Mao's initiative in ending China's isolation in the first place.

This by no means is to downplay Mao's unique yet inadvertent contribution to China's reform and opening—ostensibly not to his liking on ideological grounds—in that his engagement with the West during the Cultural Revolution had nonetheless created cordial relations in an international united front against Soviet expansionism, thereby removing the intractable ideological and psychological barriers to broad-ranging economic exchanges with the West. Mao's West-leaning strategy also led to the culmination of the Cold War in East Asia, a decade earlier than the end of the global Cold War in 1989. Although his allying with the West to oppose another socialist power seriously eroded communism in the long term,[3] the erosion per se enabled the economically backward China to extricate itself from the bondage of the communist dogma and whereby to forge ahead the much-desired market-oriented reform in a more cost-efficient way. In general, the Sino-US rapprochement served China's fundamental national interest in its quest for modernity. As Michael Yahuda put it, "the international implications of the policies of modernization called for a greater interdependence with the international economy and the pursuit of policies of accommodation with the West and the East Asian market economies in particular."[4]

Mao was an idealist communist who had fought all his life against likely "capitalist restoration" in China. He was deeply vigilant against and distrustful of Western capitalism and the capitalist global institutions prescribing market economy as the cornerstone. That is why China did not join GATT in 1971 even at virtually no cost when the USA extended the olive branch. Committed to self-reliance (*dulizizhu, ziligengsheng*), Mao's modernization agenda was clearly one of autonomous development based on autarkic import-substituting industrialization (ISI). Deng Xiaoping strictly followed Mao's united front strategy against the USSR. Yet he did not seem to care too much about the ideological ramifications. He based China's development on good relations with the West. Unlike Mao, who focused on ideological purity even at the expense of China's modernization, Deng was far more committed to materialism.[5] Beyond his expectation, nonetheless, Deng's modernization approach based on external integration eventually set China on a dependent path of development in the late 1990s.

The time when modernization was highlighted in the mid-1970s by the CCP even before the end of the Cultural Revolution saw the decline of the West and global capitalism in economic and strategic terms. The Bretton Woods System collapsed in 1971. In the years that followed, the USA was in full retreat in the face of Soviet global expansion. It was defeated in Vietnam and was forced to withdraw from Indochina. It did not get an upper hand in proxy wars against the Soviet-backed socialist-oriented nationalists in the Third World; its economic preeminence came to be challenged by Japan and West Germany, the hard core of European Economic Community (EEC). The Third World, in the aftermath of the third Middle Eastern War in 1973, launched the "Southern Challenge" in the UN calling for establishing a New International Economic Order (NIEO) in lieu of the liberal economic order so as to facilitate their national development on more just terms. With the US hegemonic world order left in tatters, the turbulent world seemed to be evolving into some kind of multipolarity. From the late 1970s until the mid-1980s, the decline of American empire seemed to be an inescapable destiny of what happened to all other empires in history under the law of "imperial overstretch."[6]

Sensing the inevitable declining trend of American power, Nixon and Kissinger, the two most renowned realist politicians in the late 1960s, started to use the Sino-Soviet split to address US strategic concerns. What made Sino-US rapprochement possible was the US objection of the Soviet threat of a surprise attack on China's nuclear facilities in 1969. The USA feared that allowing the Soviet attack to take place could destabilize the US–Soviet strategic parity to the latter's advantage. To deter the threat from the USSR, the USA and China found common strategic interests. This led to the thawing of relations in the 1970s and ensuing normalization of China's relations with the entire Western world. China's strategic reconciliation with the West paid off economically. The USA and its allies abolished the discriminatory "China differential" stipulation from the blacklist of the Coordinating Committee (CoCom) based in Paris and eased technology export controls to China. This enabled China to import a great deal of badly needed technologically advanced equipment from the Triad, which elevated the entire level of China's industrialization. In addition, military exchanges between the USA and China intensified after Nixon's visit, which ended up in the US transfer of certain advanced military technologies to China and the joint gathering and sharing of information on the Soviet Union. US military ties with China were so close that even its NATO allies and Japan were jealous. With Ronald Reagan's rise to the presidency in 1981, however, the USA reoriented its strategic focus to Japan. Coupled with this strategic shift was US's continued massive military buildup, which rendered China less important strategically despite the ongoing military exchanges between the two powers.[7] With China increasingly distancing itself from the developing nations, the USA held firm on to its position vis-à-vis the Third World that had been struggling for establishing the NIEO since the mid-1970s. Neoliberalism was on the rise and spreading globally following the eventual failure of the "Southern Challenge" in 1982. The global neoliberal turn, thus, posed tremendous pressure for the liberalization of trade and investment on the part of the Global South, including China, to be drawn into the orbit of the capitalist world-system.

These profound changes in global political economy constituted the backdrop against which China's reform and opening began to unfold in the late 1970s. Despite the fact that China and the USA viewed the USSR as the common enemy most threatening to world peace, they each had a distinct perception of and strategic agenda vis-à-vis the other. This involved certain modifications of strategic focus at different stages of the Cold War. For China under Mao, its chief motivation for engaging the USA was enhancing national security. From the late 1970s onward, the primary concern of Deng's China was creating a prolonged peaceful environment to facilitate its modernization drive. For the USA, the Sino-Soviet split made it possible to apply different strategies against the two Communist powers. "Fencing in" the industrially more powerful USSR was to ensure the survival of the West and global capitalism in high politics and low politics terms. By contrast, "drawing China out" into the international system of global capitalism was more cost effective given the acute economic backwardness of China, which resented the Soviet Union's advanced socialism so much as to no longer take the "Soviet model" as an alternative to modernity. Outliving the Cold War, "drawing China out" ended up in China's full integration into the global economy, hence becoming an active defender of the liberal order in which it has a stake at the turn of the millennium.

Benefiting from engaging the West economically in the early 1970s, the most famous example of which was the "43-plan,"[8] deepened China's interest in interacting with the Global North in order to accelerate its modernization drive in the reform era. Unlike Lenin's Russia in the 1920s and 1930s when socialism was on the rise, the 1980s saw the global decline of socialism economically and politically. A subconscious defeatism dominated Chinese reformers with regard to the feasibility of socialism as alternative altogether. This enabled the USA to exert heavy influence on Chinese reformers to further its "drawing out" strategy in terms of fostering China's embrace of liberal developmentalism in an institutionally irreversible way.

USA, Global Capitalism, and Development

The rule-based global capitalist system came into being with the ending of the World War II. With preponderant political, economic and military powers, the USA was vested with an unprecedented opportunity to create a new capitalist world order, or as Pyle put it, a "Liberal Democratic Order" as planned by the USA during the war "based on a vision of a postwar world inspired by Wilsonian goals of democratic government, free trade, collective security, and the rule of law."[9] *Pax Americana* materialized within the capitalist First World, thanks to extensive US security guarantees to its allies, ensuring their dealings with each other occurred in a peaceful way, promoting the economic integration of Europe, and guaranteeing their free access to markets and raw materials and thereby making colonial empires redundant. Viewing statism and autarky (self-sufficiency) as the root cause of the interwar Great Depression, hence the economic origin of World War II, US policymakers dismissed closed capitalist economies, Japan's wartime Greater East Asian Co-Prosperity Sphere (GEACS), for instance, as the greatest threat to its democracy and prosperity. Dedicating to rebuild the global economy, and whereby to create "a favorable international environment," US policymakers, in designing the postwar blueprint, decided to "integrate production and finance on a global scale into an interdependent world economy through the free flow of trade and capital across national boundaries in response to the laws of comparative advantage."[10]

Through "a unique blend of laissez-faire and interventionism," the USA created a "new system different than anything that the capitalist world had seen before."[11] In contrast to Stalin's Russia that imposed uniformity within its sphere of influence in Eastern Europe, the USA instead created a liberal international system in Western Europe. It tolerated and promoted European protectionism by encouraging the creation of an integrated economic system in Europe "that could effectively compete not only with the Soviet Bloc but with the colossus of the New World as well."[12] By so doing, the USA was welcomed by its European allies as "an empire by invitation."[13] The economic revival of Germany and Japan was the key to establishing a rule-based liberal order after World War II and the price the USA had to pay in its rivalry with the USSR during the Cold War. Schwarz argued that American hegemony through "globe-girdling security commitments" was the only way to address the inherent contradiction between capitalism and international politics in the sense of balancing the imperative of Germany's and Japan's economic revival with security concerns of their neighbors.[14] The USA, through providing military protection to its Western allies, kept down those former enemy allies and integrated them into the multifaceted multilateral frameworks, like the EEC and NATO for Germany, thereby maintaining its leadership by "calling the tune" politically.[15] Through these multilateral arrangements, the international relations between the industrial capitalist states were stabilized, giving rise to a postmodern Europe based on the Kantian cosmopolitan vision of perpetual peace, though under American military sponsorship. In other words, it was the US hegemonic power that managed the peaceful rise of Germany and Japan within the multilateral framework and made them reliable partners since the USA "defeated them, helped rebuild them and protected them from an outside threat."[16]

As the economic foundation of the Liberal Democratic Order, the Bretton Woods System was created with a view to "promoting international trade and economic development and the establishment of a multitude of new institutions, including the International Monetary Fund (IMF), the World Bank and the GATT."[17] Underpinning the Bretton Woods system was the dollar–gold linkage that made US dollar the "lender of last resort." Parallel to the liberal order was the Cold War Order managed almost entirely by the USA, whose containment of the USSR, nonetheless, facilitated Western Europe and Japan to focus on economic development at the US expense. *Pax Americana* therefore contains internal tensions between high politics and low politics. Extensive security commitments, soaring military expenditures in the hot war in Indochina coupled with the economic rise of Japan and West Germany served to undermine American economic competitiveness, which inevitably led to its relative decline from the late 1960s onward.

The collapse of the Bretton Woods System in 1971 and the oil shock in 1973 gave rise to global economic disorder in the years that ensued. But, ironically, the collapse of the Bretton Woods System that ended up with the "dollar standard" in lieu of the dollar–gold linkage in the global financial system only "increased Washington's power and influence" bizarrely due to its huge indebtedness.[18] And it did not lead to the loss of the US hegemony as had been expected, in that "U.S. hegemony in the 1950s and 1960s was most obviously embedded in its military commitments overseas. The U.S. has remained broadly hegemonic since 1971, but the nature of hegemony is changing in a changing global political economy."[19] This implies that the world after the Bretton Woods was still safe for Western capitalism with continued security guarantee from the USA. Nevertheless, resorting to trade protectionism as a solution to international balance of payment crisis dealt a telling blow to the "global free trade regime" that the USA had strenuously espoused since the end of World War II. The shattered US hegemonic legitimacy, coupled with the revival of Japan and Western Europe, resulted in a *condominium* of the international economic system, characterized by the power-sharing regime in international financial institutions and the coordination of macroeconomic policies through the G-7 among the industrial states. As a consequence, the rule-based global capitalist system continued to function even with the relative decline of the USA.

In short, the paradoxical consequence of *Pax Americana* that inevitably led to the relative decline of the USA was the price or even a deliberate policy of American hegemon for the creation of an open, peaceful, and economically interdependent liberal order during the Cold War. On the one hand, US hegemonic leadership based on security guarantee was crucial to the success of global free trade regime with which its allies bandwagoned to achieve prosperity in a peaceful way. On the other hand, the rise of Europe and Japan inevitably contributed to the diffusion of American economic power and undermined its hegemony. These two features were perplexing in a sense, raising the question about the limits of an American empire that was increasingly reliant on rearmament to offset its declining trends.[20] However, the peril of "imperial overstretch" was still considerably overstated given the unique vast advantages of US economy that more than offset its weaknesses.[21]

For Third World countries during the Cold War, it is "the importance of the United States to most Third World economies that counted" not the reverse.[22] Underdevelopment remained a constant phenomenon for many of the Third World economies. Development seemed possible only if late-comer industrializers were capitalist market economies allying with the USA, dependent on its protection, and geographically adjacent to communist powers at the time of unmatched US economic primacy. With US absolute economic preponderance gone forever, economic preferences of the sort of either the Marshall Plan or of the unilateral market access accorded to the East Asian developmental states were out of the question. Moreover, the "global free trade regime" as the cornerstone of US liberal order became untenable when it resorted to trade protectionism in the 1970s regardless of the potential damages done to its hegemonic legitimacy. The USA not only retaliated against the unfair trading practices of Japan and Western Europe but also began phasing out unilateral trading preferences to its East Asian allies to address the soaring trade deficits from the mid-1980s. After the Cold War and the collapse of communism, the USA became the sole superpower, which ushered in a new unipolar world order. Defeating communism and the "Southern Challenge," the USA had no difficulty creating a truly global "global economy." In contrast to the developing and transition economies having no other alternative but to embrace neoliberalism, Corporate America regained dynamism and became hugely competitive by taking the lead in the Third Industrial Revolution heralded by the information technology (IT) throughout the 1990s.[23] The USA became even more assertive "under Bush and Clinton" in pursing "the preservation of the US's preeminent global position"[24] by "precluding the emergence of any future global competitor."[25] Against such a backdrop, industrialization of late developers tempted by the prospect of "growth by invitation" but at the expense of national development, has become extremely difficult, if not entirely impossible, in the age of liberal globalization.

Inducement and Coercion: The US Grand Strategy of "Drawing China Out"

No doubt, the very few successful examples of development were closely linked with US Cold War policy, whereas the global politics after the Cold War has created an "unfavorable international environment" for global development. For China, although it reaped the dividends of the Cold War in terms of obtaining some military technology and technological equipment through allying with the USA, it did not rely on the USA for military protection. Rather, as a communist power, China continued to be strategically guarded against by the USA in economic and technological terms. For instance, the Jackson-Vanik Amendment linking the most-favored-nation (MFN) trading status to free emigration of the USSR was also applied to China, although on an entirely different conditionality. In addition, although since 1978 China has been accorded the unilateral Generalized System of Preferences (GSP) by virtually all Global North countries and even many socialist states, such as Poland and East Germany, it has never been the beneficiary of the US GSP. Furthermore, the high-technology export control regimes under the Coordinating Committee for Multilateral Export Controls (CoCom) had once loosened in the mid-1980s, with China being treated friendlier than the USSR. Yet, after the Tiananmen Incident, the USA tightened its high-tech export control against China, which did not dissipate with the demise of CoCom in 1994 but remained an outstanding issue between the two states even after China was fully integrated into the global economy and became a stakeholder of the international system.

With or without the Cold War factor, the USA had no incentive to prop up the communist China into an industrialized power of the German or Japanese kind. It became even more unlikely for the USA after the Cold War—its foreign policy priority was "precluding the emergence of any future global competitor" as stated in the classified document titled "Defense Planning Guidance" in 1992, not to mention the fact that the ideology of democracy promotion in US foreign policy eclipsed its realist tradition from time to time. As a matter of fact, the containment of China has been the dominant strategy of the USA since 1949, even if China was undergoing profound transformation from a revolutionary challenger to a stakeholder of the existing international system. Nonetheless, the USA adopted a different containment strategy on China than the one on the USSR after the Sino-Soviet split during the Cold War. This is what Nixon called "containment without isolation," or what Robert Zoellick coined "drawing China out."[26] It has been widely cited in the international history textbooks in Chinese colleges and universities that Richard Nixon cautioned in 1969 against leaving China "outside the family of nations" and leaving its most able people to "live in angry isolation." In reality, what Nixon alluded to was not merely the geopolitical importance of China that the USA could exploit from the realist perspective, but the possibility of inducing delicate change inside China to eliminate its "fantasies, hates and threats to neighbors." He argued that keeping non-communist Asian states strong "economically, politically and militarily" could stop communist China's ambition to export revolution and facilitate it to turn its energies inward. Only at this time should the USA start negotiations with China and persuade it to accept "the basic rules of international civility" in the short run and to pull it "back into the world community" in the long run.[27]

Jimmy Carter and Ronald Reagan shared Nixon's vision of integrating China into the international system. The Carter administration established diplomatic relations with China, and Reagan engaged China on bilateral basis "on a series of global issues and bringing China into several international institutions."[28] George Bush was the most committed to this vision than all his predecessors. However, he was stopped from fulfilling his mission by the decision to impose sanctions on China after the Tiananmen Incident on June 4, 1989. Bush did so out of the political necessity at home. But in just two weeks' time, he wrote a letter to the Chinese paramount leader Deng Xiaoping in strict confidentiality calling for maintaining the relationship that had been "patiently built up over the past seventeen years." Bush later recalled in his memoir:

Within twenty-four hours I had a personal reply from Deng, who accepted my idea of a personal emissary. I sent Brent Scowcroft, who asked Larry Eagleburger to go with him. Their mission was so secret that their plane was almost shot down when it entered Chinese airspace unannounced. Their trip was successful in that it conveyed to the Chinese how serious the divide was between us but also how much we respected our friendship. It kept the door open.[29]

This letter was vehemently attacked by the exiled Chinese dissidents afterward as Bush's kowtowing to Beijing for lack of will in the face of the "Chinese tyranny." What Bush actually intended to achieve was to keep the USA's ability to influence changes in China by keeping its own door open. This letter, issued on June 20, 1989, highlighted Bush's extraordinary insights in consistently seeking to integrate China into the international system of global capitalism. The content of Bush's letter is so important that it deserves quoting in full, as below.

George Bush letter to Deng Xiaoping.
His Excellency Deng Xiaoping.
People's Republic of China.
Beijing.
Dear Chairman Deng,

I write this letter to you with *a heavy heart*. I wish there was a way to discuss this matter in person, but regrettably that is not the case. First, I write in a spirit of genuine friendship, this letter coming as I'm sure you know from one who believes *with a passion* that good relations between the United States and China are in the fundamental interests of both countries. I have felt that way for many years. I feel more strongly that way today, in spite of the difficult circumstances.

Secondly, I write as one who has great respect for what you personally have done for the people of China and to help your great country move forward. There is enormous irony in the fact that you who yourself has suffered several reversals in your quest to bring reform and openness to China are now facing a situation fraught with so much danger and so much anxiety.

I recall your telling me the last time we met that you were in essence phasing out of the day-to-day management of your great country. But I also recall your unforgettable words about the need for good relations with the West, *your concerns about "encirclement"* and those who had done great harm to China, and your commitment to keeping China moving forward. By writing you I am not trying to bypass any individual leader of China. *I am simply writing as a friend, a genuine "lao pengyou."*

It is with this in mind that I write you asking for your help in preserving this relationship that we both think is very important. *I have tried very hard not to inject myself into China's internal affairs. I have tried very hard not to appear to be dictating in any way to China about how it should manage its internal crisis.* I am respectful of the differences in our two societies and in our two systems.

I have great reverence for Chinese history, culture and tradition. You have given much to the development of world civilization. But I ask you as well to remember *the principles on which my young country was founded. Those principles are democracy and freedom—freedom of speech, freedom of assemblage, freedom from arbitrary authority.* It is reverence for those principles which inevitably affects the way Americans view and react to events in other countries. *It is not a reaction of arrogance or of a desire to force others to our beliefs but of a simple faith in the enduring value of those principles and their universal applicability.*

And that leads directly to the fundamental problem. The early days of the student demonstrations, and indeed, the early treatment of the students by the Chinese Army, captured the imagination of the entire world. The wonder of TV brought the details of the events in Tiananmen Square into the homes of people not just in "Western" countries but world-wide. The early tolerance that was shown, the restraint and the generous handling of the demonstrations won worldwide respect for China's leadership. Thoughtful people all over the world try to understand and sympathize with the enormous problems being faced by those required to keep order and indeed, they saw with admiration the manifestation of policy which reflected the leaders' words: "The Army loves the people." The world cheered when the Chinese leaders were seen patiently meeting with students, even though there were "sit-ins" and even though disorder did interfere with normal functions.

I will leave what followed to the history books, but again, with their own eyes the people of the world saw the turmoil and bloodshed with which the demonstrations were ended. Various countries reacted in various ways. *Based on the principles I described above, the actions that I took as President of the United States could not be avoided. As you know, the clamor for stronger action remains intense. I have resisted that clamor, making clear that I did not want to see destroyed this relationship that you and I have worked hard to build. I explained to the American people that I did not want to unfairly burden the Chinese people through economic sanctions.*

There is also the matter of Fang Lizi.[30] The minute I heard Fang was in our Embassy, I knew there would be a high profiled wedge driven between us.

Fang was not encouraged to come to our Embassy, but under our widely accepted interpretation of international law we could not refuse him admittance.

In today's climate I know this matter is of grave importance to you and I know it presents you with an enormous problem; a problem that adversely affects my determination and, hopefully, yours to get our relationship back on track.

We cannot now put Fang out of the Embassy without some assurance that he will not be in physical danger. Similar cases elsewhere in the world have been resolved over long periods of time or through the government quietly permitting departure or through expulsion. I simply want to assure you that we want this difficult matter resolved in a way which is both satisfactory to you and does not violate our commitment to our basic principles. *When there are difficulties between friends, as now, we must find a way to talk them out.*

Your able Ambassador here represents your country firmly and faithfully. I feel that Jim Lilley does the same for us; but *if there is some special channel that you would favor, please let me know.*

I have thought of asking you to receive a special emissary who could speak with total candor to you representing my heartfelt convictions on these matters. If you feel such an emissary could be helpful, please let me know and we will work cooperatively to see that his mission is kept in total confidence. I have insisted that all departments of the U.S. Government be guided in their statements and actions from my guidance in the White House. Sometimes in an open system such as ours it is impossible to control all leaks, but *on this particular letter there are no copies, not one, outside of my own personal file....*

I send you this letter *with great respect and deep concern*. We must not let this importance relationship suffer further. Please help me to keep it strong. Any statement that could be made from China that drew upon the earlier statements about peacefully resolving further disputes with protesters would be very well received here. *Any clemency that could be shown the student demonstrators could be applauded worldwide*. We must not let the aftermath of the tragic recent events undermine a vital relationship patiently built up over the past seventeen years. I would, of course, welcome a personal reply to this letter. This matter is too important to be left to our bureaucracies.

As I said above, *I write with a heavy heart*; but I also write with *a frankness reserved for respected friends.*

Sincerely,
George Bush.[31]

Winston Lord was then in Beijing as American ambassador. As a career diplomat, he had accompanied Dr. Henry Kissinger to secretly visit Beijing via Pakistan in 1971. Lord acknowledged that US relations with China "has encouraged and strengthened the very forces for greater openness and freedom in China that shone so brightly last April and May." He dismissed those misgivings at home about China moving closer to the USSR, arguing "only the United States, Europe and Japan can provide the capital, technology, markets and managerial savvy that China urgently requires. The Soviet Union's disastrous economy, lagging technology and limited barter trade provides no alternatives." Lord was confident that China would be unable to shut up the door that had been opened to the "barbarians," since "*even hard-line leaders* understand China's desperate need for foreign capital, technology and market … No nation can prosper in the age of information and technology without opening up within and to the world outside."

Lord shared Bush's insight of preserving a long-term relationship with China as well as the latter's secret misgiving that in case of a continued chill in the bilateral relations, the USA's direct influence on China would "shrivel." He echoed Nixon's vision of getting China engaged in "international market and institutions" so that it would "have greater incentive to pursue a responsible foreign policy." Lord outlined concrete steps in an undisguised tone to entice China to move in the direction of liberal globalization by means of "keeping open U.S. markets to Chinese goods, transferring technology and encouraging China's participation in the global economy." As a quid pro quo, Lord argued that a "more enlightened" Chinese regime "will need to resume the momentum toward a pluralistic market economy and a trade and investment climate that is clear, fair and sure." For this purpose, Lord suggested that China take concrete measures of "reducing high tariffs and import barrier; loosening control over foreign exchange and import licenses; allowing competition in the services sectors; streamlining bureaucracy; ensuring consistent implementation of agreements."[32]

The prevision of Winston Lord on China's trajectory of policy changes after Tiananmen was strikingly accurate, despite the interlude when Bush's constructive engagement came to an end when he was succeeded by Bill Clinton in 1993. Partly constrained by his election campaign promises to hold the Chinese regime accountable for its human rights abuses, Clinton endorsed the Congressional approach that conditioned the granting of MFN in 1994 on China's progress in human rights and non-proliferation of nuclear weapons. This brought bilateral relations to a low point. China reacted strongly by tightening up social control, although it symbolically released some political prisoners to the USA so as to keep the MFN alive. At the same time, China began playing the Europe card, signaling to the USA that it had alternative accesses to technology. This was just an intuitive diplomatic technique of the Chinese regime to use its expanding home market as leverage to de-politicize its trade relations with the USA. By so doing, China successfully prompted US businesses to lobby at the Capitol Hill on her behalf for delinking human rights from trade.

At the urgings of the business community and the Department of Commerce supportive of US business interests in China, Bill Clinton moved his China policy back on track to Bush's constructive engagement. At this juncture, the breaking out of the Third Taiwan Strait Crisis in 1995–1996 prompted the Clinton administration to engage China, on the one hand, but to reinforce containment to underwrite its engagement policy by increasing military presence in the Asia-Pacific region, enhancing security commitments to Taiwan and resuming defense alignment with Japan, on the other. This was Clinton's so-called congagement policy on China, a hybrid of containment and engagement. From late 1996 until mid-1997, Jiang Zemin and Bill Clinton exchanged state visits to each other's capital and declared to establish a "strategic cooperative partnership" between the two nations. This implies that greater emphasis of the US–China policy had been placed on the intrusive engagement, or what Clinton termed "comprehensive engagement." It had become increasingly clear in Clinton's mind during his second term in office that an interdependent relationship with China "would lead in the long run to changes in that country that would make it more market oriented and more liberal politically."[33]

Clinton's liberal approach of "comprehensive engagement" served the purpose of fostering China's deeper integration into the global economy by first and foremost letting China to bandwagon with the liberal order to "enjoy the benefits," hence its willingness to "accept the obligations" and "adhere to international norms," as Warren Christopher suggested.[34] One such "benefit" was clearly "growth by invitation" that a country strictly following neoclassical creed of comparative advantage would hope to reap. Such export-led high growth was closely linked with the legitimacy of the Chinese regime, and thus would necessarily be strongly desired by policymakers pursuing "externally oriented" economic development. However, bandwagoning with the liberal order was by no means costless and must be paid for. Thus, inducing China to join the liberal order, allowing it to benefit therefrom, and to become dependent on the rule-based global capitalist system, would incentivize China to actively safeguard the basic order of existing international system in which it has a stake. And by so doing, the USA would be able to coerce China into renouncing economic nationalism as a quid pro quo, committing it to WTO plus deep integration. The "primary objective," as Mastanduno convincingly argued, was "to turn China into a status quo power."[35]

Integrating China into the global economy formed the bedrock of US grand strategy of "fully integrating China into the international system," which was a consistent grand strategy since the early 1970s.[36] Admitting China into the WTO on strictly commercial terms stands as one of Clinton's greatest political achievements in pursuing US national interest on a multilateral basis. In fact, US talks with China on the WTO deal encompassed nuanced psychological warfare in the sense of encouraging "a culture of compliance within China." Doing so would enable the USA to avoid the image of being the "sole demander" that imposed an unequal treaty, whereas China would in turn be tempted to conclude that the multilateral rules of the WTO would apply to Sino-US trade as well. And the WTO "might rule in favor of China" and even go against the USA that it has "become accustomed in its trade relations with other countries." To reinforce the desired market orientation of the Chinese reform, US think-tank researchers advised the administration to support "the interest-based constituencies inside China as a key element in the reform process," including "working closely with Chinese officials and interested stakeholders—universities and ministry-tied think tanks—to build the capacity to educate and encourage provincial and local officials involved in grass-roots implementation of WTO policies."[37] This ad hoc policy recommendation worked soundly as evidenced by the pervasive uncritical embrace of economic globalism across the Chinese society after China joined the WTO.[38]

"Kicking Away Its Own Ladder": External Integration as Ideology in China

Outside examples of modernization had huge psychological impacts on Chinese leaders in the late 1970s. Deng Xiaoping made two important visits in the year 1978 after he was restored in party and government positions in July 1977 after the Cultural Revolution. One was the visit to Japan in October 1977. Deng was deeply impressed by Japan's modern factories. After learning that the Nissan Auto Company produced 94 automobiles per worker each year in contrast to just one vehicle per worker a year by China's most advanced auto plant in Changchun, Deng uttered a sigh, "Now I see what modernization is." Deng was especially fascinated by the *shinkansen* bullet train, which ran at a speed of 210 km/hour. He replied to Japanese journalists that his feeling on the high-speed train was just one word—"quick."[39] It was this particular state visit to Japan that further prompted Deng Xiaoping to make up his mind to open the door to the outside world.[40] It should be noted that the *shinkansen* high-speed train impressed Deng so much that it shaped his understanding of modernization, equating it as high growth. Deng's obsession with "high speed" had deep implications on China's external-oriented development strategy (*waixiangxing zhanlue*) in the long run.

Immediately after returning from Japan, Deng made his second visit to Singapore, a newly industrialized city-state and one of the East Asian tigers that had once been regarded as the stooge of American imperialism in the Mao era. Deng was amazed by the staggering economic success of Singapore that industrialized through opening up to FDI. Prime Minister Lee Kuan Yew disapproved of Deng's overly cautious worry about China's revival, stating that the Singaporeans were mostly the descendants of emigrating farmers and fishermen from Guangdong and Fujian in the past few centuries, whereas today's mainland Chinese were the descendants of China's ancient literati, thus were more capable of catching up in the not-so-distant future. When Deng Xiaoping asked Lee Kuan Yew about China's opening policy, Lee stated frankly that China must stop exporting revolution to Southeast Asian countries. To Lee's surprise, Deng accepted his advice without the slightest hesitation. Upon returning to Beijing, Deng made two crucially important decisions with a view to facilitating the country's reform and opening: to end autarkic development and to open up to the outside world, to cease exporting revolution to Third World countries.[41]

In addition to appeasing the neighbors, Deng had a broader vision with regard to China's relations with the West that were deemed far more important to China's modernization drive. He gave up ideological confrontation and pursued economic and technological exchanges with the West from a pragmatic perspective. As he perceived it, "all having good relations with the U.S. have become rich countries."[42] In light of US dominance in East Asia and the urgency of China's modernization, Deng decided to compromise on the Taiwan issue by permitting continued US arms sales to Taiwan into an indefinite future in exchange for formal US diplomatic recognition at the end of 1978. In January 1979, Deng Xiaoping made a state visit to the USA in the capacity of Vice-Premier. Given Deng's weight in Chinese politics, Jimmy Carter greeted him as the de facto head of state of the PRC. Deng briefed Carter about China's intention to "teach Vietnam a lesson." Carter demanded China to exercise restraint, a signal understood by the Chinese side as US endorsement. Deng's objectives of launching a border war against the Vietnamese were threefold: to consolidate his authority within the party as the indispensable paramount leader; to rescue the Khmer Rouge guerrillas of Kampuchea encircled by the Vietnamese occupation forces; and most importantly, to please the USA, who had suffered a humiliating defeat in Indochina less than four years ago in an attempt to enlist sponsorship of the USA and the West camp for China's modernization.[43]

Deng's overtures to the USA paid off in economic and strategic terms. With the worsening of relations with the USSR after its invasion of Afghanistan in December 1979, Carter reacted strongly by initiating massive military buildup and strengthened cooperation with China by authorizing exportation to the PRC of "non-lethal weapons, including advanced computers and other high-technology products."[44] From 1978 until the 1980s, Japan and the USA were the two main industrial powers that were most actively involved in China's economic development. However, distrust of the Japanese for historical reasons and Japan's reluctance to transfer high technology prompted China to seek more cooperation with the USA. Images of the USA as the embodiment of wealth and power and the shining beacon of liberal democracy dominated many Chinese people toward the US and Western capitalism. Worshiping anything from the West (*chongyang meiwai*) became the mode of fashion that quickly permeated across Chinese society. The charisma of Ronald Reagan, rock music, Michael Jackson, and so on and so forth, started to dominate China's metropolitan life and captured the hearts and souls of young Chinese people, especially college students, from the early 1980s onwards.

Sensing the danger of being infiltrated by the US liberal ideology as had already been demonstrated in daily life, Deng Xiaoping issued a warning at the 12th National Party's Congress in 1982 that "(the West should) never expect China to become their dependent state and to swallow the bitter fruit of impairing our country's interests."[45] What he cautioned against was more about the danger of ideological Westernization than about the threat of a potential economic domination by the West. In fact, Chinese leaders, either Deng Xiaoping or Chen Yun, had limited knowledge of modern market economy. Their views about global capitalism were shaped by the classical Leninist depiction of imperialism as being the highest stage of capitalism. They were ignorant of how the liberal global capitalist system came about and functioned after World War II and of the likely way in which China could be economically dominated with its gradual integration into the international system. These revolutionary guards were extremely vigilant against Western ideological infiltration, viewing it as destabilizing to China's political system and national independence. They were all pragmatists whose attitudes with regard to introducing foreign capital and technology were similar and varied only on those policies in connection with the communist ideology.

Hence, the danger of dependency was more political than economic in the minds of most octogenarian politicians wielding real power on China's political arena. In 1984, Deng propounded "peace and development" as the two main issues facing the contemporary world.[46] This new notion was based on his observation of a *détente* between the USA and the USSR, which reduced the likelihood of a new world war, and hence brought China a good opportunity of peaceful development through engaging the West. Nevertheless, to increase its room for maneuvering, China began seeking rapprochement with the Soviet Union from the early 1980s onward. This led to the improvement of Sino-Soviet relations. China's reconciliation with the USSR minimized the risk of an overhead diplomacy by the superpowers at China's expense. But this rapprochement was not at all the signal of China's turning to equidistant diplomacy. Relations with the USA, which served China's fundamental national interest, were far more important. In Deng's mind, a détente between the two superpowers made peace possible, and the modernization of China also made peace possible. By reinterpreting East–West and North–South relationships, Deng overturned the classical Leninist tenet that it is revolution that stops war but that it is development that makes peace possible.

Like realist communist leaders such as Stalin and Mao, Deng subjected himself to the classical realist balance of power principle. Deng was absolutely right in this regard. However, the sort of development was paradoxically predicated on a peaceful environment in the first place through appeasing the West politically and increasing interdependence economically. Deng's approach was in no doubt to use liberal means to achieve realist ends. His vision of China's prolonged peaceful development was based on an erratic assumption of modernizing the economy through free riding on the US-condescended "Liberal Democratic Order," a wishful thinking that misperceived the experience of the East Asian tigers.

The CCP's consensus built upon Deng's vision on China's peaceful development highlighted the meager knowledge and naivety of the Chinese leadership in the 1980s in their understanding of the international system and the global political economy when the age of colonial imperialism gave way to a rule-based global capitalist system after World War II. There is no denying the fact that Deng was a communist. He regarded integration into the global capitalist system as a *modus vivendi* and a shortcut to achieve modernity. He dictated putting off developing high-tech industries in the 1980s in order to concentrate on the livelihood-connected light industries by playing to the comparative advantage in the first place. In his mindset, China would be able to develop high-tech industries only after the Chinese nation became wealthy enough. Deng's vision on peaceful development led to massive disarmament in the 1980s. This was necessary in a sense in economic and political terms; but the disarmament involved substantial reductions of investment in military technology in tandem with the diversion from the high-tech military equipment manufacturing to the low-tech civilian light-industrial goods production, known as the "military-to-civilian diversion" (*junzhuanmin*). Given his unmatched authority, Deng was capable of keeping the special interests of the military-industrial complex at bay throughout the 1980s. China and the USA were then on honeymoon. US military technology transfer left Deng at large and reinforced his pragmatic instinct that since "mortgaging ships" was far more economical, why bother "building ships" of our own?![47]

As a matter of fact, the entire leadership, not just Deng Xiaoping alone, was caught off guard by the prospect of a prolonged peace to accommodate China's economic development. Zhao Ziyang delivered a political report that was endorsed by all the octogenarian politicians beforehand to the 13th National Party's Congress in October 1987. In it, Zhao specified his plan to open the door wider in great detail. Though he mentioned import substitution in one short paragraph, this was nothing but rhetoric. In less than two months, he propounded the coastal development strategy with Deng's full backing. This sort of external integration approach of development was indeed an entirely new thinking in the eyes of the Communist leadership at the time. Reservations of Chen Yun together with Premier Li Peng and first Vice-Premier Yao Yilin focused on only the technical aspects. No one questioned his liberal grand strategy per se from the perspective of alternative import substitution in connection with self-reliance.

As a pragmatic practitioner, Zhao was exploring feasible scenarios for the deadlocked economic reform. He became increasingly obsessed with Milton Friedman's neoliberalism and the idea of "neo-authoritarianism" in the late 1980s. He was somewhat enticed by the model of the authoritarian capitalism under Chiang Ching-kuo in Taiwan, the political strongman and Kuomintang chairman. As China's political and economic situation became precarious, Zhao's liberal economic thinking received wide support of liberal intellectuals. Some prominent young economists and political scientists gathered around him and became his de facto advisers. The deadlocked economic reform radicalized many of the intellectuals including those advising Zhao. They took Zhao as the last hope of China's economic reform and were attempting to mobilize support for him in a variety of ways.

A political documentary titled Heshang, or *River Elegy*, came out in mid-1988, which created a brainstorm across the country. Many people were deeply impressed and even amazed by its most daring and subversive comments on Chinese history and in particular harsh criticism against Mao's tyranny after 1949. *River Elegy* lashed out at the "conservative" Chinese civilization, which has led to nothing but political despotism, cultural obscurantism, and lack of aggressiveness in business and conquest. This sort of agrarian civilization or "yellow civilization" lost its vigor long ago due to the Confucian ideology of great unification (*dayitong*) and commensurate super-stable superstructure, which could never spawn the industrial civilization and progressiveness of Chinese state and society. Using "blue ocean" as the metaphor of Western industrial civilization, *River Elegy* argued that "going to the ocean" or outright Westernization was the last hope of China if it did not want to be "dispelled from this planet" (*kaichu qiuji*). The documentary contended that China needed democracy yet to be realized for nearly a century and an independent intelligentsia. It urged the Chinese audience to have a strong sense of anxiety (*youhuan yishi*) and embrace the "ocean civilization" to rebuild China's national greatness. *River Elegy* argued that China was now encountering an unprecedented opportunity for development, with the West Pacific becoming a "new stage of world economy," in that Japan had suggested to the USA and the East Asian tigers to readjust their economic structure. It claimed, "This opportunity of global industrial structure adjustment might pass in a twinkling. We are late already and are still ill-prepared and immature. And now we have come to the realization that we *must develop an outward-oriented economy*. But our sole advantage is the cheap labor force. This sort of labor-intensive and low-tech industry is unlikely to make up our enduring competitiveness." Echoing Zhao's idea of expediting China's coastal development by participating in the "grand international economic cycling," *River Elegy* asserted, "We are fixing our eyes on other countries' markets, whilst we are keeping our own market closed, worrying about the outflow of wealth. We seem to have forgotten that foreign investors are willing to invest in China simply because they take a fancy to our market. *If we want China to enter the world, we must let the world to enter into China.* Otherwise, we will stand to lose another good opportunity [of development]."[48]

River Elegy is a microcosm of the trend of thought of the 1980s. It stands for the ad hoc enlightenment efforts of some avant-garde intellectuals at that time to exert their influence on China's economic reform and political transformation at a critical juncture. Except for their appeals for political reform, their economic thinking coincided with the external integration approach of development advocated by Zhao Ziyang and Deng Xiaoping. This political documentary created a great stir throughout the country with huge success. There is no evidence to show that the making of this path-breaking documentary was inspired by Zhao Ziyang, who did enjoy it anyway. As a prudent statesman, his only gesture was presenting the videotape of *River Elegy* as a gift to the visiting Singaporean Prime Minister Lee Kwan Yew.[49]

River Elegy was banned with the fall of Zhao in the aftermath of the Tiananmen Incident. Before and after Tiananmen, it was attacked by the cultural conservatives, statists like He Xin, and nationalists like Wang Xiaodong for its "contempt" of the glorious Chinese civilization. Wang vehemently attacked *River Elegy*, labeling it as a reverse racism. Revolutionary veterans such as General Wang Zhen were infuriated by the documentary's alleged humiliation of the Chinese nation. However problematic *River Elegy* was at that time, it offered new perspectives in rethinking about China and the world. This was the first and the last time of broadcasting such heretical ideas that were totally different from the dogma of the party's ideology on state television in the history of the PRC. In fact, what actually went unnoticed was the strong racist inclination displayed by the writers of *River Elegy* who spent every minute highlighting Chineseness.[50] They deplored the lack of aggressiveness of the ancestors. This paradoxically ended up with the same objective of restoring China's past glory with that of the nationalists, though on a different intellectual basis. Nonetheless, they were not the sort of nationalists or statists of Meiji Japan dedicated to building up "a rich nation and a strong army" from a mercantilist realist perspective. They were a group of free trade believers who deemed economic liberalism to be the only correct approach leading to wealth and power of China. They largely misread the economic history on the rise of Great Powers and were obviously unaware that free trade has always been the ideology of the strong. This highlighted the rapidly growing clout of neoliberalism on the path-dependent Chinese reform and development in the late 1980s.

Zhao's coastal development strategy was brought to a halt in the aftermath of the Tiananmen Incident. In fact, the West camp that imposed economic sanctions on China was not monolithic. In addition to Bush's dispatch of secret emissaries to China to mend bilateral relations, Japan played an important role in getting the sanctions collectively lifted in the 1990s.[51] Deng's southern tour in 1992 reaffirmed China's outward-oriented development strategy propounded by Zhao Ziyang four years earlier, which became a more systematic national development strategy. The only difference lay in the fact that import substitution was forsaken, accompanied by China's resort to deeper external integration on a national scale. Deng warned in harsh words in 1992, "Not a single word of the 13th National Party's Congress report was allowed to be changed."[52] What he actually alluded to was the economic not political aspects of the political report. Political reform was dead after 1989, while the collapse of Soviet communism and the breakup of the USSR, coupled with drastic transitional decline, led to divisions of the intellectuals who for the majority resented the Communist regime for its crackdown of the demonstrators. Many intellectuals modified their attitudes after 1992. Their pro-democracy radicalism began to recede, allegedly on account of the reality of the difficult transition of former communist states in the Soviet Bloc and particularly the disintegration of the USSR.[53] Deng's re-launch of the market-oriented reform was to a large extent to please the intellectuals and whereby to leave his reputation intact as the great reformer.

Indeed, after his historic southern tour in 1992, a growing number of moderate intellectuals started to cooperate with the Chinese authoritarian regime by advising it on liberal economic policymaking. By so doing, they silently abandoned their liberal political position and endorsed the official foreign policy of appeasing the USA to facilitate the market Leninist reform and deeper external integration. Those staying outside the regime acquired more chances after 1992 to enrich themselves with the deepening of the reform. Their attitudes experienced delicate change with dramatic enhancement of their economic and social status. They became much less critical and increasingly docile and cynical politically toward the regime. They endorsed the regime's efforts to maintain good relations with the USA, viewing keeping the USA deeply involved in China's internal affairs as being conducive to the peaceful evolution of China's political system. Thus, they supported China's external integration as the medium for networking the country with the outside world. In this way, they shared the authoritarian regime's pro-American foreign policy from a different perspective.

There are two additional specific reasons for the commonality between the liberal intellectuals and the authoritarian regime over the issue of external integration. One is historical reason. As Mao's harsh totalitarian rule had traumatized a vast number of intellectuals and bureaucrats, they resented virtually everything in association with Mao, particularly developmental Maoism. Against such a backdrop, deep integration into the global economy naturally became an absolute political correctness, which ironically fit well into the party's tactics of mythologizing reform and opening. Hereby, opening was mistakenly understood as deep integration only! In the minds of the liberal intellectuals and the ruling elites, the wider China's market access, the more correct it was politically. And even a shallow integration was not entirely correct. In contrast, advocates for protecting domestic industries or import substitution were synonymous to opposing reform and opening, which usually invited ideological crusades by both the party's propaganda apparatus and the liberal intellectuals. This false dichotomous understanding of opening made it extremely difficult to hold serious and in-depth discussions and debates over China's economic and foreign policies. A typical example in this regard was the debate on the discourse of so-called peace and development theme in early 2001.[54] Ironically, like the anti-communist democrats in the post-USSR era who opposed their opponents in exactly the same way as the Communist Party of the Soviet Union (CPSU), many Chinese liberalists inside or outside the party thought the way the CCP did!

The second reason relates to China's improper education system. Schooling on trade and economics in Chinese universities was overwhelmingly about the infallible comparative advantage after 1992. The disciplines of international relations (IR), international political economy (IPE), and development studies were far inferior in quality and were full of errors. Few Chinese professors had profound learning on these related disciplines. As for the IR scholars, many of them did not understand modern economics. Some even lacked basic common sense with regard to economics, let alone the much more complicated international economic relations and the economic factors behind them. And as for the economists and liberal intellectual thinkers, the great majority did not understand IR and IPE at all. Thus, Chinese IR scholars who advised government foreign policymaking or helped propagate official foreign policy intents were more often than not readily receptive to the self-praised economic achievement of the regime and were keen on designing grand diplomatic strategy for the regime, which ironically did not treat their architecture seriously. For the liberal economists and the liberal thinkers, few of them were familiar with such IR concepts of power, security dilemma or relative gains. They had no idea of how the postwar capitalist system came into being, what positive and negative roles the US hegemony played in shaping the postwar liberal order, and what such an order meant for global development, particularly for *late* late-developers, such as China. For the vast majority of non-IR liberal intellectuals, they tended to view US hegemony as being benign only, and to dismiss any mentioning of the term "hegemony" as the rejection of the progressiveness based on universal liberal values. In terms of development studies in China, very few Chinese scholars in this discipline pointed out that the WTO is not about development. Their scholarship in these social science disciplines has to date failed to substantially improve.[55] Disciplinary inadequacy was closely associated with the CCP's omnipotent political control over education that stifled freethinking and debates, as well as the powerful inertia of class-struggle mentality of the entire nation taking shape in the pre-reform era that afterward led to false dichotomous thinking among intellectuals.

Nevertheless, the support of the liberal intellectuals legitimized the regime's external integration approach. Their space of expression in the public sphere also expanded. Though they were unsatisfied with the half-hearted official propaganda of opposing US hegemonism, they intended to take advantage of the regime's appeasement with the USA to keep China connected with the outside world so as to have the Chinese regime reined in by the USA. In reality, many of the so-called liberal intellectuals were not, or no longer, democracy fighters in light of their cynicism and readiness to be co-opted by the Chinese authoritarian regime. Their attitudinal change was not so much the result of the cool-headed reassessment of China's economic reform and the unfavorable global environment after the Cold War as their adaptive resilience against the quickly changing reality—namely that external integration has kept the Chinese economy growing rapidly and made them the third largest beneficiaries after the ruling elites and business elites. In other words, they supported China's foreign policy that prioritized enhancing relations with the USA since this was compatible with their pro-American liberalism in value terms, while they supported China's external integration in that this made them winners of reform and opening. The co-option of Chinese intellectuals to a considerable extent compensated for the loss of legitimacy as a result of the market Leninist efficiency-biased reform that had marginalized the workers and peasants since the mid-1990s. They offered justifications for China's deeper integration when the economic growth became increasingly difficult to sustain in the late 1990s on account of the market Leninist reform at the expense of social justice.

Jiang Zemin became the paramount leader true to the name after Deng's death in February 1997. He seemed somewhat complacent about himself with power in hand. Jiang thrived well under the communist system, yet he was not a rejectionist with reference to Western culture and system in ideational terms. As the leader of a communist state, Jiang was not hostile to liberal democracy. Rather he tended to view these liberal values as having been crucial to US ascendance to a superpower. However, there is no evidence to suggest that Jiang intended to carry out the political reform after he consolidated power after Deng's death, as many people had anticipated. The only grand vision Jiang unfolded was to reunify Taiwan. This was in fact not his invention but one of the party's three major tasks set out in the 12th National Party's Congress in 1982. Jiang's announcement in 1995 that the PRC government would never renounce the use of force to reunify Taiwan did arouse uneasiness in the

USA, Japan, and the neighboring ASEAN countries. In addition, China's increase in defense spending at two digits per annum since 1990 gave rise to the "China Threat" rhetoric. In fact, the increase in defense spending was in large part a symbolic gesture in order to appease the military since a large portion of defense spending was used to raise the wages and benefits of the People's Liberation Army (PLA) officers. Jiang lacked the authority of Deng to rein in the army without proper compensation. As a matter of fact, China's defense spending increase has its *raison d'être*, in that all the high-ranking officers of the PLA were shocked by US global power projection, which was hugely enhanced as a result of the Revolution in Military Affairs (RMA). Even so, reunification of Taiwan was not something new, and China's enhancement of military capability was no more than a defensive reaction to US military buildup and enhancement of US–Japan realignment in the first place. China was far from being in a position to balance the USA in terms of hard power, let alone its soft power, which was negligible compared with that of the USA.

Chinese leaders felt weak in face of US preponderant hard power and soft power. Acting as a balancer did not serve China's peaceful development given the country's increasing economic interdependence with the West. Given the rampant corruption at home and the constraints of external integration upon the autonomous development of China, Jiang devoted his attention to making big money silently (*mensheng fadacai*) by continually free riding on the international system. In this sense, Deng's vision fell apart as China was getting increasingly dependent not only economically but politically. This once again highlighted the inherent tension between the (realist) ends and the (liberal) means of Deng's logic of peaceful development. It was thus not Jiang's fault if he was regarded by the nationalists and leftists as being too pro-American, but the inherent incompatibility of realism in high politics and liberalism in low politics, so long as he followed Deng's approach of external integration as the basis of China's national development.

Jiang's knowledge of international politics was rather limited. He was politically incapable of revising the foundation of Deng's legacy, which is exactly the source of his legitimacy as the successor and the core of the third-generation leadership. The inexorable dependence of China on the international system to ensure continued free riding and *mensheng fadacai* prompted Jiang and the CCP regime to silently forsake Deng's vision on the ends of peaceful development since the growing dependence had made China a fragile great power unable to hard balance the USA. Jiang's solution was soft balancing within certain limits by uniting with developing countries to resist US pressures on human rights in the UN and calling for democracy in international relations. Besides, Jiang seemed to hold a constructivist view: as long as inter-state relations were de-ideologized, world peace would be preserved through the deepening economic interdependence between nation-states. This idea was made public through his close aide Liu Ji on May 27, 1997, on the eve of his state visit to the USA with an aim to conclude a constructive strategic partnership.

Liu Ji was then the vice-chairman of the Chinese Academy of Social Sciences (CASS). He addressed the audience that included important figures in intelligentsia, foreign policy and political communities at the Fairbank East Asia Research Centre of Harvard University. Liu's speech had a huge impact on the US decision-making body. Liu started with his observation that the USA, though the No.1 superpower in the world, was in decline. China was focusing on economic development in order to realize modernity. China sincerely wished to have a peaceful, friendly, and cooperative international environment. He quoted Deng Xiaoping's assertion that "Sino-US relations must improve anyway," arguing that the US opportunity of maintaining its No. 1 status lay in using its capital and technology to combine with China's emerging market. Liu contended that China's 1.2 billion population amounted to a super-scale global market. International experience has told us that a possible solution was that the USA adopted the sort of aInternational experience has told us that a possible solution *would have been for* the USA to adopt the sort of a Marshall Plan in Europe in the late 1940s to provide US$100 billion or more in assistance programs to China at the beginning of the twenty-first century. China *could then* use this amount to purchase Marshall Plan in Europe in the late 1940s to provide US $100 billion or more in assistance programs to China at the beginning of the twenty-first century. And China would use this amount to purchase technologically advanced US products in order to promote the economic development of China and the economic growth of the USA. An expanded market of China would be able to suck in more capital, technology and products from the USA and in turn sustain US economic prosperity and preserve its No. 1 status.

Liu Ji asked the key question, "Who is the Marshall today?" Liu hinted to the USA that the exportation of revolution or ideology was wrong. It was up to the host country people to decide which ideology was feasible. In this regard, Liu Ji seemed to be utterly unclear about how important ideology has been in American foreign policy. He tried to assuage the US concern on China's socialism, arguing, "Whatever means to enable China's modernization, to make Chinese people rich, will be adopted. This is what we understand of socialism." He advised the USA not to look at China from the Cold War perspective but to give China "understanding, sympathy and support."[56]

Liu Ji's remarks were suggestive of his romantic understanding of IR and international history. The de-ideologization of IR and a new Marshall Plan in the post-Cold War era were illusory and impractical simply because IR has always been value-laden and the Marshall Plan was deeply ideology-biased to contain communism. The US policy of integrating China into the international system has been a consistent strategy since Nixon as a "containment without isolation," not to mention the fact that the US foreign policy after the Cold War was heavily influenced by the highly ideological "democratic peace" thesis. Meanwhile, its foreign policy priority in the post-Cold War era was to prevent any emerging power from challenging its leadership. Nonetheless, for Chinese leaders and their advisors, their perception of a benevolent American hegemony sparked a high expectation of an enduring solid relationship with the USA and the liberal order that closer economic interdependence would entail.

The Cold War and the global trading regimes under US sponsorship created a handful of late-industrializers in East Asia that allied with the USA as bulwark against communism. The US strategy of "containment without isolation," or "drawing China out" since 1972 was aimed at transforming China into a stakeholder of the international system rather than to help build China into a powerful industrial nation like Germany or Japan. Unclear of how the postwar global capitalism evolved and what it meant to China's development, the Chinese decision-makers misread the East Asian model and based China's development strategy on deeper integration. In the aftermath of the Global 1989, the Chinese leaders found it difficult to resist the coercion and inducement of the USA in offering "growth by invitation," on the condition, nonetheless, that China relinquish economic nationalism as a quid pro quo. By the late 1990s, Chinese leaders were immersed with some sort of idealist pacifism, not because of the country's increased capabilities in hard power terms but because of its deepening economic dependence on the USA. They had neither the resolve nor the capacity to change the country's peripheral status in the global economy but were satisfied with it. What made the matters worse was that dependency was accompanied by the rise of crony capitalism at home. In this setting, what dominated the leaders' mindset was to securitize China's dependent development through deeper integration into the global economy and continually appeasing the USA in strategic terms accordingly. Thus, China's fateful choice of institutionalizing dependent development signifies the completion of the transformation of China's socialism into crony comprador capitalism in both form and substance. China's desperate accession to the WTO stands for the culmination of this particular transformative process. And its "turn to globalization has been one of the greatest foreign policy triumphs of American history."[57]

Notes

1. Dai Chaowu (2010), "U.S. 'Trade Liberalization' Policy and China's 'Reform and Opening' (1969–1975)," *shixue yuekan (History Studies Monthly)*, No. 2.
2. Chen Jian of Cornell University gave high evaluation on Mao's role. "The Great Transformation: How China Changed in the Long 1970s," LSE Public Lecture, 22/01/2009. http://www.lse.ac.uk/website-archive/newsAndMedia/videoAndAudio/channels/publicLecturesAndEvents/player.aspx?id=92
3. Chen Jian (2001), *Mao's China and the Cold War*, Chapel Hill & London: The University of North Carolina Press, p. 278.
4. Michael Yahuda (2003), *The International Politics of the Asia-Pacific* (2nd and revised ed.), New York: Routledge, p. 180.
5. Deng's Works, vol. 3, p. 274.
6. Paul Kennedy (1987), *The Rise and Fall of the Great Powers: Economic Change and Military Conflict from 1500 to 2000*, NY: Random House, p. 609, note 18.

7. Yahuda (2003), p. 73.
8. "The Little Known '43-Plan,'" *China News Week*, 13/02/2012. http://focus.news.163.com/12/0213/21/7Q61AE8800011SM9.html
9. Pyle, K (2008), *Japan Rising*, p. 211.
10. Benjamin Schwarz (1996), "Why America Thinks It Has to Run the World," *The Atlantic Monthly*, June, pp. 92–102.
11. John Ikenberry (1992), "A World Economy Restored: Expert Consensus and the Anglo-American Postwar Settlement," *International Organization*, 46:1, pp. 289–321.
12. Randall B, Woods (2000), "The Trials of Multilateralism: America, Britain, and the New Economic Order, 1941–1947," in *From War to Peace*, ed. Paul Kennedy and William I. Hitchcock, Yale, p. 122.
13. Geir Lundestad (1986), "Empire by Invitation: The United States and Western Europe, 1945–1952," *Journal of Peace Research*, 23:3, September, pp. 263–277.
14. Schwarz (1996), pp. 92–102.
15. Marc Trachtenberg, *The Making of a Political System: The German Question in International Politics, 1945–1963*, ed. Kennedy and Hitchcock, Yale 2000, p. 117.
16. Harper (1997), "The Dream of Democratic Peace—Americans are Not Asleep," *Foreign Affairs*, 76:3, May/June, pp. 117–121.
17. Pyle (2008), *Japan Rising*, p. 211.
18. Diane B. Kunz (2000), *The International Financial System and the Nation-State*, ed. Kennedy and Hitchcock, p. 221.
19. Stuart Corbridge (1994), "Bretton Woods Revisited: Hegemony, Stability, and Territory," *Environment & Planning*, A1994, v. 26, pp. 1829–1859.
20. Robert Kagan, "No Time to Cut Defense," *Washington Post*, 3/02/2009; Robert Kaplan, "Where's the American Empire when We Need It?" *Washington Post*, 2/12/2010. Cited from Paul K. MacDonald and Joseph M. Parent (2011), "Graceful Decline? The Surprising Success of Great Power Retrenchment," *International Security*, 35:4, Spring, pp. 7–44.
21. Susan Strange (1987), "The Persistent Myth of Lost Hegemony," *International Organization*, 41:4, pp. 551–574.
22. Odd Arne Westad (2007), *The Global Cold War*, p. 50.
23. Nolan (2001), *China and Global Economy*, p. 99.
24. Michael Mastanduno (1997), "Preserving the Unipolar Moment: Realist Theories and US Grand Strategy after the Cold War," *International Security*, 21:4, pp. 49–88.

25. "Excerpts from Pentagon's Plan: Prevent the Re-emergence of a New Rival," *New York Times*, 8/03/1992. http://www.nytimes.com/1992/03/08/world/excerpts-from-pentagon-s-plan-prevent-the-re-emergence-of-a-new-rival.html?pagewanted=all
26. "Whither China: From Membership to Responsibility?" Robert Zoellick, Deputy Secretary of State Remarks to National Committee on U.S.-China Relations, 21/09/2005. https://2001-2009.state.gov/s/d/former/zoellick/rem/53682.htm
27. Richard Nixon (1967), "Asia after Vietnam," *Foreign Affairs*, 46:1, October, pp. 111–125.
28. David Shambaugh (2005), "The New Strategic Triangle: U.S. and European Reactions to China's Rise," *The Washington Quarterly*, 28:3, Summer, pp. 7–25.
29. http://www.64memo.com/b5/1571.htm
30. The dissident Fang had taken refuge in the American embassy in Beijing. Eventually China expelled him and he came to the USA.
31. This letter was issued on June 20, 1989, the same day he announced a series of sanctions against China. http://www.64memo.com/b5/1571.htm
32. Winston Lord (1989), "China and America: Beyond the Big Chill," *Foreign Affairs*, 68:4, Fall, pp. 1–26.
33. Yahuda (2003), pp. 256–257.
34. Cited from Mastanduno (1997), p. 71: footnote 75.
35. Mastanduno (1997), p. 71.
36. US Deputy Secretary of State Robert Zoellick pointed out in 2005, "For fifty years, our policy was to *fence in* the Soviet Union while its own internal contradictions undermined it. For thirty years, our policy has been to *draw* out the People's Republic of China. As a result, the China of today is simply not the Soviet Union of the late 1940s … Chinese leaders have decided that their success depends on being networked with the modern world." "Wither China: From Membership to Responsibility?" Robert Zoellick, Deputy Secretary of State, Remarks to National Committee on US–China Relations, September 21, 2005.
37. Robert D. Hormats, et al. (2001), "Task Force Report: Beginning the Journal—China, the United States, and the WTO," Report of an Independent Task Force sponsored by the Council on Foreign Relations.
38. Fu Bo (2003), "China Hides Its Intentions Again," *Le Monde Diplomatique*, March.

39. Li Lanqing (2008), *Breaking the Siege*, p. 58.
40. Wu Guangxiang (2008), "Journey of Peace to Japan, Deng Xiaoping Made Up His Mind to Launch Reform and Opening," *dangshi zongheng*, No. 8.
41. Regarding Deng's obsession with the "Singapore Model," please see special report on *China Business Daily*, 20/05/2011. http://www.cb.com.cn/opinion/2011_0520/211293.html; "Lee Kwan Yew's Intercourses with Five Generations of Chinese leaders," *Wenweipo* (Hong Kong), 23/03/2015. http://news.wenweipo.com/2015/03/23/IN1503230015.htm; Liang Heng (2008), "Deng Xiaoping's Modest Apology Moved Lee Kwan Yew," *Party Construct (dangjian)*, No. 10.
42. Zhao Kejin, "The Fact Is the US Is No Worse Than Other Great Powers," *Global Times*, 18/01/2012. http://world.huanqiu.com/roll/2012-01/2367088.html
43. General Liu Yazhou listed the first and third factors in his speech titled "Belief and Ethics (*xinnian yu daode*)": http://military.china.com/zh_cn/hostory2/03/11027561/20070731/14251621.html; or http://www.chinathintank.cn/ShowArticle.asp?ArticleID=5242
44. Yahuda (2003), p. 85.
45. Deng's Works, vol. 3, p. 3.
46. Deng's Works, vol. 3, pp. 104–106.
47. There is a famous debate in 1974 when Deng was called back by Mao to preside over economic rectification. Deng conflicted with the Gang of Four very soon on whether China should rely on itself to build ships or mortgage ships from world market at much cheaper cost. The Gang of Four asserted that the "mortgaging" argument was a traitorous behavior and labeled it as a "slavish comprador philosophy" (*yangnu zhexue*). This is the famous "Fengqinglun Incident" during the Cultural Revolution. This event added to Deng's resentment of developmental Maoism in its entirety, prompting his rejection of self-reliance in the post-Mao era.
48. The fourth episode of *River Elegy*: New Era, 1988.
49. Xie Xuanjun, one of the authors of *River Elegy* disclosed this information at a public lecture in Beijing Foreign Studies University in August 1988.
50. Cheng Yinghong (2011), "The Racist Views in Contemporary China," *Beijing Cultural Review (wenhua zongheng)*, No. 4.
51. Drifte (2003), *From Balancing to Bandwagoning?* p. 30.
52. Deng's Works, vol. 3, p. 296.

53. Kang Xiaoguang (2002), "An Analysis of China's Stability in the Next 3–5 Years," *Strategy and Management*, No. 3.
54. Zhang Ruizhuang (2001), "Peace and Development is Not Main Theme of Contemporary World," *Strategy and Development*, No. 1.
55. Many development studies scholars in one very famous Chinese university are even unclear of what a "developmental state" is. An interview with an insider, 10/07/2013, Beijing, China.
56. Liu Ji, "The Choice of Sino-U.S. Relations in the 21st Century," *Zaobao* (Singapore), 23/10/1997.
57. William Overholt (2005), *China and Globalization—Testimony before the U.S.-China Economic and Security Review Commission*, RAND, released on May 19, 2005.

7

After the WTO: Rise or New Dependency?

China's national development was in a dilemma when it joined the WTO. On the one hand, the market Leninist reform irrespective of social justice and human rights gave rise to a quickly enlarging income gap, leading to enduring underconsumption, which therefore rendered the economy increasingly dependent on export and foreign direct investment (FDI). On the other hand, deep integration entailed low wages for workers that paradoxically enabled an export-driven economic growth by "having foreign firms fit China into the newly globalized division of labor."[1] The "reform and opening," thus, institutionalized demand shortfall and exacerbated the structural weakness of the Chinese economy. This in turn eroded internal integration on which China's autonomous modernization was supposedly predicated. Rejecting democratic power-sharing created an even more predatory state after China joined the WTO. But rising tensions and global imbalance eventually joined hands to backfire from the last quarter of 2008, bringing the Ricardian economic miracle to an abrupt end. Stuck in a quagmire of dependent development, the Chinese economy and the destiny of the country were at stake.

J. Yue, *China's Rise in the Age of Globalization*, Palgrave Studies in Economic History, https://doi.org/10.1007/978-3-319-63997-0_7

Rich But Soft State: Crisis in Accumulation After Accession

China's dilemma of development in globalization resulted in a positive feedback loop of underconsumption and dependent development. This vicious cycle was hard to reverse since the market Leninist reforms had produced powerful vested interests that enriched themselves by dint of their close connections with the power elites. The market Leninist reform since 1992 had alienated the Chinese socialist system into crony capitalism, which made the economic reform a zero-sum game in the 1990s. Completely losing faith in socialism, the ruling elites subject to no external checks or balances became extremely greedy economically and fearless politically. They captured most of the benefits and opportunities of economic development through absolute monopoly of power. Their predominance forestalled upward social mobility and thus made the country's political system increasingly closed and resistant to change. The closeness of this special community reinforced institutional corruption of the party-state. The elite community became so decadent and corrosive that other members of the society, once absorbed into this "black hole," would stop complaining about social injustice. Few of them would care about the destiny of the underclass people outside the community any longer.[2] Like the old community elites, the few fortunate new members, tempted by power and corruption, were content with the status quo and in particular the privileged accesses to proprietary opportunities for wealth creation. The majority of them consciously shared the outlook of the ruling elites and was inclined to resist political changes. Once in power, these people became no less corrupt than the old political elites. Thus, the institutional corruption arising from the capitalization of power held the Chinese elites together. As a Chinese political novelist presciently put it in the 1990s, "corruption makes our rule more solid."[3]

Added to the interest-related political conservatism was the fact that China's rapid economic growth reinforced the ruling elites' confidence in authoritarianism. Yet, the economic success was founded on institutional disrespect of labor rights, thus making its development model difficult to translate into the soft power of China. To moderate Western criticism, hired scholars within the regime talked about democracy in a rarely outspoken language and even hailed democracy as "a good thing."[4] Nonetheless, in the face of fast-growing social unrest or rights movements (*weiquan yundong*) and criticism by the international community on China's deteriorating human rights since 2005, the Chinese regime played double-faced tactics. On the one hand, Chinese leaders continued to talk about democracy in the world arena, claiming that there could be no modernization without democracy;[5] on the other hand, they argued assertively at home that they would never undertake separations of power that characterized the liberal democracies in the West.[6] With US neoliberal capitalism severely weakened by the financial crisis in 2008, China's hired scholars denounced the Western multiparty system and the cosmopolitan values of liberty, human rights and democracy without hesitation.[7] This made the prospect of a political transformation from within the regime illusory.

The consolidation of the regime was also embodied by the formation of an alliance of the political elites with the business and intellectual elites by the late 1990s. Their joint forces were so powerful that they were able to block any reversion of the path dependence of China's reform and development to the detriment of their interests. Yet this elite coalition does not imply an equal cooperative partnership between the social elites and the ruling political elites. As Kang pointed out, "the political elites sit above all social classes and exercise 'authoritarian rule' upon all of them. The non-political elites are never allowed to dip their fingers into the political power." Kang shrewdly observed that through effective control over all political, social and economic resources that could be mobilized to make collective actions possible, the Chinese authoritarian regime placed the business and intellectual elites in a state of "a dish of loose sand."[8] This implies that by subjugating the social elites through coercion and co-option, the Chinese regime successfully dominated the society in the post-Deng era. Sun Liping looked into the more complicated relationship between the elites. As he saw it, business elites and political elites were interchangeable. What he referred to is the same category of people who could be officials at one time or business people at another, depending on their personal choice and relations with the power-holders.[9] This particular group of elites was essentially a derivative of the political elites.

Other business elites had no chance to penetrate into the core of the power system, though they could either buy into or be co-opted into decorative institutions like the people's congress or political consultative conference at local or national level.

The docility of the social elites, especially the intellectual elites, was displayed as a universal cynicism in their political attitudes. As winners of the zero-sum economic reform, they deemed social stability to be the source of profitability and an imperative to rapid accumulation of wealth. They arrived at the consensus that the political reform aimed at ending the Chinese Communist Party (CCP)'s monopoly of power was destabilizing and must be averted. Those intellectual elites that closely cooperated with the Chinese regime, either liberal economists or new left scholars, were also against the political reform. Recognizing that political reform had become "impossible" because both officials and intellectuals were beneficiaries of the marketization economic reform and would never risk losing what they had reaped in the past decades, these bureaucratic-affiliated intellectuals bet the country's future on the systemic self-perfection by the authoritarian regime itself. To this end, their solution to the "capitalism with Chinese characteristics," as coined by Yasheng Huang, was not to press the regime to wage the perilous political reform but, ironically, to admonish the over-exploited underclass with whom they often claimed to sympathize to restrain and be patient.[10]

This self-perfection story was totally illusory in that the coalition of elites and the formation of an increasingly closed elite community generated the most powerful interest groups who captured the state by means of influencing public policies to their benefits. First of all, as political stability is essentially regime stability, the purpose of development first and foremost served the state interest rather than the national interest. Therefore, the bureaucracy as a whole evolved into a self-serving institution, making the Chinese party-state increasingly predatory. In 2009, China's fiscal revenue reached 6.85 trillion yuan, an increase of over five-fold compared with 1999 when it for the first time rose over 1 trillion yuan. But behind the richer state was the fact that about 80 million peasants had lost their land and large numbers of urban dwellers were forced to relocate for a low-compensation price set by the local authorities who colluded with the developers in the name of speeding up urbanization and industrialization.[11] In 2009, revenues from the land-related transactions went up by 140% to 1.5 trillion yuan in the localities, which amounted to about 4.4% of China's GDP and nearly half of local fiscal revenue.[12] What's more, to speed up local economic development and increase fiscal revenue, local authorities were competing to introduce heavily polluted yet highly lucrative industrial projects with the endorsement of central government regardless of oppositions by the local residents. The dramatically enhanced extractive capacity of the self-serving bureaucracy created a predatory state. In total, 58% of the fiscal revenue was consumed by the 70-million-strong civil servants and public service staff, instead of being used to improve people's welfare.[13] National development in the form of industrial projects or infrastructure building was promoted most actively by the bureaucrats out of self-interested motivation rather than their dedication to China's modernization drive in the first place, and was more often than not associated with corruption.[14]

Secondly, state autonomy in formulating the rightful social policies to address the increasingly unfair redistribution of wealth was severely eroded.[15] On the one hand, the bureaucracy was not monolithic, and state interest was by no means the simple aggregation of the interest of its constituent sectors. Conversely, all the sectors were endeavoring to maximize their respective interest even at the expense of state or national interest. The property boom that emerged in the wake of the SARS pandemic in 2003 was a typical example in which the Ministry of Construction, local governments, the state bank branches in the localities, and the developers collaborated closely to circumvent the central bank's effort to curb inflation at an earlier stage.[16] National interest was thus eclipsed by state interest, which was eventually reduced to sectoral interest in a normative legitimate manner. On the other hand, interest groups that benefited from the marketization reform exerted huge influence to cripple the efforts of central authorities to launch remedial or corrective reforms in public interest. The privatization of housing and medicare and charged education did little harm to the interest groups. Rather, the "three heavy mountains" captured the second largest share of the ordinary people's consumption, which significantly depressed domestic demand since the mid-1990s. Thus, the Chinese party-state is both strong and soft. It is extremely strong in extractive and repressive capacities to serve the interest of the elites, but it is rather soft in boosting demand and fostering social justice given its weakened autonomy as a result of being captured by the interest groups.

China's intensifying crony capitalism in this institutional context developed much faster than and went far beyond what Deng Xiaoping could have anticipated in the early 1980s. Deng was then in the belief that development by letting a part of the people to get rich in the first place was the hard truth that would eventually lead to a common prosperity. It was somewhat too late when he sensed the perilous trend of an accelerating income disparity in 1993 shortly after his fateful southern tour to encourage an efficiency-biased marketization reform and outward-oriented development. As a socialist in the abstract sense, Deng was rather uneasy and somewhat deplored his radical market reform at the expense of social justice. He shrewdly acknowledged that his pragmatic approach of economic development had created more problems than no development, which, as he feared, would "run into big trouble" (*chu dawenti*).[17] Nevertheless, Deng was being unable to cope with the issue of unfair redistribution of wealth, precisely because an entirely different path dependence of reform and development had taken shape and institutionalized the societal polarization ever since. Social unrest emerged in the mid-1990s and increased rapidly after China joined the WTO.[18] These mass events (*quntixing shijian*) had in large part to do with the infringement of people's basic human rights of subsistence, most notably forced relocation and nomenclatura privatization.[19] With pervasive corruption and increasing repressiveness of the Chinese regime, the social situation became more and more tense as evidenced by rapidly growing protests and demonstrations that mainly targeted the local governments in the new century.[20]

By 2010, the Chinese authoritarian regime was apparently having a hard time. Pacifying the masses by holding the officials accountable to the constituencies would risk instability of the regime and the loss of cohesion of the bureaucracy as a whole, while appeasing the bureaucracy could only result in "volcanic stability."[21] The heightened social strains discredited the party's commitment to "building a harmonious society." Contrary to the optimism of the self-complacent middle-ranking officials, well-informed official think tank advisors close to the top leadership were rather pessimistic. Their argument was that

> many of our problems nowadays are institutional. Corruption is so serious, especially in the military, and income gap is so great that the interests of the workers and peasants are not well protected. The masses do not trust the government which has lost hearts and minds of the people. If there is an economic crisis, the situation will change drastically. And now the odds of a major economic crisis is great ... The crisis will surely occur ... and social instability will follow. It's not just a matter of probability, but a matter of time.[22]

The well-informed Chinese leaders were not muddle-headed. They were entirely clear that they were racing against time. Though some measures had been taken to alleviate the miserable conditions of the underclass since the late 2000s, such as exemptions from rural taxes and increases in subsistence allowance for urban dwellers, and so on, these limited improvements in the underclass people's welfare did not suffice to offset the much faster wealth accumulation among the business and political elites, and they did not alter the megatrends of quickly enlarging income disparity either. Documented billionaires continued to increase in numbers very rapidly from 100 in 2004 to 1000 in 2009. Of all the bank deposits of 21.8 trillion yuan in 2008, 40.37% were owned by the rich people with assets over 10 million yuan.[23] Thus, the Gini coefficient kept climbing up from 0.48 in 2007 to more than 0.5 in 2008 and 2009.[24] It further rose to 0.61 in 2010.[25] Accordingly, the percentage of household final consumption expenditure in GDP declined from 52.5% in 1981 to the record low of just 35% in 2010 (Table 7.1).[26] It rose only slightly to 37.1% in the year of 2015, much lower than the world average of 58.1%, the OECD average of 60.5%, and even BRICS average (excluding China) of 58.5%.

The Chinese leaders were fully aware of the peril of persistent underconsumption to the economy and social stability. They called for expanding domestic demand as early as 1998 when Premier Zhu Rongji was completely in charge. Yet, domestic demand has remained sluggish until the present day. It is clear that without the introduction of some sort of democratic power-sharing, or political reform to ensure institutionalized fairer distribution of wealth, there is no way to address the issue of underconsumption. However, the Chinese regime was intransigent not to give

Table 7.1 China's household final consumption expenditure (% of GDP): 1978–2015

Year	Household consumption	Year	Household consumption
1978	48.8	2007	36
1981	52.5	2008	35.1
1991	47.5	2009	35.1
2001	45.2	2010	35
2002	43.7	2011	35.7
2003	41.7	2012	36.0
2004	39.8	2013	36.2
2005	37.7	2014	36.2
2006	36.2	2015	37.1 (World Bank)

Source: China statistics yearbook; World Bank national accounts data (http://data.worldbank.org/indicator/NE.CON.PETC.ZS)

the slightest political concession to the people. The National People's Congress (NPC) has been resisting ratifying the United Nations Convention on Civil Rights and Political Rights that the government of China signed in 1998. And based on the lessons drawn from the 1989 Tiananmen Incident that all potential destabilizing factors must be wiped out in their infancy, the overriding reaction of the Chinese regime to the growing social unrest was to toughen its position vis-à-vis the people by sharply increasing outlays on maintaining internal stability (*weiwen*).

Under harsh orders of the central government, the top priority of local authorities has fundamentally changed since early 2009. Their top priority was no longer placed on development but rather on maintaining social stability. The *weiwen* has since become the overriding task of the local government.[27] In 2009, expenditure on internal public security (*weiwen*) increased by 16% to 472 billion yuan.[28] In 2010, *weiwen* spending grew by 15.6% to 549 billion yuan, in excess of the defense spending at 433.4 billion yuan, which grew by 7.8%. Deeply worried about the spread of the "Jasmine Revolution" in the Middle East to China, the Chinese regime increased the budget on *weiwen* at 624 billion yuan, which for the second year outpaced defense spending at 602 billion yuan and would be "greater than the combined budgets for healthcare, diplomacy and financial oversight."[29] This highlighted the assertiveness of the Chinese authoritarian regime, which regarded any expression of interest by the underclass as threatening to the regime stability in its handling of social unrests at home. In the absence of institutional expression of interest by the vulnerable underclass, *weiwen* has essentially become the instrument of the privileged elites to protect their vested interests.[30]

Meanwhile, the Chinese leadership had taken note of the peril of excessive trade dependence of the country's economy in the late 1990s. They were fully aware of the vital importance of stimulating domestic demand to enable a self-sustaining economic growth. However, as observed by *Caijing*, China's most influential liberal journal, in late 2005, three years after the transition period ended, "Data suggest that China's economic growth has become even more dependent on the external demand than any period in the last few years."[31] With the "rise of China" becoming a global consensus soon after it joined the WTO,[32] China's trade dependence did not decline but has stood at 60%, which is far above the world's average. The CCP's main mouthpiece, the *People's Daily* warned in early March 2010, "Lacking of innovation capability, core technology and proprietary property rights, our country's enterprises rely more on the comparative advantage in cheap labor, massive inputs of resources and energies to reap just negligible profits at the low end of the global value chain. The luminous ring of 'World Factory' cannot eclipse the predicament that 90% of our exports are Original Equipment Manufacturing (OEM) products."[33] Despite these acknowledgments, the Chinese leaders are reluctant to face squarely the institutional root cause of sluggish domestic demand. Nor are they capable of rivaling institutions in which they have crucial stakes and their families are the largest beneficiaries. Hence, the political barriers to a fairer redistribution of wealth institutionalized an ever-enlarging income disparity and societal polarization, rendering China's economy inexorably dependent on the *domestic demand* of the advanced economies.

The paradox of economic development in China's ad hoc institutional context seems to be that only by keeping the people relatively poor can the country's sole comparative advantage in cheap labor be maintained so that the economy is able to continue to prosper on the premise that customers in the advanced economies, in particular the USA, with the assistance of China's massive investment in US Treasury Bonds, continue to "save less and spend more." But the hard constraints of global imbalance had backfired through either forcing renminbi to revaluate or deficit countries to resort to trade protectionism. The perverse economic interdependence between China and the USA is collapsing with Trump's rise to the presidency. This implies that China's highly export-dependent economy is being exposed to greater risks in case of a substantial policy reversal by the USA. Yu Yongding argued in 2010 that the China model itself as featured by "anemic innovation, slow tech upgrades, and social tensions" had become unsustainable and needed painful readjustments.[34] As this author will argue, the self-defeating China model ended in the last quarter of 2008. The global recession that began in 2007 did not cause China's economic plight, but exacerbated it.

The Rise of China, the Decline of Chinese Manufacturers

Despite the neoclassical optimism on China's long-term economic development at home and abroad prior to its WTO accession, suspicions were rampant on whether China could manage the impacts in the initial years after the accession. Predictions of an economically failing China were logically sound and empirically grounded given the structural weakness of the Chinese economy. Most of the suspicions came from the leftists. Han Deqiang quoted Lardy by arguing that the impacts from cheap foreign imports would kill quite a number of domestic enterprises, leading exports from these impacted industries to shrink by 20%.[35] Cui Zhiyuan used the Kalecki model to postulate that the pressure of profit repatriation by foreign investors could erode China's trade surplus and reduce its forex reserve, thus worsening China's balance of payments.[36] One famous new left economist made similar projections. He asserted that the Chinese economy would collapse in five years after the WTO accession.[37] Gordon Chang, an anti-communist lawyer residing in the USA, also voiced doubts about China's capacity to manage the impacts of deep integration. He made the most systematic analysis in 2001 on "The Coming Collapse of China" in the wake of the accession. Chang argued that with the state-owned enterprises (SOEs) dying and state banks getting insolvent, the

Chinese economy would stagnate. Against the backdrop of an explosive social situation, the accession would trigger off the collapse of Chinese communist regime and the disintegration of the Chinese state.[38]

However, all these arguments or predictions on China's post-accession economic failings turned out to be mistaken. Though the non-performing loans of China's state banks continued to build up,[39] the economic situation was taking a turn for the better after the SARS pandemic ended in June 2003. Property prices hiked up. Exports soared and FDI flooded in. China's foreign currency reserve piled up rapidly. Most remarkably, the performance of the SOEs improved. China's booming economy after its accession to the WTO impressed the whole world. Of particular importance is that the Chinese economy continued to prosper in 2009 when the world economy was devastated by the sub-prime crisis that broke out in the USA in late 2007 and worsened again in November 2008. These are definitely not the indications of a collapsing economy. The party state is not disintegrating either. Rather, the rise of China has since been widely recognized and has become a global consensus.

Nonetheless, the mistaken "disintegration thesis" does not suffice to justify the neoclassical dogma on China's economic success thanks to liberal globalization. Underneath the economic miracle, China's low-tech manufacturing industries went into deep crisis since early 2007 due to the revaluation of renminbi, spiraling inflation, and an increasing number of quality defects in the export products. Lacking innovation capability, China's manufacturing enterprises had no way to offset the quickly rising production costs by relocating their operations to lower-income countries (*zou chuqu*). In the year 2008 alone, more than 100,000 SMEs went bankrupt. About 20 million migrant workers were laid off.[40] The Chinese Academy of Social Sciences (CASS) *Blue Paper on China's Social Situation* published on December 16, 2008, demonstrated that the actual unemployment rate had reached 9.4%, well above the internationally recognized alert level of 7% and more than doubled the officially claimed "registered unemployment rate" (*dengji shiyelv*) of 4.0%.[41] Yet, China's exports kept flourishing. The sub-prime crisis taking place in late 2007 in the USA did not spread to the real economy until December 2008. Hence, the impasse of China's manufacturing operations had little to do with the global financial crisis. It was the second wave of the globalized financial crisis that severely impacted Chinese exports.[42] One CASS report showed that until the first half of 2009, 40% of China's SMEs went broke, 40% were on the verge of collapse, and only 20% were unaffected.[43] The Chinese regime promptly used the global financial crisis as the scapegoat for the country's economic hardship to divert public attention from their blunt reaction.

The hastily formulated 4-trillion yuan (US $585 billion) stimulus package at the end of 2008 gave a strong impetus to the economic growth. GDP grew at 9.1% in 2009 in excess of the preset target of 8% by the Chinese government. This was the only bright spot in the gloomiest global economy. By the year's end, China declared confidently that it would move ahead of others to step out of the shadow of global recession and expect to make significant contribution to the global economic recovery.[44] However, unlike in 1998 when Premier Zhu Rongji used the Keynesian approach to stimulate the economy under deflation, combat against inflation in early 2008 gave way to the politicized target of GDP growth by the year's end through expansionary fiscal and monetary policies. Similar to what happened in 1998, the stimulus package generated a "crowd-out effect" against private-sector investment, since a large proportion of the state investments and assorted bank loans went to the cash-rich oligopolistic SOEs in either the construction of infrastructure or the capacity rebuilding in heavy industries. The non–publicly owned small- and medium-sized enterprises (SMEs) were not on the agenda of the state bail-out scheme. Without state-sponsored financial support, these SMEs, which produced 60% of China's GDP and absorbed more than 70% of the labor force, kept declining. Ironically, the official figure of "registered unemployment rate" has consistently hovered around 4% since 2002.[45] Premier Wen Jiabao informed the attendants at the China Development Executive Forum held in Beijing on March 22, 2010, that China at that moment had an *underemployed* population of 200 million.[46] This candid statement was misreported as China having 200 million jobless people and caused huge panic in the domestic media.

Amid the global eulogy of China's successful market authoritarianism as a unique alternative approach to the Washington consensus neoliberalism, new concepts were invented such as the "Beijing Consensus," "the China Model," "the Chinese century," and so on. Niall Ferguson even used "Chimerica" to describe China's crucial importance to the global economy and its symbiotic economic relations with the USA.[47] However, the perceptions of Chinese leaders on the country's economic situation and prospects were entirely different. In February 2009, the Politburo meeting judged that the year 2009 could be the *most difficult year* for China's economic development in the new century. The Chinese leadership called for "mobilizing the people and joining hands to pass through the hardships" (*gongke shijian*).[48] Wen Jiabao repeated this judgment about the gloomiest economic situation in 2009 at the annual NPC session in March 2010.[49] More importantly, Chinese leaders sensed the "riskiness" and "unsustainability" of the country's development model based on "massive inputs of resources ... at the expense of the most fragile ecology in Chinese history."[50] They came to realize that this sort of development was quintessentially a "path of low end production" (*diduan zhilu*) in the international division of labor that has to date impeded the enhancement of China's global competitiveness.[51] Hence, it was rather uncommon that China's top leaders Hu Jintao, Wen Jiabao, and First-Deputy Premier Li Keqiang simultaneously turned out at the Central Party School in early February 2010 to address high-ranking officials at ministerial and provincial level on the crucial importance of transforming the mode of economic development.[52]

China's entrapment in the *diduan zhili* is in no sense the symbol of an emerging industrial power. Paradoxically, the Chinese leadership did not seem to establish a link between China's persistent entrapment in *diduan zhilu* and globalization. Contrary to the iron rule that free trade has been the ideology of the strong, the Chinese leaders became the most ardent eulogists of free trade on world arena. At the press conference after the closing annual NPC session in March, 2010, Premier Wen Jiabao reaffirmed China's "staunchest support" for free trade and its adamant opposition to "all forms of trade protectionism."[53] What's more, during the second round of the Sino-US Strategic and Economic Dialogue (S&ED) held in Beijing on May 24 and 25, 2010, China committed to submitting "a robust revised Agreement on Government Procurement (GPA) offer before the July 2010 meeting of the WTO Government Procurement Committee." In addition, China promised to allow the Qualified Foreign Institutional Investors (QFII) to "invest in stock index futures products," and "make more and more SOEs market-oriented legal entities … continue to reform the SOEs by promoting further investor diversification, including issuing publicly traded shares and inviting strategic investors, including non-public and foreign investors, to take equity stakes."[54]

These ad hoc concessions on investment and financial liberalization suggest that the rise of China embodied by continuing rapid economic growth did not significantly increase China's bargaining power in its relations with the declining USA. The timing of commitment on GPA was ostensibly to assuage US concern on China's innovation policies, which were understood by foreign investors and Western media at the start of the year as an emerging economic nationalism, the symbol of worsening investment environment.[55] China promised the USA that it would "revise its Catalogue Guiding Foreign Investment in Industries and 'encourage and expand areas that are open to foreign investment in high-end manufacturing, high-tech industries, modern services, new energy, energy savings and environmental protection sectors.'" Both states agreed that

> their innovation policies will be consistent with the following principles: non-discrimination; support for market competition and open international trade and investment; strong enforcement of intellectual property rights; and; consistent with WTO rules, leaving the terms and conditions of technology transfer, production processes and other proprietary information to agreement between individual enterprises.

This was a reminder of the Trade-related Investment Measurement (TRIMs) agreement China had committed to honor upon accession and to wipe out any gray areas or loopholes in the WTO rules of which China could take advantage by imposing local content or technology transfer requirements upon foreign investors, in particular the multinational corporations (MNCs) from the USA.

As a matter of fact, China's compromise on innovation policies was not the product of bargaining with the USA at the negotiating table, but was preceded by its new policies on FDI with roughly the same contents promulgated by the State Council on April 6, 2010.[56] China's new policies on FDI and its commitment to joining the Agreement on Government Procurement (GPA) were hard evidence of its coherent conversion to economic liberalism rather than a breach of its WTO commitments and a reorientation to economic nationalism. Both states committed to "building a more open system of global trade and investment and opposing trade and investment protectionism," and stressed "the importance of open trade and investment in fostering economic growth, job creation and innovation in the United States and China."[57]

These liberalization promises offset against the indigenous innovation (*zizhu chuangxin*) policies advocated by Chinese leaders imply that they had no intention to embrace economic nationalism. The concessions China made on the fateful innovation policies highlighted the greater dependence of the Chinese economy on the US market rather than the reverse. In this regard, heavy purchases of US Treasury Bonds did not seem to furnish China with the necessary means to devastate the US economy and extract equivalent concessions from the USA. Given the enormous difficulties in technological upgrading of domestic firms, Chinese leaders had to choose between RMB revaluation and the withdrawal of free trade by the USA in accordance with the terms (non-market economy) China accepted prior to the WTO accession. Either option was poised to incur huge damage to China's labor-intensive exports and the large labor force behind them. After successive revaluation of RMB since July 2005, domestic firms cannot afford further substantial revaluation, a consequence, as Wen conceded during his visit to Washington in September 2010 that will plunge the country into "a new cycle of disorder."[58] Thus, China has no other choice but to compromise on its innovation policies to exchange for moderation on China's forex policy and continued access to US market.

It is no more pronounced that FDI has played a key role in prompting China to compromise on GPA and its innovation policies. On the one hand, FDI has become too important to the Chinese economy to be neglected. In 2009, the foreign-invested enterprises (FIEs) accounted for 28% of China's industrial output, 22.7% of its tax revenues, and 55.9% of the total exports and engaged 45 million Chinese staff.[59] On the other hand, despite the global economic slump, US global firms operating in China "improved their profit margins compared to their margins in other markets." According to the AmCham-China's 2010 *Business Climate Survey*, 71% of US companies were profitable or very profitable in 2009; and 81% were optimistic about China's economic future in year 2010, which is twice

Table 7.2 The proportion of the FIEs in China's fixed-asset investment (FAI), industrial output, profits, and tax contribution (excl. import duties and land fees) (unit: US $100 million; %): 1992–2015

Year	FDI	FAI (%)	Industrial output (%)	Profits (%)	Tax contribution
1992	110.08	7.51	7.09	4.25	3.96
1993	275.15	12.13	9.14	5.71	5.67
1994	337.67	17.08	11.25	8.51	8.29
1995	375.21	15.65	14.30	10.96	10.52
1996	417.26	15.10	15.14	11.87	11.56
1997	452.57	14.79	18.57	13.16	12.55
1998	454.63	13.23	24.34	14.38	13.74
1999	403.19	11.17	27.75	15.99	16.29
2000	407.15	10.32	31.29	17.5	18.74
2001	468.78	10.51	27.98	19.01	19.94
2002	527.43	10.10	33.37	20.52	20.59
2003	535.05	8.03	35.87	20.86	22.35
2004	606.30	7.16	31.43	20.81	23.16
2005	724.06	6.69	31.41	20.71	23.06
2006	727.15	5.28	31.50	21.19	23.70
2007	835.21	4.63	30.91	20.17	22.57
2008	923.95	4.37	29.74	20.94	23.10
2009	900.30	2.86	28.00	22.70	23.46
2010	1057.35	3.09	27.1	–	23.03
2011	1160.11	2.57	26.11	–	22.53
2012	1117.16	2.04	–	–	22.25
2013	1175.86	1.72	–	–	20.92
2014	1195.62	1.54	–	–	21.42
2015	1262.27	1.5	–	–	19.87

Source: Statistics of the Ministry of Commerce, PRC

the figure the *Survey* found in 2009. In total, 91% of US companies were optimistic about their five-year outlook, which was "notably higher than the 81%" in 2009.[60] This contrasts sharply with the many Chinese SMEs in the manufacturing sector. Lucrative business in China has made US global firms natural allies of the Chinese government to lobby at Capitol Hill for maintaining free trade between the two trading powers (Table 7.2).

The renewed investment boom driven by the massive influx of FDI made China the "Factory of the World." However, as the world's leading manufacturing powerhouse, China is in no sense comparable to Great Britain in the nineteenth century, which took the lead in industrial innovation. The technologically dependent China in the twenty-first century was but the most ideal production site of the global value chain. China reaped just a small portion of value added at the final stage of labor-intensive assembling, while the FIEs in China or foreign importers that outsourced from China captured the lion's share of the profits. According to a survey carried out by the China Customs in Shanghai, the HP laptop manufactured in China was sold at US $1000 in the US market. Profits incurred at the chain of distribution in the USA were as high as US $169.6. China gained only US $30.3 of processing expenses, which amounts to just 3% of the retail price.[61] This is among the numerous examples of Chinese indigenous firms engaging in low-end commodity manufacturing. The relative gain of this type from the global division of labor that China has fostered through the trade and investment liberalization was so small as to generate larger technological gaps with the advanced economies.

The wholly owned FIEs dominated China's new and high-tech exports in the late 1990s. The dramatic increase of the wholly owned FIEs reinforced their inclination to safeguard technological know-how. In addition, banning "local contents" in already opened sectors facilitated the MNCs to make full use of their global procurement system for profit maximization at the expense of China's backward linkage, hence industrial deepening. These developments increased domestic firms' dependence on importation of "designs, critical components, and manufacturing equipment" from the advanced economies.[62] Data show that about 40% to 50% of Chinese exports are the parts and components imported from the developed countries, and "the proportion of import content is particularly high in the high-end manufactures as opposed to that in the low-skilled exports."[63] Whatever high-tech or low-tech indigenous firms appeared to be, they engaged in the least profitable part of the commodity manufacturing. Thus, they were financially incapable of massively investing in research and development (R&D) for the purpose of technological upgrading.[64] Except the Taiwanese firms that have managed to upgrade technologically, China's indigenous firms have failed to upgrade. Most of them were strong in reverse engineering but weak in innovation and system integration. In the face of the FIEs that dominated the high-end product market, domestic firms, even if they imported cutting-edge equipment to manufacture new products, had little choice but to focus on the commodity-focused production of undifferentiated and standardized products. According to Steinfeld, this sort of commodification production lowered the entry barriers and sharply reduced profit margins of domestic firms as a whole. With the detachment of manufacturing from innovation in the global supply chain driven by China's WTO accession, "leading global competitors race forward into something yet more sophisticated and more difficult to replicate."[65] By so doing, Western countries, in particular the USA, "have done equally well or even better" in globalization.

Added to the innovative weakness of domestic firms are the institutional barriers that favor foreign investors at the expense of domestic ones after China joined the WTO. The appeals for unifying the income tax rate to be applied to all industrial firms operating in China were strongly resisted by interest groups at Moftec (MOFCOM from 2003) and local governments that accorded the FIEs a great variety of preferences, in particular tax breaks and concessions since China opened the door to the outside world. It was not until March 2007 that the draft new law was passed by the NPC; it entered into force on January 1, 2008. To sustain rapid economic growth and to create more jobs, the new administration under Premier Wen Jiabao adopted more radical measures to liberalize inward foreign investment in China. These measures went far beyond what had been committed by his predecessor Zhu Rongji who in 1999 refused to compromise in certain key areas where the weak domestic firms were unable to compete.[66] Though Zhu was the main propeller of China's deep integration, he was doing his utmost to win as much time as possible for domestic firms to grow into stronger competitors during the transition period. In contrast, Wen seemed to be preoccupied with job creation via economic growth in the initial years after the accession.

From 2003 onward, mergers and acquisitions (M&A) by foreign investors were encouraged as the new way of attracting FDI by the Chinese government. According to Gao Liang, M&A has grown rapidly and has accounted for about half of the FDI since 2004. Most of the M&A cases targeted China's leading capital goods producers (equipment manufacturers), a situation deemed by economic nationalists as having endangered China's economic security.[67] By the end of 2008, 300 domestic equipment manufacturers became subsidiaries of MNCs as a result of

Table 7.3 China's new and high-tech imports/exports by ownership (2005) (unit: US $100 million)

Firms	Exp	(%)	IMP	(%)	Trade balance
FIEs	1920.0	88.0	1579.8	79.9	340.2
SOEs	161.5	7.4	282.2	14.3	-120.7
Collectively-owned	39.8	1.8	30.8	1.6	9.0
private	61.1	2.8	83.4	4.2	-22.3
Other types	0.059	0.0027	0.895	0.045	-0.84
Local firms sub-total	262.5	12.0	397.3	20.1	-134.8
Total	2182.5	100.0	1977.1	100.0	205.4

Source: MOFCOM data

the M&A. Yet, it was not until March 18, 2009, the anti-monopoly law (AML) enacted on August 1, 2008, was invoked for the first time against Coca Cola's M&A of Huiyuan Juice Company under massive pressures of public opinion.[68]

As a result, China's domestic industries declined in relative terms as opposed to the FIEs (Table 7.3).[69] The high-end capital goods sector remained weak in technological terms. The 2005 official data showed that 95% of the integrated circuits (IC), more than 70% of the highly sophisticated digital-control machine tools, 100% of the photo-electronics facilities, and 70% of car manufacturing equipment and textile machineries relied on imports from the advanced economies.[70] The State Administration of Industry and Commerce (SAIC) issued warnings against the market monopoly by the FIEs in May 2004, stating "the monopoly of market by the FIEs has become very conspicuous in recent years. The MNCs are using their advantages in technology, brand and scale to expand their monopoly and have created high entry barriers."[71]

"Indigenous Innovation": The Myth of Techno-nationalism

The perilous trends of market domination by the technologically advanced FIEs upset the Chinese leadership. They started to introduce a set of industrial policies in an attempt to mitigate technological dependence on foreign powers. In February 2006, the Ministry of Science and Technology (MOST) released the "The National Medium- and Long-Term Plan

(MLP) for the Development of Science and Technology" to echo the appeal of the top leadership one month ago for building China into an innovative state (*chuangxinxing guojia)* by 2020. This plan involves a massive increase in R&D spending and state sponsorship of "indigenous innovation" (*zizhu chuangxin*) of the domestic firms, in particular the SOEs. For this purpose, the MLP aims to elevate the S&T (science and technology) contribution to the economic growth from 39% in 2006 to above 60% in 2020, and the whole-nation R&D outlay as a percentage of GDP from 1.35% to 2.5%, and to reduce technological dependence on foreign sources from 50% to 30%.[72] In November 2012, the CCP put forward the "Innovation-driven Development Strategy," vowing to further cut down China's technological dependency ratio to below 20% by 2020.[73]

The pressing need for "indigenous innovation" was further verified by the State Council's Development and Research Center (DRC) report issued in August 2006 in which similar conclusions to those of SAIC were reached with regard to the industry control by the FIEs.[74] Given the resurgence of economic nationalism sparked off by the perceived MNCs' hostile takeover of Chinese industries, as well as the frustrations of China's M&As in those MNCs' mother countries, most notably the failure of the CNOOC's acquisition of Unocal, legislation on M&A became imperative politically and economically in the wider context of President Hu Jintao's proclamation to build up an innovative state by 2020. In the same month of the DRC report, six Ministries and Commissions of the central government gathered around to work out regulations on M&A by foreign investors. However, this law was aimed at encouraging further foreign investment in the form of M&A of Chinese enterprises, which paradoxically went against the tenet of indigenous innovation with a view to building an innovative state. The drafting of this allegedly "most important law" was ironically presided over by Mr. Guo Jingyi, a high-ranking MOFCOM official in charge of treaties and laws. He was arrested two years later for taking bribery from the MNCs and acting as their agent.[75] Paradoxically, despite Guo's arrest and the uproar of public opinion against the foreign takeover of Chinese lead firms, policies of promoting M&A by foreign investors were unaffected and even continued to be encouraged by the central government.[76]

Indigenous innovation is the key to the building of an innovative state. It is defined by the MOST as the "enhancement of original innovation through co-innovation and re-innovation based on assimilation of imported technologies." Given the past lessons of importing technology without proper absorption and assimilation, the MLP placed the emphasis on strengthening the absorptive capacity of domestic enterprises through "international cooperation." This implies that indigenous innovation is not essentially a self-reliant approach of technological development, but one premised upon the technology transfer from foreign partners with market share as a quid pro quo.

This spectacular plan aroused global attention. The allusion to technology transfer as the key approach to enhancing China's original innovation alerted quite a number of the MNCs who considered the MLP to be "a blueprint for technology theft on a scale the world has never seen before."[77] This overstated China's ambition to catch up with the West simply because without substantial enhancement of domestic firms' absorptive capacity, especially a highly efficient national system of innovation (NSI), there is no way for China to out-innovate the West in long-term economic rivalry even if it manages to get access to sophisticated technologies of the West through industrial espionage one way or another. What is at issue is that institutional barriers remain in place to discourage innovation, as mentioned above. In addition, the "softness" of the Chinese state, though still strong in extraction and repression, is no more pronounced in its being not monolithic in promoting national industrial development. A most typical example is the law on government procurement enacted in 2002, which came into being a few years earlier than the MLP. The PRC's Government Procurement Law (GPL) vexed the global firms who were deeply worried about China's massive state sponsorship of domestic industries at their expense. Their protectionist fear reached a climax over China's stimulus package in 2009.[78] But in reality, the implementation of GPL, in most cases, ended up with open and *rampant* discrimination of domestic rather than foreign firms for many years in China.[79] This has in large part to do with the incompatibility of policies made by the central government; quality inferiority of the domestically made products bidding for the government procurement; and corruption in various levels of government.[80]

Since 2008, the central government has intervened in an attempt to redress improper practices of local authorities with regard to government procurement, but this has largely been in vain. As a matter of fact, the GPL, even if it has been properly implemented, is by no means a protectionist mechanism that violated China's WTO commitments. The GPL, together with government subsidies in R&D, is the legal industrial policy instrument, as per the WTO rules. However, bowing to US pressure, China agreed to delink government procurement from its indigenous innovation policies. In June 2011, The Ministry of Finance decided to cease implementing measures for government procurement-related management of budgets.[81] Moreover, from 2010 China made repeated assurances that it did not impose technology transfer requirements on the foreign investors as it had committed before to accede to the WTO.[82]

Market-seeking MNCs are very sensitive to and particularly annoyed by the imposition of local content requirement by the Chinese central government to leverage technology transfer from foreign investors by dint of its market size. Yet, despite the fact that China had taken advantage of a *gray area* in international economic law by rejecting a key clause of the WTO agreement that banned "its top planning agency from making such demands, and government negotiators have continued to ask foreign companies to transfer technology to local partners or to set up research centers to train local engineers,"[83] the TRIMs agreement China had committed to honor upon accession strictly prohibited such imposition in general. Therefore, China is not seeking alternatives to the liberal globalization approach in technological development but is rather attempting to modernize the country within the bounds of the WTO rules. Equally important is the limited industry coverage of indigenous innovation policy. China's approach of technology-import-based indigenous innovation did not cover those industries that had already been opened for foreign investment such as the auto industry, but did cover those *yet-to-open* areas in "high-end manufacturing, high-tech industries, modern services, new energy, energy savings and environmental protection sectors." These new high-tech industries were the areas of particular concern to the USA during the S&ED negotiations in 2009 and 2010.

Generally speaking, China's indigenous innovation has, since its inception in 2006, made significant headway in certain yet-to-open areas in securing the transfer of advanced technologies from the West, exclusively in development of wind turbines and high-speed trains. This is primarily because the central government intervened more directly to enforce industrial policies through government procurement and imposition of local content requirement, which as a result significantly enhanced efficiency and effectiveness in terms of negotiating technology transfer from foreign partners. These "two arms" of the indigenous innovation are what distinguished indigenous innovation from the ETMA in the 1990s. In addition, what made Chinese tactics work is the fact that the sluggish market demand at home inclined the global leading manufacturers to trade off "short-term sales for long-term competition."[84] Henceforth, China not only managed to obtain advanced technologies but even started to export the high-tech products at extremely competitive prices to the global market that was traditionally dominated by its foreign partners.

Is technological leapfrogging this way sustainable? A Wall Street Journal (WSJ) article asserted, "after the partnerships expired, many of the Chinese partners couldn't succeed independently."[85] This raised deeper questions with regard to the efficacy of indigenous innovation based on technology transfer by foreign investors. How on earth "advanced" is the technology transferred to the Chinese partners? How much "indigenous" is the innovation made by the Chinese firms on the basis of transferred technologies? As in the case of wind turbines, the local content requirement raised by the National Development and Reform Commission (NDRC) did force global leading wind turbine manufacturers to source their engines locally. But many of them "have opted to not partner with Chinese-owned companies except for some smaller components, and have not transferred know-how or intellectual property rights as a license."[86] General Electric (GE) as the leading producer of the most sophisticated gas-fired wind turbines eventually decided to cooperate given the attraction of China's sizable wind market. Yet GE did not transfer "the most secret elements of the turbine, including the design of the cooling system for the first row of blades and the technology behind a thermal protective coating for those blades." Jeffrey R. Immelt, GE's Chairman and CEO told the WSJ that the company's turbine designs were "at least two generations ahead" of the turbine sold to China.[87]

The local content requirement was abandoned by China in 2009 as a result of the S&ED between China and the USA. The withdrawal of this policy seemed to be associated with the possibility that the domestic manufacturers have grown up.[88] That might be true, but in what sense or to what extent have the Chinese firms "grown up"? Evidence is weak in supporting such an allegation. In fact, the technological gap with the West remains large, as evidenced by China's much smaller share in exports due to their quality deficiency. The Kellogg School of Management research stated, "The Chinese industry lags technologically behind foreign wind equipment producers in several important categories, including offshore wind equipment, control systems, and software supporting turbines."[89] Whether the "grown-up" Chinese firms will be able to catch up through self-reliant innovation and even outcompete foreign players on the global market afterward remains an outstanding issue.

The leapfrogging of the high-speed train (*gaotie*) seems more encouraging. It was reported that China has managed to obtain the most advanced technologies at a cheaper cost from Western countries based on a set of exquisite negotiation tactics since 2004. Fierce competition between global firms and the blueprint of China's grand railway network building in the next decade were what made the expected technology transfer possible. China was reported to have not only assimilated the imported technologies, but also started to export high-speed trains to a couple of countries, including the USA, at the expense of its foreign partners.[90] The conflict of interests with foreign partners over the latter's traditional market and its consequences were eclipsed by a national pride associated with the rise of China arising from the "indigenous innovation" that had been deemed successful. However, as time passed by, more and more problems concerning the financial risk of the high-speed train project began to emerge. Domestic media revealed that a large portion of the stimulus package was invested in the construction of national rail networks, in particular the *gaotie*. Interest expenses incurred per annum were so huge as to drive the Ministry of Railway (MOR) financially insolvent.[91] The likely insolvency of China's *gaotie* project was complicated by the arrest of Minister Liu Zhijun in early 2011, a national hero who gave birth to China's *gaotie*. He was charged with having accepted huge bribes from a businesswoman called Ding Shumiao in Shanxi Province in the process of public bidding. More tellingly, the corruption scandal did not involve Liu alone, but implicated his entire project team. The most notable figure was Liu's closest aide Zhang Shuguang, deputy Chief Engineer of the project. Zhang was said to have taken kickbacks and secretly deposited US $2.8 billion in the USA and Switzerland.[92]

The downfall of Liu and his team is among the numerous scandals of collective corruptions that are usually linked with big state projects in infrastructure. In a sense, China's spectacular economic growth after it joined the WTO was fueled by a *special* investment hunger driven by the corruption motivations of the insiders of SOEs and the bureaucracy rather than being driven by the "soft constraint" that characterized the shortage economies of the socialist states. More than that, as corruption pushed up the total cost of the *gaotie* project, China needed overseas market to subsidize the costly *gaotie* operations at home. In this regard, the export dynamo was driven not so much by China's ambition to outcompete foreign partners globally as by the heavy pressure of debt repayment domestically. The severity of corruption in China's high-speed train project undoubtedly eroded its techno-economic performance in the long term. But legacies are manifold. Fairly speaking, this case is not simply a corruption-associated image project propped up by the MOR. Mr. Liu has arguably managed to promote the technological progress of the country's entire railway system in one great stride. Liu came to office as a cabinet member of Premier Wen Jiabao in 2003 when the "China Star" (*zhonghua zhixing*), the first domestically designed high-speed train with proprietary intellectual property rights, was under scrutiny. Irrespective of oppositions from within the MOR, Liu made the crucial decision to terminate the China Star project in favor of the ETMA option by negotiating with the leading manufacturers of high-speed train in France, Germany, and Japan. This adversely caused a massive drain-out of technical staff from the China Star project. But Liu went on his way. He turned out to be a master strategist in playing one foreign firm off against the other to substantially bring down the total cost of technology transfer.

Prior to Liu's fall, state media depicted the *gaotie* story as the template of China's indigenous innovation. Doubts were rare and were suppressed intentionally. Since his fall, more and more problems concerning the technological development and financial management have been exposed.

This is the irony of Chinese politics. In fact, as early as 2006, MOR insiders, to be more exact, those involved in the "China Star" project, indicated that key technologies from Japan's Kawasaki Company had been transferred to its subsidiary in the form of joint ventures established with the Chinese partners.[93] The most cutting-edge technologies remained firmly under the control of the Japanese. The Chinese partners were devoted to assembling the less-sophisticated secondary components. Bai Yimin, a well-known business analyst who had worked in Mitsui for years, described such adaptive strategies of Japanese firms' technology transfer as "Made in China, but Made by Japan."[94]

Chinese media noted that Siemens, though having licensed the production of 57 of the 60 bidder-trains in China, retained some key components manufacturing within Germany.[95] *Handelsblatt*, one of Germany's most influential commercial newspapers cited internal sources of Siemens as saying, "Siemens hold exactly the same attitudes as those of Tysen Krupp and Airbus … will not and never concede core technologies (to China)."[96] It is now clear what these global firms had transferred were less critical technologies to meet China's local content requirement, while they retained the most sophisticated technological know-how and intellectual property rights with their home companies. In terms of the ETMA-based indigenous innovation on the part of China, the share of entirely proprietary intellectual property rights China commanded did not exceed 20%, according to many high-speed train experts.[97] Internal sources confirmed that the absorptive capacities of indigenous locomotive manufacturers were below the expectation. Large numbers of domestically made parts and components did not meet the appropriate quality standard.[98] Therefore, China has to import many key parts and components from abroad, in particular all the specialty bearings from SKF of Sweden, FAG of Germany or NTN of Japan, and so on, which control 80% of global markets.[99]

Nevertheless, the technological capabilities of Chinese firms have increased significantly with the enforcement of indigenous innovation. Their competitiveness in undercutting global firms on the basis of the latter's (limited) technology transfer and comparative advantage in cheap labor has upset and even to some extent horrified the global firms. Though the global firms dominate the high-end manufacturing and monopolize key technologies, they are increasingly sensitive to the likelihood that China will catch up much quicker than expected through whatever means and become their most dreadful competitor in the near future. There is evidence to suggest that industrial powers, in particular the USA, have sensed the danger of China using the rivalry between the USA and EU to secure the most advanced technologies to accelerate the country's industrial development. Evidence shows that global firms in industrial countries, coordinated by their governments behind, were considering joining hands to circumvent China's tactics to extract the largest concessions on technology transfer.[100] In fact, the USA has taken actions with regard to China's indigenous innovation on a bilateral basis. During the two S&EDs held in 2009 and 2010 and the Sino-US Joint Commission on Commerce and Trade (JCCT) in 2010, the USA has managed to press China into renouncing the local content requirement and to commit to joining the GPA of the WTO as early as possible without discriminating against foreign producers in China. In the third meeting of the S&ED on May 10, 2011, China "pledged to eliminate all of its government procurement indigenous innovation products catalogues and revise Article 9 of the draft Government Procurement Law Implementing Regulations as part of its implementation of President Hu's January 2011 commitment not to link Chinese innovation policies to government procurement preferences."[101] These fateful commitments have deep implications for China's development in globalization. With these "two arms" of indigenous innovation being crippled, can China's domestic firms out-innovate global firms on a self-reliant basis in an increasingly hostile international environment?

This relates to the general technological performance of Chinese enterprises as a whole during the 11th and 12th Five-Year Plans (2006–2010; 2011–2015). Chinese enterprises, in particular the large-sized SOEs, have achieved notable technological advancements during this period in areas like chip-making, petrochemicals, transport equipment, nuclear technology, high-speed trains, and high-voltage electrical transmission (2006–2010); and lunar exploration project, deep-dive technology, satellite application, and supercomputing (2011–2015). Those SOEs are the national teams of China's industrial development, not simply because of their size and significance in the national economy, but because they work like a team and share technologies between themselves at virtually no cost. Financially, China's R&D spending as a percentage of GDP rose from 1.35% in 2005 to 2.1% in 2016.[102] R&D spending of the central government-owned SOEs (*yangqi*) grew by 28.5% annually from 2006–2009.

Its proportion in sales revenue has climbed to 2.1% in 2009, well above China's average R&D ratio.[103] China's total R&D spending has increased far more rapidly than the rest of the world and has exceeded any single member of the EU, ranking only after that of the USA in 2015.[104]

Despite these technological advancements, innovative weakness can be found in a number of ways. Firstly, the size of R&D outlay per se does not make much sense, given the rampant and serious corruption within China's science community,[105] low quality of patents, and the reluctance of Chinese firms to invest in R&D,[106] as well as the improper *composition* of R&D outlay in particular. According to Steinfeld, R&D can be divided into three categories: "research on fundamental, new-to-the-world technologies (basic research); research and development for new product platforms (applied research); and research and development for existing products that need to be adapted to specific customer or country-level requirements."[107] The first two categories fall into the realm of the science and technology (S&T) activities. They represent a nation's original innovation capabilities, which are in most cases financed by the government. Based on data of China's second R&D census released on 23/11/2010, in 2009, China's R&D spending reached 580.21 billion yuan, including 27.03 billion yuan (4.7%) on basic research and 73.08 billion yuan (12.6%) on applied research. By contrast, the two categories account for more than 10% and 20% of R&D, respectively, in the developed countries (Table 7.4).[108]

However, in spite of the importance of the intensity of government financing the R&D, the most cost-effective measure, Yusuf and Nabeshima argued, is "absorptive capacity which is a function of the volume and quality of talent and the depth as well as the heterogeneity of research experi-

Table 7.4 S&T of China compared with the USA and Japan (% R&D)

Country	Basic research	Applied research	S&T combined
China (2009)	4.7	12.6	17.3
USA (2008)	17	22	39
Japan (2005)	12.7	22.2	34.9

Source: China's Statistics Bureau, 23/11/2010. In 2016, China's R&D expenditure rose to 1567.67 billion yuan, of which basic research accounted for 5.2% (82.29 billion yuan), and applied research 10.3% (161.05 billion yuan). The ratio of S&T combined was 15.5%, even lower than the 2009 figure of 17.3%. Source: China's State Statistics Bureau, 10/10/2017. http://www.stats.gov.cn/tjsj/zxfb/201710/t20171009_1540386.html

ence. It is also a function of how companies maximize the commercial benefits of research and development, and the coordination of research with production and marketing."[109] The third category of R&D is what Chinese enterprises have been engaging in most actively in recent years. Spending in this category grew faster than the first two. Hence, the level of innovation in this category is rather low. By 2010, only 0.03% of Chinese enterprises had proprietary intellectual property rights. Average R&D spending as a percentage of sales revenues was merely 0.56%. The top 500 Chinese enterprises had a R&D ratio of sales revenue at 1.88%, 2.29%, 2.41%, 2.13%, 1.95%, and 2.03% from 2005 to 2010, respectively, far below the average level of the global giants, which normally spend no less than 5%, or even as high as 10–15% of revenues in innovation. At present, in 2017, only 4.1% Chinese firms are investing more than 5 million yuan in R&D, while as high as 67% of Chinese firms are investing less than 1 million yuan on R&D.[110] Therefore, Chinese enterprises have found it very difficult to enhance their assimilation and absorptive capacity.[111]

With intensifying global competition, technological progress, as Nolan et al. argued, constitutes the main source of competitive advantage "driven by oligopolistic competition" in the age of globalization.[112] The BEER annual report of 2008 indicates that the total R&D expenditure of the 1400 global giants reached US $545 billion. The top 50 accounted for 45% of all the R&D inputs, the top 100 accounted for 60%, and the bottom 100 accounted for less than 1%. For the four emerging developing countries of Brazil, Russia, India and China (BRIC), only 37 companies ranked among the global 1400. China's total R&D expenditure is just about 5% of that of the USA and 9% of that of Japan. The patents granted in China are just 1/30 of that in the USA or Japan and 1/6 of that in South Korea.[113] The highly authoritative China Stats Survey Bulletin issued in 2010 show that only 4.7% (1893) of the large and medium-sized enterprises (LMEs) were granted invention patents totaling 14,277 in 2009.[114] Things seem to have improved remarkably since then. However, despite the explosive patents applications by China's local firms from then on until the present day (2017), their conversion rate is rather low and the duration of patent enforceability is short.[115]

China's weakness in innovation was further substantiated by its performance in innovation on the global playing field within the advanced economies. China's share of patents granted by US Patent and Trademark

Table 7.5 Share of patents issued to residents of foreign countries/areas by the USA (2006–2010, 2015)

Country	2006	2007	2008	2009	2010	2015
China	**868 (0.47%)**	**1139 (0.62%)**	**1684 (0.92%)**	**2195 (1.2%)**	**3060 (1.31%)**	**9004 (2.8%)**
Taiwan	7356 (4.0%)	7569 (4.1%)	7424 (4.1%)	7958 (4.2%)	9202 (4.0%)	12,575 (3.9%)
Japan	36,482 (19.9%)	36,658 (19.9%)	35,847 (19.6%)	37,879 (19.9%)	44,893 (19.3%)	54,422 (16.7%)
Germany	10,083 (5.5%)	10,256 (5.6%)	9794 (5.4%)	10,279 (5.4%)	12,916 (5.5%)	17,752 (5.4%)
UK	3978 (2.2%)	4100 (2.2%)	3882 (2.1%)	3904 (2.1%)	4830 (2.1%)	7167 (2.2%)
France	3542 (1.9%)	3757 (2.0%)	3683 (2.0%)	3836 (2.0%)	4835 (2.1%)	7026 (2.2%)
India	470 (0.26%)	560 (0.3%)	650 (0.36%)	678 (0.36%)	1076 (0.46%)	3415 (1.0%)
Russia	169 (0.09%)	183 (0.1%)	186 (0.10%)	206 (0.11%)	246 (0.11%)	–

Source: US Patent and Trademark Office—performance and accountability report year 2010; data 2010 is temporary; source for year 2015: https://www.uspto.gov/web/offices/ac/ido/oeip/taf/pat_tr15.htm

Office kept climbing up in the past five years. However, China's share is negligible compared with that of the industrial powers in the world's most competitive and innovative market. Its position exactly reflected China's global competitiveness in innovation. China's share still ranked far behind that of Japan and Germany, which it has overtaken in the past decade in GDP terms, and was even behind that of Taiwan (Table 7.5), leaving aside the quality differentials of the patents concerned. This highlights China's immense technological gap with the industrial West. Catching up is rather difficult even though the output of China's manufacturing surpassed that of the USA in March 2011 to become the No. 1 goods producer.[116]

Thus, despite massive state sponsorship of the indigenous innovation of domestic firms, the general trend of market domination by the FIEs has not diminished but rather has intensified since the second half of the 2000s. The official "China Report 2009 on the Industry Control by the FIEs" claimed that until 2009, market control by the FIEs on China's secondary industry "has increased steadily" since 1998, and the control ratio remains above 30%, which exceeded the alert level of China's indus-

Table 7.6 China's import and export by ownership in 2015 (unit: US $100 million)

Jan–Dec 2015	Export	(%)	Import	(%)	Trade balance
FIEs	10,047.3	**44.1**	8298.9	49.3	**1748.4**
SOEs	2423.9	10.6	4078.4	24.2	−1654.5
Other enterprises	10,294.5	45.3	4443.4	26.5	5851.1
Chinese enterprises (subtotal)	12,718.4	**55.9**	8521.8	**50.7**	**4196.6**
Import/export total	22,765.7	**100.0**	16,820.7	**100.0**	**5945**

Source: China's customs statistics

try security. The report indicated that among all of the 600,000 FIEs, the world's top 500 MNCs have invested in China. Manufacturing is the area the FIEs have controlled most effectively; while in the electronic information industry, the market control rate of FIEs has stayed at more than 80% after 2004. Most importantly, foreign control of China's high-tech industry has approached 70% in recent years.[117]

China's persistent technological dependency and excessively high ratio of FIEs in China's foreign trade and, in particular, the high-tech exports (Table 7.6) highlighted not the economic strength of China but rather its substantial economic weakness in globalization. However, the recommendation of the 2009 report was a standard cliché that echoed China's consistent policy on FDI. Although it called for establishing an early-warning regime on FDI, it suggested that China maintain a "reasonable increase" of FDI while making every effort to "enhance the quality and level" of the utilization of FDI and strengthening the policies to promote "substantive technology transfer" from the MNCs. These pointless recommendations are not fresh ideas at all and have been repeated many times since the 1990s. This implies that external integration is not identified by the official think tanks as one of the origins of China's developmental quandary, but rather continues to be identified as the solution.

The Chinese regime is no smarter in this regard. Though it recognized in early 2010 that the existing mode of development is "a low-end path that makes it difficult to enhance China's global competitiveness," and "transforming the mode of economic development has reached a critical juncture,"[118] it considered further liberalization as the only feasible approach to industrialization. The First-Deputy Premier Li Keqiang, during his visit to Germany in January 2010, pledged to increase openness to foreign investors so as to "keep Western companies more committed to China." To enable the completion of industrialization by 2020, Li said that China will "pursue a much more active policy of openness" to import "leading technologies, management expertise, highly skilled labor and capital."[119]

The Premier's inadvertent revelations of China's continued reliance on skill-importation are sheer reflections of the enduring dependency of China as a semi-peripheral state that, after three-decade strong growth, still has a huge gap in technological capabilities (Tables 7.7a, 7.7b, 7.7c, 7.8, and 7.9 are self-explanatory) and thus it has a long way to "catch up and get even" with the advanced economies. The leaders' myopia is highlighted not only by their lack of will to develop but also by the acute underinvestment in technical education in the last decades whose outcome—acute shortage of high-skill labor force—had become a nightmare for China attempting to eschew the "middle-income trap." The *Workers' Daily* wrote, "In Japan, high-skilled labor (HSL) account for 40% of the entire work force; and the ratio reaches as high as 50% in Germany. But in

Table 7.7a China's import and export of aerospace and aeronautic products (2002–2013) (unit: US $100 million)

Year	Export	(%)	Import	(%)	Balance
2002	5.94	0.9	46.02	5.6	−40.07
2003	7.55	0.7	55.01	4.6	−47.46
2004	9.96	0.6	63.66	3.9	−53.70
2005	14.11	0.6	87.14	4.4	−73.03
2006	24.36	0.9	131.58	5.3	−107.22
2007	25.18	0.7	129.16	4.5	−103.98
2008	32.13	0.8	131.35	3.8	−99.22
2009	26.84	0.7	140.34	4.5	−113.5
2010	34.94	0.71	169.99	4.05	−132.05
2011	45.99	0.84	190.15	4.10	−144.16
2012	44.37	0.7	242.07	4.8	−197.70
2013	51.12	0.8	301.90	5.4	−250.78

Source: MOST (Ministry of Science and Technology) statistics

Table 7.7b Two largest sources of technology imports of China's aerospace and aeronautics 2013

Source of technology	(%)
USA	55.6
EU	35.8

Source: MOST data on China's two biggest sources of technology (2014), p. 28

Table 7.7c Sources of technology imports for China's aerospace and aeronautics industries (2002–2013) (unit: %)

Year	No. 1	No. 2	No. 3	Year	No. 1	No. 2	No. 3
2002	USA: 53.77	Russia: 23.2]	Germany: 6	2008	EU: 49.9	USA: 41.0	Brazil: 2.8
2003	USA: 49.1	France: 21.4]	Russia: 12.4	2009	USA: 50.2	EU: 40.9	Brazil: 2.8
2004	USA: 49.3	EU: 39.9]	Russia: 4.9	2010	USA: 48.6	EU: 42.0	Japan: 2.6
2005	USA: 50.1	EU: 42.8]	Japan: 2.6	2011	EU: 43.0	USA: 42.5	Japan: 3.24
2006	USA: 50.6	EU: 44]	Japan: 3.1	2012	EU: 45.0	USA: 43.5	Brazil: 3.9
2007	USA: 49.2	EU: 44.8]	Canada: 2.1	2013	USA: 55.6	EU: 35.8	-

Source: MOST statistics
No.1, 2 and 3 indicate the top three sources of technology

Table 7.8 New and high-tech (NHT) exports as a percentage of total exports (2005–2013) (unit: US $100 million)

Year	NHT exports	Total export	%
2005	2182.5	7620.0	28.6
2006	2814.7	9690.8	29.1
2007	3675.0	12,180.2	30.2
2008	4156.1	14,285.5	29.1
2009	3769.3	12,016.6	31.4
2010	4924.0	15,779.3	31.2
2011	5487.9	18,986.0	28.9
2012	6012.0	20,489.3	29.3
2013	6603.4	22,100.4	29.9

Source: MOFCOM statistics

China, the ratio only stands at 5%. The HSL-gap across the country approximates 10 million strong." Citing the Blue Paper issued by CASS 2017, it showed that according to a survey carried out a decade ago, among the HSL, high-level technical workers account for only 0.1%, and middle- and lower-level HSL account for 1.1% and 6.1%, respectively.[120]

In the face of strong appeals from both Global North and South countries for correcting global imbalance for which China's Ricardian export-led growth miracle was arguably responsible, China, "increasingly isolated" at the G-20 meeting in late February 2011,[121] had to trade off between a stable exchange rate poised to trigger trade retaliation globally and more imports. In fact, on December 12, 2010, the Central

Table 7.9 China's big plane, regional jet ARJ21. system suppliers

Systems	Suppliers	Supplier locations	Systems	Suppliers	Supplier locations
Avionic system	Rockwell Collins	USA	Flight deck control	SAGEM	France
Electrical system/APU/ high-lift device	Hamilton Sundstrand	USA	Emergency equipment	ZODIAC air Cruisers	France
Fuel system/ hydraulic system/flight control actuators	Parker Aerospace	USA	Fire protection system	Kidde Aerospace	USA
Air management system	Liebherr Toulouse	France	Lighting equipment	Goodrich Hella	USA
Landing gear	Liebherr Lindenberg	Germany	Interior	Fischer Adv. Comp	Austria
Primary flight control	Honeywell	USA	Oxygen equipment	B/E Aerospace	France

Source: COMAC handbook 2012

Economic Conference held in Beijing stressed the need to sharply increase imports of "advanced technological [equipment], key parts and components, and energy and raw materials."[122] Accordingly, a new trade strategy unveiled in January 2011 underscored a balanced trade by "giving imports and exports an equal weight" with an aim to reduce frictions with the main trading partners.[123] The real focus was on the first two categories to serve the purpose of speeding up industrialization. Thus, China was ready to "do … good public relation work towards the EU, the U.S. and Japan."[124] Meanwhile, economic retrenchment caused by the misplaced stimulus package (2009) prompted the Chinese regime to revise "Catalogue Guiding Foreign Investment in Industries" in March 2015, lifting the ban (issued in 2005) on FDI in steel industry—previously identified as China's "strategic industry."[125] One year later, M&A of Chinese SOEs by the global firms was encouraged again by MOFCOM in order to "elevate the general level of economic opening."[126] In June 2017, China further liberalized foreign investment under the updated "Guidance Catalogue," for the sake of FDI facilitation.[127]

Taken together, the reinforcement of technological dependency and deepening trade and investment liberalization strongly suggests that globalization has created a developmental quandary for the part of China, a new dependency or dependent development characterized by a "growth without development" (narrowly defined as "catch-up") that highlights the twofold effect of globalization on the Chinese economy: a stimulation of growth, and an inhibition of catch-up. In other words, China has fallen into the pitfall of liberal globalization and cannot easily escape from it.

Neixiang and Waixiang: Uncompetitiveness of Chinese Firms versus the FIEs

The SOEs' reform that followed the guideline of "to grasp the big and let go the small" (*zhuada fangxiao*) accelerated after the Fourth Plenary Session of the 15th National Party's Congress in September 1999. The thrust of the SOEs' "strategic regrouping" was to concentrate large-sized SOEs in non-competitive areas in a bid to "optimize the distribution and structure of the state-owned economy" and to withdraw large numbers of state-owned SMEs from the "general competitive areas."[128] The 16th National Party's Congress held in November 2002 decided that the ownership of part of the SOE assets should be devolved to the sub-national governments.[129] This implied that nearly half of the 10 trillion yuan-worth state asset stocks would be owned by and at the disposal of local governments. This ad hoc "reform" was said to be the conspiracy of the interest groups that were resolved to take exclusive possession of the last "free lunch" of socialism.[130] Consequently, state assets at the localities fell easy prey to the SOE insiders who colluded with the local corrupt officials to enrich themselves.[131] "To let go the small" (*fangxiao*) by devolving ownership of state-owned SMEs legitimized the spontaneous nomenclatura privatization in practical terms by means of the so-called management buy-out (MBO). Heavy losses from privatizing state assets through the MBO forced the Ministry of Finance (MOF) to put urgent brakes on the MBO in January 2003.[132] But the MOF alone was unable to monitor the *fangxiao* and to prevent the pillage of state assets in a variety of hidden ways. The privatization of state-owned SMEs was largely completed when the State-owned Assets Supervision and Administration Commission (SASAC) and MOF attempted to regulate the MBO only two years later.[133]

Unlike the MOF that is more concerned about asset losses from the spontaneous privatization, the SASAC as the competent authorities of large-sized SOEs focuses on building up large companies or company groups through cross-region, cross-industry M&A. The aim of SASAC was to reduce the quantity of the nominally owned SOEs by the central government from 9000 to 1200. In accordance with the principle of "divided ownership" as set out in the 16th National Party's Congress held in 2002, the 100 extra large-sized SOEs with all or with controlling shares held by the state were to be classified as "central SOEs," or *yangqi* monitored directly by the SASAC. As state ownership characterized Chinese market socialism in political and ideological terms, the Chinese regime has to bolster these carefully selected large-sized SOEs at all costs. Sponsoring the SOE giants was also imperative politically for the Chinese regime to appease the special interests of SOEs that had resisted the WTO accession as well as to use them as the foundation of national development. Given the fact that the accession commitments had made it illegal for the Chinese regime to provide special protection for the SOEs, its intuitive response was to make the SOEs "bigger and stronger." To this end, the most convenient way was the establishment of oligopoly by the SOE conglomerates under state administrative sponsorship.

Data show that the surge of profitability of the SOEs after the WTO accession was due to the skyrocketing energy prices and their high degree of market monopoly. SOE profits soared to 1430 billion yuan in 2004, more than double those in 1998. Yet a large part of the profits was accrued to the oligopolistic state industries, such as oil, petrochemicals, telecom and tobacco, and so on. Among the *yangqi* under the SASAC, seven SOEs of PetroChina, Sinopec, CNOOC, Baogang Steel, China Mobile, China Unicom and China Telecom accounted for as much as 78% of all the *yangqi's* profits combined. In 2005, the concentration of profits into the hands of the *yangqi* intensified. Their profits reached 641 billion yuan, more than 70% of all the profits of SOEs nationwide. The top ten *yangqi* reaped 55% of all the profits of SOEs.[134] The corporatization reform and the Westernization of corporate governance played some part in enabling SOEs' remarkable efficiency gains.[135] It was primarily the state-controlled financial system, the transfer of non-performing loans (NPLs) to the state asset management companies (AMC), and the direct financing through the IPOs that bailed out the heavily indebted SOEs and contributed to their improved performance afterward.

However, asset losses of the SOEs due to mismanagement continued to build up despite massive state sponsorship.[136] In its annual Global Non-Performing Loan (NPL) Report released on May 3, 2006, Ernst & Young estimated the NPLs of China's four big state banks and other financial institutions to have nearly doubled from US $480 billion in 2002 to US $911 billion in 2005,[137] which amounted to some 40% of GDP in 2005.[138] This contentious report enraged the People's Bank of China (PBOC), which claimed the amount of NPLs at just US $162.5 billion, of which the NPLs of the big four state banks stood at US $133 billion. This official figure was largely understated given the authenticity of China's statistics. The *Economist* made a more prudent estimation of China's NPLs at around US $300–500 billion.[139] In fact, the continued buildup of NPLs compelled the Chinese regime to make a second round of massive "write-off" by transferring a book value of US $153 billion-worth of NPLs to the AMCs in 2004 and 2005.[140] Even so, the NPLs of all China's commercial banks were reported at US $177 billion by the end of 2007, according to the China Banking Regulatory Commission (CBRC).[141]

A dramatic change occurred after 2007. Both the NPL amount and NPL ratio of the four state banks declined from 8.05% in 2007 to 1.31% in 2010 (Table 7.10). During this period, however, the "fundamentals" at the micro-level had been turning for the worse in the context of inflation at home and global financial crisis abroad.[142] The only plausible explanation seems to be that the largest proportion of bank loans were released to the SOEs to finance massive state investment in infrastructures in order to stimulate the economy that all of a sudden lost momentum after the Olympic Games. Many of these loans financed long-term projects and did not reflect the potential risk of payback in the future with the implicit warranty of the Ministry of Finance (MOF). Local governments acutely used the "4-trillion-yuan stimulus package" to revive the defunct

Table 7.10 NPL ratio of China's five big state banks (2006–2016)

Year	NPL ratio (%)
2006	9.22
2007	8.05
2008	2.81
2009	1.80
2010	1.31
2011	1.78
2012	1.56
2013	1.0
2014	1.3
2015	1.7
2016	1.74

Source: CBRC database

model of "*tics*" (trust and investment companies) in the form of a "financing platform" to finance investments in infrastructure and "image projects." The multiplier effect of credit ease caused Chinese economy to boom again in 2009 and enabled its GDP to overtake Japan as the second largest economy in 2010. However, this miracle was achieved on the basis of a rapid buildup of debts at national and sub-national levels of government, which exacerbated inflation and property bubbles, putting China's financial system at stake in the long term (Table 7.10).[143] Despite the low official figures which put the NPL rate at 1.74% by the end of 2016, the actual size of China's NPL might be ten times larger which "has reached between 15pc and 21pc and is rising fast as the country delays serious reform." according to Fitch Ratings.[144]

The corporatization reform and conglomerization made those *yangqi* formidable special interests that were far more powerful than a decade earlier when Zhu Rongji was the economic tsar who had both the will and artifice to rein in the SOEs' interests. Corporatization facilitated the SOE conglomerates to derail state regulations in public interest under the pretext of maximizing shareholders' value. The tax reform in 1994 permitted the SOEs to retain post-tax profits for reinvestment and technological innovation. This revived the investment hunger that characterized the old SOEs subject to the "soft budget constraints" in pre-reform era. Meanwhile, the SOEs' management used the retained post-tax super-profits to benefit themselves and employees and to promote internal cohesion. The average salary of CEOs of the oligopolistic *yangqi* is disclosed to be 128 times greater than that of average social salary level.[145] The wage and extra-wage incomes of the employees working in those monopolistic or oligopolistic SOEs such as electric power, telecom, oil, finance, insurance, water and electricity supply, tobacco, and so on accounted for 55% of the total payroll, although they only numbered less than 8% of the national employment.[146] Thus, shareholders' value was maximized to the greatest benefit of the management at the expense of interest of the largest "state shareholder," or tax payers represented by the state. This "internal loot-sharing" (*neibu fenzang*) at the expense of consumer surplus created a monolithic interest entity (*liyi gongtongti*), which strengthened not only the "insider control" by SOEs' management but their bargaining position vis-à-vis the state. The Chinese state was thus obliged to not only accommodate the SOEs' tough demands for an expanding monopoly but also provide subsidies to the underperforming SOEs at the expense of taxpayers' interest. As a result, the state autonomy in making public policies in national interest was severely eroded. The escalating inflation in the aftermath of the SARS pandemic is the best example of a weakened state capacity in regulating the macro-economy.[147]

In the years of 2004 and 2005, some peculiar two-way changes emerged when the FIEs continued to expand their operations and the oligopolistic SOEs became increasingly profitable. The changes were characterized by renationalization on the one hand and privatization on the other. The highly oligopolistic SOEs in "resource-intensive and basic industrial areas"[148] started to encroach upon the "competitive areas" left over to privately owned enterprises (POEs) by using coercive or even political means to force the latter to exit from competition. One of the most famous examples is the "Oilfield Event at North Shaanxi Province" (*shanbei youtian shijian*), in which a few hundred private shareholders were compelled to sell their shares at an extremely low price to one oligopolistic SOE that coveted the huge profits of an oil refinery in the backdrop of a growing shortage of energy supply on the domestic market. The event was masterminded by the Shaanxi provincial authorities and the SOE concerned at the connivance of the central government.[149]

Concomitant to the renationalization of lucrative businesses operated by private proprietors, state-owned SMEs continued to be privatized. Yet, the layoff of workers involved not only those in privatized SMEs, but also those in the oligopolistic SOEs that substantially raised wages and benefits after sacking redundant staff.[150] The two-way changes not only exposed the extreme opportunism of the Chinese regime with regard to the reform on state-owned SMEs (to control them when they make money and to discard them when they lose money), but also highlighted the degeneration of the POEs from their peak at the turn of the century when being flattered by the party as "having become [an] important constituent part of the socialist market economy" enshrined in the revised constitution in 1999. Private entrepreneurs were even allowed to join the party after General Secretary Jiang Zemin made the groundbreaking speech on July 1, 2001. The purpose of extending an olive branch to private business was ostensibly to entice the POEs to increase investment and create more jobs at the time when the economy was deflationary and the SOEs were in a quagmire. The new changes implied that the POEs were after all a "vulnerable group" (*ruoshi qunti*) politically in the face of a Leninist Leviathan, even if they had been indispensable to the Chinese economy. With the "advancement of SOEs and retreat of POEs" (*guojin mintui*) commencing from 2004, the POEs continued to be prejudiced and were practically impeded by the institutional barriers to enter into strategic industries where the SOEs predominate. These limitations upon POEs were designed on purpose to prevent the private capitalist class from becoming intractable political rivals later on.[151]

In contrast, there were relatively much fewer entry barriers imposed upon foreign investors. The Chinese regime even took the initiative to invite foreign investors as "strategic investors" of certain key industries, such as banking, on extremely generous terms in an attempt to prompt them to lobby with their home country's government or legislature to bolster the stability of the regime. Conceding vital national interest to foreigners on issues concerning the destiny of the country's modernization is the best testimony of China's crony comprador capitalism sponsored by the market Leninist regime. As a matter of fact, the Chinese bureaucrats nowadays make no attempt to disguise their value belief that state (regime) interest takes precedence over national interest. During the first round of S&ED held in Washington on July 28, 2009, Dai Bingguo, China's State Councilor in charge of foreign affairs, defined China's "core interest" with the USA in the sequence of (1) safeguarding the basic system and national security; (2) safeguarding national sovereignty and territorial integrity; and (3) promoting sustained and stable economic and social development.[152] The real "core" is unequivocally the viability of the regime. Dai's definition of "core interest" stands for China's enhanced confidence in dealing with the USA being plagued in the quagmire of Iraq and the economic disaster in the wake of the financial crisis. China's request for respect for its core interest is in no doubt to obtain reassurance from the perceived declining American empire that a regime change through a peaceful color revolution must not be plotted. Except this, all else in the list of S&ED can be negotiated.

Prior to the 2009 S&ED, the Chinese authoritarian regime had been deeply upset by regime changes in the Ukraine and particularly the neighboring Central Asian states in the mid-2000s. Since then, the Chinese leadership seemed to have been enormously relieved, until the most recent Jasmine Revolution in the Middle East in early 2011. They felt they had seen through the hypocrisy of Western democracies that preferred profits to justice in the face of China's vast domestic market. By staking the West in its expanding market, the Chinese regime was hugely successful in dispelling external challenges in ideological terms, so that it is now in a much advantageous position to devote all the resources to quell discontent at home to ensure that her "basic system" is intact. It was exactly during this short interval that China was on the offensive diplomatically. Its foreign policy, to some extent, deviated from its past strategy of "bide the time to build up our national strength" (*taoguang yanghui*) that Deng Xiaoping dictated after Tiananmen in 1989. China, in the eyes of foreigners, is getting increasingly assertive and acting, on many occasions, like a challenger. Examples are many, such as China's unprecedented defiance at the Copenhagen climate summit in December 2009, its tough positions over the disputed Diaoyu/Senkaku Island with Japan and the South China Sea (Spratly Islands) with ASEAN countries, its partiality with the DPRK on the latter's clashes with South Korea, the perceived clandestine sponsorship of anti-West nationalism at home, and so on. Yet, these are just episodes that reflect either the preferences of individual leaders, such as Hu Jintao's fondness of Kim Jong-Il regime of DPRK,[153] or a sheer misjudgment of the *realpolitik* across the region on account of overrating China's own strength and influence. US tough reactions and the resultant US "pivot to Asia" and reinforced alliance with Chinese neighbors,[154] including intended alignment with Vietnam, added to China's frustration and fear of encirclement by the USA. Against this backdrop and the rapidly worsening socioeconomic situation at home, the Chinese regime silently moved back to the policy of *taoguang-yanghui* around late December 2010.[155]

This implies that the intuition of the Chinese leadership has informed them at this juncture where *raison d'état* lies. They must avoid a "two-front war" against the US hegemon and the increasingly enlightened and restless people at home simultaneously. Without social justice in place, the rise of China failed to hold the people together to back up the regime. More and more, the Chinese are becoming increasingly suspicious of the economic wonder that benefited not the majority of the people but the New Class, particularly a small number of privileged families. The illusion that China would turn for the better after the Olympics in 2008 and allow greater political freedom quickly evaporated with the regime's tighter control of the society. Against this backdrop, nationalism is not easily manipulated to the benefit of the regime. People are indifferent to the news that China overtook Japan to become the world's No. 2 economic power. They resent the economically predatory and politically repressive state to such an extent that the Chinese authoritarian regime at all levels of administration has lost all its public credibility.[156] Consequently, the Chinese regime found it rather difficult and risky politically to mobilize public support in case of a large-scale confrontation with the USA in military terms. The Chinese regime cannot afford it economically either. This can be seen clearly from Xi Jinping's remarks during his first face-to-face meeting with the newly elected US president Donald Trump at Mar-a-Lago on April 6, 2017, that "There are a thousand reasons to make the China–US relationship a success, and not a single reason to break it."[157] After all, the viability of the regime is the top priority for the CCP, and it is the economy that is the most crucial. Thus, a "restless empire" abroad is in any sense counterproductive, despite the nationalist rebound after Xi rose to power in November 2012. A continued access to the US market is indispensable to the Chinese economy particularly at the critical juncture of painful structural adjustment for fulfilling the desired economic transition.

Back to early 2009 when Obama began his second term in office, his top concern or dominant strategy was to restore the impaired legitimacy of US leadership through a revived multilateralism. For this purpose, as Kitchen and Cox argues, the USA must "prevent other powers from seeking or offering an alternative. Gaining China's assent for renewed American leadership is the first and most fundamental step in that strategy."[158] Hence, "staking" China in the rule-based global capitalist system serves the purpose of locking in China's liberal pathway of development, thereby making the rising China not a challenger but a stakeholder of the international system. This is congruent with China's "peaceful rise" argument propounded a few years earlier.[159] For China, "peaceful rise" as a political strategy is consistent with economically "staking the West" to serve the purpose of maintaining stability at home and continuing bandwagoning with rather than overturning the liberal order dominated by the USA. Nonetheless, relative to the economically fragile and technologically dependent "rising" China, the USA has *ostensibly* far more leverages and is consistently assertive in integrating China into the liberal global economy. Thus, the interaction of the two staking strategies that served fundamentally different "core interests" resulted in a landslide diplomatic victory of the USA in the three S&EDs from 2009 to 2011, evidenced by China's de facto renouncement of key policy instruments to promote indigenous innovation. This was poised to reinforce rather than reduce China's technological dependence under the shadow of liberal globalization. Paradoxically for US strategists, judging otherwise that

> the American effort to 'integrate' China into the liberal international order has now generated new threats to U.S. primacy in Asia—and could result in a consequential challenge to American power globally—Washington needs a new grand strategy toward China that centers on balancing the rise of Chinese power rather than continuing to assist its ascendancy.[160]

China's dependent development suffices to render Nixon's worry that "We may have created a Frankenstein"[161] ultimately unnecessary.

Domestically, *guojin mintui* is not the indication of enhanced competitiveness of the SOEs. In 2003, the SOEs for the first time posted a trade deficit of US $4.45 billion (Table 7.11a and 7.11b). Two years later,

Table 7.11a Trade balance by ownership (2001–2013) (unit: US $100 million)

Firms/year	2001	2002	2003	2004	2005	2006	2007	2008	2009	2010	2011	2012	2013
SOEs		83.7	−44.5	−228.6	**−283.9**	−338.9	−449.1	−965.8	**−974.8**	**−1532.0**	**−2261.8**	**−2391.3**	**−2500.0**
FIEs	73.72	96.6	84.3	140.4	**566.9**	912.2	1361.1	1706.6	**1270.2**	**1243.1**	**1305.0**	**1515.1**	**1694.4**
FDI	468.78	527.43	535.05	606.3	724.1	727.2	845.2	924.0	900.3	1057.3	1160.1	1117.2	1175.86

Source: China customs statistics

Table 7.11b Chinese new and hi-tech exports by ownership (2002–2013) (unit: %)

Firms/year	2002	2003	2004	2005	2006	2007	2008	2009	2010	2011	2012	2013
SOEs	15.1	10.4	8.5	7.4	6.9	7.3	7.4	6.9	6.9	5.8	5.7	5.6
FIEs	79.3	83.3	85.6	86.3	86.2	85.2	83.9	83.2	82.2	82.5	77.5	72.1
Others	5.7	6.3	5.9	6.2	6.8	7.6	8.7	9.9	10.9	11.7	16.9	22.2

Source: MOFCOM and MOST statistics

the trade deficit surged to US $38.39 billion and continued to grow by a large margin in the years that followed. Since "global market serves as benchmark for cost and quality,"[162] export performance is used as a good measure of competitiveness for "its simplicity and clear connection" to the latter.[163] As the technologically and managerially advanced domestic players compared with the POEs, the SOEs experienced drastic decline in export proportion from 32% in 2003 to 10.6% in 2015. The SOEs had just 14.85% of its total exports that were new and high-tech, which accounted for only 1.67% of China's total exports (2013 figure).

In 2009, China's top 500 enterprises, predominantly the large-sized SOEs, posted net profits at an impressive US $179.6 billion, which for the first time exceeded those of the US top 500 at US $98.9 billion.[164] However, as the SASAC Minister Li Rongrong frankly admitted, "new and high-tech firms are rare, new energy firms are rare, firms with global brands are rare, and the real-sense MNCs are rare too."[165] In contrast to booming export surplus for the country as a whole, the SOEs recorded soaring trade deficits that derived mainly from the massive importation of technological equipment from the advanced economies and of raw materials and energy from the resource-rich countries. The sharply decreased share of export and soaring trade deficits highlighted the across-the-board uncompetitiveness of the SOEs on the global market. They were forced to "look inward" (*neixiang*) by overwhelmingly eyeing the home market.

While the POEs, pressured by the *guojin mintui* and the technologically advanced FIEs, had no other choices but to focus on the low-end production by exploiting the country's comparative advantage in cheap labor. They tended to be "outward looking" (*waixiang*) by eyeing the overseas markets. This is due to the fact that in order to bring down the production costs, the POEs were competing to expand production in a bid to realize the economies of scale. Excessive investment for this purpose is susceptible to overcapacity, leading the POEs to an internecine strife at home and abroad. Yet, it is good news for oligopolistic SOEs predominantly lying at the upstream of the industrial production. The only way for the POEs to address overcapacity is export large quantities of low-tech products to global markets at an extremely low price. This has turned out to be another major source of China's trade surplus and foreign currency reserve (Table 7.6). These unprofitable low-tech POEs are in a more difficult position than the SOEs to upgrade technologically and thus are unable to relocate their operations abroad (*zou chuqu*) to offset the rising human costs. They are bound for failure in case of inflation or decline of external demand, as has been substantiated by the crisis in the manufacturing sector starting from 2007.

Thus, neither the trade deficit of the SOEs nor the trade surplus of the POEs has, from totally different technological perspectives, testified to the global competitiveness of China's yet-to-be-fully-industrialized economy. The myth of the China's "rise" or the economic miracle after the WTO accession lies in the fact that the economy was driven by an investment and export boom catalyzed by an expansionary monetary policy since 2002. However, the investment boom was not entirely pushed by the state, but more importantly internally driven by all types of enterprises in China. The lucrative market of China, as well as its position as the key knot of the global supply chain incentivized the FIEs to expand their operations for global markets. Huge retained profits drove the oligopolistic SOEs to invest heavily regardless of state efforts to combat inflation; while the POEs, under freer registration systems after the WTO accession and de facto insurmountable entry barriers to strategic industries monopolized by the SOEs, tended to expand production for cost-cutting. These joint forces to a large extent contributed to continued extensive growth of the Chinese economy that was achieved unexceptionally based on excess drain on natural resources and at the expense of the country's extremely fragile ecological system.

The 4-trillion stimulus package in early 2009 came to the rescue of the oligopolistic SOEs that had been affected by the withering demand of POEs at the downstream. Such Keynesian approach adopted at the time when the Chinese economy was inflationary rather than deflationary did not help to redress the country's hugely distorted economic and industry structure. Rather, it refueled the property and stock bubbles. Inflation loomed as early as 2003 and accelerated as of late 2007 due arguably to China's huge trade surplus and rapid buildup of foreign currency reserve, a phenomenon similar to what had happened to Japan in the late 1980s. It is by no means inevitable theoretically and practically.

Similar phenomenon appeared in the mid-1990s when Zhu Rongji was in charge. Yet China experienced long-time deflation. Substantial credit easing was the root cause. But the main driver for the policy overhaul was political rather than economic. The 9/11 incident led the Chinese leadership to conclude that China was being presented with a "rare strategic opportunity of development" with the USA turning all its attention to global war on terror. Thus, China seized this critical moment to achieve faster economic growth through an expansionary monetary policy. The SARS epidemic in the first half of 2003 catalyzed such policy change. This specific inside–outside interaction of international politics and Chinese domestic politics is what prompted the key economic policies of the early 2000s.[166] With overcapacity in the real economy getting even more severe than ever before, the odds of the bubble bursting in the virtual sector are increasing rapidly. Once the bubble has burst, bad assets of state banks will be skyrocketing given the heavy indebtedness of the national economy. A hard landing will be inevitable and a long-term recession will naturally follow. This will be the last straw for the explosive social situation.

Hu Jintao declared at the 16th National Party's Congress in November 2002, one year after China joined the WTO, that China must "focus on 'construction and development'" (*jujinghuishen gaojianshe, yixinyiyi moufazhan*) to "build a socialism ***of*** Chinese characteristics."[167] The delicate changing of the term "**OF**" from the original one of "**WITH**" highlights the confidence of the new leadership that a correct pathway of development—the liberal globalization approach—has been found and must be upheld. They did have good reason to be self-complacent with the matrimony of China's market Leninist crony capitalism and global capitalism that soon drove a Chinese export-led *wirtschaftswunder*. Yet underneath the Ricardian growth miracle, an ever-enlarging wealth gap significantly eroded China's internal integration in socioeconomic terms and solidified an already abnormal economic structure excessively dependent on exports. Although quite a number of the Chinese firms, particularly large monopolistic and oligopolistic SOEs, have thus far achieved significant expansion in size, their autonomous capacity of science and technology innovation is still very much in question. Only one Chinese firm was ranked among the 2016 Top 100 Global Innovators, among which 39 were from the USA, 34 from Japan, 3 from South Korea, and 1 from Taiwan.[168] The official Economic Blue Paper 2014 issued by CASS admitted,

> the high-end chains of many Chinese industrial sectors are heavily dependent on import. For instance, 90% of chips are imported from foreign manufacturers, the total cost of which has exceeded that of oil. China today still falls short of core technologies in those key parts and components such as engine, hydraulic devices, transmission devices, control technologies, etc., which are critically dependent on imports; 70–80% of expensive high-end medical [equipment] have to be imported from abroad or sourced from the MNCs in China.[169]

As a result, China's technology dependency ratio did not even drop slightly from the 2006 level but remains above 50%, much higher than that of the USA and Japan, which remain below 5%.[170]

"Growth without development" or dependent development distinguishes China from most of the developing nations in the post-Cold War era of globalization. However significantly China may matter in economic and strategic terms, given its "empire" size, its acute innovation shortfall by no means testifies to the economic rise of China. The globalization of the Chinese economy has not pushed China any closer to being an emerging industrial power comparable to Germany or Japan after World War Two, nor has it made the nominally Communist regime more democratic as both market liberals and Marxists have predicted. An illusory global power shift from the USA to China, and resultant US "pivot to Asia," however, coupled with a "volcanic stability"[171] at home has fostered the Communist regime's recent totalitarian turn. "A 'Frankenstein' or a 'Paper Tiger'?" Nevertheless, what a hybrid of an economic giant with feet of clay and a Leninist leviathan means for China and the world remains to be seen.

Notes

1. Edward Steinfeld (2010), *Playing Our Game—Why China's Rise doesn't Threaten the West*, NY: Oxford University Press, p. 25.

2. Interviews with youthful officials within the central and local bureaucracies from June 2006 until March 2008.
3. Chen Fang (1997), *The Wrath of Heaven (tiannu)*, Hohhot: yuanfang chubanshe (Chap. 17), p. 283.
4. Yu Keping (2007), "Democracy is a Good Thing (minzhu shige haodongxi)," *Study Times (xuexi shibao)*, No. 367. http://theory.people.com.cn/GB/49150/49152/5224247.html
5. Hu Jintao's speech addressed to Yale University on April 21, 2006. *People's Daily*, 24/04/2006. http://www.china.com.cn/chinese/news/1199378.htm
6. Wu Bangguo, "juebuneng zhaoban xifang gao duodang lunliu zhizheng (We will Never Practice Western Multi-party System)," CCTV.com, 9/03/2009. http://news.cctv.com/china/20090309/102808.shtml
7. "The Central Propaganda Department of the CCP Explains Six Fundamental Questions Concerning the Construction of the Core Socialist Value System," *People's Daily*, Jan 5–Feb 16, 2009. http://theory.people.com.cn/GB/40557/145802/
8. Kang Xiaoguang (2002), "An Analysis of China's Political Stability in the Next 3–5 Years," *Strategy and Management*, No. 3.
9. Sun Liping et al. (1998), "The Mid-Term and Long-Term Trends and Hidden Danger of the Transformation of China's Social Structure," *Strategy and Management*, No. 5.
10. Taishi Jian, "A Comment on Wen Tiejun's Recent Speech in Fujian," *huaxia dianzibao*, No. 122, 1/12/2006. http://www.huaxiabao.org/article.asp?IssueId=122&ArtNb=1
11. Jiang Xun, "Chinese Peasants Become Shareholders and Appeal for Land Revolution," *Asia Weekly*, No. 11, 15/03/2008. http://www.yzzk.com/cfm/Content_Archive.cfm?Channel=ag&Path=385827171/11ag1a.cfm
12. *New Beijing Daily (xinjingbao)*, 9/01/2010. http://news.xinhuanet.com/house/2010-01/09/content_12780512.htm; In 2010, land revenues further increased by 70.4% to 2.7 trillion yuan. *Southern Weekend*, 11/01/2011. http://www.infzm.com/content/54397
13. *New Beijing Daily (xinjingbao)*, 9/01/2010. http://news.sohu.com/20100109/n269465598.shtml
14. A most typical example is the high-speed train development. "Behind the Fall of Liu Zhijun (Minister of Railway)," *China Business Daily (zhongguo jingyingbao)*, 19/02/2011. http://www.cb.com.cn/1634427/20110219/185888.html

15. Sun Liping (2002), p. 365.
16. Yue Jianyong and Chen Man (2008), "What Caused the Inflation?" *Modern China Studies*, No. 1.
17. Song Fufan, "Deng Xiaoping Rethinks of China's Path of Development in His Late Years," *Study Times (xuexi shibao)*, 29/06/2009. http://dangshi.people.com.cn/GB/138903/141370/9562577.html
18. Yan Jijian (2010), "The Causes and Solutions to Mass Incidents," *Theory Guide (lilun daokan)*, No. 5.
19. Sun Liping, "The Chinese Society is Racing towards Decadence," 21ccom.net, 10/01/2010. http://new.21ccom.net/plus/view.php?aid=7550
20. Yu Jianrong, "Safeguard the Bottom-Line of Social Stability," a speech addressed to Beijing Lawyers' Association, 26/12/2009. http://www.chinaelections.org/newsinfo.asp?newsid=169507
21. He Qinglian (2003), "China's Changing of the Guard: A Volcanic Stability," *Journal of Democracy*, 14:1, January, pp. 66–72.
22. Yu Jianrong, "Safeguard the Bottom-line of Social Stability," a speech addressed to Beijing Lawyers' Association, 26/12/2009.
23. "zhongguo caifu kuaisu xiang shaoshuren jizhong (China's Wealth Concentrated rapidly into Small Number of People)," *Liaowang Weekly (Outlook)*, 13/02/2010. http://finance.people.com.cn/GB/10977869.html
24. *Economic Reference News (jingji cankaobao)*, 21/05/2010.
25. *Jinghua shibao*, 10/12/2012. http://news.sina.com.cn/c/2012-12-10/075225771850.shtml
26. The Chinese government decided to elevate the starting point of individual income taxation to 3,500 yuan per month on July 1, 2011. *Economic Reference News (jingji cankaobao)*, 1/07/2011. http://www.jjckb.cn/2011-07/01/content_318835.htm.This implies that only 24 million people would be covered under the new regulation. Cheng Xiaonong argued that the starting point of the taxable income usually stands for the low income line. The 24 million taxable people accounts for just 3% of the 800 million working population. This is the most convincing evidence for what caused underconsumption. http://biweekly.hrchina.org/article/1141 (this hyperlink carrying Cheng's analysis no longer exists). Based on "2013 figures from China NBS, CNPolitics, Goldman Sachs Global Investment Research, US Bureau of Labor Statistics, US Department of Defense," Goldman Sachs

claimed, "Today's China consumer market is dominated by a relatively narrow middle class. Less than 2% of workers earn enough even to pay income tax. 11% of China's population can be considered middle class," whose "average daily spending was just $7 as opposed to $97 of US consumers." http://www.goldmansachs.com/our-thinking/macro-economic-insights/growth-of-china/chinese-consumer/

27. Xiong Chuandong, "How Deep is the Bottomless Pit of the 'Costly Stability,'" *Guangming Guancha*, 13/06/2010. http://www.chinare-form.net/2010/0611/17888.html
28. "weichi wending, zhongguo baoan yusuan zengfu chaoguo junfei (Maintaining Stability, China's Budget growth on Public Security greater than on Defense)," 6/03/2010. http://www.afinance.cn/new/gncj/201003/257419.html
29. Leslie Hook, "Beijing Raises Spending on Internal Security," *Financial Times*, 6/03/2011.
30. Sun Liping, et al. (2010), Tsinghua University Research Group, "To Realize Long-Term Stability through Institutionalized Expression of Interest," *Leaders (lingdaozhe)*, No. 33, April.
31. "Consulting China's Economy," *Caijing*, Issue 143, 3/10/2005.
32. Robert Sutter (2003), "Why does China Matter?" *The Washington Quarterly*, 27:1, (Winter 2003–2004), pp. 75–89.
33. Ren Zhongping, "A Great Choice on the Destiny of Modernization—On the Transformation of the Mode of Economic Development," *People's Daily*, 1/03/2010.
34. Yu Yongding, "A Different Road Forward," *China Daily*, 23/12/2010. http://www.chinadaily.com.cn/opinion/2010-12/23/content_11742757.htm
35. Cited from Di Yingqing, "A Discussion with Long Yongtu," *China and the World* (online), No. 12, December, 1999. http://chicagoguangzhou.com/zgysj/99/zs9912a.htm#2
36. Cui Zhiyuan (1999), "Expanding Domestic Demand is a Deep Revolution," *Dushu*, No. 4.
37. Roundtable Discussion in December 1999, Beijing.
38. Gordon, G. Chang (2001), *The Coming Collapse of China*, London: Arrow.
39. For instance, by the end of 2002, the non-performing loans of the four state banks posted at 26.1%, despite that 1.4 trillion yuan had been transferred to the State Asset Management Companies (AMCs), which

brought down the NPL ratio by 10 percentage point (Yue and Chen 2003, pp. 83–89).

40. "Chen Xiwen: Around 20 million migrant workers lost their jobs due to global financial crisis and went back to the countryside," News Briefing by the State Council's Information Office, 2/02/2009. http://www.china.com.cn/economic/txt/2009-02/02/content_17209939.htm
41. *China News Networks*, 15/12/2008. http://news.cnfol.com/081215/101,1277,5207566,00.shtml
42. Yue Jianyong, "Going out of the Pitfall of 'Technologyless Industrialization,'" *Nanfengchuang*, No. 1, 1/01/2009.
43. "CASS Expert Chen Naixing: 40% SMEs Go Broke in Crisis," *Dongfang Daily*, 12/06/2009. http://www.dfdaily.com/node2/node27/node119/userobject1ai173466.shtml
44. The Social Blue Paper 2010 issued by CASS asserted, "Our Country will be the First Nation to Step Out of the Financial Crisis and into a New Growth Stage," *renminwang*, Beijing, 22/12/2009. http://npc.people.com.cn/GB/14840/10628150.html
45. "Different Data on Unemployment Rate Arouse Dispute," *China Economic Weekly (zhongguo jingji zhoukan)*, 7/04/2009.
46. Wen was quoted as saying, "I know there is an unemployed population of 2 million in the US, which makes the government very anxious. But the figure for the Chinese government when it comes to providing jobs to our people is 200 million, and there's a huge gap between urban and rural areas." See report "Wen upbeat on US relations despite strains," *China Daily*, 23/02/2010. http://www.chinadaily.com.cn/china/2010-03/23/content_9625455.htm
47. Niall Ferguson, "Not Two Countries, But One: Chimerica," 4/03/2007. http://www.niallferguson.com/Site/FERG/Templates/ArticleItem.aspx?pageid=95
48. cpc-news (online), 25/02/2009. http://cpc.people.com.cn/GB/64093/64103/8870435.html
49. *People's Daily*, 6/03/2010.
50. In 2009, China's GDP reached US $4.7 trillion, about 8% of the world GDP, but China consumed 18% of the world's energy, 44% of steel and 53% of cement. Zhang Xiaoqiang and Ma Xiuhong on the State Council's New Policy on FDI on April 14, 2010. http://financial.people.com.cn/GB/11368944.html

51. *People's Daily*, 1/03/2010.
52. *Xinhua*, Beijing, 3–5/02/2010.
53. *People's Daily*, 15/03/2010.
54. Second Meeting of the U.S.-China Strategic & Economic Dialogue Joint U.S.-China Economic Track Fact Sheet. http://www.ustreas.gov/press/releases/tg722.htm
55. The official *Liaowang Weekly (Outlook)* quoted an investigation report of a Western Chamber of Commerce in Beijing that some restrictive measures taken by the Chinese government that precluded foreign investors entering some robust market areas have aroused mounting dissatisfaction of the MNCs in China. "China Readjust Policy on FDI, FIEs' Era of Extra-National Treatment is Over," *Liaowang Weekly (Outlook)*, 25/04/2010.
56. "A Set of Opinions on Taking Better Advantage of Foreign Investment of the State Council," Source: The General Office of the State Council, 13/04/2010. http://financial.people.com.cn/GB/11368944.html
57. Second Meeting of the U.S.-China Strategic & Economic Dialogue Joint U.S.-China Economic Track Fact Sheet.
58. "Wen Jiabao: RMB Revaluation by 20% will Incur Severe Unemployment," *jingji guanchawang*, 23/09/2010. http://www.eeo.com.cn/Politics/international/2010/09/23/181542.shtml
59. Zhang Xiaoqiang, "Vice-Minister of the National Development and Reform Commission (NDRC) on China's New FDI Policy," 14/04/2010. http://finance.people.com.cn/GB/113689944.html
60. AmCham-China's 2010 Business Climate Survey. http://users.cla.umn.edu/~erm/data/sr486/govdocs/AMCHAM2010.pdf
61. "The FIEs are the Main Creators and Beneficiaries of China's Trade Surplus," *The Legal Daily*, 14/04/2010. http://www.legaldaily.com.cn/bm/content/2010-04/14/content_2112297.htm
62. George J. Gilboy (2004), "The Myth behind China's Miracle," *Foreign Affairs*, 83:4, July/August, pp. 33–48.
63. Yılmaz Akyüz, "Export Dependence and Sustainability of Growth in China and the East Asian Production Network," Research Paper 27, April 2010. http://www.southcentre.org/index.php?option=com_content&view=article&id=1326%3Aexport-dependence-and-sustainability-of-growth-in-china-and-the-east-asian-production-network&catid=142%3Aglobal-financial-and-economic-crisis&lang=en
64. According to Hu Chunli, deputy director of the Research Institute of Industrial Economy and Technology Economy under the NDRC, the

profitability of China's manufacturing industries as a whole was 5–6%, while profitability of the high-tech industries was only 2–3%. "How China's Manufacturing Industries Break Besiege of Foreign Capital?" http://www.ca800.com/news/html/2005-4-5/n21679_0.htm

65. Steinfeld (2010), p. 105.
66. Eric Ng, "Vehicle Policy Raises Threshold for Entry into Crowded Sector," *SCMP*, 2/06/2004; David Murphy, "Cars: Driving Ambitions," *Far Eastern Economic Review* covered dated 27/05/2004.
67. Gao Liang, "waizi zaihua binggou ji guojia anquan xingshi (Foreign M&As in China and the Situation of National Security)," *Global View*, No. 283, 9/03/2010. http://www.globalview.cn/ReadNews.asp?NewsID=20647
68. Su Fenyong (2009), "How Many Lessons are Needed for China's Equipment Manufacturers to Become Clever enough to Cope with Foreign M&As?" *Electric China (dianqi zhongguo)*, No. 12.
69. "How China's Manufacturing Industries Break Besiege of Foreign Capital," http://www.ca800.com//05/4-5/n21679.asp
70. Wang Sirui, "Experts Warn against International Gap of China's Manufacturing," *diyi caijing ribao*, 23/11/2005; Xu Kuangdi (president of the Chinese Academy of Engineering), "The Current Situation and Challenges of China's Manufacturing Industries," China Development Observation webpage, the Development and Research Center of the State Council, 26/04/2005. http://www.chinado.cn/ReadNews.asp?NewsID=299
71. The SAIC report shows that absolute monopoly has been established by the FIEs in computer operating system, soft packaging products, photosensitive materials, meridian tires and mobile phones, while in light industry, chemical industry, pharmaceuticals, and machinery and electronics, FIEs' products had captured more than one third of the market share. *21st Century Business Herald*, 16/05/2004.
72. "Constructing an Innovative State," http://news.xinhuanet.com/ziliao/2006-01/12/content_4043283.htm
73. *Xinhua*, 17/11/2012.
74. *Nanfengchuang*, 28/08/2006.
75. *Xinhua*-net article written by Zhu Jidong, "Why Foreign M&As Go Ahead against the Will of the People?" 4/09/2008. http://xinhuashe2007.home.news.cn/blog/a/0101000029400 3E77224FD9B.html
76. *Xinhua*, Beijing, 30/11/2009.

77. "China's Drive for 'Indigenous Innovation—A Web of Industrial Policies,'" APCO Worldwide 2010. https://www.uschamber.com/report/china%E2%80%99s-drive-indigenous-innovation-web-industrial-policies
78. *The Financial Times*, 28/05/2009.
79. *China Economic Weekly*, 15/06/2009; Also *China Youth Daily* commentary, 16/06/2009: "The 4-Trllion Buy-Local is Not Trade Protectionism," http://www.chinanews.com/cj/cj-plgd/news/2009/06-16/1735157.shtml. A good example of such reverse discrimination was the Ministry of Agriculture public procurement of instruments in 2015, of which 97.8% were imports, only 2.2% were domestically made products. *China Science News (zhongguo kexuebao)*, 10/06/2015. http://news.sciencenet.cn/htmlnews/2015/6/320588.shtm
80. "How the Government Procurement should Avoid '*Discrimination against the Local Products*'?" *People's Daily* (overseas edition), 1/07/2009. http://paper.people.com.cn/rmrbhwb/html/2009-07/01/content_286089.htm
81. Notice of Ceasing to Implement *Measures for Management of Budgets of Government Procurement of Indigenous Innovation Products* (issued by the Ministry of Finance, 23/06/2011). http://gks.mof.gov.cn/redianzhuanti/zhengfucaigouguanli/201106/t20110628_567649.html
82. "Minister of Commerce (Chen Deming), China's Indigenous Innovation never linked with trade policy," *Xinhua* (Xiamen), 9/09/2010. http://news.xinhuanet.com/fortune/2010-09/09/c_12537031.htm; also "Chen Deming: Access to Chinese Market Not Conditioned on Technology Transfer," *zhongguangwang* (Beijing), 9/02/2012. http://china.cnr.cn/gdgg/201202/t20120209_509144668.shtml
83. "China's Price for Market Entry: Give us Your Technology, Too," *The Wall Street Journal*, 26/02/2004.
84. Ibid.
85. Ibid.
86. Dewey & Leboef LLP, "China's Promotion of the Renewable Electric Power Equipment Industry, Hydro, Wind, Solar, Biomass," March 2010.
87. "China's Price for Market Entry: Give us Your Technology, Too," *The Wall Street Journal*, 26/02/2004.

88. Dewey & Leboef LLP, "China's Promotion of the Renewable Electric Power Equipment Industry, Hydro, Wind, Solar, Biomass," March 2010.
89. Ibid.
90. "The 'Grown-up' History of the High-Speed Train," *China Economic Weekly*, No. 5 & 6, 14/02/2011. http://www.ceweekly.cn/html/Article/2011021481724704324492.html
91. "Trillion-Debt Qualm of High-Speed Train," *Caijing*, No. 4, 2011 (14/02/2011).
92. *Mingpao*, 19/02/2011.
93. *China Business Weekly (shangwu zhoukan)*, March 2006.
94. Bai Yimin (2008), *Mutsui Empire in Action*, Beijing: China Economic Publishing House, p. 262.
95. *21st Century Business Herald*, 23/03/2011.
96. Cited from the *21st Century Business Herald*, 23/03/2011. http://www.21cbh.com/HTML/2011-3-24/wNMDAwMDIyODUwNA.html?source=hp&position=focus_xg
97. *New Beijing Daily* (xiningbao), 14/06/2011. http://www.china.com.cn/economic/txt/2011-06/14/content_22777587.htm
98. "The Big Crumble," *Caixin-New Century (xinshiji)*, No. 30, 2011 (published on 1/08/2011). http://magazine.caing.com/2011-07-30/100285595.html
99. Ibid. and *21st Century Business Herald*, 6/01/2011. http://www.21cbh.com/HTML/2011-1-7/xNMDAwMDIxNDkxNg.html?source=hp&position=focus
100. Testimony of Owen E. Herrnstadt, Director of Trade and Globalization International Association of Machinists and Aerospace Workers before the US–China Economic and Security Review Commission's Hearing: "China's Emergent Military Aerospace and Commercial Aviation Capabilities," 20/05/2010. Washington, DC.
101. The 2011 US–China Strategic and Economic Dialogue U.S. Fact Sheet—Economic Tract 5/10/2011. Source: U.S. Department of Treasury. https://www.treasury.gov/press-center/press-releases/Pages/TG1172.aspx
102. *21st Century Business Herald*, 11/01/2017. http://epaper.21jingji.com/html/2017-01/11/content_54451.htm
103. "Guiding 'Made in China' towards 'Created in China'—Recalling 11th Five and Looking forward to 12th Five," *People's Daily*, 27/02/2011. Accounting for more than one fourth of China's all-nation R&D expendi-

tures, nonetheless, the central *yangqi's* R&D outlay declined to 1.41% in proportion to their sales revenues in 2014. *The China Youth Daily*, 25/07/2016. http://zqb.cyol.com/html/2016-07/25/nw.D110000zgqnb_20160725_2-07.htm

104. *Xinhua*, 23/02/2016.
105. *Caixin*, 12/10/2013. http://china.caixin.com/2013-10-12/100590867.html; "Fraud Scandals Sap China's Dream of Becoming a Science Superpower," *The New York Times*, 13/10/2017. https://www.nytimes.com/2017/10/13/world/asia/china-science-fraud-scandals.html
106. *The Legal Daily*, 4/04/2017. http://www.chinanews.com/gn/2017/04-04/8190785.shtml
107. Steinfeld (2010), p. 150.
108. http://www.stats.gov.cn/tjfx/fxbg/t20101123_402685243.htm
109. Yusuf, S and Nabeshima, K (2007), "Strengthening China's Technological Capability," World Bank Policy Research Working Paper No. 4309.
110. *The Legal Daily*, 4/04/2017. http://www.chinanews.com/gn/2017/04-04/8190785.shtml
111. "'Made in China' Face Five Big Soft Underbellies, Chinese Enterprises Big but not Strong," *The Economic Reference News (jingji cankaobao)*, 11/10/2010. http://ccnews.people.com.cn/GB/12914512.html
112. Peter Nolan et al. (2010), "Global Competition after the Financial Crisis," *New Left Review*, 64, July–August.
113. Gao Liang, "On Globalization, Mental Emancipation and Transformation of Mode of Development," *Hong Kong Fax*, No. HK2009–07, 27/10/2009.
114. The Second Nationwide Resource Survey Bulletin on Scientific Research and R&D Demonstrated Our Nation's Strength and Level, *zhongguo tongji xinxiwang*, 23/11/2010. http://www.stats.gov.cn/tjfx/fxbg/t20101123_402685243.htm
115. "China's Patents' Purity Yet to Be Improved," *zhongguo chanjing xinwenbao*, 14/04/2017. http://www.cnipr.com/yysw/zscqycx/201704/t20170414_201930.htm
116. Peter Marsh, "China Noses ahead as Top Goods Producer," *The Financial Times*, 13/03/2011.
117. "China's Industry Security Break Alert Level, Foreign Control Exceed One-Third," *zhongguangwang*, Beijing, 30/11/2009. http://news.sohu.com/20091130/n268578182.shtml
118. *People's Daily*, 1/03/2010.

119. "Li calls for Deeper Ties with Germany," *The Financial Times*, 7/01/2011.
120. *The Workers' Daily*, 13/03/2017. http://ah.workercn.cn/14839/201703/13/170313144322829.shtml
121. "China Blinks on Yuan in Late G-20 Deal," *The Wall Street Journal Asia*, 21/02/2011.
122. *China News Agency*, Beijing, 13/12/2010.
123. *Xinhuawang*, 5/03/2011.
124. "New Foreign Trade Strategy Pursue Global Win-Win," *Outlook (liaowang)*, 4/01/2011.
125. *Xinhua*, 14/03/2015.
126. *Xinhua*, 2/03/2016; *Sina Caijing*, 21/03/2016.
127. *Caixin*, 29/06/2017. http://companies.caixin.com/2017-06-29/101107271.html
128. Wu Jinglian, et al. (1999), "Realizing the Strategic Regroupings of the State-Owned Economy," Working Paper.
129. *Xinhua*, Beijing, 17/11/2002. http://cpc.people.com.cn/GB/64162/64168/64569/65444/4429120.html
130. Interview with an informed source at the official think tank, 18/02/2003.
131. Interviews with SOE insiders in December 2003.
132. *China Economic Times*, 18/12/2003.
133. Shuipi, "What is the Essence of Chinese-style MBO?" *China Business Daily*, 19/04/2005.
134. Kong Shanguang, "Where did the 5-Trillion Profits of SOEs Go?," *Guangming Guancha*, 11/02/2007. http://guancha.gmw.cn/show.aspx?id=3445
135. Interview with a management consultant who spent a whole year in a listed SOE to investigate the efficacy of the SOE management reform, 21/09/2001.
136. *Economic Reference News (jingji cankaobao)*, 8/11/2005.
137. Jack Rodman, "China: NPL Market Report," Global Nonperforming Loan Report 2006, Ernst & Young, 3/05/2006. This report enraged the Chinese government. Two weeks later, E&Y had to declare to withdraw the report. *The Economist*, 15/05/2006.
138. Jonathan Richter (2008), "Circumscribing China's NPL 'Puzzle,'" Wharton School, University of Pennsylvania. http://repository.upenn.edu/wharton_research_scholars/54
139. *The Economist*, 20/05/2006, p. 78.

140. http://www.pwccn.com/webmedia/doc/633090682731395808_nplasia_newsletter_mar2007_chi.pdf
141. http://www.cbrc.gov.cn/english/home/jsp/docView.jsp?docID=2007051774830DBD1F20010BFFD7F4A6791F6F00
142. Economist Lang Xianping made an in-depth and comprehensive survey on China's manufacturing industries since 2007. His finding is that the rapidly worsening investment environment for China's SMEs in the manufacturing sector forced them to relocate investment in property and stock markets, which as a result pushed up the bubble in the virtual economy. http://www.folcn.com/news/caijingguancha/20080123/37031.html
143. "A Conservative Estimate of China's Local Debts at 10 Trillion Yuan," *New Century Weekly*, 7/03/2011.
144. "Fitch Reveals the $2trillion Black Hole in China's Economy that Heralds a Lost Decade," *The Telegraph*, 22/09/2016. http://www.telegraph.co.uk/business/2016/09/22/fitch-warns-bad-debts-in-china-are-ten-times-official-claims-sta/
145. *Economic Reference News (jingji cankaobao)*, 10/05/2010.
146. *Economic Reference News (jingji cankaobao)*, 21/05/2010.
147. The half-heartedness of the central government in combating inflation is partly to blame; since after 9/11, the Chinese leaders saw a rare "strategic opportunity of development" (*zhanlue jiyuqi*) in the context of improved Sino-US relations. They decided to further loosen credit control and implemented an expansionary monetary policy to stimulate the economy. Yue and Chen (2008), "What Caused China's Inflation?" *Modern China Studies*, No. 1.
148. The Unirule Institute of Economics, "The Nature, Performance, and Reform of the State-Owned Enterprises," p. 82, 12/04/2011.
149. *The Phoenix TV*, 14/07/2005. http://www.phoenixtv.com/phoenixtv/74312739631136768/index.shtml. Full text: http://www.xzzg.org/Article_View.asp?id=1906
150. http://pioneer-worker.forums-free.com/topic-t344.html; http://www.xinmiao.com.hk/0004/0100-0041S.htm
151. Yue Jianyong (2011), "The Myth of the Chinese Model," *Leaders (lingdaozhe)*, No. 40, June.
152. *China News Network*, 29/07/2009. http://www.chinanews.com.cn/gn/news/2009/07-29/1794984.shtml
153. An Exclusive Report by *Boxun News*. http://www.peacehall.com/news/gb/pubvp/2010/12/201012090529.shtml

154. This is best summarized by "The National Military Strategy of the United States of America 2011—Redefining America's Military Leadership," 8/02/2011.
155. The landmark event symbolizing this policy re-reversal is State Councilor Dai Binguo's article published on the website of the PRC's Ministry of Foreign Affairs (MFA), titled "Adhering to the Road of Peaceful Development." http://www.mfa.gov.cn/chn/gxh/tyb/zyxw/t774662.htm. Shortly after that, General Xiong Guangkai, who used to be regarded as a hawkish figure within the PLA, wrote an article on an influential newspaper with the title, "China's Security Image Distorted." In it, Xiong strongly criticized "Unhappy China," a best-selling book in 2010 preaching near-militaristic nationalism written by a couple of nationalists and New-Left scholars. *Diyi caijing ribao*, 21/02/2011. http://dycj.ynet.com/article.jsp?oid=76806547. General Chen Bingde, Chief of the General Staff of the PLA, said during his visit to the USA on May 19, 2011, "China never intends to challenge the US. Although China's defense and military development has come a long way in recent years, a gaping gap between you and us remains." http://www.bbc.co.uk/news/mobile/world-asia-pacific-13450316
156. Chinese scholars such as Yu Jianrong and Sun Liping made strong arguments in this regard. This author has similar findings through interviews with many insiders of Chinese government and public institutions in recent years.
157. "Xi: 'A Thousand Reasons' to Build Ties," *China Daily*, 8/04/2017. http://www.chinadaily.com.cn/world/2017-04/08/content_28840787.htm
158. Nicholas Kitchen and Michael Cox, "Driving Decline? Economic Crisis and the Rise of China," from the Special Report: "Obama Nation? U.S. Foreign Policy One Year On," LSE Ideas, January 2010.
159. In fact, China has made it clear to the USA in the mid-2000s that plagued by the increasingly acute resource shortages, environmental worsening, and social strains, China focused all attention to domestic issues. It viewed a cooperative partnership with the USA vital to its economic development. China respected the USA as the guarantor of international order in the Far East and had no intention to seek hegemony in world affairs. China regarded itself as the beneficiary of globalization and the international system. Hence, it expected to rise peacefully within the international framework. Zheng Bijian (2005), "China's 'Peaceful Rise' to Great-Power Status," *Foreign Affairs*, 84:5,

September/October; Wang Jisi (2005), "China's Search for Stability with America," *Foreign Affairs*, 84:5, Sep/Oct.

160. "Revising U.S. Grand Strategy toward China," Council on Foreign Relations Special Report released in April 2015. https://www.cfr.org/report/revising-us-grand-strategy-toward-china
161. "The Biggest Vote," *The New York Times*, 18/05/2000. http://www.nytimes.com/2000/05/18/opinion/essay-the-biggest-vote.html; Joseph Bosco, "The One China Policy: What Would Nixon Do?" *The Diplomat*, 5/01/2017. http://thediplomat.com/2017/01/the-one-china-policy-what-would-nixon-do/
162. Steinfeld (2010), p. 83.
163. Wade (2003), p. 372.
164. *Xinhuanet*, 5/09/2009. http://news.xinhuanet.com/fortune/2009-09/05/content_12001982.htm
165. "Are China's Top 500 that Strong?" *Beijing Business Daily (Beijing shangbao)*, 19/09/2009.
166. Yue, J and Chen, M (2008), "What Caused China's Inflation?" *Modern China Studies*, No. 1.
167. The Constitution of the CCP (revised in 2002). http://news.12371.cn/2015/03/11/ARTI1426058071921337.shtml
168. 2016 Top 100 Global Innovators Report issued by Clarivate Analytics. http://top100innovators.stateofinnovation.com/sites/default/files/content/top100/L178_Cvt_Top_100_Innovators_Report_008.pdf
169. *Xinhuawang*, Beijing, 10/12/2013. http://news.xinhuanet.com/world/2013-12/11/c_125838153.htm
170. Wang Bao'an (PRC's Deputy Minister of Finance), "How to Forge an Upgrading of the Chinese Economy?" *Qiushi (Seeking Truth, one of the most authoritative mouthpieces of the CCP)*, 1/01/2014. http://www.qstheory.cn/zxdk/2014/201401/201312/t20131230_307459.htm
171. He, Q (2011), "A Volcanic Stability," http://hqlenglish.blogspot.com/2011/06/volcanic-stability.html

8

Conclusion

The Chinese economy began to take off since the late 1970s after the end of the Cultural Revolution. Due to far-reaching market reform and external integration, an over-three-decade-long strong growth has made China the second largest economy in 2010, which is poised to overtake the USA shortly. This sort of externally oriented growth miracle was achieved at huge social, economic, and environmental cost and through excessive and premature depletion of indigenous resources. Yet China remains a semi-peripheral state whose various efforts to upgrade into a high-income "core" economy has been unsuccessful. Trapped in an unsustainable and prohibitively cost dependent development, China has failed to provide a successful modern alternative for other developing nations to emulate.

Such a developmental quandary is by no means predetermined or inevitable. China's liberal globalization approach was shaped by both the domestic and international forces that interacted to incline China for "external orientation" in an institutionally irreversible way by the closing years of the 1990s. It is nonetheless the first and foremost autonomous choice of the Communist regime basing its legitimacy on sustained high GDP growth after Tiananmen that made China's radical external integration a necessity. Deng Xiaoping's particular way of drawing lessons from the Tiananmen Incident and the Global 1989 and Zhu Rongji's deficient

J. Yue, *China's Rise in the Age of Globalization*, Palgrave Studies in Economic History, https://doi.org/10.1007/978-3-319-63997-0_8

statecraft prescribed the abandoning of socialism and self-reliance as the underpinning of China's new path-dependent market Leninist reforms and development strategy along neoliberal lines. Meanwhile, the USA played a crucial role in inducing China's active participation in the global economy as part of its grand strategy for fully integrating China into the international system of global capitalism. By the late 1990s, the unholy alliance between China's crony capitalism and global capitalism set China on a dependent path of development that continued well into the twenty-first century.

The backward socialism that Mao created after 1949 and the devastating Cultural Revolution made economic reform not only necessary but also a lot easier than in the Soviet Union, both ideationally and practically. For China's post-Mao leadership, reform was "self-help" in nature whose ultimate aim was to strengthen rather than undermine the Communist regime per se. Believing in the reformability of Communism, the reformers, moderates, or radicals, were committed to the "self-perfection of socialism," an idealistic conviction that drove the regime's post-totalitarian turn and state normalization in its quest for modernization in the initial years of "reform and opening." The "birdcage" as espoused by Chen Yun was the consensual limit set on the market-oriented reform within the confines of state socialism. Nevertheless, based on sheer Machiavellian pragmatism, Deng Xiaoping's radical approach of "perestroika without glasnost" drove him at loggerheads with both the central planners and the intellectuals, leading to the breakdown of the reform consensus in the mid-1980s.

Throughout the 1980s, remarkable progress had been made in poverty alleviation. This was in large part due to the socially costless decollectivization reform in the rural areas and the redemption policy in the urban areas by reversing Mao's coercive high accumulation policies even at the expense of state financial health. The market-oriented reform in the urban public sector achieved only limited success and did not make the SOEs noticeably more efficient. Not going beyond Lenin's New Economic Policy (NEP) in the 1920s' Soviet Russia, the Chinese reform dwarfed that in the Soviet Bloc in terms of greater tolerance for private businesses and greater economic openness, especially in opening up to foreign investment. Yet what actually amplified the effectiveness of Chinese reform was the consumption-led boom caused not by an effective market reform but by the regime's deliberate policy of deindustrialization in the capital goods sector, hence over-investment in light industry. In the absence of a technological leapfrogging, prosperity created on such basis was conceivably unsustainable which came to an end by the late 1980s. In fact, there was no clear-cut grand strategy throughout the 1980s. Opportunism dominated the senior leaders; no matter whether they were market reformers or central planners, none of whom had extraordinary insights into how to modernize the economy or through what kind of reform and opening. As Deng's protégé, Zhao Ziyang was the de facto chief architect of China's economic reform in the 1980s. Endorsed ironically by the central planners, Zhao's reform of fiscal decentralization and coastal development strategy, both meant for undermining central planning in important ways, inspired local economic dynamism but at the expense of China's national economic reintegration. Fostering economic feudalism, the market reformers paradoxically inherited Mao's legacy of provincial autarky in an allegedly "creative" way. The failed price reform in the summer of 1988 nonetheless not only cost Zhao his political life, but also led to the central planners' full economic takeover.

The Chinese Communist Party (CCP) survived the domino effect of the collapse of Communism in the Global 1989, thanks to Deng's determination, for good or bad. 1989–1992 was the "stabilization period" after Tiananmen that witnessed a temporary backsliding of "reform and opening" due to backlash at home from ideologues and central planners on the one hand, and Western-imposed economic sanctions on the other. The discrediting of Communism nonetheless freed Deng entirely from ideological bondage. The tremendous impact of the Global 1989, his eagerness to rebuild legitimacy for the Communist regime, and the personal need to institutionalize his reform legacies prompted Deng, with the backing of the People's Liberation Army (PLA), to impose radical marketization reform upon the party in 1992. Deng drew three major lessons from the Tiananmen Incident: no political reform, no appeasing the people, and appeasing the West. To put it in another way: no democracy (and Gorbachev), no socialism, and embracing of global capitalism. Committed to an "ideology of no ideology," the party state institutionalized Deng's reform legacies by instantly legalizing the "market economy" and constitutionalizing the so-called Deng Xiaoping Theory, five years later (1997), whereby to silently reinvent itself from a "left-wing dictatorship" to a "right-wing dictatorship" in the long 1990s. By making high growth the overriding political goal, Deng based the legitimacy of the Communist regime on sustained rapid economic growth *at all costs*.

1992 marks the changing character of the Communist party state, hence the changing path-dependent reform and development along neoliberal lines. The radicalization of reform and opening after 1992 manifests itself in the building of a "socialist market economy without socialism." In lieu of market socialism prior to 1992, market Leninism set in and allied itself with global capitalism. An efficiency-biased marketization reform began to unfold at the expense of social justice. Zhu Rongji was in full charge of China's reform and development. He was not the kind of Gorbachevite humanist socialist; nor was he a social democrat like Ludwig Erhard. As a statist, Zhu went out of his way to build up a strong central state through fiscal recentralization in 1994. However, he never seemed to have pondered over dismantling provincial autarky to spur national economic reintegration as the foundation for China's autonomous development. Compared with his reformist predecessor Zhao Ziyang, Zhu was in an ostensibly much more favorable position to seek a "planning-rational" approach to "managed marketization," joining it with internal integration by increasing state capacity to foster social justice on the one hand, and unifying the domestic market on the other. As a matter of fact, it was not Zhu Rongji alone, but the entire technocratic third-generation leadership, out of a deep sense of inferiority, who had neither the grand vision nor the strong "will to develop," despite their nationalist rhetoric. Opportunistically mythologizing "reform and opening," they instead eschewed, consciously or not, internal integration as an alternative option.

Abandoning socialism and self-reliance was what underpinned the Chinese market Leninist reform and neoclassical development strategy after 1992. As the economic tsar, Zhu engineered radical price liberalization (1993–1994) and the privatization of state-owned small- and medium-sized enterprises (SMEs), typical shock therapy scenarios with Chinese characteristics. The "shock and awe" effect of the Tiananmen crackdown enabled the nomenclatura privatization to go virtually unimpeded, resulting in massive layoffs of urban industrial workers. Meanwhile,

Zhu liberalized trade and investment on a massive scale in the hope of securing technology transfer from foreign investors by conceding the vast domestic market as a quid pro quo. The exchange for technology with market access (ETMA) strategy led to an influx of market-seeking foreign investors from the advanced economies. They posed deadly threat to the local firms, especially the state-owned SMEs struggling to survive the *gaizhi* (restructuring) and the *zhuada fangxiao* (grasp the big, let go the small) initiative. Their displacement of the SOEs rendered China's industrialization essentially stagnant at the turn of the century. Thus, the reform and opening interacted with each other to the great detriment of the local firms, particularly the SOEs. Yet with limited technology spillovers from the multinational corporations (MNCs), the ETMA virtually came to naught, which ended up in the foreign-invested enterprises (FIEs) (the MNCs included) dominating Chinese market and foreign trade from 1998.

The intensifying dependency on external markets and FDI driven by the enduring underconsumption and flagging industrialization highlighted the substantial structural weakness of the Chinese economy. It is paradoxically the "double dependency" that kept the Chinese economy growing robustly under the shadow of deflation and capital flight. And this positive effect of external integration enabling China to avoid "transitional decline" during the tumultuous marketization process in the 1990s inclined Chinese leaders to further confuse "growth" with "development," hence more firmly eschew "catch-up" in favor of "comparative advantage." More assuaging to the regime is the fact that the consolidation of the regime through embracing global capitalism benefited the middle class and the intellectuals and induced their docility and collaboration. The resultant elite coalition established between the three greatest vested interests, though hierarchical, further bolstered the regime. But the regime consolidation this way rendered the strong state soft thanks to the state capture by the vested interests. A soft state, although still strong in its extractive capacity, served first and foremost the purpose of self-enrichment rather than social justice and national development. A good example of this was the three de-socialist reforms in education, medicare, and housing carried out forcefully by Zhu Rongji after he took office in March 1998 as the Premier. Thus, by making China one of the most unequal societies in the world, the market Leninist reforms eventually backfired in the late 1990s to cause household consumption as a percentage of GDP to further decline to the point of an incoming economic recession. Eschewing internal integration, nonetheless, the decision makers, imbued with the political correctness of reform and opening, had no other option but to seek the WTO plus deep integration—a greater degree of "external orientation"—in a bid to address the legitimacy crisis evoked paradoxically by a decelerating "externally oriented" economy.

The USA played a crucial role in integrating China into the global economy. This is part and parcel of its grand strategy of transforming China from a challenger of the rule-based international system of global capitalism into a stakeholder. The Sino-Soviet split in the late 1960s offered the USA a rare opportunity to "draw China out" into the international system. Since Nixon visited China in 1972, "containment without isolation" has been the consistent American strategy. The USA played an active role in helping China to join the global institutions in the 1980s, contributing to China's transition from a revolutionary state to a normal state. The strategy nonetheless did not have a domestic agenda given the country's shallow integration at the time. Although an intensifying US–Soviet rivalry in the second Cold War (1979–1985) cemented Sino-US strategic partnership, the huge soft power clout of the USA could be strongly felt in China, which effectively catalyzed discrediting of Communism as both a belief system and an alternative to modernity.

The end of the Cold War in 1989 brought Sino-US strategic partnership to an abrupt end. The diminishing strategic value of China to the USA and the Tiananmen crackdown, however, did not deflect the US–China policy of not isolating China. Rather, the Global 1989 and its aftermath enabled the USA to shape the future of China in an unprecedented way by dint of economic engagement. Seeing that China had no other alternative but to embrace global capitalism after Tiananmen, President Bush, despite having to impose the economic sanctions, kept the door open to China, believing that doing so would induce China to keep networking itself with the outside world. From the mid-1990s, President Clinton combined realist containment with liberal engagement, a policy called "congagement." More proactive than that of "containment without isolation" as espoused by Nixon, this policy was designed to "bring China into the current international system while both preparing for a possible Chinese challenge to it and seeking to convince the Chinese leadership that a challenge would be difficult and extremely risky to pursue."[1] The "congagement" policy served three purposes: promoting US security and economic interests; forcing China to relinquish economic nationalism; and making China dependent on the international system economically and politically. In other words, the USA has never had the intention to make China another Germany or Japan with or without the Cold War factor, and this has nothing to do with whether China would transform into a democracy or not. Creating an inducement of "growth by invitation," nonetheless the USA allowed China to bandwagon with the liberal order that was "easy to join but hard to overturn," whereby China could achieve a Ricardian growth miracle at the expense of autonomous national development. The trajectory of China's deepening integration into the global economy since 1992 strictly follows such a roadmap. This is further evidenced by the Chinese leaders' deep faith in economic globalism that is rarely seen in other parts of world despite the country's inexorable dependency on the "core," and by the US firm resolve to prevent China from seeking alternatives, even to the present day.

Amid the euphoria of China's entry into the WTO in 2001, the dominant view at home and abroad then was that the accession would transform China into a liberal democracy based on a functioning market economy in the long term despite likely adverse impact in the short run. The pessimists, the minority, argued that the accession would soon trigger off a regime implosion following an inevitable economic collapse. China far outperformed these projections in strictly economic terms. Its economic momentum was swiftly resumed after the SARS pandemic in 2003. GDP grew at an average annual rate of some 10%. State finance improved and the export boom made China the largest creditor in the world. China's outbound FDI also increased exponentially and invested heavily in the resource-rich countries. Given its rapid economic expansion regionally and globally, China's diplomacy became more proactive and even assertive sometimes. From 2005 onward, the "rise of China" has been widely recognized by the international community. The country's seeming immunity from the global financial crisis since 2007 further made the broadly perceived state-capitalist China model under a "resilient authoritarianism"[2] the template for economic success.

Entry into the WTO symbolizes the matrimony of China's crony capitalism (market Leninism) and global capitalism. The Chinese state, reluctant to enforce strong protection of intellectual property (IP) and human rights, remains both soft and repressive. This, nonetheless, enabled a Ricardian growth miracle to take place. As the liberal order could only "accommodate one or two Japans," given China's size, its accommodation symbolized the formation of the global supply chain premised precisely upon China's full conversion to the neoliberal development paradigm. For the MNCs, producing in China for global markets meant creating global economies of scale through which profits could be maximized on an unprecedented scale. This constituted the main driver of the massive FDI influx that made China the "Factory of the World." However, the outlawing of "local contents" in fully opened domestic sectors under the WTO agreement facilitated the MNCs to take advantage of their global procurement system to forestall backward linkages across the value chain in China, hence industrial deepening and economic sophistication. For the local firms squeezed to the low end of the global value chain, they mainly engaged in final assembly with razor-thin profitability, and thus stood little chance of moving up the technological ladder in order to make themselves top-tier suppliers or system integrators. Such a presumed transformation is exactly what characterizes industrialization. The local firms' staggering industrial expansion without catch-up, thus, reinforced their dependency on importing key parts, components and capital goods from advanced economies, making China not the classical "Factory of the World" in which the nationally owned enterprises (NOEs) presumably predominated, but rather the "Assembly Plant of the World." In other words, as one of the defining features of dependent development in the age of liberal globalization, "Made in China" has given way to "Assembled in China."

"Growth without development (narrowly defined as catch-up)" testifies to China's unsuccessful industrial upgrading, and henceforth incomplete economic transformation into a high-income industrial economy. Underpinning China's dependent development is the country's distorted sectoral structure in which a rigid division of labor between different ownership types of enterprises took shape and became entrenched shortly after China joined the WTO. In the first instance, the privatization of the state-owned SMEs was largely completed by 2005. The large-sized SOEs were condensed into a handful of oligopolistic conglomerates dominating the upstream basic and certain key capital goods sectors. They ballooned in size and became hugely lucrative thanks to the state-sanctioned administrative monopoly. Since 2006, these SOEs have achieved remarkable technological progress under the policy of so-called indigenous innovation. But except in very few shining examples, such as the high-speed train, most SOEs remain uncompetitive on global markets, and hence become increasingly "internally orientated." By contrast, the FIEs remain the market leader dominating China's high-tech sectors and foreign trade. For those private enterprises squeezed by the SOEs and the FIEs to the excessively competitive downstream sectors, they were forced to move towards external orientation to export large quantities of low-tech products to global markets at extremely low prices. As opposed to the SOEs suffering spiraling trade deficits from 2002, it is the non-SOEs that drove the export boom and huge stock of foreign currency reserve. As always, the market Leninist regime used but discriminated against the domestic "private capital." It did so not for socialist purposes but for regime security. First and foremost, its sponsorship of large-sized SOEs did not serve public purposes. Instead, the regime made the SOEs more an instrument of state-enrichment than that of national development. Most crucially, its "unholy alliance" with the profit-seeking yet politically docile global capitalists fostered the joint domination of the domestic market by the oligopolistic SOEs and the MNCs to the great detriment of the country's fundamental national interests, thereby institutionalizing China's "growth without development" under crony comprador capitalism.

Although a self-defeating strategy in developmental terms, China's liberal globalization approach that generated the Ricardian growth miracle in the first post-9/11 decade was bound to create an economic bubble.[3] And given the country's economic size and the sheer magnitude of global imbalance, its export-led growth spurt necessarily engendered after the WTO entry would sooner or later backfire to force the *renminbi* to strongly revaluate. Both trends were meant to undercut China's competitiveness, causing the real economy to deindustrialize by way of either plant closure or relocation to other low-wage economies. And things did happen that way from the last quarter of 2008 onward, implying that the globalization-led prosperity has gone and perhaps gone forever. As a matter of fact, China's mounting strategic vulnerability in resource and foodstuff shortages—prompted or exacerbated by its long-lasting mode of extensive growth suffices to and has in practical terms called the country's deep integration into serious question.[4] Last but not least, as an alternative engine of growth after 2003, the property bubble, closely linked with the economic bubble,[5] from which local administrations have been financing to invest in infrastructure, drove debt to the level of 2.77 times GDP at the end of 2016, prone to burst at any time.[6] All these developments cast a long shadow on China's economic prospects.

Ostensibly, China's continued rise is unlikely unless the country achieves profound transition of the mode of development from extensive export- and investment-driven growth to intensive consumption- and innovation-driven growth. Such transition, however, seems increasingly a "mission impossible." First of all, the entrenchment of an "unholy alliance" of China's crony capitalism and global capitalism that assuaged the regime's fear of a Western-instigated regime change drove the Chinese state to be even more predatory and repressive after the WTO accession. Income inequality continued to rise at an accelerated rate. Real Gini coefficient reached 0.61 in 2010, which was only slightly lower than that of South Africa.[7] The top 1% of the families seized control of more than a third of the national wealth. "The poorest 25 per cent of Chinese households own just 1 per cent of the country's total wealth,"[8] according to one recent independent research. Still, there were over 200 million people living in poverty at or below the World Bank standard of US $2 per day.[9] Thus, the fear of approaching "revolutionary turmoil"[10] prompted massive capital flight[11] and exacerbated indiscernible kleptocratic transformation. Out of a deep sense of insecurity, the Chinese rulers tightened their grip on the society. Internal security (*weiwen*) outlays increased exponentially and for the first time exceeded the defense budget in the year of 2011.[12] A "Great Leap Backward" of the rule of law naturally ensued.[13] Following Hu Jintao's affirmation of continuing commitment to the "Deng Xiaoping Road" in terms of rejecting developmental Maoism (autarkic self-reliance) and Western-style democracy altogether at the end of 2008,[14] Wu Bangguo, head of the Chinese legislature (the NPC), declared "five Nos"[15] to underscore the leadership's explicit and firm commitment to absolute monopoly on power.

Table 8.1 GDP growth rate (2007–2016)

Year	2007	2008	2009	2010	2011	2012	2013	2014	2015	2016
GDP (%)	14.2	9.7	9.4	10.6	9.5	7.9	7.8	7.3	6.9	6.7

Source: The State Bureau of Statistics

Behind the Brezhnevite conservatism is unequivocally the irreversible decline of the Chinese economy since the last quarter of 2008. The regime's "shot in the arm" in 2009, a totally misplaced Keynesian stimulus package, although having propped up a short-lived rebound in 2010, resulted in severe overcapacity in many industries and soaring debt levels, making the situation even worse (Table 8.1). With a major economic crisis looming large, the rising social tensions drove the "authoritarian resilience" into an intense power struggle that accompanied the rise and fall of Bo Xilai (2007–2012). As a princeling and the son of Bo Yibo, one of the *balao* in the 1980s, Bo was a Politburo member and the party boss of the Chongqing Municipality where he had attempted at a hugely controversial populist "socialism 3.0" drive. His alleged vying for leadership nearly derailed the "smooth" transition of power at the 18th National Party's Congress in November 2012. The impact of Bo Xilai, even prior to his downfall, had sparked a fierce intra-party debate over which path the CCP should follow after Hu Jintao stepped down: the "Deng Xiaoping Road," the "Mao Zedong Road," or whatever. For many Chinese, as far as the country's future was concerned, reform or revolution—"that is the question!" For the deeply anti-revolutionary market Leninist regime that brought down Bo Xilai, nonetheless, the logical way out is an "anti-(Dengist) reform" under the "right-wing dictatorship," in other words, controlling capital and corruption by an omnipresent and omnipotent Leninist Leviathan.

Thus, despite the "rule of law" rhetoric after Xi Jinping rose to power, it only stands for the CCP resorting to the traditional legalist "rule by law." And inspired by Tocqueville's *The Old Regime and Revolution* (1856), the new leadership recognized that the Chinese Tocquevillian Moment had befallen on the increasingly kleptocratic Communist regime. Against the backdrop of an economic downturn, it is just such a collective awareness that prompted the CCP's sudden totalitarian turn and political-ideological repression. Being not a belief system after all, this sort of opportunistic market totalitarianism is marked by the regime's blatant imperiousness and avarice. Alienating the collaborators, the new totalitarian leaders are risking destroying the elite coalition that had effectively bolstered the regime in the past two decades. Moreover, composed mainly of former Red Guards of the Cultural Revolution imbued with Maoist anti-intellectualism, the new leadership are no less myopic intellectually, yet far more arrogant and self-important than their mediocre predecessors. They have neither the grand vision nor outstanding statecraft to seek alternative pathways of development. That is why the growing economic hardship due to being trapped in dependent development did not lead them to question the globalization myth, but rather further reinforced their belief in it.[16] Ironically, the illusion of a power shift from the USA to China is creating a self-fulfilling prophecy of a so-called Thucydides Trap in great power relations, making China's continued bandwagoning with the liberal order to accommodate its dependent development increasingly less likely. This, along with the regime's totalitarian turn, has undercut the prospect of lasting peace, the country's democratic transition, and China's modernization per se. Thus, rather than being a solid global power candidate, China is instead an inward-looking "restless empire" focusing on internal security and continuing to rule its own people in the way that is bound to fail in the age of the Internet. But whether that endgame will be naturally followed by modernization and democracy, or by a revival of Maoism, remains an open question.

History did not end in 1989, and does not end!

Notes

1. Rand Report (1999), Zalmay Khalilzad, Abram N. Shulsky, Daniel Byman, Roger Cliff, David T. Orletsky, The United States and a Rising China—Strategic and Military Implications.
2. Andrew Nathan (2003), "Authoritarian Resilience," *Journal of Democracy*, 14:1, pp. 6–17.
3. Yue, J and Chen, M (2008), "What Caused China's Inflation?" *Modern China Studies*, No. 1.

4. China's import dependency ratios (IDR) of five major mineral products are: oil 60%; iron ore 53.6%; refined aluminum 52.9%; refined copper 69%; potassium 52.4%. *China Economic Herald*, 12/12/2014. http://lib.cet.com.cn/paper/szb_con/335799.html; "Food Security Cannot Be Bought," *People's Daily* (Overseas edition), 6/01/2014. http://paper.people.com.cn/rmrbhwb/html/2014-01/06/content_1372063.htm
5. Yue, J and Chen, M (2008), "What Caused China's Inflation?"
6. "RPT-SPECIAL REPORT-'Ghost Collateral' Haunts Loans Across China's Banking System," *Reuters*, 31/05/2017. http://www.reuters.com/article/china-collateral-fake-idUSL3N1IY1UM
7. "China's Gini Index at 0.61, University Report Says," *Caixin*, 10/12/2012. http://english.caixin.com/2012-12-10/100470648.html
8. "China Income Inequality among World's Worst," *The Financial Times*, 14/01/2016. https://www.ft.com/content/3c521faa-baa6-11e5-a7cc-280dfe875e28?mhq5j=e3
9. "The State Council Information Office of the PRC," 17/10/2014. http://www.scio.gov.cn/zhzc/8/4/Document/1383409/1383409.htm; *Caixin*, 15/02/2016. http://china.caixin.com/2016-02-15/100855986.html
10. "China Insider Sees Revolution Brewing," *The Sydney Morning Herald*, 27/02/2010. http://www.smh.com.au/world/china-insider-sees-revolution-brewing-20100226-p92d.html
11. "Capital Exodus from China Reaches $800bn as Crisis Deepens," *The Telegraph*, 22/07/2015. http://www.telegraph.co.uk/finance/economics/11756858/Capital-exodus-from-China-reaches-800bn-as-crisis-deepens.html; "China's Capital Flight—Money is Pouring Out of China as Rapidly as it Once Poured In, That's a Dilemma for Xi Jinping," *Bloomberg*, 14/01/2016. https://www.bloomberg.com/news/articles/2016-01-14/china-s-capital-flight; "China's Capital Flight: Far More Serious than Imagined," *wangyi pinglun*, 13/06/2016. http://view.163.com/16/0613/05/BPDS57J600015AAR.html
12. March 6, 2011, *Deutsche Welle* (Mandarin). http://www.dw.com/zh/%E4%B8%AD%E5%9B%BD%E7%BB%B4%E7%A8%B3%E7%BB%8F%E8%B4%B9%E9%A6%96%E6%AC%A1%E8%B6%85%E8%BF%87%E5%9B%BD%E9%98%B2%E9%A2%84%E7%AE%97/a-14892486?&zhongwen=simp
13. *Jiang Ping*, https://www.voachinese.com/a/article-20100303-chinarulelawullretreat-86185087/462920.html

14. *People's Daily*, 19/12/2008. http://cpc.people.com.cn/GB/64093/64094/8544901.html
15. Wu Bangguo remarks, 27/01/2011. http://www.npc.gov.cn/npc/sjb/2011-01/27/content_1620264.htm
16. Li Keqiang, "Safeguard Economic Globalization, Support Free Trade," *Takungpao*, 15/03/2017. http://news.takungpao.com/hkol/headline/2017-03/3430791_wap.html; "China's Xi Jinping Defends Globalization from the Davos Stage," *Financial Times*, 17/01/2017. https://www.weforum.org/agenda/2017/01/chinas-xi-jinping-defends-globalization-from-the-davos-stage/

References

Amsden, A. 2001. *The Rise of "The Rest": Challenges to the West from Late-Industrializing Economies*. New York: Oxford University Press.

———. 2007. *Escape from Empire—The Developing World's Journey through Heaven and Hell*. Cambridge: MIT Press.

Anderson, Jonathan. 2004. A Fresh Challenge to the 'China Miracle'. *Bi Jiao (Comparison)* (Beijing), No. 14, September 1.

Bai, Yimin. 2008. *Mutsui Empire in Action*. Beijing: China Economic Publishing House.

Bensel, R.F. 2000. *The Political Economy of Industrialization, 1877–1900*. New York: Cambridge University Press.

Bernstein, T., and H. Li, eds. 2010. *China Learns from the Soviet Union, 1949–Present*. Plymouth: Lexington Books.

Bhala, R. 2000. Enter the Dragon: An Essay on China's WTO Accession Saga. https://law.drupal.ku.edu/sites/law.drupal.ku.edu/files/docs/resources/library/IntlTradeLaw/Enter%20the%20Dragon%20PDF.pdf

Bhalla, A.S., and S. Qiu. 2004. *The Employment Impact of China's WTO Accession*. London and New York: RoutledgeCurzon.

Bienefel, Manfred. 2006. The Challenge of China: Bringing Latent Contradictions to a Head. LSE DESTIN lecture series on Pandora's World: *Why We are Failing to Meet the Challenge of Global Development*, November 28.

Braham, Laurence. 2002. *Zhu Rongji & the Transformation of Modern China*. Singapore: John Wiley & Sons (Asia) Pte Ltd.

J. Yue, *China's Rise in the Age of Globalization*, Palgrave Studies in Economic History, https://doi.org/10.1007/978-3-319-63997-0

Breslin, S. 2005. Power and Production: Rethinking China's Global Economic Role. *Review of International Studies* 31 (4): 735–753.

Bruton, H. 1998. A Reconsideration of Import Substitution. *Journal of Economic Literature* 36 (2, Jun.): 903–936.

Burczak, T.A. 2006. *Socialism after Hayek*. Ann Arbor, MI: Michigan University Press.

Cave, M. 1980. *Computers and Economic Planning: The Soviet Experience*. Cambridge: Cambridge University Press.

Chang, Gordon G. 2001. *The Coming Collapse of China*. London: Arrow.

Chang, Ha-Joon. 2003. *Kicking Away the Ladder: Development Strategy in Historical Perspective*. London: Anthem Press.

———. 2009. Hamlet without the Prince of Denmark: How Development has Disappeared from the 'Development' Discourse? 15/02/2009. http://hajoonchang.net/wp-content/uploads/2012/01/HamletwithoutthePrinceofDenmark-revised.pdf

Chang, J., and J. Haliday. 2006. *Mao, The Unknown Story*. Hong Kong: Open Press.

Chen, Donglin. 1997. A Realistic Critique of the Economic Construction during the Cultural Revolution. *Studies on China's Economic History*, No. 4.

Chen, M. 2001a. A Comprehensive Analysis on the Effect of FDI on Chinese Economy. *Strategy and Management* (Beijing), No. 3.

Chen, Jian. 2001b. *Mao's China & the Cold War*. Chapel Hill and London: The University of North Carolina Press.

Chen, Yan. 2006a. *China's Awakening: An Evolution of Chinese Thoughts after the Cultural Revolution (1976–2002)*. Hong Kong: Tianyuan.

———. 2006b. The Democracy Wall Movement and Its Historical Status. *Modern China Studies*, No. 2.

Chen, C. 2007. *The Prospects for Liberal Nationalism in Post-Leninist States*. University Park: Pennsylvania State University Press.

Chen, Man, and Jianyong Yue. 2002. Exchange for Technology with Market Access. *Modern China Studies*, No. 3, Princeton, NJ.

Cheng, X. 1995. Decision and Miscarriage: Radical Price Reform in the Summer of 1988. In *Decision-Making in Deng's China: Perspectives from Insiders*, ed. Carol Lee Hamrin and Suisheng Zhao, 189–206. Armonk, NY: M. E. Sharpe.

Cheng, Xiaonong. 1996. Where the Prosperity Comes from? *Modern China Studies*, No. 3.

———. 2003. Reinterpreting China's Economy: Dynamism and Consequence of Economic Growth. *Modern China Studies* 1: 25–46.

———. 2009a. Dilemma of Development: The Logical Result of Social Unfairness. *Modern China Studies*, No. 3.

Cheng, Yinghong. 2009b. Socialist China: The Terminator of World Communist Movement. *Modern China Studies*, No. 3, Princeton, NJ.

Cheng, X. 2015. Capitalism Making and Its Political Consequences: A Comparative Political Economy of China's Communist Capitalism. In *China's Transition from Communism—New Perspectives*, ed. G. Wu and H. Lansdowne. Oxon: Routledge.

Cheng, Tun-Jen, Stephen Haggard, and David Kang. 1996. *Institutions, Economic Policy and Growth in the Republic of Korea and Taiwan Province of China*. Geneva: United Nations.

Chen Yun, nianpu. 2000. *A Chronicle of Chen Yun*. Vol. 3. Beijing: zhonggong zhongyang wenxian yanjiushi.

China Labor Bulletin. 2005. Report on Chinese Workers' Movement (2000–2004). Hong Kong. http://www.clb.org.hk/sites/default/files/archive/en/File/No.4%20labourmovement%28S%29.pdf

Communist and Post-Communist Studies. 2016. Special issue on Putin's Russia and Re-Stalinization, March 2016, pp. 1–112.

Corbridge, Stuart. 1994. Bretton Woods Revisited: Hegemony, Stability, and Territory. *Environment & Planning A* 26: 1829–1859.

Cox, Michael. 1996. *U.S. Foreign Policy after the Cold War*. London: Chatham House Press.

Cui, Zhiyuan. 1999a. Joining the WTO is Not China's Pressing Task. *Zaobao*, July 6.

———. 1999b. Stimulating Domestic Demand is a Revolution. *Guoji jingi pinglun [Review of International Economics]*, No. 5–6.

Cumings, B. 1984. The Origins and Development of the Northeast Asian Political Economy. *International Organization* 38 (1): 1–40.

Dai, C. 2010. U.S. 'Trade Liberalization' Policy and China's 'Reform and Opening' (1969–1975). *shixue yuekan [History Studies Monthly]*, No. 2.

Datta, A. 1973. *Perspectives of Economic Development*. London and Basingstoke: Macmillan.

Deng, Liqun. 2006. *Twelve Years*. Hong Kong: Strong Wind Press.

Deng, K. 2012. *China's Political Economy in Modern Times: Changes and Economic Consequences, 1800–2000*. Oxon: Routledge.

Deng Xiaoping, nianpu. 1975–1997. *A Chronicle of Deng Xiaoping*. Beijing: zhongyang wenxian chubanshe (2004).

De Sanctis, S. 1993. Legal and Criminal Law Reform: Another Failure of Perestroika? In *The Soviet Transition: From Gorbachev to Yeltsin* (Special Issue of the "*Journal of Communist Studies*" 9:1), co-ed. Stephen White, Rita Di Le, and Ottorino Cappelli, 152. London: Routledge.

Di, Yinqing. 1999a. A Critique on Long Yongtu's Article 'Entry into WTO is Not Equal to Full Open-up'. *China and the World (e-journal)*, December.

———. 1999b. A Critique on Sino–U.S. Agreement on China's WTO Accession. *China and the World (e-journal)*, No. 41, December.

Dore, R. 1987. *Taking Japan Seriously: A Confucian Perspective on Leading Economic Issues*. Redwood: Stanford University Press.

Dos Santos, Theotonio. 1971. The Structure of Dependence. *American Economic Review* 60 (1970): 231–236.

Drifte, R. 2003. *Japan's Security Relations with China since 1989: From Balancing to Bandwagoning? (The Nissan Institute/Routledgecurzon Japanese Studies)*. 1st ed. Oxon: Routledge.

Du, D. 2008. How to Look on Deng Xiaoping Today? *Caijing*, 05/12/2008.

Economides, Spyros, and Peter Wilson. 2001. *The Economic Factor in International Relations: A Brief Introduction*. London and New York: I.B. Tauris.

Evans, P. 1979. *Dependent Development: The Alliance of Multinational, State, and Local Capital in Brazil*. Princeton, NJ: Princeton University Press.

Fan, B., and G. Zhou. 2011. *tongchou guonei fazhan he duiwai kaifang [Coordinating Domestic Development and International Integration]*. Beijing: zhongguo caizheng jingji chubanshe.

Fang, M. 2016. Hua Guofeng and China's Open-Door. *yanhuang chunqiu*, No. 5.

Feng, H. 2006. *The Politics of China's Accession to the WTO*. New York: Routledge.

Ferguson, Niall. 2007. Not Two Countries, But One: Chimerica. 04/03/2007. http://www.niallferguson.com/Site/FERG/Templates/ArticleItem.aspx?pageid=95

Ferraro, V. 2008. Dependency Theory: An Introduction. In *The Development Economics Reader*, ed. Giorgio Secondi, 58–64. London: Routledge.

Finlay, D. 2012. Gorbachev's Miscalculation and the Collapse of the Soviet Union. *Foreign Policy*, November 22. https://thestateofthecentury.wordpress.com/2012/11/22/gorbachevs-miscalculation-and-the-collapse-of-the-soviet-union/

Fligstein, N. 2008. *Euroclash: The EU, European Identity, and the Future of Europe*. Oxford: Oxford University Press.

Frank, Andre Gunder. 1972. The Development of Underdevelopment. In *Dependence and Underdevelopment*, ed. James D. Cockcroft, Andre Gunder Frank, and Dale Johnson. Garden City, NY: Anchor Books.

Frieden, J. 2006. *Global Capitalism—Its Rise and Fall in the Twentieth Century*. New York: Norton.

Fu, Bo. 2003. China Hides Its Intentions Again. *Le Monde Diplomatique*, March.

Fukuyama, Francis. 1989. The End of History? *The National Interest*, Summer.

Gao, W. 2003. *Zhou Enlai in His Late Years*. New York: Mirror Books.

Gao, Liang. 2009. On Globalization, Mental Emancipation and Transformation of Mode of Development. Hong Kong Fax. No. HK2009-07, October 27.

Gao, W. 2016. Mao's Cultural Revolution Legacy and Xi Jinping's Statecraft. An essay delivered to the academic seminar on the fiftieth anniversary of the start of the Cultural Revolution, VOA, 6/05/2016. https://www.voachinese.com/a/gao-wenqian-cultural-revolution-part1-20160505/3317245.html

Gao, X., and P. He. 1993. *Biography of Zhu Rongji*. Taipei: The Journalist.

Gerovitch, S. 2008. InterNyet: Why the Soviet Union did Not Build a Nationwide Computer Network. *History and Technology* 24 (4): 335–350.

Gilboy, G.J. 2004. The Myth behind China's Miracle. *Foreign Affairs*, July/August, pp. 33–48.

Gilpin, R. 2001. *Global Political Economy: Understanding the International Economic Order*. Princeton, NJ: Princeton University Press.

Goldman, M.I. 1983. *USSR in Crisis—The Failure of an Economic System*. New York: Norton.

———. 1992. *What Went Wrong with Perestroika* (updated). New York: Norton.

Golub. 2013. From the New International Economic Order to the G20. *Third World Quarterly* 34 (6): 1000–1015.

Gore, C. 2000. The Rise and Fall of the Washington Consensus as a Paradigm for Developing Countries. *World Development* 28 (5): 789–804.

Grant, C., and T. Valasek. 2011. *Preparing for the Multipolar World—European Foreign and Security Policy in 2020*. London: Centre for European Reform.

Gruber, Lloyd. 2000. *Ruling the World: Power Politics and the Rise of Supranational Institutions*. Princeton, NJ: Princeton University Press.

Guo, S. 1992. sannian zhili zhengdun yu zhongguo jingji gaige [Three-year Rectification and Improvement and China's Economic Reform]. *shengchanli yanjiu [Productivity Research]* 5: 18–32.

Guo, R. 2017. *An Economic Inquiry into the Nonlinear Behaviors of Nations: Dynamic Developments and the Origins of Civilizations*. London: Palgrave Macmillan.

Han, D. 2000. *Collision—The Pitfall of Globalization and China's Realistic Choice*. Beijing: jingji guanli chubanshe.

Han, Deqiang. 2001. Pros and Cons of China's Accession to the WTO, Dynamics and Debates. A speech at the European Parliament, 26/06/2001. http://www.wyzxsx.com/Article/Class17/200411/845.html
Hao, Y. 2007. China's Foreign Economic Policy in the Past Fifty Years. *Beijing: waijiao pinglun (Review of Foreign Affairs)* 5: 57–63.
Harper, John L. 1997. The Dream of Democratic Peace—Americans are Not Asleep. *Foreign Affairs* 76 (3, May/Jun.): 117–121.
Harvey, David. 2007. *A Brief History of Neoliberalism.* Oxford and London: Oxford University Press.
Hatch, Walter, and Kozo Yamamura. 1996. *Asia in Japan's Embrace—Building a Regional Production Alliance.* New York: Cambridge.
Hayhoe, R. 1992. Book Review: The Confucian Ethic and the Spirit of Capitalism. *Curriculum Inquiry* 22 (4): 425–431.
He, Qinglian. 1998. *The Pitfall of Modernization.* Beijing: jinri zhongguo chubanshe. New edition in 2003, Sunnydale: Broad Press.
———. 2000a. A Comprehensive Analysis of the Evolution of China's Social Structure. *Book-house*, No. 3, Hunan, China.
———. 2000b. What is the Goodness of Joining the WTO? *Duowei News*, April 2.
———. 2003. China's Changing of the Guard: A Volcanic Stability. *Journal of Democracy* 14 (1, Jan.): 66–72.
———. 2006. *A Revelation of the Strategy of Media Control in Mainland China.* Taipei: Liming Culture.
———. 2008. Thirty Years of Reform: The Abnormal Development of State Capacity and Its Consequence. *Modern China Studies*, No. 4.
He, W. 2015. *Unfinished Manuscripts.* Hong Kong: Strong Wind Press.
Hirschman, A.O. 1968. The Political Economy of Import-Substituting Industrialization in Latin America. *The Quarterly Journal of Economics* 82 (1): 1–22.
Hitchcock, William I. 2004. *The History of the Continent since 1945.* London: Profile Books.
Hodges, D.C. 1981. *The Bureaucratization of Socialism.* Amherst: University of Massachusetts Press.
Hormats, Robert D. 2001. *Task Force Report: Beginning the Journey—China, the United States, and the WTO.* Report of an Independent Task Force sponsored by the Council on Foreign Relations.
Hu, S., ed. 1991. *Seventy Years of the CCP.* Beijing: zhongyang dangshi chubanshe.

Hu, Peizhao. 1994. Impediments of Reverse Growth of China's Modern Enterprise System. *jingji yanjiu [Economic Research]* (Beijing), No. 7.

Hu, Angang. 1999. The Greatest Challenge in the New Century: China Enters into the Stage of High Unemployment. Working Paper.

Hu, A. 2012. The Global Spread of Neo-Liberalism and China's Pension Reform since 1978. *Journal of World History* 23 (3): 609–638.

Hu, Ping. 2017. A Review of Yang Jisheng's New Book on the History of the Cultural Revolution. *China Human Rights Bi-weekly*, No. 201. http://www.hrichina.org/chs/zhong-guo-ren-quan-shuang-zhou-kan/hu-ping-da-li-tui-jian-yang-ji-sheng-xian-sheng-xin-zhu-tian-di

Huang, Yasheng. 2003. *Selling China—Foreign Direct Investment during the Reform Era*. New York: Cambridge University Press.

Hughes, Chris. 1997. *Taiwan and Chinese Nationalism—National Identity and Status in International Society*. London: Routledge.

Huntington, S. 1965. Political Development and Political Decay. *World Politics* 17 (2): 386–430.

Ikenberry, J. 1992. A World Economy Restored: Expert Consensus and the Anglo-American Postwar Settlement. *International Organization* 46 (1): 289–321.

———. 2011. *Liberal Levithan: The Origins, Crisis, and Transformation of the American World Order*. Princeton, NJ: Princeton University Press.

Jin, C. 2011. *The Biography of Mao Zedong*. Vol. 6. Beijing: zhongyang wenxian chubanshe.

Johnson, C. 1982. *MITI and the Japanese Miracle: The Growth of Industrial Policy, 1925–1975*. Redwood: Stanford University Press.

———. 1999. The Developmental State: Odyssey of a Concept. In *The Developmental State*, ed. Meredith Woo-Cumings. Ithaca and London: Cornell University Press.

Kagan, R. 2008. *The Return of History and the End of Dreams*. London: Atlantic Books.

Kang, Xiaoguang. 2002. An Analysis of China's Stability in the Next 3–5 Years. *Strategy and Management* (Beijing), No. 3.

Katsiaficas, G. 2006. Neoliberalism and the Gwangju Uprising. http://www.eroseffect.com/articles/neoliberalismgwangju.htm

Kay, C. 2002. Why East Asia Overtook Latin America. *Third World Quarterly* 23 (6): 1073–1102.

Kennedy, Paul. 1987. *The Rise and Fall of the Great Powers: Economic Change and Military Conflict from 1500 to 2000*. New York: Random House.

Kennedy, S. 2002. *China Cross Talk: The American Debate over China Policy since Normalization*. Lanham: Rowman & Littlefield Publishers.

Kennedy, Paul, and William I. Hitchcock, eds. 2000. *From War to Peace: Altered Strategic Landscapes in the Twentieth Century*. New Haven and London: Yale.

Khanin, G.I. 2003. The 1950s: The Triumph of the Soviet Economy. *Europe-Asia Studies* 55 (8): 1187–1211.

Kiely, R. 2006. *New Political Economy of Development: Globalization, Imperialism, Hegemony*. Oxon: Palgrave.

Kitchen, Nicholas, and Michael Cox. 2010. *Driving Decline? Economic Crisis and the Rise of China*. Special Report: '*Obama Nation? U.S. Foreign Policy One Year On*', LSE Ideas, January.

Klare, Michael. 2005. *Blood and Oil: The Dangers and Consequences of America's Growing Petroleum Dependency*. London: Penguin.

Komaiko, R. 2007. An Innovative Perspective on US–China Ties. U.S.–China Economic and Security Review Commission, July 25.

Kong, Q. 2002. *China and the World Trade Organization: A Legal Perspective*. Singapore: World Scientific Publishing Co Pte Ltd.

Kornai, J. 1979. Resource-Constrained Versus Demand-Constrained Systems. *Econometrica* 47 (4): 801–819.

Kornai, Janos. 1992. *The Socialist System: The Political Economy of Communism*. Oxford: Clarendon Press.

Krastev, I. 2008. The Crisis of the Post-Cold War European Order. 10/09/2008. http://www.eurozine.com/the-crisis-of-the-post-cold-war-european-order/

Krugman, P. 1994. The Myth of Asia's Miracle. *Foreign Affairs* 73 (6, Nov./Dec.): 62–78.

Kueh, Y.Y. 2008. *China's New Industrialization Strategy: Was Chairman Mao Really Necessary?* Cheltenham: Edward Elgar Publishing Limited.

Lall, S. 2004. Reinventing Industrial Strategy: The Role of Government Policy in Building Industrial Competitiveness. UNCTAD G-24 Discussion Paper Series No. 28, April, pp. 1–46.

Lapres, D.A. 2000. The EU–China WTO Deal Compared. *China Business Review* 27 (4): 8–14. (2001). EU Deal Paves the Way for China to finally Join the WTO. European Report, June 23, pp. 507.

Lardy, Nicholas. 1995. The Role of Foreign Trade and Investment in China's Economic Transformation. *The China Quarterly* 144 (Dec.): 1065–1082.

———. 2002. *Integrating China into the Global Economy*. Washington: Brookings Institution Press.

Latham, M. 2011. *The Right Kind of Revolution: Modernization, Development, and US Foreign Policy from the Cold War to the Present*. Ithaca: Cornell University Press.

Lawson, G., C. Armbruster, and M. Cox, eds. 2010. *The Global 1989—Continuity and Change in World Politics*. Cambridge: Cambridge University Press.

Ledovsky, Andrei. 1995. Mao's Telegram on November 30, 1947 in '*Mikoyan's Secret Mission to China in January and February 1949*'. *Far Eastern Affairs* (Moscow) 2: 72–94. Chinese translation: see *Study of CPC History Abroad*, No. 5, 1995.

Lenin, V.I. 1956. *The Development of Capitalism in Russia*. Moscow: Foreign Languages Publishing House.

Li, C. 1989. An Externally-Oriented Strategy Should Not Be the General Development Strategy of China as a Big Country. *jingji lilun yu jingji guanli [Economic Theory and Economic Management]*, No. 5.

Li, H. 2001. The Political Stalinization of China: The Establishment of One-Party Constitutionalism, 1948–54. *Journal of Cold War Studies* 3 (2): 28–47.

Li, S. 2002. The PRC's Foreign Policy. March. http://paper.usc.cuhk.edu.hk/Details.aspx?id=2200

Li, H. 2006. *Mao and the Economic Stalinization of China, 1948–1953*. Lanham, MD: Rowman & Littlefield.

Li, Lanqing. 2008a. *Breaking the Siege—Days when the Door Started to Open*. Beijing: zhongyang wenxian chubanshe.

Li, J. 2008b. Deng Xiaoping's Meeting with Gorbachev Remembered. *bainianchao* (Beijing), No. 3.

Li, H. 2010. Instilling Stalinism in Chinese Party Members: Absorbing Stalin's Short Course in the 1950s. In *China Learns from the Soviet Union, 1949–Present*, ed. T. Bernstein and H. Li. Lanham, MD: Lexington Books.

Li, X. 2016. huiyi yiwei zhanzai gaige qianyan de zhangzhe [A Forerunner of Reform Remembered]. *yanhuang chunqiu*, No. 2. http://www.yhcqw.com/html/hyp/2016/29/1629152821DIF7810084A898K0F55BJ8G4A.html

Liang, H. 2008. Deng Xiaoping's Modest Apology Moved Lee Kwan Yew. *dangjian [Party Construct]*, No. 10.

Lieven, Dominic. 2003. *Empire*. London: Pimlico.

Liew, L. 2005. China's Engagement with Neo-liberalism: Path Dependency, Geography and Party Self-Reinvention. *The Journal of Development Studies* 41 (2): 331–352.

Lin, C. 2008a. China: Changing the Rules of the Game. *Soundings* 39 (1): 7–19.

———. 2008b. Against Privatization in China: A Historical and Empirical Argument. *Journal of Chinese Political Science* 13 (1): 1–27.

Lin, Justin Yifu, et al. 1999. Comparative Advantage and Development Strategy—A Reinterpretation of the East Asian Miracle. CCER No. C1999006, Peking University.

Lind, M. 2016. Taking Modernization Seriously—How to Think About Global Industrialization. *Breakthrough Journal*, No. 6, Summer. https://thebreakthrough.org/index.php/journal/issue-6/taking-modernization-seriously

List, Friedrich. 1909. *The National System of Political Economy*. Translated by Sampson S. Lloyd. London: Longmans, Green.

Liu, L. 1992. *The Transformation of China's Economic Development Strategy and Its Problems*. The State Council's Development and Research Centre (DRC) internal report, No. 43, 25/09/1992.

Liu, Y. 1999. The Segmentation of China's Domestic Market—The Institutional Legacy of the Planning Economy. *Journal of Sociology of NCCU* 29 (Oct.): 1–32.

Liu, J. 2007. An Interpretation of the 'Judicial Review Clause' of the Accession Protocol of the People's Republic of China. http://www.iolaw.org.cn/showArticle.aspx?id=2133

Lord, Winston. 1989. China and America: Beyond the Big Chill. *Foreign Affairs* 68 (4, Fall): 1–26.

Lundestad, Geir. 1986. Empire by Invitation: The United States and Western Europe, 1945–1952. *Journal of Peace Research* 23 (3, Sep.): 263–277.

Luo, Y. 2015. *Farewell to the General Staff.* Hong Kong: Open Press.

Ma, Guochuan. 2008. *fengyujiancheng: zhongguo zhuming jingjixuejia fangtanlu [A Collection of Interviews with Chinese Economists]*. Beijing: SDX Joint Publishing House.

Ma, L., and Z. Lin. 1998. *jiaofeng [Cross Sword]*. Beijing: Today's China Press.

MacDonald, P., and J.M. Parent. 2011. Graceful Decline? The Surprising Success of Great Power Retrenchment. *International Security* 35 (4, Spring): 7–44.

MacFarquhar, R., and M. Schoenhals. 2006. *Mao's Last Revolution*. Cambridge: Belknap Harvard.

Marx, Karl, and Friedrich Engels. 2004. *The Communist Manifesto*. Penguin: Longman.

Mastanduno, M. 1997. Preserving the Unipolar Moment: Realist Theories and US Grand Strategy after the Cold War. *International Security* 21 (4): 49–88.

Miller, C. 2016. Could Mikhail Gorbachev Have Saved the Soviet Union? *Foreign Policy*, 21/12/2016. http://foreignpolicy.com/2016/12/21/could-mikhail-gorbachev-have-saved-the-soviet-union/

Moghadam, V.M. 2005. *Globalizing Women: Transnational Feminist Networks*. Baltimore, MD: The Johns Hopkins University Press.

Munck, R. 2012. *Contemporary Latin America*. 3rd ed. New York: Palgrave Macmillan.

Myrdal. 1968. *Asian Drama: An Inquiry into the Poverty of Nations*. London: Allen Lane The Penguin Press.

Nathan, A. 2003. Authoritarian Resilience. *Journal of Democracy* 14 (1): 6–17.

Nixon, R. 1967. Asia after Vietnam. *Foreign Affairs* 46 (1, Oct.): 111–125.

Nolan, P. 1995. *China's Rise, Russia's Fall: Politics, Economics and Planning in the Transition from Stalinism*. New York: St. Martin's Press.

———. 2001a. *China and Global Economy*. New York: Palgrave.

———. 2001b. China, the US and the WTO: Battle of the Giants or Defeat of the Pygmies? (manuscript).

———. 2002. China and the Global Business Revolution. *Cambridge Journal of Economics* 26 (1): 119–137.

Nolan, P., and J. Zhang. 2010. Global Competition after the Financial Crisis. *New Left Review* 64, July–August.

North, Douglass. 1990. *Institutions, Institutional Change and Economic Performance*. Cambridge: Cambridge University Press.

Oshima, H. 1986. The Transition from an Agricultural to an Industrial Economy in East Asia. *Economic Development and Cultural Change* 34 (4): 783–809.

Overholt, W. 2005. China and Globalization—Testimony before the U.S.-China Economic and Security Review Commission. RAND, released on 19/05/2005.

Pei, Y. 2015. *The Disillusion of Utopia*. Taipei: Independent & Unique.

Pierenkemper, T., and R. Tilly. 2004. Chap 10: The International Economy. In *The German Economy during the Nineteenth Century*, 145–156. London: Berghahn Books.

Pierson, Paul. 2000. Increasing Returns, Path Dependence, and the Studies of Politics. *The American Political Science Review* 94 (2, Jun.): 251–267.

Pillsbury, M. 2014. *The Hundred-Year Marathon: China's Secret Strategy to Replace America as the Global Superpower*. New York: Henry Holt and Co.

Pomeranz, K. 2001. Is there an East Asian Development Path? *Journal of the Economic and Social History of the Orient* 44 (3): 322–362.

Prebisch, Rail. 1959. Commercial Policy in Underdeveloped Countries. *American Economic Review* 49 (2): 251–273.

Prebisch, Raul. 1981. *Peripheral States: Crisis and Transformation*. Chinese version 1990. Beijing: shangwu yinshuguan.

Preston, P. 2011. *Theories of Development*. London: Routledge.

Pyle, B.K. 2008. *Japan Rising: The Resurgence of Japanese Power and Purpose*. New York: Public Affairs.

Qiu, X., and Y. Du. 1994. The Potential and Development Thinking on China's Rural Market. *jingji yanjiu [Economic Research]* (Beijing), No. 8.

Qu (Chu), Wan-wen. 2009a. The China Factor in Taiwan's Economic Miracle. *Taiwan Social Studies Quarterly* 74 (Jun.): 49–93.

———. 2009b. The China Model of Industrial Policy under the Catch-up Consensus: The Case of the Automobile Industry. *China Economic Quarterly* 8 (2): 501–532.

Quah. 2011. The Global Economy's Shifting Centre of Gravity. *Global Policy* 2 (1): 3–9.

Radice, H. 2015. Chap 5: Britain in the World Economy: National Decline, Capitalist Success. In *Global Capitalism: Selected Essays*, 91–107. Oxon: Routledge.

Rawski, Thomas G. 2001. What's Happening to China's GDP Statistics? September 12. http://www.pitt.edu/~tgrawski/papers2001/gdp912f.pdf

Reinert, Kenneth A., and Ramkishen S. Rajan, eds. 2009. *The Princeton Encyclopedia of the World Economy (Two Volume Set)*. Princeton, NJ: Princeton University Press.

Rice, Condoleezza. 2000. Campaign 2000: Promoting the National Interest. *Foreign Affairs* 79 (1, Jan./Feb.): 45–62.

Rodrik, Dani. 2000. Development Strategies for the Next Century. http://siteresources.worldbank.org/DEC/Resources/84797-1251813753820/6415739-1251814020192/rodrik_japan.pdf

Rodrik, D. 2011. *The Globalization Paradox*. Oxford: Oxford University Press.

Sanchez, O. 2003. The Rise and Fall of the Dependency Movement: Does it inform Underdevelopment Today? *EIAL (Estudios Interdisciplinarios de América Latina y el Caribe)* 14 (2, Jul./Dec.): 31–50.

Schwarz, B. 1996. Why America Thinks It Has to Run the World. *The Atlantic Monthly*, June, pp. 92–102.

Segal, Gerald. 1999. Does China Matter? *Foreign Affairs* 78 (5, Sep.–Oct.): 24–36.

Selected Works of Chen Yun. 1995. Vol. 3, Beijing: renmin chubanshe.
Selected Works of Deng Xiaoping. 1983. Vol. 2, Beijing: renmin chubanshe.
———. 1993. Vol. 3, Beijing: renmin chubanshe.
Shambaugh, D. 1996. *China and Europe: 1949–1995*. London: Contemporary China Institute, SOAS, University of London.
———. 2005. The New Strategic Triangle: U.S. and European Reactions to China's Rise. *The Washington Quarterly* 28 (3, Summer): 7–25.
Shen, Jiru. 1999. Several Thinkings on the Kosovo Question. *World Economics and Politics*, No. 7.
Shen, Z. 2009. From Xibaipo to Moscow: Mao Declared 'Leaning to One Side'. *Journal of Chinese Communist Party History Studies*, No. 4.
Shi, Guangshen. 2009. A Review of Negotiations on China's 'Reentry' into the GATT and Accession to the WTO. *Bainianchao [Hundred-Year Tide]*. No. 7.
Shirk, S.L. 1993. *The Political Logic of Economic Reform in China*. Berkeley: University of California Press.
Smith, D. 1991. *The Confucian Continuum: Educational Modernization in Taiwan*. New York: Praeger.
Song, Y. and D. Sun, ed. 1999. *The Cultural Revolution and Its Heresies* (online).
Stanley, T., and A. Lee. 2014. It's Still Not the End of History. *The Atlantic Monthly*, September 1.
Steinfeld, E. 2010. *Playing Our Game—Why China's Rise Doesn't Threaten the West*. New York: Oxford University Press.
Stiglitz, J. 2002. *Globalization and Its Discontents*. London: Penguin Books.
———. 2007. *Making Globalization Work: The Next Steps to Global Justice*. London: Penguin Books.
Stokes, B. 1999. Taming the Dragon: Integrating China into the Global Trading System. In *Partners or Competitors: The Prospects for U.S.–European Cooperation on Asian Trade*, ed. R.H. Steinberg and B. Stokes, 177–192. Lanham, MD: Rowman & Littlefield.
Strange, S. 1987. The Persistent Myth of Lost Hegemony. *International Organization* 41 (4): 551–574.
Strayer, R. 1998. *Why did the Soviet Union Collapse? Understanding Historical Change*, 191–193. Oxon: Routledge.
Su, S. 1999. Theory and Practice of Political System Reform in the Deng Xiaoping Era. *Modern China Studies*, No. 3.
———. 2006. *Democracy Cannot Wait*. Hong Kong: Greenfield Bookstore.
Sun, Liping. 2002. The New Trends of the Evolution of China's Social Structure since the mid-1990s. *Modern China Studies*, No. 3.

Sun, Liping, et al. 1998. The Mid-term and Long-term Trends and Hidden Danger of the Transformation of China's Social Structure. *Strategy and Management*, No. 5.

———. 2010. Tsinghua University Research Group: 'To Realize Lon-term Stability through Institutionalized Expression of Interest'. *lingdaozhe [Leaders]*, No. 33, April.

Sutter, Robert. 2003. Why does China Matter? *The Washington Quarterly* 27 (1, Winter 2003–2004): 75–89.

Szelenyi, Ivan, et al. 1994. The Socialist Economic System. In *The Handbook of Economic Sociology*, ed. Neil J. Smelser and Richard Swedberg. Princeton, NJ: Princeton University Press.

Thun, E. 2006. *Changing Lanes in China: Foreign Direct Investment, Local Governments, and Auto Sector Development*. New York: Cambridge University Press.

Thurow, L. 2007. A Chinese Century? Maybe It's the Next One. *New York Times*, August 19.

Tian, J. 2015. The Formation and Implementation of the Coastal Development Strategy. *yanhuang chunqiu*, No. 3. http://www.yhcqw.com/html/cqb/2015/39/15391919259H8E597782DI69GEE3384DKC.html

Tsou, Tang. 1994. *Chinese Politics in the Twentieth Century*. Hong Kong: Oxford University Press.

UN. 2009. Rethinking Poverty—Report on the World Social Situation 2010. http://www.un.org/esa/socdev/rwss/docs/2010/fullreport.pdf

UNCTAD. 2001. Transfer of Technology—UNCTAD Series on Issues in International Investment Agreements. http://unctad.org/en/docs/psiteiitd28.en.pdf

———. 2009. *The Least Developed Countries Report 2009: The State and Development Governance*. New York and Geneva.

———. 2013. The Asian Developmental State and the Flying Geese Paradigm. November. http://unctad.org/en/PublicationsLibrary/osgdp20133_en.pdf

UNDP-GCPSE. 2015. Is the Private Sector more Efficient? A Cautionary Tale.

Vogel, E. 2013. *Deng Xiaoping and the Transformation of China*. Chinese ed. Hong Kong: CUHK Press.

Wade, R. 1996. Japan, the World Bank, and the Art of Paradigm Maintenance: The East Asian Miracle in Political Perspective. *New Left Review* 1 (217, May–Jun.): 3–36.

———. 2003. *Governing the Market: Economic Theory and the Role of Government in East Asian Industrialization*. 2nd ed. Princeton, NJ: Princeton University Press.

Walder, A.G. 1983. Organized Dependency and Cultures of. Authority in Chinese Industry. *The Journal of Asian Studies* 43 (1): 51–76.

Wallerstein, I. 1979. *The Capitalist World-Economy*. Cambridge: Cambridge University Press.

———. 1992. The Concept of National Development. *The American Behavioral Scientist* 35 (4): 517–529.

Walter, A., and G. Sen. 2009. *Analyzing the Global Political Economy*. Princeton, NJ: Princeton University Press.

Wan, M. 2007. The United Stated States, Japan, and the European Union: Comparing Political Economy Approaches to China. *The Pacific Review* 20 (3): 397–421.

Wang Xiaoqiang. 1980. A Critique of Agrarian Socialism. *Problems of Rural Economy*, No. 2.

Wang, Xiaodong. (Shi Zhong). Why has Socialism Suffered Setbacks? *neibu canyue* (Beijing), 25/05/1991.

——— (Shi Zhong). 1995. The Logic of Comparative Advantage Should Not Be Pushed to the Extreme. *Strategy and Management* (Beijing), No. 3.

Wang, Lixiong. 2000. The Mao Zedong Mentality and Its Undercurrents. *Modern China Studies*, No. 2.

Wang, Shaoguang. 2002. When the Pie is Made Bigger… *Dushu*, No. 2.

Wang, Jisi. 2005. China's Search for Stability with America. *Foreign Affairs* 84 (5, Sep./Oct.): 39–48.

Wang, Y. 2006. *In the Days of Negotiating China's Entry into GATT/WTO*. Beijing: zhonggong zhongyang dangxiao chubanshe.

Wang, Xiaodong. 2008. *China: A Predestinate Great Power*. Nanjing: Jiangsu renmin chubanshe.

Wang, Xiaodong, and Ning Fang. 1999. *The Chinese Road under the Shadow of Globalization*. Beijing: zhongguo shehui kexue chubanshe.

Wang, Xiaoqiang, and Peter Nolan. 1999. China's Aviation Industries: What Course to Follow? *Strategy and Management* (Beijing), No. 5.

Wehler, Hans-Ulrich. 1985. *The German Empire*. Oxford: Berg.

Wei, X. 2010. Chen Yun's Thought on Planning vs. Market is the Forerunner of China's Economic Reform. *Social Sciences Journal of Universities in Shanxi* 22 (9, Sep.): 1–5.

Wen, T. 2004. Impact of WTO Entry on Chinese Peasants, Agriculture, and Rural Development. http://www.moa.gov.cn/fwllm/jjps/200405/t20040509_201786.htm

Westad, Odd Arne. 1993. *Soviet–American Rivalry and the Origins of the Chinese Civil War*. New York: Columbia University Press.

———. 2007. *The Global Cold War*. New York: Cambridge University Press.
Wolf, M. 2004. *Why Globalization Works—The Case for the Global Market Economy*. New Haven and London: Yale University Press.
Woo, W.T. 2001. Recent Claims of China's Economic Exceptionalism—Reflections Inspired by WTO Accession. *China Business Review* 12 (2/3): 107–136.
Woo-Cuming, M. 1999. Introduction: Charmers Johnson and the Politics of Nationalism and Development. In *The Developmental State*, ed. M. Woo-Cumings. Ithaca and London: Cornell University Press.
World Bank. 1993. *The East Asian Miracle: Economic Growth and Public Policy*. World Bank Policy Research Report, September.
Wu, Jinglian. 1999. *Studies on China's Economic Development*. Shanghai: yuan-dong chubanshe.
Wu, Si. 2003. Empire and Its Destiny of Variation. Blog article.
Wu, Y. 2004. The Ideological Battle between 1978 and 1988. *Modern China Studies*, No. 3. http://www.modernchinastudies.org/cn/issues/past-issues/85-mcs-2004-issue-3/875-19781988.html
Wu, Guangxiang. 2008. Journey of Peace to Japan, Deng Xiaoping Made up His Mind to Launch Reform and Opening. *dangshi zongheng*, No. 8.
Wu, W. 2014. Two Different Roadmaps of Political Reform between Deng Xiaoping and Zhao Ziyang. *New York Times* (Chinese online), 15/12/2014. https://cn.nytimes.com/china/20141215/cc15wuwei41/
———. 2015. Decision Making behind the 1988 Price Reform. *yanhuang chunqiu*, No. 12. http://www.yhcqw.com/html/cqb/2015/129/1512918131 3AIJ1410032B9DBK8329E88IGJ.html
Wu, J., et al. 1995. On the Establishment of a Modern Enterprise System: Selections from 'Reform in Large-Scale and Medium-Size Enterprises'. *International Journal of Political Economy* 25 (1): 7–45.
Wu, Jinglian, et al. 1999. Realizing the Strategic Regroupings of the State-Owned Economy. Working Paper.
Xing, Zhaoliang. 2008. dangdai zhongguo gonggong zhishifenzi qunti queshi de yuanyin [The Cause of the Loss of Public Intellectuals in Contemporary China]. *Modern China Studies*, No. 2, Princeton, NJ.
Xu, Zerong. 2000. China's Role in the Korean War. *Modern China Studies*, No. 2, Princeton, NJ.
Yahuda, Michael. 2003. *The International Politics of the Asia-Pacific*. 2nd and revised ed. New York: Routledge.

Yan, C. 2005. The Inside Story about the Use and Annulment of the Appellation of 'Shanghai Commune'. *bainianchao* (Beijing), No. 8. http://www.hprc.org.cn/pdf/BNCH200508008.pdf

Yan, Jijian. 2010. The Causes and Solutions to Mass Incidents. *Theory Guide (lilun daokan)*, No. 5.

Yang, Xiaokai. 2000. The Two Possible Outcomes of China's Accession to the WTO. http://www.boxun.com/hero/yangxk/45_1shtml

Yang, J. 2004. *The Political Struggle in the Era of Reform*. Hong Kong: Excellent Cultural Press.

———. 2015. How China Dealt with Mao's Legacies after the Cultural Revolution? Speech at the seminar on "*Maoism: Perspectives Half a Century Later*", Keio University, Tokyo, Japan, 27/12/2015. http://yangjs001.jigsy.com/entries/general/%E6%9D%A8%E7%BB%A7%E7%BB%B3%EF%BC%9A%E6%96%87%E9%9D%A9%E5%90%8E%E4%B8%AD%E5%9B%BD%E6%80%8E%E6%A0%B7%E5%AF%B9%E5%BE%85%E6%AF%9B%E6%B3%BD%E4%B8%9C%E7%9A%84%E2%80%9C%E9%81%97%E4%BA%A7%E2%80%9D

Yu, Keping. 2006. *Democracy is a Good Thing*. Beijing: shehuikexue wenxian chubanshe.

Yu, Y., and B. Zheng. 2000. *A Research Report on China's Accession to the WTO: China's Industries*. Beijing: shehui kexue wenxian chubanshe.

Yuan, M. 2005. The U.S. Factor in the Process of China's Modernization. *Diplomatic Review*, No. 3.

Yue, Jianyong. 2004. A Bleak Prospect of China's Industrialization. *Dushu* (Beijing), July.

———. 2008. Peaceful Rise of China: Myth or Reality? *London: International Politics* 45 (4, Jul.): 439–456.

Yue, J. 2011. The Myth of the Chinese Model. *Leaders* (Hong Kong), No. 40, June, pp. 11–27.

———. 2013. Behind the WTO Entry—The Neoliberal Logic of China's Developmentalism. *Twenty-first Century* (Hong Kong), June, pp. 83–94.

———. 2016. China, Global Capitalism, and the Quest for Political Legitimacy. *International Politics* 53 (6, Nov.): 752–774.

Yue, J., and M. Chen. 2003. Why did China Strive for FDI in Full Drive? *Modern China Studies*, No. 3, Princeton, NJ, pp. 83–89.

Yue, Jianyong, and Man Chen. 2008. What Caused the Inflation? *Modern China Studies*, No. 1, Princeton, NJ.

Yusuf, S., et al. 2007a. Strengthening China's Technological Capability. World Bank Policy Research Working Paper, WPS4309.

———. 2007b. *Under New Ownership: Privatizing China's State-owned Enterprises*. Stanford: The World Bank and Stanford University Press.

Zhang, Shuguang. 1994. An Economic Analysis of Corruption and Bribery. *China Social Science Quarterly* 1(6).

Zhang, Hanlin. 1999. *A Guiding Book on the World Trade Organization*. Beijing: duiwai jingji maoyi daxue chubanshe.

Zhang, Ruizhuang. 2001. A Critique on the Theme of Peace and Development—Reassessing China's International Environment. *Strategy and Management* (Beijing), No. 1.

Zhang, N. 2011a. On the Changes of Chinese Legal System for Implementing the WTO Laws. *The Legist (faxuejia)*, No. 1, pp. 9–18. http://article.chinalawinfo.com/ArticleHtml/Article_59681.shtml

Zhang, B., ed. 2011b. *Zhao Ziyang's Road*. Hong Kong: Morning Bell Press.

Zhao, Ziyang. 2009. *The Secret Journal*. Hong Kong: New Century Press.

Zheng, Bijian. 2005. China's "Peaceful Rise" to Great-Power Status. *Foreign Affairs* 84 (5): 18–24.

Zhu, Rongji. 2009. *Zhu Rongji's Answers to Journalists' Questions*. Beijing: renmin chubanshe.

Zhu, G., et al., eds. 2003. *China's Manufacturing in the Age of Globalization (tuwei)*. Beijing: shehui kexue wenxian chubanshe.

Zhu's Remarks. 2011. *A Record of Zhu Rongji's Remarks*. Vol. 1–4. Beijing: renmin chubanshe.

Zhu's Shanghai Remarks. 2013. *A Record of Zhu Rongji's Remarks during his Tenure in Shanghai*. Beijing: renmin chubanshe.

Zong, F. 2007. *Zhao Ziyang: Captive Conversation*. Hong Kong: Open Press.

Zubok, V. 2009. *Zhivago's Children*. Cambridge, MA: Harvard University Press.

Zweig, D., and J. Bi. 2005. China's Global Search for Energy. *Foreign Affairs* 84 (5, Sep./Oct.): 25–38.

Index[1]

[1]Note: Page number followed by 'n' refers to notes.

J. Yue, *China's Rise in the Age of Globalization*, Palgrave Studies in Economic History, https://doi.org/10.1007/978-3-319-63997-0

The manufacturer's authorised representative in the EU is Springer Nature Customer Service Centre GmbH, Europaplatz 3, 69115 Heidelberg, Germany. If you have any concerns regarding our products, please contact ProductSafety@springernature.com

Printed and bound by CPI Group (UK) Ltd, Croydon, CR0 4YY

30/09/2026

02225228-0004